1988 Lassen Volcanic National Park update

p. 9: Add this entry to the list of campgrounds. **Cassel Campground** (B2). P.G.& E. From the Cassel Post Office, drive about 0.2 mile on a road that goes 1.0 mile north to Baum Lake.

p. 12: Areas closed to camping. Add Cold Spring (near Butte Lake Campground).

p. 13: Changes and additions to regulations. Pack out all trash—don't bury it. This includes toilet paper. Also, bury feces at least 8 inches deep. Campfires are now prohibited. Finally, no bikes are allowed on the park's trails.

p. 86: ROCK AVALANCHE HAZARD NEXT 2.3 MILES. This sign still exists, but you can now stop at posts 63 through 66 along this 2.3-mile stretch. While a rock avalanche may accompany a future eruption, the chance of one occurring without warning is extremely remote. The U.S. Geological Survey and National Park Service had greatly exaggerated the risk.

p. 93: Sandy and Sugarloaf picnic grounds. Both have been removed, but there is still ample parking space at the latter, and it is frequented by fishermen.

p. 95: Hat Creek Ranger Station. This is now the Hat Creek Work Center. Also, wilderness permits aren't required for Thousand Lakes Wilderness or for Caribou Wilderness.

p. 96: Cassel Road. As stated, this leads 1.9 miles to Rising River, then 1.3 miles more to Cassel, on the Cassel-Fall River Mills Road. However, the quickest way to the Crystal Lake State Fish Hatchery, by Baum Lake, is to take a P.G.& E. road from the Cassel Post Office north one mile to its end, passing Cassel Campground along the way.

p. 135: After about one mile of essentially level walking, we pass a shallow pond. This is seasonal, and when it dries up, so do the springs in the nearby area just west of Badger Flat. Also, the old spur trail that once left a saddle is now obscured by fallen snags, the charred remains from a 1984 fire. You'll see ample evidence of this fire in this area and on land just north of the nearby park boundary. In 1988, the burned area outside the park was being logged.

p. 174-75: PCT, Domingo Spring north to Drakesbad. As before, you follow a road, which is now closed, 0.4 mile. The road then ends abruptly at a clearcut. Timber was cut in 1986, the debris was burned in 1988, and trees will be planted in 1989. Just north of this clearcut is a second one, where the easily followed PCT climbs to a ridge. Also note that from the viewpoint you can't see either a pond or a lakelet lying just to the east. The pond, like the one just west of the trail before the viewpoint, is seasonal. The lakelet, while permanent, is grassy and shallow, and for most people is not worth the visit. Finally, where the PCT meets the descending, private road, you cross it and walk 45 yards west-northwest on an abandoned spur road before relocating the obvious trail along this road's south side.

p. 197 & 198: Sugarloaf Picnic Ground no longer exists.

p. 198: Hat Creek Valley Loop. In 1987, lightning strikes ignited devastating fires in drought-stricken California. One of several fires in our area began in Hat Creek Valley and it climbed eastward up to the Hat Creek Rim. Most of the land lying east of Highway 89 and between Highway 44 and Road 22 was burned. Consequently, the northern third of this loop trail is charred and not worth hiking. Indeed, along the rim, the trail can be hard to follow.

p. 201: PCT, Road 32N12 north. Baker Spring is seasonal, as is nearby Baker Lake. Neither can be relied on from about June through November.

p. 201: PCT, Highway 44 north. The 1987 fire burned rim lands from the Plum Valley vicinity to about 1/2 mile north of the Hat Creek Rim Fire Lookout. The trail's tread was eradicated in many places, but will be rebuilt. The Forest Service plans to have the trail open in 1990, and then it will install a water tank at the lookout. The lookout was largely destroyed by the fire, but it may eventually be rebuilt.

p. 202: PCT to Highway 299 (and beyond to Highway 89). Just after the PCT crosses Highway 89 in McArthur-Burney Falls Memorial State Park, it spans Burney Creek on a substantial bridge. About 0.2 mile beyond it the trail reaches a large camp for trail users and for bicyclists.

Lassen

Volcanic National Park & Vicinity

A natural-history guide to Lassen Volcanic National Park, Caribou Wilderness, Thousand Lakes Wilderness, Hat Creek Valley and McArthur-Burney Falls State Park

Jeffrey P. Schaffer

First edition 1981
SECOND EDITION 1986
Second printing August 1988

Copyright © 1981, 1986 by Wilderness Press
Photos and maps by the author
Design by the author

Library of Congress Card Catalog Number 85-41054
International Standard Book Number 0-89997-059-1

Manufactured in the United States of America

Published by Wilderness Press
2440 Bancroft Way
Berkeley, CA 94704

Free catalog on request

Library of Congress Cataloging-in-Publication Data

Schaffer, Jeffrey P.
   Lassen Volcanic National Park & vicinity.

   Bibliography: p.
   Includes index.
   1. Hiking--California--Lassen Volcanic National Park--
Guide-books. 2. Natural history--California--Lassen
Volcanic National Park. 3. Lassen Volcanic National
Park (Calif.)--Guide-books. I. Title. II. Title: Lassen
Volcanic National Park and vicinity.
GV199.42.C22L377 1986   917.94'24   85-41054
ISBN 0-89997-059-1

Front cover: Lassen Peak rising above Upper Kings Creek Meadow.

Title page: Lassen Peak reflected in Manzanita Lake.

iv

Acknowledgments

An author who attempts to cover an area's roads, trails, campgrounds, resorts, fishing potential, climate, geography, geology, zoology and botany often ends up pushing the limits of his knowledge and resources, for it is difficult, if not impossible, to be an expert in all these subjects. The author can claim to be a specialist only in physical geography and cartography, so he has relied on a number of authorities to examine various sections of the manuscript. Such examination proved to be necessary.

I am particularly indebted to Richard L. Vance, the chief park naturalist at Lassen Volcanic National Park, who read virtually the entire manuscript. Ron Warfield, his assistant, also gave corrections to Chapter 10, the nature trails. Maryann Showers, a park botanist, checked my collection of wildflower slides and made a few necessary corrections in my sometimes erroneous identifications.

The most useful criticism came from Michael Clynne, a geologist at the U.S. Geological Survey in Menlo Park. Mr. Clynne, who began mapping the Lassen area in the mid-1970s, critically reviewed *all* of the book's geology, which is, admittedly, rather profuse in places. In addition, Prof. Phil Kane of California State University, Northridge, reviewed the geology chapter and the Lassen Park Road log. Prof. Kane is *the* expert on the park's glacial history.

Chapters 15-19, dealing with areas outside the park, were sent to appropriate government agencies for review. The author extends his thanks to Bill Westmoreland, of Chester's Almanor Ranger District, Philip Carlson and Chuck Rowe of Fall River Mills' Hat Creek Ranger District, Jack Sanders, of McArthur-Burney Falls Memorial State Park, and Gene Arnold, of Crystal Lake State Fish Hatchery.

Finally, I would like to express my gratitude to Thomas Winnett, of Wilderness Press, who financed and supervised the project, and to my wife, Bonnie, who patiently endured the days alone while I was in the mountains and the hours alone while I was working nights and weekends at home.

—Jeffrey P. Schaffer
Boyes Hot Springs, CA
February 17, 1981

Contents

1 The Lassen Area

The Park and Related Lands

ntroduction Less than a tankful of gas from San Francisco and Sacramento, the ·elatively uncrowded Lassen area provides an alternative mountain-recreation ?xperience for hikers and horsemen, sightseers and rock hounds, botanists and)irdwatchers, fishermen and hunters. Compared with the High Sierra, this area has ,varmer days, longer summers, fewer people and more campgrounds and resorts ,vith available space. The Lassen area also contains a volcano that was active early .n this century and could erupt again at any time. The area is one of the more active /olcanic areas in all of California.

Lassen Volcanic National Park is the primary attraction of a larger mountain landscape known as "the Lassen area." The Lassen area, as used in this book, ?xtends roughly from Highway 36 north to Highway 299 and from Forest Service Road 17 west to Lassen County Road A21. McArthur-Burney Falls Memorial State Park lies a few miles north of Highway 299, but is included because many people visiting Hat Creek Valley also visit this state park.

The Lassen area, as defined in this book, is composed of the following geographic units: foremost, Lassen Volcanic National Park (usually called "Lassen Park," for brevity, in this book); Lassen Park's south and west borderlands; Caribou Wilderness; Thousand Lakes Wilderness; Hat Creek Valley; and McArthur-Burney Falls Memorial State Park ("Burney Falls State Park").

Lassen Volcanic National Park (Chapters 8 and 10-14) Lassen Park typically receives close to half a million visitors each year, which is considerably less than its larger relative, Yosemite National Park, in the central Sierra Nevada. In Yosemite, usage is concentrated in Yosemite Valley and, to a lesser extent, Tuolumne Meadows. Lassen has a similar pattern, with the Lassen Park Road bearing the brunt of the traffic and the Lassen Peak and Bumpass Hell trails bearing the tread of the hikers. These two trails, accounting for only 3% of the park's total trail mileage, handle more hikers than all the other miles of trail combined. Of the half million or so annual park visitors, only about 15-20% camp overnight in the park, and of these, only about 15% backpack overnight in the park's wilderness. Hence, on a typical summer night, there is about *one backpacker*

1

Top left: lodgepole pines are reflected in a typical, unnamed lake in Caribou Wilderness. Top right: Everett Lake, in Thousand Lakes Wilderness, has a spectacular backdrop. Bottom left: wildflowers bloom briefly on the usually dry Hat Creek Rim. Bottom right: Burney Falls thunders year round.

for every square mile of Lassen wilderness—though backpackers do tend to congregate at the park's major lakes. Nevertheless, the potential for solitude is high, and this is also true for Caribou Wilderness and Thousand Lakes Wilderness. If you are in good shape, you can day-hike to *any* spot in the Lassen backcountry or to any in either wilderness. Backpacking is not required to reach a destination, but rather is undertaken by those who want to camp alone or with friends.

Most visitors come not for solitude but rather for the scenic attractions, mainly Lassen Peak and the park's hydrothermal areas. The park's visitors generally come with a family outing in mind, and look forward to enjoyable times relaxing or playing in a campground, hiking a short trail, or fishing and/or swimming in a readily accessible lake. The scenery almost always pleases, for the summer weather is usually cooperative. Camping is quite pleasant, once you get a campsite. Plan to get one early in the day, if possible, but by 5 p.m. at the latest. This does not apply to the park's remote campgrounds—Butte Lake, Juniper Lake, Warner Valley—since you can usually find a site at these no matter how late in the day. See Chapter 2 for campgrounds, their size, and their location.

Fishing in the Lassen area is best *outside* the park—see Chapter 4. It is, nevertheless, a popular activity at lakes with adjacent campgrounds—Manzanita, Summit, Butte and Juniper lakes. Nonmotorized boats are fairly common on these lakes. If you use one, be sure your party has life vests—a park requirement. Swimming at these roadside lakes is acceptable, but is inferior compared to that at some of the lakes reached by trail. Most of the wilderness lakes are shallow and therefore offer enjoyable swimming from about late July to mid-August. Several, such as Snag, Sifford and Soap lakes, are warm enough for comfortable swimming from late June through early September.

Lassen Park's south and west borderlands (Chapter 15) This landscape, dominated by forested, rolling hills rather than by prominent peaks, attracts campers, fishermen, hunters and, in winter, snowmobilers. Trails are few, the scenery second-rate, and trail usage light. Private property becomes pervasive several miles from the park boundary.

Caribou Wilderness (Chapter 16) This wilderness area is a logical eastern addition to the Lassen Park backcountry, though no trail connects the two. Compared to High Sierra hiking, hiking in Caribou Wilderness is almost effortless, for the landscape is subdued and the area small. It is therefore an ideal place for adults to introduce the joys of hiking and backpacking to children. Most lakes are stocked with trout, adding another incentive to visit the area.

Thousand Lakes Wilderness (Chapter 17) Despite its name, this wilderness has few lakes, and most of these are disappointingly shallow. Still, folks do swim and do catch trout. The scenery is more rugged and varied than that of Caribou, and views from its high, glaciated summits are excellent.

Hat Creek Valley (Chapters 9 and 18) This book focuses on the valley's designated recreation area, which, during the summer season, attracts many campers and fishermen. The campgrounds in this area can and do hold more campers than those of Lassen Park. Hiking is usually minimal, typically done just to reach a better fishing spot. The Pacific Crest Trail, mostly along the Hat Creek Rim in this area, accounts for the bulk of this area's trail miles, but in the summer it is hot and dry, and therefore little used. Subway Cave and the Spatter Cones appeal to children—and to many adults.

McArthur-Burney Falls Memorial State Park (Chapter 19) Most of the park's visitors stay only long enough to view Burney Falls or hike the falls' nature trail. Due to the park's relatively low elevation, summer days are hot and therefore the pace is lazy. Camping, boating, fishing and swimming are the rule of the day. Fishing, however, is better at other nearby locations—see Chapter 4.

Seasons and Seasonal Sports

Climate The climate of the Lassen area creates two tourist seasons. The primary one is the summer season, which is in full swing from about the Fourth of July through the Labor Day weekend. The secondary one is the snowy winter season, from about Thanksgiving through April. The following table presents a few basic statistics of two Lassen Park locations, and we can generalize from them.

Lassen Park Headquarters, near Mineral, at 4850 feet elevation

	Jan.	Feb.	Mar.	Apr.	May	Jun.	Jul.	Aug.	Sep.	Oct.	Nov.	Dec.
Av. max. temp.	40	44	46	54	63	72	81	81	75	63	50	42
Av. min. temp.	21	23	24	28	34	40	44	42	39	34	29	24
Av. snowfall (in.)	40	30	31	16	5	.2	--	--	.2	.6	11	27

Manzanita Lake, in northwestern Lassen Park, at 5850 elevation

	Jan.	Feb.	Mar.	Apr.	May	Jun.	Jul.	Aug.	Sep.	Oct.	Nov.	Dec.
Av. max. temp.	39	42	43	50	60	70	80	78	71	60	47	41
Av. min. temp.	19	20	22	28	35	42	46	45	41	33	27	23
Av. snowfall (in.)	40	31	37	23	9	1	--	.1	.6	3	20	34

In general the summer season is quite mild, neither too hot nor too cold, and precipitation is uncommon. As a rule, the lower a spot is, the warmer it is. Hence the temperatures at Burney Falls State Park and Hat Creek Valley tend to be about 5-10° warmer than those at Mineral, at least during the summer. Early morning is about 40-50°F, and afternoon about 85, although July and August have many days in the 90s.

Most of Lassen's campgrounds and lakes are higher than the Manzanita Lake weather station, so summer days are cooler. Caribou Wilderness and Thousand Lakes Wilderness experience similar temperatures. June mornings can dawn near freezing, though they are usually in the high 30s. By afternoon, the days reach the high 60s, though a passing storm may drop the temperature 10-15 degrees. Snow is rare after summer officially begins. The warmest period is roughly from about July 10 to August 15, with dawns usually in the high 30s to mid 40s and afternoons in the low 70s. Because air is thinner in the park than at sea level, solar radiation is greater. Hence, 70°F can feel more like 80°F. As you climb higher, the radiation increases, and you can find yourself uncomfortably hot at 60°F atop Lassen Peak.

By the Labor Day weekend, temperatures have dropped markedly. Autumn is in the air and fall colors appear. Days typically climb into the high 60s. Lakes, which got into the mid-to-upper 60s a few weeks earlier, are now in the low 60s, which is too cool for most swimmers. The first snow storm can appear, giving the park and the wilderness areas a momentary ermine coat. Fall is a pleasant time in the mountains, for most of the people are gone, yet the days are mild enough for one to enjoy the quiet solitude.

About mid-October, the first major storm sweeps through, closing the Lassen Park Road and most of the Lassen area's trails.

Winter typically arrives in the Lassen area by Thanksgiving. At about 6000 feet, the snowpack usually lasts through April; at 7000 feet, through May; and at 8000 feet, through June. Some snowfields last into August, and the one atop Lassen Peak is perennial. Highways and major roads—except the Lassen Park Road—are usually kept open during winter, and they provide access to many winter-recreation sites. If you plan on winter recreation, be aware that temperatures can drop, on occasion, to sub-zero in December through March.

Hiking season At Burney Falls State Park you can hike year-round, though snow may sporadically cover the ground from December through February. In Hat Creek Valley, a bit higher, the season is a bit shorter, from about April through Thanksgiving. The lowest trails in Lassen Park and the wilderness areas are mostly snow-free by early June, though most of the trails don't reach this condition until late June. Some of the higher trails, such as the trails to Bumpass Hell, Brokeoff Mountain, Magee Peak and Lassen Peak, may have substantial snow patches even in mid and late July. Nevertheless, by July 15, nearly every trail is quite easy to follow.

Generally, below 6000 feet elevation, wildflowers are at their best in June; above it they are best in July. Mosquitoes go hand in hand with the beautiful wildflower displays, so be prepared. By late July most mosquitoes have died and lakes reach their maximum temperatures, which they maintain until about August 10. This is prime time for swim-oriented hikers—though lakes above

7500 feet rarely warm up enough for an enjoyable swim. By early September, many of the Lassen area's shallower lakes have shrunk substantially, a few even drying completely.

Hiking in the park or the wilderness areas is usually quite safe in September and early October, but still you should check the weather report before you start. A sudden snowstorm may occur, but rarely does one drop enough snow to prevent a retreat to the trailhead. Outside Lassen Park, hunters armed with bows and arrows hunt deer in September, and those with guns hunt from the last weekend in September on through October. Nonhunting hikers should then stick to the park.

Camping season As a rule, campgrounds at higher elevations open later and close sooner. The one at Burney Falls State Park is open all year, but the Forest Service campgrounds below 5000 feet typically open mid-May and close at the end of October. Higher up, they open by Memorial Day weekend or early June and close in late September or mid-October.

In Lassen Park, both Manzanita Lake and Butte Lake campgrounds have a fairly long season, from about late May through October 15. Summit Lake, one of the highest, has the shortest season, from June 15 through September 15. The park's other campgrounds' seasons lie somewhere between.

Winter-sports season As previously stated, the area is usually covered with snow from late November through April. However, Burney Falls State Park and much of Hat Creek Valley are too low to offer substantial winter sports. In upper Hat Creek Valley, however, snow is much more abundant, due to higher elevation and to the absence of any mountain range to block incoming snow storms. Eskimo Hill Summit, 1.3 miles north of Highway 44's junction with the Lassen Park Road (Highway 89), is a grand place for families to play in the snow. Just 2.7 miles north of it, at USFS Road 16, is Ashpan Snowmobile Park. Miles of roads await snowmobilers. They will will also find miles of roads along the park's southern and western borderlands and along roads striking west from Chester.

Downhill skiers can expect a late-November through April season at the park's ski area, just beyond the park's Southwest Entrance Station. Use is family-oriented and very popular. Good weekends, unfortunately, attract overflow crowds.

Cross-country skiers have the longest season, for Lassen Park and the two wilderness areas are usually mostly snowbound until late May. Above 7000 feet, skiing is practical through mid-June, and above 8000 feet, through early July. Caribou Wilderness, with its gentle topography, is particularly well suited for cross-country skiing.

Burney Falls Campground, packed full during the summer season, is pleasingly quiet the rest of the year.

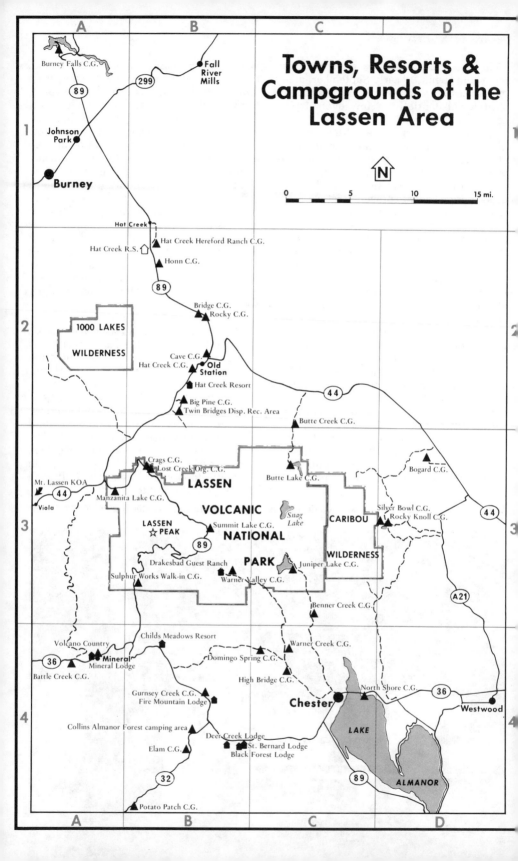

Towns, Resorts & Campgrounds of the Lassen Area

N

0   5   10   15 mi.

Burney Falls C.G.

299

89

Fall River Mills

Johnson Park

Burney

Hat Creek

Hat Creek Hereford Ranch C.G.

Hat Creek R.S.

Honn C.G.

89

1000 LAKES

WILDERNESS

Bridge C.G.
Rocky C.G.

Cave C.G.
Hat Creek C.G.
Old Station

Hat Creek Resort

Big Pine C.G.
Twin Bridges Disp. Rec. Area

44

Butte Creek C.G.

Crags C.G.
Lost Creek Org. C.G.

Bogard C.G.

LASSEN

Butte Lake C.G.

Mt. Lassen KOA

44

Manzanita Lake C.G.

Viola

VOLCANIC

Snag Lake

CARIBOU

Silver Bowl C.G.
Rocky Knoll C.G.

44

LASSEN PEAK

Summit Lake C.G.

89

NATIONAL

WILDERNESS

Drakesbad Guest Ranch

PARK

Juniper Lake C.G.

Sulphur Works Walk-in C.G.

Warner Valley C.G.

A21

Benner Creek C.G.

Childs Meadows Resort

Volcano Country

Warner Creek C.G.

36

Mineral
Mineral Lodge

Domingo Spring C.G.

Battle Creek C.G.

High Bridge C.G.

North Shore C.G.

36

Gurnsey Creek C.G.
Fire Mountain Lodge

Chester

Westwood

Collins Almanor Forest camping area

LAKE

Deer Creek Lodge

Elam C.G.

St. Bernard Lodge
Black Forest Lodge

32

ALMANOR

89

Potato Patch C.G.

2 Towns, Resorts and Campgrounds

Towns

Burney and its northeast outlier, **Johnson Park**, offer a complete range of gas, food, lodging, supplies and services for visitors to Hat Creek Valley, Thousand Lakes Wilderness and Burney Falls State Park. It is also the closest major settlement to Lassen Volcanic National Park's Manzanita Lake area (40 miles) and its Butte Lake area (44½ miles). **Redding**, far larger than Burney, is a bit farther from the Manzanita Lake area (45½ miles).

Chester compares favorably with Burney in gas, food, lodging, supplies and services, and it is convenient to visitors going to Lake Almanor, Caribou Wilderness and Lassen Park's southeastern section. **Westwood**, about 13 miles east of Chester, provides some basic services, but it is not really tourist-oriented. **Susanville**, 21½ miles east of Westwood, is very complete, and it serves those driving north from Reno.

Mineral, near the southwestern border of Lassen Park, is a small community offering few services except those at Mineral Lodge, described below.

Old Station, in upper Hat Creek Valley, offers meals and gas. See also Hat Creek Resort, below.

Resorts and Lodges

Of the resorts and lodges serving the Lassen area, all but two lie along Highway 36. The letter-number combination after the name of each refers to its grid location on this chapter's map of resorts, lodges and campgrounds.

Mineral Lodge (A4), in the center of Mineral, is a very complete resort with rooms, meals, store, post office, pool, tennis and other attractions. Volcano Country, a campground, is just east of it, and a gas station is just across from it.

Childs Meadows Resort (B4), 4.6 miles east of the Lassen Park junction and 7.6 miles northwest of the Highway 32 junction, rivals Mineral Lodge in completeness. It also has a trailer park, is close to fishing, and offers horseback rides.

Fire Mountain Lodge (B4), 5.8 miles southeast of Childs Meadows Resort and 1.8 miles northwest of the Highway 32 junction, is not as large or complete as the two above, but it does have cabins, meals, gas, a small store and a trailer park. This resort too is close to good fishing.

Deer Creek Lodge (B4), is the first of three Highway 36 lodges lying east of the Highway 32 junction. Each has rooms and serves meals. This first lodge is 1.9 miles east of the junction.

Black Forest Lodge (B4), 2.9 miles east of the Highway 32 junction, specializes in fine German dinners.

St. Bernard Lodge (B4), is 3.1 miles east of the Highway 32 junction. Camping.

Drakesbad Guest Ranch (B3) is the only resort operating in Lassen Park. It has cabins, meals, a thermal pool and horseback rides. Reservations usually must be made several years in advance: California Guest Services, Inc., Adobe Plaza, 2150 Main Street, Suite 7, Red Bluff, CA 96080.

Hat Creek Resort (B2), on Highway 89, is located in upper Hat Creek Valley. It is 10.4 miles northeast of the Highway 44 junction near Lassen Park and 3.0 miles southwest of the Highway 44 junction near Old Station. This resort has cabins, a small store, gas, and a post office. A trout-stocked stream is across the road.

Campgrounds

These are listed alphabetically, since there are a few that won't fit neatly into any kind of geographical arrangement. As with the preceding resorts and lodges, the following campgrounds have a letter-number combination after their names to help you find them on this chapter's map. The number of campsites in each campground is not given for privately operated campgrounds. Where given, the numbers are approximate and subject to change.

Battle Creek Campground (A4). U.S. Forest Service. 50 sites. Along Highway 36 immediately west of Battle Creek bridge and 1.2 miles west of Lassen Park headquarters.

Benner Creek Campground (C3). U.S. Forest Service. 4 sites. Leave Chester on Feather River Drive, branch right after ⅔ mile, and drive 6⅓ miles north.

Big Pine Campground (B2). U.S. Forest Service. 19 sites. One-half mile east of Highway 89 in upper Hat Creek Valley. The campground's road leaves Highway 89 just 0.5 mile north of a signed Vista Point and 1.6 miles south of Hat Creek Resort.

Bogard Campground (D3). U.S. Forest Service. 22 sites. West of Highway 44. Road 31N26 to this campground leaves Highway 44 2.8 miles north of the Lassen County Road A21 junction and 1.9 miles south of the highway's Bogard Work Center. Drive 1.5 miles west, then 0.5 mile northwest to campground's entrance.

Bridge Campground (B2). U.S. Forest Service. 25 sites. Along Highway 89 in Hat Creek Valley, 4.0 miles north of the Highway 44 junction and 17.7 miles south of the Highway 299 junction.

Burney Falls Campground (A1). State operated. 118 sites. In McArthur-Burney Falls Memorial State Park. Hot showers from about late April through October 15; cold showers rest of year. Reservations, available through Ticketron, are recommended for summer season.

Butte Creek Campground (C2). U.S. Forest Service. 14 sites. Along Road 32N21, which leaves Highway 44 11.0 miles east of its Highway 89 junction in Hat Creek Valley and 16.8 miles northwest of its junction with Lassen County Road A21. The campground is 2.4 miles up Road 32N21.

Butte Lake Campground (C3). National Park Service. 98 sites. In northeastern Lassen Park near end of Road 32N21, 6.5 miles from Highway 44. See preceding entry for directions. Horse corral near camp.

Cave Campground (B2). U.S. Forest Service. 45 sites. Along Highway 89 in Hat Creek Valley, 0.3 mile north of the Highway 44 junction and 21.4 miles south of the Highway 299 junction.

Collins Almanor Forest camping area (B4). This lumber company allows camping on its land along the upper part of Highway 32, near the Highway 36 junction. No facilities exist. Haul out all trash.

Crags Campground (B3). National Park Service. 45 sites. In northern Lassen Park, 4.4 miles east of the Manzanita Lake Entrance station. Overflow use only.

Domingo Spring Campground (C4). U.S. Forest Service. 18 sites. Leave Chester on Feather River Drive, branch left after ⅔ mile, and drive 7¾ miles west.

Elam Campground (B4). U.S. Forest Service. 17 sites. Along Highway 32, 49 miles northeast of Chico and 3.4 miles southwest of the Highway 36 junction.

Gurnsey Creek Campground (B4). U.S. Forest Service. 52 sites. Along Highway 36, 2.4 miles north of the Highway 32 junction and 9.8 miles southeast of the Lassen Park Road junction.

Hat Creek Campground (B2). U.S. Forest Service. 73 sites. Along Highway 89 in Hat Creek Valley, 1.5 miles north of Hat Creek Resort and 0.9 mile south of Uncle Runts Place (restaurant) in Old Station.

Hat Creek Hereford Ranch Campground (B2). Privately operated. About ¼ mile east of Highway 89 in Hat Creek Valley. The road to this campground is 0.2 mile north of the Hat Creek Ranger Station and 10.6 miles south of the Highway 299 junction. Hot showers. Cafe, store, gas close by. Reservations recommended: Hat Creek Hereford Ranch, P.O. Box 35, Hat Creek, CA 96040.

High Bridge Campground (C4). U.S. Forest Service. 12 sites. Leave Chester on Feather River Drive and branch left after ⅔ mile. Continue for 4.9 miles, branch left immediately past the Warner Creek bridge, and drive 0.2 mile south.

Honn Campground (B2). U.S. Forest Service. 6 sites. Along Highway 89 in Hat Creek Valley, 9.1 miles north of the Highway 44 junction and 12.6 miles south of the Highway 299 junction.

Juniper Lake Campground (C3). National Park Service. 18 sites plus group sites. In southeastern Lassen Park, 11.7 miles from Chester. Leave town on Feather River Drive and branch right after ⅔ mile. Horse corral near camp. Reservations must be made in advance for group sites: Lassen Volcanic National Park, Mineral, CA 96063.

Lost Creek Organization Campground (B3). National Park Service. 10 group sites. In northern Lassen Park, 4.6 miles east of the Manzanita Lake Entrance Station. Reservations must be made in advance: Lassen Volcanic National Park, Mineral, CA 96063.

Manzanita Lake Campground (A3). National Park Service. 181 sites. In northwestern Lassen Park. The campground's road leaves the Lassen Park Road (Highway 89) just 0.6 mile east of the park's Manzanita Lake Entrance Station.

Mt. Lassen KOA (A3). Privately operated. Along Highway 44, about 4.2 miles east of Shingletown and 6.9 miles west of Viola. Hot showers.

North Shore Campground (C4). Privately operated. Along north shore of Lake Almanor. Road to campground branches south from Highway 36. 2.0 miles east of Feather River Drive in Chester and 2.9 miles west of the highway's junction with Plumas County Road A13. Many features, including hot showers and boat rentals.

Potato Patch Campground (B4). U.S. Forest Service. 32 sites. On Highway 32 42¼ miles northeast of Chico and 10¼ miles southwest of the Highway 36 junction.

Rocky Campground (B2). U.S. Forest Service. 8 sites. Along Highway 89 in Hat Creek Valley, 3.3 miles north of the Highway 44 junction and 18.4 miles south of the Highway 299 junction.

Rocky Knoll Campground (D3). U.S. Forest Service. 18 sites. Above northeast shore of Silver Lake. From Highway 36 near Westwood, drive 13.8 miles north on Lassen County Road A21, then 5.1 miles west up Road 110.

Silver Bowl Campground (D3). U.S. Forest Service. 18 sites. Above north shore of Silver Lake. From Highway 36 near Westwood, drive 13.8 miles north on Lassen Country Road A21, then 5.0 miles west up Road 110, branching right onto Road 10 just 0.1 mile before Rocky Knoll Campground. In 0.5 mile branch left and drive 0.4 mile to campground.

Sulphur Works Walk-in Campground (B3). National Park Service. 24 sites. In southwestern Lassen Park, immediately north of the Southwest Entrance Station.

Summit Lake Campground (B3). National Park Service. 93 sites. In central Lassen Park, 12.4 miles from the Southwest Entrance Station and 15.6 miles from the Manzanita Lake Entrance Station. Horse corral near camp.

Twin Bridges Dispersed Recreation Area (B2). Undeveloped camping area on U.S. Forest Service lands. East of Highway 89 in upper Hat Creek Valley, located along Hat Creek between Twin Bridges and Big Pine campgrounds. Road to first is 0.2 mile south of a signed Vista Point; road to second is 0.5 mile north of it.

Volcano Country (A4). Privately operated. Along Highway 36, 0.2 mile east of Mineral Lodge. Hot showers.

Warner Creek Campground (C4). U.S. Forest Service. 11 sites. In lower Warner Valley. Leave Chester on Feather River Drive and branch left after ⅔ mile. In 5½ miles, branch right and drive north 1.1 miles.

Warner Valley Campground (B3). National Park Service. 15 sites. Drive 8.8 miles beyond Warner Creek Campground, the previous entry.

3 Exploring the Lassen Area on Foot, Horseback or Skis

Introduction   Over half of this book is devoted to trails—where they go, what they are like, what lakes, peaks or views you'll see, and what significant plants, animals or geologic formations you're likely to encounter. This book is aimed mainly at hikers, not at equestrians or skiers, though they will find some merit in the book and its map. In Lassen Park, horses are definitely discouraged, though allowed, so equestrians might plan to visit areas outside the park (Chapters 14-18), particularly Caribou Wilderness or Thousand Lakes Wilderness. The rules that apply to hikers also apply to equestrians and skiers, though they have a few more points to consider, which are mentioned at the end of this chapter. Perhaps the most important point for all is that you'll need a wilderness permit to camp in the Lassen Park backcountry.

Wilderness Permits

For what areas   In Lassen Park, permits are required year-round for those who plan to camp overnight in the park's wilderness—that is, outside its campgrounds. Equestrians must get a permit for day use. Outside the park wilderness permits are not required, though campfire permits are if you want to build a fire. These can be obtained at the Forest Service headquarters or at its ranger stations, listed below. If you use a stove and don't build any fires, you won't need a campfire permit.

Size of party   In either wilderness you can have up to 25 people in your party; in Lassen Park, the limit is 20. Generally, the smaller the party, the better, since large groups can be quite noisy or conspicuous, and this is counterproductive to the feeling that you are alone in the wilderness.

How to get a permit   The best way to get a permit is to write or phone for one in advance, though you can also get one in person. Write or phone within two weeks to two months of your proposed trip. For Lassen Park, write or phone:

Superintendent
Lassen Volcanic National Park
Mineral, CA 96063
(916) 595-4444

For a campfire permit or for information about Caribou Wilderness or Thousand Lakes Wilderness, contact:

Forest Supervisor
Lassen National Forest
55 S. Sacramento Street
Susanville, CA 96130
(916) 257-2151

or

Almanor Ranger District
Lassen National Forest
P.O. Box 767
Chester, CA 96020
(916) 258-2141
(best for Caribou Wilderness)

or

Hat Creek Ranger District
Lassen National Forest
P.O. Box 220
Fall River Mills, CA 96028
(916) 336-5521
(best for Thousand Lakes Wilderness)

In person, you can pick up campfire permits at the above locations or, for either wilderness, at Hat Creek Ranger Station, on Highway 89 in Hat Creek Valley. This station is 10.9 miles north of the Highway 44E junction near Subway Cave and 10.8 miles south of the Highway 299 intersection.

During the summer you can get wilderness permits for Lassen Park at its Visitor Center near Manzanita Lake, at the Lassen Chalet near the Southwest Entrance Station, and supposedly at all its ranger stations (Butte Lake, Juniper Lake, Summit Lake and Warner Valley). The author says "supposedly" because every station was closed when he visited each during the summer of 1980; rangers are usually out on patrol.

Regardless of where or how you get a permit, you'll have to supply the following information: trip dates, size of hiking party, and proposed hiking itinerary (for example: 7/18: Butte Lake trailhead to Snag Lake; 7/19: Snag Lake to Horseshoe Lake; 7/20: Horseshoe Lake to Lower Twin Lake; 7/21: Lower Twin Lake to Butte Lake trailhead). If an area is too popular, you may be asked to hike in a different area.

In planning your hike in Lassen Park, be aware that many areas, most of them by lakes, are closed to camping. These are alphabetically listed below, and you can camp no closer than ¼ mile to any one of them.

Anklin Meadow	Hat Creek: West Fork
Bathtub Lake (and	between park road
adjacent lake)	and its confluence
Boiling Springs Lake	with East Fork
Bumpass Hell	Hat Creek cabin area,
Butte Lake (except	near road's creek
south end and in	crossing
campground)	Hat Lake
Cascade Springs	Hemlock Lake
Chaos Jumbles	Hot Rock
Cinder Cone	Hot Springs Creek
Cliff Lake	(Devils Kitchen to
Cold Boiling Lake	south boundary)
Crags Lake	Ink Lake
Crumbaugh Lake	Inspiration Point
Crystal Lake	Juniper Lake (except in
Dersch Meadows	campground)
Devils Kitchen	Kings Creek Falls
Diamond Peak	Kings Creek Meadows
Drakesbad	(all)
Dream Lake	Lake Helen
Dwarf Forest	Lassen Peak (trail and
Echo Lake	summit)
Emerald Lake	Lily Pond
Emigrant Pass	Little Hot Springs
Hat Creek: East Fork	Valley

Lost Creek (north of	Mt. Harkness (summit)
Park Road)	Old Boundary Spring
Lost Creek Diversion	Paradise Meadow
Flume	Reflection Lake
Manzanita Creek	Shadow Lake
(below bridge to	Summit Lake (except
Section 29)	in campground)
Manzanita Lake	Sunflower Flat
(except in	Terrace Lake
campground)	Warner Valley

Day Hiking
and Backpacking

General   Most, if not all, of the hikes in this book can be done as day hikes rather than as overnight hikes—although you may want to take more than one day to do many of them. Generally, however, many are suitable day hikes and you can do them with very little planning or preparation. Novices to hiking and backpacking can learn the art by reading Thomas Winnett's *Backpacking Basics*—aimed directly at them.

Because an accurate, up-to-date map is included in this guide, mileage figures within the text are kept at a minimum. Those at the beginning of each hike are strictly those of the author's, based on his field mapping and measurements.

If you're hiking in early season or in winter, you can often follow a trail even when it is under several feet of snow. Trails in Lassen Park are marked by red or yellow metal disks nailed to trees. Outside the park, some trails are marked with blazes. A *blaze* is a spot on a tree's trunk where a patch or two of bark has been removed to leave a conspicuous, manmade scar.

Minimum-impact hiking   If thousands of hikers walk through a mountain landscape, with its fragile soils, they are almost bound to degrade it. The following suggestions are offered in the hope they will reduce man's imprint on the landscape, thus keeping it attractive for those who might follow.

First, if you're healthy enough to make an outdoor trip into a wilderness area, you're in good enough condition to do so on foot. If possible, leave horses behind. (However, some hunters who enter Caribou Wilderness, Thousand Lakes Wilderness and any other mountain area in late September or early October may certainly object to carrying a deer out on their shoulders.) One horse can do more damage than a dozen backpackers. It will contribute at least as much excrement as all of them, but moreover, it will do so indiscriminately, sometimes in creeks or on lakeshores. Another problem with horses is that they can trample meadow trails into a string of muddy ruts, particularly in early season. And they selectively graze the meadows, causing a change in the native flora. No grazing is permitted in park or wilderness.

On foot, if at all possible, day-hike rather than overnight-hike. In one day's time you can reach *any* destination in Lassen Park, Caribou Wilderness or Thousand Lakes Wilderness and return to your trailhead. Most lakes are an easy-to-moderate hike, round trip. No lake in this entire area is more than 5½ miles from the nearest trailhead; most are 4 or less. Fishermen may object to day-hiking since the best times for fishing are early morning and in the evening. And who wants to get up at four in the morning to fish a lake at dawn? For them, backpacking is a must.

Why do day-hikers have less impact on the environment? For one thing, they usually use toilets near trailheads rather than soil near lakes. A month's worth of backpackers in the Lassen Park wilderness contribute about a ton of human waste to the area, and the bulk of this is within 100 yards of a lake, stream or trail. Around a popular lake, excrement can lead to deterioration of its water quality. Always defecate *at least 50 yards* away from any lake or stream and bury feces 6-8 inches deep.

If, in order to have a satisfactory wilderness experience, you decide to backpack, you might consider the following advice.
1. Pack out toilet paper. Popular lakes can receive hundreds of visitors during summer, and there's a limit to how much paper can be buried.
2. Don't build a campfire unless you absolutely have to do so, as in an emergency. They aren't prohibited, but downed wood is already too scarce at popular sites, and cutting or defacing standing vegetation, whether living or dead, is strictly prohbited. Use a stove instead. Stoves cook meals faster, leave pots and pans cleaner, and save downed wood for the soil's organisms, which are, in turn, food for larger animals. Campfires can leave an unsightly mess and, as winter's snowpack melts, campfire ashes

can be carried into lakes, reducing their water quality.
3. Don't pollute lakes and streams by washing clothes or dishes in them or throwing fish guts into them. And don't lather up in them, even with biodegradable soap. *All* soaps pollute. Do your washing and pot scrubbing well away from streams and lakes, and bury fish entrails ashore rather than throwing them back into the water.
4. Set up camp at least 100 feet from streams, trails and lakeshores. Always camp on mineral soil (or perhaps even on bedrock, if you've brought sufficient padding), but never in meadows or other soft, vegetated areas. It's best to use a site already in existence rather than to brush out a new campsite. That would result in one more human mark upon the landscape.
5. Leave your campsite clean. Don't leave scraps of food behind, for this only attracts mice, bears and other camp marauders. If you can carry it in, you can carry it out. After all, your pack is lighter on the way out.
6. Don't build structures. Rock walls, large fireplaces and bough beds were fine in the last century, but not today. There are just too many humans on this planet, and one goes up into the wilderness for a bit of solitude. The hiker shouldn't have to be confronted with continual reminders of man's presence. Leave the wilderness at least as pure as you found it.
7. Noise and loud conversations, like motor vehicles, are inappropriate. Have some consideration for other campers in the vicinity. Also, camp far enough from others to assure privacy to both them and you.

Regardless if you are day-hiking or backpacking, you should observe the following advice.

1. If you are 16 or older, you will need a California fishing license if you plan to fish—see next chapter.
2. Destruction, injury, defacement, removal or disturbance in any manner of any natural feature or public property is prohibited. This includes molesting any animal, picking flowers or other plants; cutting, blazing, marking, driving nails in, or otherwise damaging growing trees or standing snags; writing, carving or painting names or other inscriptions anywhere; destroying, defacing or moving of signs; collecting rocks or minerals.

3. Smoking is not allowed while traveling through vegetated areas. You may stop and smoke in a safe place.

4. Although you are unlikely to meet any pack or saddle animals on a trail, they do have the right of way. Hikers should get completely off the trail, on the downhill side if possible, and remain quiet until the stock has passed.

5. When traveling on a trail, stay on the trail. Don't cut switchbacks, since this destroys trails. When going cross-country, don't mark your route in any way. Let the next person find his way as you did. Use a compass and map.

6. Be prepared for sudden, adverse weather. It's good to carry a poncho even on a sunny day hike. It can also double as a ground cloth or emergency tent. A space blanket (2 oz. light) is also useful. Some day hikes accidentally turn into overnight trips, due to injury, getting lost or bad weather. Early-season and late-season hikers may encounter snow flurries and, rarely, full-fledged storms; and if they plan to camp out overnight, they should have a tent or at least a tube tent. Before you drive off to your trailhead, find out what the weather is supposed to be like, but be prepared for the worst. Never climb to a mountaintop if clouds are building above it, particularly if you hear thunder in the cloudy distance. And if you see lightning, turn back.

7. The farther you are from your trailhead, the greater is the problem if you are injured. You shouldn't hike alone, since you might have no one but yourself to rescue you in an emergency. However, most of the trails covered in this book are popular enough that you are likely to meet other hikers, should you need help.

8. Vehicles, including bicycles and motorcycles, are not permitted on trails in Lassen Park or on those of either wilderness area. Motor vehicles are also banned from any part of the Pacific Crest Trail.

The following regulations apply to Lassen Park *only*.

1. Dogs, cats and other pets are not permitted in the backcountry or on any trail.

2. Firearms and other hunting devices are prohibited.

The cross-country ski season in the park's downhill ski area often lasts well into May.

Equestrians

In the 1950s and 60s, with an increase in mountain roads and the development of reliable lightweight backpacking equipment, every mountain destination became attainable on foot. Horses were no longer needed. Some people still prefer to pack in with horses, and they can do so, particularly in Caribou Wilderness and Thousand Lakes Wilderness. If you take in horses, you are required to pack in feed for them and see that they stay away from lakeshores.

Lassen Park policy is generally anti-horse. Officials allow, but don't encourage, their use. You must bring in all necessary feed and then remove any residual feed when you leave the park. No grazing is permitted. Horses can be used for day-use only, except at the Hat Creek horse camp beside the park's northern border (see map). This site, however, is really intended for those equestrians riding the Pacific Crest Trail. The park has horse corrals near three of its campgrounds: Butte Lake, Juniper Lake and Summit Lake. Your party may take a maximum of 15 animals along the park's trails. A wilderness permit is required, and advance reservations are recommended. Some trails are closed to horses, so make sure you clear your itinerary with a park ranger before you proceed.

Cross-Country Skiers

From November through May, Lassen Park, Caribou Wilderness and Thousand Lakes Wilderness are largely mantled with snow. For some folks, this is the best time to experience wilderness, for solitude abounds and the marks of man are largely buried beneath the snow. The same rules that applied to hikers apply to ski tourers. In addition, if you start near the Manzanita Lake or Southwest entrance station in Lassen Park, you are required to sign in before entering and sign out upon leaving.

Much of the Lassen backcountry and all of Caribou Wilderness is subdued topography, lacking prominent landmarks. If you are not expert with map and compass, you could easily get lost. In a blinding snowstorm, you could get lost no matter how expert you are. Never travel alone. If you are unfamiliar with the area or with mountain navigation and winter survival, restrict your activities to the shorter, more popular routes, and do so after mid-March, when there's little chance of subzero weather. Isolated winter camping can be either rewarding or deadly.

Giardiasis

Our clear mountain lakes and streams unfortunately sometimes contain disease-producing organisms. One hidden hazard you should particularly know about is a disease called giardiasis (jee-ar-dye-a-sis). It can cause severe intestinal discomfort. The disease is caused by a microscopic organism, Giardia lamblia. The cystic form of giardia can be found in mountain streams and lakes. These natural waters may be clear, cold and free-running; they may look, smell and taste fine; you may see wildlife drinking without hesitation from these sources. All of these indicators sometimes lead people mistakenly to assume that these natural waters are safe to drink. Giardia may or may not be present, but you should be aware of the danger.

Although giardiasis can be incapacitating, it is not usually life-threatening. After ingestion by humans, giardia organisms normally attach themselves to the small intestine. Disease symptoms usually include diarrhea, gas, loss of appetite, abdominal cramps and bloating. Weight loss may occur from nausea and loss of appetite. These discomforts may last up to six weeks. Most people are unaware that they have been infected, and often return home from vacation before the onset of symptoms. If not treated, the symptoms may disappear on their own, only to recur intermittently over a period of many months. Other diseases can have similar symptoms, but if you drank untreated water, you should suspect giardiasis and so inform your doctor. If properly diagnosed, the disease is curable with medication prescribed by a physician.

There are several ways for you to treat raw water to make it relatively safe to drink. The treatment most certain to destroy giardia is to boil the water, preferably for 3-5 minutes. Chemical disinfectants, such as iodine or chlorine, are not as reliable as boiling unless you use them for a long time, such as an hour. This, obviously, is a long time to wait for a drink, so carry two water bottles. While you're drinking from one, the second can be sitting in your pack, with the disinfectant working in it. The recommended dosages, per quart, for these substances are: 5 tablets of chlorine or 4 drops of household bleach or 2 tablets of iodine or 10 drops of 2% tincture of iodine.

4 Fishing

Where to fish Many visitors expect Lassen Park, with all its lakes and streams, to be prime trout country. This was true until the mid-1970s, when the Park Service decided to stop stocking most of the park's lakes. Today, only 17 of the lakes contain fish, and only 7 of these have self-sustaining populations. However, some of the lakes that contain fish are readily accessible. These are Manzanita, Reflection and Summit lakes, all along the Park Road; Dream Lake, near the Drakesbad Guest Ranch; Juniper Lake and close-by Crystal Lake, near the Juniper Lake Campground; and Butte Lake, near the Butte Lake Campground. Manzanita, Summit, and Butte lakes all receive heavy fishing pressure, but only Butte Lake is regularly stocked.

If you want some fine backcountry fishing, try Caribou Wilderness. The area is lightly used, relatively speaking, and most of its lakes are stocked with either fingerlings or catchables. Thousand Lakes Wilderness is also stocked, but the area, despite its name, has many fewer lakes than Caribou, so fishing pressure is greater.

Silver, Caribou and Echo lakes are three rather large lakes lying near the boundary of Caribou Wilderness. They are stocked, but because fishermen can drive up to them and camp at or near them, they receive heavy use. Consequently, fishing at them tends to be poorer than at lakes in Caribou Wilderness.

Two excellent fishing areas lie just beyond this book's area of coverage; Lake Almanor and Deer Creek. The large lake, of course, is best suited for those with seaworthy boats, for on some days the winds can whip up a real choppy surface. Southwest from the Highway 36/89 junction, Highway 32 soon comes alongside Deer Creek and stays with it for about 10 miles. This stretch can be crawling with fishermen during the summer, though most congregate in or near its campgrounds. Turnouts along the narrow highway are few.

Unquestionably the most popular fishing area lying within the area covered by this book is Hat Creek, particularly the stretch from Big Springs north to the northern boundary of the Hat Creek Recreation Area. During the summer, Hat Creek Valley's campgrounds are overflowing with fishermen, and for good reason. The valley's Crystal Lake State Fish Hatchery plants this creek about once or twice a week during the summer, the plantings of catchables usually being at or near the creekside campgrounds. Although you can't fish at the state fish hatchery, you can fish next to it, at Baum Lake.

Lake Britton, north of Highway 299, attracts a fair number of fishermen, but trout do poorly here, competing poorly with the lake's "rough" fish. Consequently, trout are no longer planted. Lower Burney Creek offers some trout fishing, but the best is along the stretch of Pit River above Lake Britton. Fishing there is perhaps the area's best, though boaters may find Lake Almanor better.

Fishing regulations and restrictions If the following information doesn't answer all your questions, write, phone or visit the Department of Fish and Game. The office nearest the Lassen area is at 601 Locust Street, Redding, CA 96001; phone (916) 225-2300.

1. If you are 16 years of age or older, you'll need a fishing license. Resident, nonresident and short-term nonresident licenses are available. (The license also applies to mollusks, crustaceans, amphibians and reptiles—other than rattlesnakes.)

2. You may fish for trout and salmon from one hour before sunrise to one hour after sunset.

3. Fishing regulations and special restrictions may change from year to year. Therefore obtain a copy of the latest regulations from your local sporting goods store or license agent.

Cinder Cone, the Lassen area's youngest volcano, viewed from Butte Lake's east shore.

5 Geology

Introduction   If you could have flown over the Sierra Nevada about 250,000 years ago, you'd have seen that it looked much as it does today. The range stood just about as high, and the glaciated canyons were only slightly narrower and a bit shallower. Glaciation had already been an active force in those mountains for perhaps 2 million years, possibly longer.

But if you could have flown over Lassen Volcanic National Park about 250,000 years ago, you'd probably have flown right over it without recognizing it, because the park's scenery has radically changed over the last 250,000 years. Back then, Lassen Peak did not exist, nor did Chaos Crags, the Prospect Peaks, Mt. Harkness, Sifford Mountain, Crescent Crater, Hat Mountain, Fairfield Peak, Crater Butte, Cinder Cone and a few others. Juniper, Snag, Manzanita and Reflection lakes certainly did not exist, and many of the other park lakes you see today either did not exist or were significantly different. These additions to the landscape were mainly the result of volcanism and glaciation. The latter had a significant effect in a relatively short time due to the relatively easy erodability of the area's volcanic rocks, which is very great, compared to that of the Sierra's resistant, granitic rocks.

Lassen's oldest rocks   The oldest rocks in the Lassen area, like those of the Sierra Nevada and the Klamath Mountains, may date back several hundred million years or more, and they might have been deposited on a marine shelf just west of the shore of an ancient continent. No trace of these rocks exists in the Lassen area, for younger rocks have buried them hundreds-to-thousands of feet deep. However, old marine sedimentary rocks are abundantly exposed east and south of Lake Almanor, and we can safely infer that they extend northwest under the Lassen area.

But we cannot infer that Lake Almanor's igneous granitic rocks, about 90-130 million years old, extend northwest under the Lassen area. Although geologic maps tend to imply that granitic rocks underlie the area, some geologists believe that these rocks have been faulted about 100 miles westward, and that today they lie in the Klamath Mountains. These rocks began as molten material—magma—rising through the earth's crust, and finally solidified in it to form *plutons* near the earth's surface. Some of the magma probably reached the surface and erupted, creating volcanoes and lava flows similar to those seen today. Granitic rocks are generally referred to as plutonic rocks, and they are essentially similar to volcanic rocks in chemical composition. However, the latter usually have smaller crystals, due to their rapid solidification on the earth's surface, whereas magma can take thousands of years to cool to a body of solid rock, and so the crystals have time to grow larger. Another difference between plutonic and volcanic rocks is that the former, solidifying underground, incorporate trapped gases into their structure. At the surface, these gases, under tremendous heat and pressure, violently escape, causing explosive eruptions. The following table of igneous rocks shows the approximate equivalents of volcanic and plutonic rocks.

IGNEOUS ROCKS

generally increasing oxides of
silicon, sodium and potassium

Volcanic Rocks		Plutonic Rocks
rhyolite	approximately equals	granite
rhyodacite	approximately equals	quartz monzonite
latite	approximately equals	monzonite
dacite	approximately equals	granodiorite
andesite	approximately equals	diorite
basaltic andesite	approximately equals	
basalt	approximately equals	gabbro

generally increasing oxides of
magnesium, iron and calcium;
also, increasing melting point
and increasing density

During the extensive time when granitic plutons were being formed, the Lassen landscape lay very close to sea level. Part of it may have been a shallow sea, part of it a lowland swamp. By 35-40 million years ago the land had been raised a bit, though swamps still prevailed locally. Vegetation flourished in a tropical climate, and the swamps accumulated deposits that later turned to coal. About 20-30 million years ago, more uplift occurred, and the climate became subtropical. During this period, the area experienced its first major eruptions of volcanic rock, mostly fluid lava flows of basalt and basaltic andesite. Such flows gradually buried the older landscape under hundreds of feet of lava. Although extensive, these flows probably erupted at a rate no greater than that occurring in the Cascade Range today; still, over millions of years such eruptions can significantly change the landscape.

The Lassen area's oldest volcanic rocks As mentioned above, Lassen Park itself has seen a lot of volcanic activity in the last 250,000 years. In fact, the whole Lassen area, from Highway 36 north to about Highway 299, experienced a lot of volcanism. Consequently, the area's oldest volcanic rocks are buried under younger volcanic rocks. The oldest ones exposed are in the Burney Falls-Lake Britton area, just north of Highway 299. These may be about 5-10 million years old.

Within Lassen Park, all the volcanic rocks may be 2 million years old or less, most of them considerably less. Between Burney

Falls and Lassen Park lie rocks generally of intermediate age. Those making up the east and west sides of fault-dropped Hat Creek Valley may be 2-5 million years old. During this time span—the Pliocene epoch—extensive eruptions occurred and buried most of the earlier volcanic rocks. Several large volcanoes may have existed, erupting lava from their summits as well as from feeder vents on their lower flanks. Lava also flowed from major fissures—cracks in the earth's crust.

Major Ice Age volcanoes Due to continuing eruptions in the Lassen area, evidence of the Pliocene-age volcanoes is mostly buried. However, one volcano, known as Mt. Maidu, has been studied fairly well, for Battle Creek—and the glaciers that descended to it—eroded away much of the overlying rocks, exposing the volcano's innards. This volcano seems to span Pliocene-Pleistocene time, the boundary between the two epochs being put at 1.8 million years ago. The Pleistocene epoch is essentially synonymous with the Ice Age, which we'll soon look at.

Mt. Maidu may have first began eruption 2-2¼ million years ago, slowly building up to a large volcano that may have towered a vertical mile or more above the town of Mineral by 1.3 million years ago. Later in its life, about 1.2-.8 million years ago, great quantities of rhyolite and dacite lava erupted on the volcano's flanks—more than eight cubic miles of volcanic rock, if you also include erupted ash.

Considerable time elapsed before the next known volcano began to grow. This one was

Mt. Tehama, which originated about 600,000 years ago, slowly growing to a sizable mountain that stood about 10 miles northeast of eroded Mt. Maidu. Mt. Tehama's summit may have grown to 11,000 feet elevation, more or less, and it probably existed as a significant landmark up to about 360,000 years ago. This volcano, more than Mt. Maidu, was a child of the Ice Age, and glaciers repeatedly developed on its flanks, gnawing deeper and deeper into the peak. Roughly 250,000 to 200,000 years ago, the peak's northeast flank became the site of several eruptions. Large amounts of dacite oozed upon the land, creating Bumpass Mountain and its associated flow, the domes of Reading Peak, Flatiron Ridge above Warner Valley, Ski Heil Peak northwest of Lake Helen, and an unnamed dome immediately east of Lake Helen. In the past some geologists had suggested that this localized outpouring of dacite led to the collapse of Mt. Tehama's summit. The amount of dacite, however, was small, so if there was a summit collapse, it would have been relatively minor. There is no convincing evidence to indicate a major collapse took place.

Both during and after periods of Mt. Tehama's flank eruptions, glaciers continued to eat away at the volcano, and by 100,000 years ago, they may have eaten back into its very core. By this date, Mill Creek canyon, up which the Park Road climbs, had probably already come into existence, for glaciers that were to follow definitely flowed south down it. Today, only the flanks of Mt. Tehama remain, Brokeoff Mountain ranking as the largest, highest remnant. Mt. Diller, just north of it, together with Pilot Pinnacle, Diamond Peak and Mt. Conard, are also remnants of this large volcano, whose summit once centered about 4000 feet above today's Sulphur Works.

While Mt. Tehama was dominating the Lassen Park area, another volcano was dominating the Hat Creek Valley area. This was the Thousand Lakes volcano, which stood about 17 miles north-northwest of Mt. Tehama and may have risen to an elevation of 9000-10,000 feet. Like Tehama, this volcano was gutted through repeated episodes of glaciation, almost entirely on its northeast slopes. Today only its southern and western flanks remain, and these are crowned by Crater, Magee and Fredonyer peaks. That volcano, or what is left of it, occupies all but the eastern third of Thousand Lakes Wilderness.

Other Ice Age volcanism Although Mt. Tehama and the Thousand Lakes volcano may have stolen the show with impressive "fireworks" from their lofty summits, they

Brokeoff Mountain, center, and Mt. Diller, right, are remnants of Mt. Tehama. Lake Helen, in foreground, came into existence only after Mt. Tehama had been mostly eroded away by glaciers.

weren't the only eruptive sites. The region as a whole experienced considerable volcanism throughout the Ice Age, burying most of the pre-Ice Age rocks. Perhaps during or after the middle of the Ice Age, roughly one million years or less, the vast lava plateau north of Lassen Park began to rift, and a large, complex block gradually dropped, bringing Hat Creek Valley into existence. Faulting had been going on for millions of years, with uplifted blocks subjected to more aggressive erosion and downdropped blocks subjected to burial by incoming sediments and lava flows.

Also about one million years ago, volcanic activity was occurring at the head of Hat Creek Valley. Near what is the park's north boundary today, two vents spilled forth andesite and basalt lava, constructing, over time, two volcanoes: Table Mountain and Badger Mountain.

By the time of the eruption of Mt. Tehama's dacite domes about ¼ million years ago, the lands of the Lassen area *outside* the park had largely taken on the appearance of today's landscape. Ensuing glaciers pruned the higher landscape, accentuating hills and ridges and leaving lakes after the area's glaciers disappeared at the end of each episode. Inside the park a significant glacial episode began perhaps about 215,000 years ago and lasted until about 140,000 years ago. Quite likely during this time, or shortly thereafter, some prominent Lassen Park volcanoes were born and then matured: Mt. Harkness, above Juniper Lake; Sifford (Red) Peak, above Warner Valley; Prospect Peak, dominating the park's northeast corner; and, mostly outside the park, West Prospect Peak.

The youngest major glacial period, the Wisconsin, lasted from about 80,000 to 10,000 years ago. Three relatively small volcanoes probably formed during this time, giving rise to extensive lava flows between the Lassen Park Road, on the west, and Horseshoe, Snag and Butte lakes, on the east. These three were Hat Mountain, Fairfield Peak and Crater Butte. In this area, as in Hat Creek Valley, volcanism could occur anytime in the very near future.

Minor eruptions 20,000-2000 years ago Despite the eruption of massive Lassen Peak during this period, it can be called the age of cinder cones and lava flows. In eastern

Thousand Lakes Wilderness about a dozen cinder cones erupted along a 7-mile-long line, perhaps a fault. Lava flows accompanied the eruptions, and several of them spilled into upper Hat Creek Valley. The cones appear to be mostly less than 10,000 years old—that is, postglacial—and their latest eruptions may have occurred only a few hundred years ago.

The activity in and just beyond the northern part of Caribou Wilderness is even more impressive. The main line of cones, stretching 10 miles south-southeast from Highway 44's Poison Lake, is composed of about two dozen cones. More than a dozen others lie west of it.

Lassen Park developed fewer cones. Possibly during this time the plateau containing Hat Mountain, Fairfield Peak and Crater Butte may have experienced some eruptions, and so might have Prospect Peak. Crescent Crater, a decapitated dacite dome on the northeast flank of Lassen Peak, probably erupted during this period, just before or after Lassen Peak did.

Lassen Peak Were it not for Lassen Peak, the national park probably would not exist. This monstrous dacite dome, one of the world's largest, welled up on the scene about 11,000 years ago, pouring out thick, pasty lava for perhaps only a year or two before quieting down. At that time, most of the park had been buried under an ice cap, and Lassen erupted right on the ice cap's divide. This action cut off the source areas of glaciers that had flowed away from the divide, and consequently they were severely reduced in size. Glaciers soon began to form on the very rubbly slopes of Lassen Peak, but the end of the Wisconsin ice age was near only 1000-2000 years away. In that time—brief by geological standards—the glaciers may have transported a quarter billion tons of Lassen's loose dacite debris, dumping it a few miles east of the source. Perhaps because of the loose nature of Lassen's slopes and/or because of the short time involved, glaciers only scalloped the peak.

The importance of glaciers Although America's glaciers mostly retreated into extinction from 12,000 to 8000 years ago, we are probably still living in the Ice Age. In the last 2 million years there have been dozens of interglacial periods such as ours. A new gla-

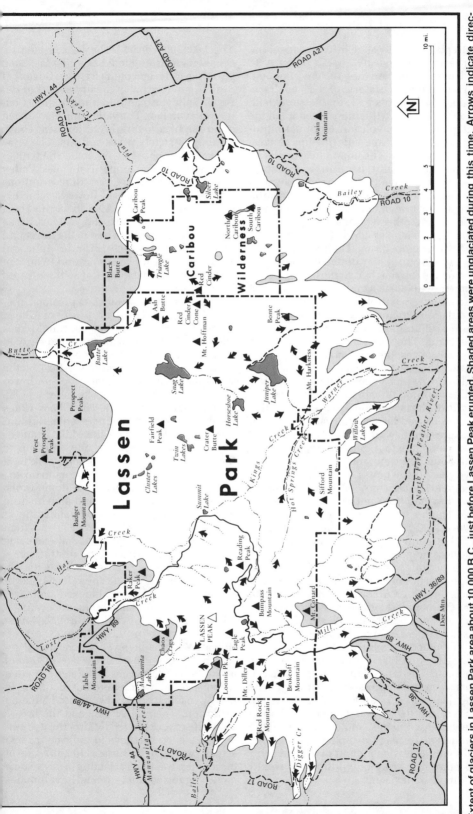

Extent of glaciers in Lassen Park area about 10,000 B.C., just before Lassen Peak erupted. Shaded areas were unglaciated during this time. Arrows indicate direction of ice movement. Lakes came into existence after glaciers disappeared. Some earlier glaciations were more extensive, with glaciers filling almost the entire area shown on this map. Author's map modified from those of Kane (1980) and Crandell (1972).

cial episode could start in the near future, perhaps induced by man's failure to understand—or care for—the environment.

The geologic history of Lassen Park, Caribou Wilderness and, to a lesser extent, Thousand Lakes Wilderness is a story of the interplay between volcanic eruptions building up the landscape and flowing glaciers grinding it down. The importance of glacial action should not be underestimated. Glaciers may have begun gnawing away at Mt. Tehama even before it reached its zenith. The same is true of the Thousand Lakes volcano or any other volcano that grew over 8000 feet above sea level. On such peaks, glaciers developed, small at first, but gradually growing until they united with others to form an ice cap that buried most of the landscape above 6000 feet under hundreds of feet of ice. Glaciers with large sources of ice accumulation extended beyond the general ice cap, descending as low as 4500 feet elevation (see map). They carved large canyons in some instances, the most notable one along Warner Creek. This creek cut down along a fault, and Warner Valley is in part the result of this faulting, though most of its seems to be due to glacial erosion. Quarter-mile-thick glaciers flowed through the valley, exerting pressures on the valley floor in excess of 30 *tons* per square *foot*. Such force, combined with abundant sand and rock for abrasion, gave glaciers the power, over countless millennia, to cut canyons 500-1000 feet deeper than they had been in preglacial times.

When the last glaciers retreated, about 9000-11,000 years ago in the Lassen area, they left behind about six hundred basins that became ponds or lakes. Some of the e are in part due to lava-flow dams or dams by volcanoes, but most are largely the result of glacial erosion. Without glaciers, the Lassen Park-Caribou Wilderness area would have perhaps only a dozen or so lakes. Thousand Lakes Wilderness would have only one, lava-dammed Lake Eiler.

While glaciers plucked away at mountainsides and canyon walls, making them steep and impressive, they transported their load of rocks and debris downslope. Most of the debris was composed of relatively fine sediments, and these became the foundation of many a mountain meadow. Without glaciers, mountain meadows, with their dazzling array of wildflowers, would be almost nonexistent.

The last 2000 years The Lassen area received its finishing touches in the last 2000 years. Near the end of the Ice Age, Sugarloaf Peak began to grow in the upper part of Hat Creek Valley, expanding until it almost cut the valley in two. The valley must have been quite a sight, a youthful volcano rising above a valley of stately pines and firs. The view dramatically changed on some date 1000-2000 years ago, as upper Hat Creek Valley broke out in a rash of very fluid eruptions from a fissure, the basalt flows burying everything in their path. Also about this time, or perhaps several thousand years earlier, a series of eruptions occurred in the lower end of the valley, constructing Cinder Butte and spreading lava for miles around. You can make a sure bet that the valley will see future faulting, eruptions and flows.

In Lassen Park, violent explosions preceded the imminent eruption of Chaos Crags, a cluster of several volcanic domes whose dacite lava was too thick and pasty to flow anywhere. These massive domes lie between even more massive Lassen Peak, to the south, and a cluster of domes, the Sunflower Flat domes, to the north. The latter may be 12,000-25,000 years old. The Chaos Crags are much younger, having erupted around 900 A.D. or shortly thereafter. Like dacite or rhyolite domes, these probably built up to their present height very quickly, taking a few months or at most a few years to do so.

About 1670 A.D., part of a dome broke loose, crashing downward and then rushing west across a gently sloped landscape at speeds well over 100 miles per hour. When the 200 million cubic yards of material came to a rest, it left an area of total destruction—the Chaos Jumbles. Manzanita Lake, Reflection Lake and Lily Pond then developed in response to the altered, blocked drainage. The author believes this traumatic event—a quick series of rockfall-avalanches—was caused by a volcanic explosion, as Prof. Howel Williams believed when he did research in this area back in the late 1920s and early 1930s. Superheated steam, created when ground water percolated down to nearby magma, could have caused such an explosion. There is evidence at the breakaway site of rock altered by superheated water; there is no evidence to indicate magma actually reached the surface. In 1857, one of the domes was still steaming away. Some have suggested that rockfall-avalanches might have been earthquake-triggered, but there is absolutely no evidence for this, nor can an earthquake hypothesis account for the presence of a crater at the base of the breakaway site—but a violent explosion can.

East of Chaos Crags, a rather fluid lava flow spilled across the land in the Butte Lake area about 1567 A.D. The flow was followed, perhaps only days or weeks later, by the construction of a cinder cone. At least three more flows and two more cinder-cone eruptions followed, the last flow and eruption happening during the winter of 1850-51. Today these fresh landmarks are called Cinder Cone and its Fantastic Lava Beds. Some of the lava flows reached Butte Lake and greatly altered its shape. One of the flows, perhaps one of about 1720 A.D., blocked a creek draining north into Butte Lake. Snag Lake pooled up behind the flow.

The final volcanic events—the ones that ultimately led to the establishment of Lassen Volcanic National Park—were a series of eruptions that began on Memorial Day, 1914, when Lassen Peak let the surrounding countryside know it had awakened from its long sleep. The activity reached catastrophic proportions on May 19 and 22, 1915. A mudflow, generated by a summit lava flow pouring onto an ash-laden snowfield, rumbled down the peak's northeast side on the night of the 19th, leaving a several-mile-long area of desolation down both Hat Creek and Lost Creek. On the 22nd, Lassen had its fiercest eruption, the 174th recorded, and it totally destroyed an area about 3 miles long by 1 mile wide. This is the Devastated Area shown on your book's map. After the May 22nd eruption, the volcano began to calm down, and after 1917 it went into dormancy—but it could awake again.

The next million years The Cascade Range consists of a series of active volcanoes stretching from southernmost British Columbia down to California's Lassen Park. However, in the near future, geologically speaking, eruptions in the park will cease, and over time the park will be eroded to resemble the volcanic landscape south of it. This demise will be due to the northward migration of the source responsible for the volcanism. This is the Juan de Fuca Plate, a chunk of the earth's crust that is diving under northern California, Oregon, Washington and southern British Columbia. The diving part of the plate melts when it reaches some depth, and part of that melt rises, reaching the earth's surface as lava or some other product. Because the Juan de Fuca Plate is drifting north as it dives, it is, over time, producing a melt in increasingly northern latitudes. About 4 million years ago, the Cascade Range's active southern end lay around Sonora Pass, near Yosemite National Park. Two million years ago, it was just south of Interstate 80's Donner Pass. One million years into the future, it will be around Burney Falls.

Millions of years ago giant sequoias migrating southwest from northern Nevada were destroyed by the volcanic activity of the southern Cascade Range; only migrating groves from Lake Tahoe south got through. Today, volcanism no longer exists between Lake Tahoe and Lassen Park, and there are numerous shallow canyons between 4500 and 5500 feet elevation in this area that could support these magnificent trees. Since the Cascade Range has "moved onward" beyond this area, foresters can plant groves of sequoia seedlings with the assurance they won't be exterminated by volcanic activity. Man has brought about the extermination of many plants and animals; now he has a chance to right a "natural" wrong.

If you'd like to know more about Lassen's geology (and its biology), drive the Park Road, using Chapter 8's road log. This road log, like the following one on Hat Creek Valley, *interprets* as well as identifies what you see. Likewise, Chapter 10's nature trails to Bumpass Hell, Boiling Springs Lake and Cinder Cone do the same. The book's remaining chapters describe hikes in the park, the wilderness areas, Hat Creek Valley and Burney Falls Park, and each hike identifies significant geological or biological points of interest. Take the time to hike this area's trails and learn first-hand about this fascinating land of fire and ice.

Common trees of Lassen Park: red fir (top left), western white pine (top right), lodgepole pine (bottom left) and Jeffrey pine (bottom right).

6 Botany

Introduction   The author, a naturalist specializing in the study of landforms, was fascinated more by this area's wildflowers than by its landforms. The landforms are, with the exception of Lassen Peak, Chaos Crags and Cinder Cone, quite ordinary for the Cascade Range. Of course, one could rightly argue that Lassen's wildflowers are quite ordinary for a mountain range. Still, the typical hiking experience in Lassen Park, Caribou Wilderness and Thousand Lakes Wilderness is a walk through a usually viewless forest, and it is largely the wildflowers that add color and diversity to the scene. Because to many visitors the wildflowers are second only to the mountains and lakes, they are extensively described here.

Plant diversity   Lassen Park hosts about 700 species of vascular plants—ferns, herbs, shrubs and trees—grouped into about 75 plant families. In comparison, Mt. Shasta, to the north, hosts about 485 species from about 60 families, and Crater Lake National Park, in southern Oregon, hosts about 570 species, also from about 60 families. All three areas are about equal in size, are volcanic, and have substantial ranges in elevation. In all three, ponderosa pines are found at the lowest elevations, matted alpine wildflowers at the highest. So why does Lassen excel in diversity? The answers are park location and geologic history.

Lassen Park and its surrounding lands lie at the north end of the Sierra Nevada floral province, the south end of the Cascade Range floral province and the west edge of the Great Basin floral province. The area is, in short, a melting pot for plants, receiving immigrants from three major, different areas.

Lassen Park and vicinity is an area of active, though sporadic, vulcanism. Geologically recent volcanoes and lava flows bury older volcanic rocks. The result is that the area is a collage of very different soils ranging from fresh lava, pumice and ash to deep, weathered, organically rich sediments. As at Mt. Shasta and Crater Lake, glaciers flowed through the area, creating canyons and meadows. Unlike the glaciers of those two areas, however, the Lassen glaciers left behind dozens of lakes of all sizes and depths, thereby creating additional environments to be exploited by plants. Lassen, with its greater number of environments, has been invaded by plants from very diverse environments. Consequently, every Lassen environment, no matter how extreme and uninviting, has found some willing takers.

27

Each plant growing in Lassen today has certain water, temperature and minera requirements, and these limit its distribution. Such wildflowers as sticky cinque foil and sulfur flower have wide tolerances and consequently enjoy greater-than average distribution. The sulfur flower grows in dry soil from about sea level up t 9200 feet, successfully competing over its elevation range with foothill plants a well as alpine plants. The cinquefoil is even more ambitious, spanning the sam elevation range, and also growing in soils ranging from dry to wet. In contrast t these two species, the skunk-leaved polemonium grows only at or near the top o Lassen Peak, and the hot-springs panic grass grows only around hot springs. Wha will happen to these plants if Lassen Peak blows its top and the hot springs coo down? They'll probably go extinct.

Overspecialization leads to extinction, yet nonspecialization leads to loss o habitat to more-specialized, better-adapted species. Plants, like animals, mus evolve along a careful path if their lines are to survive through the ages. Generally, a plant tends to prefer a fairly specific environment, which is usually called it habitat, and plants of similar habitats collectively make up a group called a plan community.

Plant communities   If you started a trip in the Burney Falls area, roughly at 300(feet elevation, and drove south up Highway 89 to the base of Lassen Peak, ther climbed the trail to its summit, at 10,457 feet, you would pass through or close t every plant community found in the area covered by this book. On such a trip you would ascend through the following major plant communities.

1. **Ponderosa Pine Forest.** Lowest in elevation, this community has the longest growing season, roughly 9 months long. Winters are relatively mild, and ample precipitation comes in the forms of rain and snow. The snow usually disappears by early or mid-spring, and by early summer the land can be fairly dry. Wildflowers, therefore, usually go to seed before the hot summer drought.

2. **Sagebrush-Juniper Woodland.** As you drive south up Hat Creek Valley, you stay near Hat Creek and often in a ponderosa-pine forest. The mountains to the west, which increase in height as you travel southward, intercept most of the moisture of incoming storms, depriving eastern lands of the life-giving moisture. Consequently, a community of sagebrush and junipers flourishes to the east, up on hot, dry Hat Creek Rim. Conditions in the valley are even more severe in many places, for recent lava flows flooded most of the valley's floor, burying creeks, streams and wet meadows. Water still flows, but beneath the lava. The young, sterile lava, parched in the summer, offers sustenance only to the hardiest species.

3. **Greenleaf Manzanita.** Where soils ar thin and dry, there is a potential for exten sive tracts of brush dominated by greenlea manzanita. These start around 4000 feet along the east base of Sugarloaf Peak in Ha Creek Valley, but are best developed jus outside Lassen Park's northwest corner, between 5000 and 6000 feet. Large fires are usually the instrument that converts an open forest into a pure brushland, though extensive logging can produce the same result. These lands provide deer with extensive forage and excellent fawning sites. The brush can grow so dense that it prevents reforestation by pines for a century or more; in places the brush lasts almost indefinitely.

4. **Jeffrey Pine Forest.** Roughly between 5000 and 6000 feet, ponderosa pines yield to Jeffrey pines. You see fine groves of mature Jeffrey pines in the Manzanita Lake area and in the park's northeastern Butte Lake area. The trees and their associated vegetation, which varies considerably from place to place, grow up to 8000 feet in places with gravelly, well-drained soils. Such places are usually slopes, though the pines are doing well in the large, flat area buried by Lassen

'eak's 1915 mudflow. This mudflow flat, owever, is a special case.

. White Fir Forest. Beyond Manzanita ake and Chaos Crags you enter a white-fir orest. Soils are deep but well-drained, and lopes vary from gentle to moderate. The orests are cool and shady, causing snow to emain on the ground through June, about a nonth or so longer than it does under Jeffrey ines on drier slopes of a similar elevation. n a prime white-fir forest, shrubs and wildflowers are few, due to lack of light, and herefore root parasites such as snow plant nd pinedrops do well, living off other lants rather than off sunlight.

. Lodgepole Pine Forest. Between 5500 nd 7500 feet, where ground water is abun-lant, lodgepole pines flourish. You first neet these trees near the Lost Creek bridge, hen see many more of them as you drive east o the Devastated Area scenic turnout. This stretch of terrain appears dry, but ground water is abundant only 5-10 feet below the surface—here, the top of a mudflow. Lodgepoles do very well along streams and around meadows and lakes. Almost every ake in Lassen Park, Caribou Wilderness and Thousand Lakes Wilderness has its share of odgepoles. The wildflowers in a lodge-pole-pine forest receive more light than do hose in a white-fir forest, and they can be quite dense along streams. But where the ground water is several feet below the surface, the ground cover changes to drought-tolerant species such as spreading phlox. Lodgepole-pine forests, due to their intimate association with abundant water, are, like meadows, areas of usually high mosquito populations.

7. Mountain Meadows. Your road to Lassen Peak passes through two fine sets of mountain meadows: Dersch Meadows, between the Devastated Area and Summit lake, and Kings Creek Meadows, higher up, between Summit Lake and Lassen Peak. Although most meadows can be quite dry in late summer, they are usually boggy enough in early summer to resist invasion from threatening lodgepole pines. Willows and alders, being a bit more water-tolerant than lodgepoles, often grow in meadows. Sedges, grasses and rushes dominate the meadows, in contrast to tree-lined stream banks, where wildflowers are the rule. As with *all* plant

communities, boundaries are vague, one community merging into another.

8. Red Fir Forest. This forest clothes almost half of Lassen Park. In Caribou Wilderness it mingles extensively with the lodgepole-pine forest, and together they blanket at least three fourths of the terrain. The bulk of both forests lies between 6000 and 8000 feet, though, as usual, a few specimens exist outside the general elevation range. The red fir and its associate, the western white pine, replace the white fir and its associate, the sugar pine. Being higher, the red-fir forest is cooler and has longer-lasting snow, some patches lasting well into July. Due to this harsher environment, the firs and pines don't grow as tall as their counterparts in the white-fir forest. Waist-high shrubs lower down have been replaced largely by foot-high pinemat manzanita. Where red firs form dense, nearly pure stands, the forest floor is almost barren. Animal life is then largely confined to the crowns of the trees.

9. Subalpine Slopes. As your road climbs to an 8500-foot pass, you enter a harsher climate. Snowpacks average about 15 feet—a bit more than in a red-fir forest—but snow can drift up to 25 feet or more and last into August. Therefore, the growing season is only 3-4 months long. Winter winds are extremely fierce, and only the hardiest plants survive. The two dominant trees are the mountain hemlock and the whitebark pine. The first avoids winter storms by growing in areas of dense snow, thereby getting buried under a protective layer of snow. These trees grow to about 9200 feet. The whitebark pine is hardier, but at higher, progressively more severe sites, the tree becomes dwarfed, being no more than a dense, prostrate bush at its upper extreme, about 10,000 feet. Both species of trees tend to grow in clusters or small groves, the environment being too severe to support a dense forest. There is plenty of rocky and gravelly open space that supports a thin cover of perennial wildflowers, grasses and sedges. Shrubs are few.

10. Alpine Wildflowers. If you hike the Lassen Peak Trail, you start up through a subalpine-slopes plant community and around 9000 feet encounter your first truly alpine species. At about 10,000 feet, the last of the trees, grasses and sedges disappear and the remaining distance to the summit lies in the domain of the alpine wildflowers. Winter winds can get unbelievably fierce, blowing away protective snow and exposing plants to windchill temperatures of -50°F and below. The wildflowers, therefore, are small and matted, most of them on the peak's summit being only an inch or two tall. During the 1-2 month frost-free growing season, they quickly shoot up flower stalks that dot the bleak environment with color. Besides humans (and ground squirrels that rely on them for food), the only vertebrates to visit—and relish—such an inhospitable environment are gray-crowned rosy finches, who seem to be nature's supreme masochists.

Herbs

Introduction Herbs are seed-producing annuals, biennials or perennials that are *usually* not woody and that *usually* die back at the end of the growing season. As one might expect, there are a number of exceptions. Nature, it seems, has no absolute categories, but rather evolves life into various grades, one form leading on to the next. The word "evolution" disturbs some people who have fundamentalist convictions, but it can disturb botanists even more—though in a diferent sense. Botanists have to deal with the *reality* of evolution. Plants have been, and still are, evolving, giving rise over long periods of time to new forms. Botanists have arrived at the scene right in the middle of this ongoing flux and they are supposed to draw artificial lines between species, defining the characteristics of one species in contrast to those of a similar one. This is far easier said than done, and botanists have taken to splitting hairs, dividing a species (sp.) into subspecies (ssp.) and varieties (var.). We can make an analogy between plants and colors. In the color spectrum, we think we see yellow next to orange, orange next to red, and so on, yet the color spectrum is continuous. Our classification is artificial and *culturally* biased. The Navaho Indians, after all, recognized dozens of colors that we would classify as only shades of blue.

Hair splitting is found not only at the species level. Species are grouped into *genera* (singular is "*genus*"), and genera into *families*. You would think that botanists could agree on these larger categories, but

they can't. There are the "lumpers" and th "splitters," the former group creating few genera and families, the latter, more. Georg Gillett, who wrote the most comprehensiv study of Lassen Park's plants, is a lumpe Ted Niehaus, who wrote the best pock guide to wildflowers of the Pacific States, is splitter. Phillip Munz, who wrote the sta dard, though now dated, guide to Californ plants, lies somewhere in between, as do Norman Weeden, who wrote the standar guide to Sierra Nevada plants. The auth has generally followed Munz and Weede for scientific names, though he has occ sionally sided with Niehaus.

Common names are even more muddle than scientific names. Gillett, the park e pert, gave common names to a fair number species, but these often disagree with tho of Weeden, Niehaus and others. The auth has tried to give the most widely used most appropriate name.

Now that the problems with terminolog are out of the way, we can get back to herb The ones in this section are typically calle "wildflowers," which implies that the r maining herbs—mostly grasses, sedges an rushes (photos on p. 148)—are not wild an lack flowers. But in fact they are equally wil and flowered, some of their flowers bein more conspicuous than those of some wil flowers. Few visitors, however, are intereste in such herbs, so they are omitted.

Identifying a wildflower If you're not ver familiar with mountain wildflowers, the your best bet is to turn to the wildflowe plates and look through them. Note th grouping of plants on each plate. The fir plate is a special case, dealing with aquati plants and parasitic plants, but the remai ing plates are of plants grouped by elevatior habitat and sometimes by color and siz Plates 2 and 3 cover plants usually foun below Lassen Park, that is, usually belov 6000 feet elevation. Plates 4-14 cover plant to be expected in Lassen Park, Caribo Wilderness and Thousand Lakes Wilde ness. These plates are broken down int three habitats: wet places such as spring creeks, lakeshores and meadows (Plates 4-8 wooded or forested places (Plates 9-11); an dry, open, usually gravelly or rocky place (Plates 12-14). The "wet places" habita which abounds in species, is further divide by plant size. The last two plates, 15 and 1 leal respectively with subalpine and alpine plants. Check Plate 15 if you're climbing Brokeoff Mountain; check both if you're climbing Lassen Peak.

Once you find a suitable candidate on a plate, note its family and its scientific name. Both are listed alphabetically in the following list, which includes a common name, a few key plant characteristics, and an elevation range for each photographed species.

In using the plates, be aware of two limitations. First, there are over 500 species of wildflowers in the area covered by this book. Many of these species lie in the 3000-6000' elevation zone below the park, yet the plates show only a few dozen of the plants to be found in that zone. Therefore, if you do serious botanizing down there, you'll find many species not found on the plates. The bulk of the plates cover Lassen Park wildflowers, and you should be able to identify almost all the ones you'll see. Still, about half of the park's wildflowers are not mentioned—plants that are uncommon or very hard to identify. These are beyond the scope of this book.

The second limitation to the plates' use is that some species occupy several habitats or have a large elevation range, and these could be shown on any of several plates. Therefore, check other plates. For example, Plates 12-14 show plants of dry, open areas, but since these often grow up in the subalpine zone, you should refer to these plates, and not just Plates 15 and 16, when you hike at high elevations.

Experienced botanists, recognizing the family that a particular candidate belongs to, may find it easier to turn directly to that family, read the plant descriptions, and then turn to the proper plate for visual confirmation.

WILDFLOWERS

Amaryllidaceae (Amaryllis Family)

Allium campanulatum, **Sierra onion.** Flowers rosy, star-shaped. Leaves narrow, onion-scented. Plant 3-12" tall. On dry, wooded slopes, up to 8000'. **Plate 11.**

Brodiaea hyacinthina, **white brodiaea.** Flowers white, bowl-shaped, in cluster. Leaves grasslike. Plant 1-2' tall. In dry-to-moist places, up to 6000'. **Plate 11.**

Dichelostemma congestum, **fork-toothed ookow.** Flowers blue-violet, in compact cluster of several flowers. Leaves grasslike. Plant 1-3' tall. In dry, open places, up to 6500'. **Plate 14.**

Triteleia ixioides ssp. *analina,* **mountain pretty face.** Flowers yellow, in open, umbrellalike cluster. Leaves onionlike. In dry places, from 4000-6500'. **Plate 10.**

Apocynaceae (Dogbane Family)

Apocynum pumilum, **mountain dogbane.** Flowers, usually absent, are white-to-pink and urn-shaped. Leaves bright yellow in fall. Common on dry forest floors, from 2500-7500'. **Plate 9.**

Cycladenia humilis, **cycladenia.** Flowers ½-¾" long, funnel-shaped, magenta. Leaves thick. Plant low, spreading. In gravelly or rocky places, from 3500-9000'. **Plate 14.**

Boraginaceae (Borage Family)

Hackelia californica, **California stickseed.** Flowers white, changing to sticking seeds. Plant 1½-2½' tall. In open forests, from 4000-7000'. **Plate 11.**

H. floribunda, **many-flowered stickseed.** Flowers many, ¼" wide, blue with white centers. Plant 1½-4' tall. In moist-to-wet places, from 4000-8000'. **Plate 7.** *H. nervosa,* **Sierra stickseed,** is similar, but flowers are fewer and ⅓-½" wide. Plant 1-2' tall, from 6500-8000'.

Caryophyllacae (Pink Family)

Arenaria Kingii var. *glabrescens,* **King's sandwort.** Flowers small, white. Plant 4-8" tall. In rocky places, from 6000-8000'. **Plate 12.**

Silene californica, **California Indian pink.** Petals multilobed, scarlet or bright red. In woods, up to 5000'. **Plate 2.**

S. Douglasii, **Douglas' catchfly.** Flowers striped, tubular, with creamy petals at tip. Plant 4-16" tall. In dry places, from 5000-9500'. **Plate 15.**

S. Lemmonii, **Lemmon's catchfly.** Flowers hanging, yellowish or white-to-pink. Stem usually leaning, not vertical. Plant ½-1½' tall. In open forest, up to 6500'. **Plate 10.**

Stellaria longipes, **long-stalked starwort.** Petals white, cleft in two, resulting in 10 "petals." Leaves pointed, narrow, ascending. Usually in meadows, from 4500-8000'. **Plate 4.**

Chenopodiaceae (Goosefoot Family)

Chenopodium incognitum, **unrecognized pigweed.** Flowers greenish white, ball-like, without petals. Leaves gray-green. Plant 1-4' tall. In dry places, from 6000-8000'. **Plate 12.**

Compositae (Sunflower Family)
(Also known as Asteraceae)

Note: These flowers are usually "daisy-like." Each "sunflower" is usually composed of numerous *ray flowers,* the "petals," and several to many central *disk flowers.* In some species the ray flowers may be lacking; in others, the disk flowers may be lacking.

Achillea lanulosa, **yarrow.** Flowers small, whitish, in dense, umbrellalike clusters. Leaves lacy, highly divided. Plant 2-24" tall. Common in moist, open places, up to 9000'. **Plate 6.**

Anaphalis margaritacea, **pearly everlasting.** Disk flowers only, small and yellow, surrounded by white, paperlike bracts. Leaves dull-green. Plant 1-3' tall. In many places, up to 7500'. **Plate 10.**

Antennaria alpina var. *media,* **alpine everlasting.** Disk flowers only, white-to-pink. Leaves silvery green. Plant 2-4" tall. In rocky or gravelly places, from 6000-8500'. **Plate 12.** *A. rosea,* **rosy everlasting,** is similar, with dull-green leaves. Plant is 6-10" tall. From 5000-7500'.

Arnica Chamissonis ssp. *foliosa,* **meadow arnica.** Flowers yellow. Leaves at base large, bright green; smaller leaves in pairs on stem. In wet places, from 5000-7000'. **Plate 6.**

Balsamorhiza sagittata, **arrow-leaved balsamroot.** Flowers large, yellow. Leaves large, arrow-shaped. Plant 1-2' tall. On sunny slopes, from 4000-8000'. **Plate 13.**

Brickellia Greenei, **mountain brickellbush.** Flowers tiny, late-blooming, in many small clusters. Plant ½-1½' tall. In rocky places, from 3000-8000'. **Plate 12.**

Chaenactis nevadensis, **Sierra pincushion.** Disk flowers only several per head, creamy yellow, fading to brick-red. Leaves hairy, lobed, silvery green. Plant 1-4" tall. In dry, often subalpine places, from 6500-9500'. **Plate 15.**

Chrysanthemum Leucanthemum, **ox-eye daisy.** Ray flowers white, disk flowers yellow. Usually by roads and in fields, up to 6000'. **Plate 3.**

Cichorium Intybus, **chicory.** Ray flowers only, toothed, light-blue to violet. Usually by roads and in fields, up to 5500'. **Plate 3.**

Cirsium Douglasii var. *canescens,* **swamp thistle.** Flowers creamy white to reddish purple. Leaves hairy, whitish green. In wet places, up to 7500'. **Plate 8.** *C. Andersonii* **Anderson's thistle,** is similar, but has green leaves and grows in dry places, from 4000-7000'.

C. foliosum, **leafy thistle.** Plant prostrate with large, spiny leaves. In moist-to-dry places, from 5000-9200'. **Plate 12.**

C. vulgare, **bull thistle.** Flowers reddish purple. Leaves with coarse, rough hairs on upper surface and with long spines. In moist-to-dry places, up to 7000'. **Plate 3.**

Erigeron peregrinus ssp. *callianthemus,* **wandering daisy.** Ray flowers violet, disk flowers yellow. Easily the commonest of Lassen's violet-and-yellow daisies. In wet places, from 5500-8500'. **Plate 7.**

Eriophyllum lanatum, **woolly sunflower.** Flowers yellow, numerous, each on a tall stem. Leaves mainly at base and, like stems, hairy. In dry, open places, up to 7000'. **Plate 2.**

Helenium Bigelovii, **Bigelow's sneezeweed.** Ray flowers yellow, disk flowers brown. Usually in wet meadows, up to 6500'. **Plate 2.**

Hieracium albiflorum, **white hawkweed.** Ray flowers only, small and white. On dry forest floors, up to 7500'. **Plate 9**

H. horridum, **shaggy hawkweed.** Ray flowers only, small and yellow. Leaves very hairy. Plant 3-12" tall. In dry places, from 5000-8500". **Plate 13.**

Madia elegans, **common madia.** Ray flowers many, narrow, lemon-yellow, each with rusty spot at base; disk flowers few. In open places, often roadsides, up to 5500'. **Plate 2.**

Microseris nutans, **nodding microseris.** Ray flowers only, bright yellow. Flower nods before it blooms. Leaves grasslike. Plant 4-10" tall. In moist woods and grassy meadows, from 4000-7000'. **Plate 10.**

Raillardella argentea, **silky raillardella.** Disk flowers only, few in number, composing solitary "sunflower." Leaves basal, hairy, gray-green. Plant ½-4" tall. In rocky, usually subalpine places, from 7500-9000'. **Plate 15.**

Senecio aronicoides, **California butterweed.** Flowers small, yellow, in a dense, umbrel-alike cluster on a single stem. Leaves dull-green, mostly basal. Plant 1-3' tall. Common in a variety of fairly dry places, up to 8000'. **Plate 10.**

S. canus, **woolly butterweed.** Similar to next species, but with silvery green leaves. Plant 3-18" tall. On dry slopes and ridges, from 6800-8000'. **Plate 13.**

S. Fremontii, **Fremont's butterweed.** Sunflowers yellow, composed of both disk and ray flowers, but ray flowers fall off early and may be lacking. Leaves bright yellow-green. Plant 2-12" tall. In rocky alpine and subalpine places, from 8000-10,400'. **Plate 16.**

S. triangularis, **arrowhead butterweed.** Flowers like those of California butterweed. Leaves bright green, arrowhead-shaped. Usually along streams, from 4000-7000'. **Plate 8.**

Stephanomeria lactucina, **large-flowered stephanomeria.** Ray flowers only, pink, magenta or rose, and late blooming. Plant 4-12" tall. In forests, from 4000-7000'. **Plate 11.**

Taraxacum officinale, **common dandelion.** Ray flowers only, yellow. Leaves basal, long and notched. Plant 2-8" tall. Common in moist places, up to 7000'. **Plate 6.**

Tragopogon dubius, **yellow salsify.** Ray flowers only, lemon-yellow. Leaves grasslike. In dry, open places, up to 5000'. **Plate 2.**

Whitneya dealbata, **whitneya.** Flowers golden yellow. Leaves gray-green. Plant ½-1½' tall. In moist, open places, from 4000-7000'. **Plate 10.**

Wyethia mollis, **mountain mule ears.** Flowers large, yellow. Leaves size and shape of mule's ears. Plant 1-3' tall. In dry, open places, from 5000-8000'. **Plate 13.**

Convolvulaceae (Morning Glory Family)

Calystegia malacophylla, **Sierra morning glory.** Flowers creamy. Leaves hairy, dull-green, arrowhead-shaped. Plants low. On dry slopes, up to 6800'. **Plate 3.**

Cruciferae (Mustard Family)
(Also known as Brassicaceae)

Arabis platysperma, **pioneer rock cress.** Flowers 4-petaled, pink-to-white. Seed pods flat, ascending. Plant 2-16" tall. Usually in alpine or subalpine rocky places, from 5500-10,400'. **Plate 16.**

Cardamine bellidifolia var. *pachyphylla*, **thick-leaved alpine bittercress.** Flowers 4-petaled, white. Leaves bright green, fleshy, spoon-shaped. Plant 1-4" tall. In alpine and subalpine rocky places, from 7500-10,400'. **Plate 16.**

C. Breweri, **Brewer's bittercress.** Flowers 4-petaled, white. Seed pods long, upright. Leaves mainly composed of one large, broad leaflet and a pair of smaller leaflets. In very wet places, from 4000-7000'. **Plate 6.**

Draba aureola, **golden draba.** Flowers 4-petaled, in yellow clusters. Seed pods short, in dense cluster. Leaves fleshy, gray-green. Plant 1-4" tall. In dry, alpine places above 9000'. **Plate 16.**

Erysimum capitatum, **Douglas' wallflower.** Flowers 4-petaled, yellow-to-orange. Seed pods long, ascending. Plant ½-2' tall. On fairly open slopes, up to 8000'. **Plate 11.**

Streptanthus tortuosus var. *orbiculatus*, **mountain jewel flower.** Flowers tiny, drab. Stems 4-8" long with round or elliptical leaves usually encircling stem. In open, usually subalpine places, from 6500-9200'. **Plate 15.**

Fumariaceae (Bleeding Heart Family)

Corydalis Caseana, **Sierra corydalis.** Flowers white-to-pink, horizontal, with end spur. Leaves composed of many small leaflets. Usually along streams, from 4000-7000'. **Plate 8.**

Dicentra formosa, **bleeding heart.** Flowers violet, heart-shaped. Leaves fernlike. In wet, shady places, up to 8000'. **Plate 7.**

Gentianaceae (Gentian Family)

Gentiana Newberryi, **Newberry's gentian.** Flowers grayish white, 1-1¼" long. Leaves small. Plants 3-6" tall. In meadows, from 6000-7500'. **Plate 4.**

G. simplex, **hiker's gentian.** Flowers 4-petaled, blue-violet or dark blue. Plant 2-8" tall. In wet meadows, from 4000-7000'. **Plate 5.**

Hydrophyllaceae (Waterleaf Family)

Nama Lobbii, **Lobb's nama.** Flowers tubular, red-violet. Leaves light-green, slightly toothed. Plants spreading, 2-12" tall. In sandy or rocky places, from 4000-8000'. **Plate 14.**

Phacelia frigida, **timberline phacelia.** Flowers violet, clustered. Leaves hairy, pale green. Plant matted, 1-4" tall. In alpine and subalpine places, from 7000-10,400'. **Plate 16.**

P. mutabilis, **changeable phacelia.** Flowers violet, in a coil. Plant 4-18" tall. On open slopes, from 4000-8000'. **Plate 11.** *P. hydrophylloides*, **waterleaf phacelia,** is similar, but with broad, lobed leaves. From 5000-8800'.

Iridaceae (Iris Family)

Sisyrinchium bellum, **California blue-eyed grass.** Flowers blue-to-purple, with yellow throats. Leaves grasslike. In wet, grassy places, up to 6000'. **Plate 7.**

Labiatae (Mint Family)
(Also known as Lamiaceae)

Monardella odoratissima ssp. *pallida*, **coyote mint.** Flowers white-to-violet. Plant ½-2' tall. Common on open slopes, up to 9000'. **Plate 12.**

Prunella vulgaris var. *lanceolata*, **selfheal.** Flowers magenta-to-purple, in terminal clusters. Leaves paired, lack mint odor. Plant 4-20" tall. In wet places, up to 7500'. **Plate 7.**

Stachys rigida ssp. *rivularis*, **rigid hedge nettle.** Flowers white-to-orchid, in terminal cluster. Leaves paired, with strong mint odor. Plant 6-16" tall. In moist places, from 2500-7500'. **Plate 6.**

Leguminosae (Pea Family)
(Also known as Fabaceae)

Lotus oblongifolius var. *nevadensis*, **narrow-leaved lotus.** Flowers pealike, upper half yellow, lower half white. In wet places, up to 7500'. **Plate 4.**

Lupinus Andersonii var. *Christinae*, **Christine's lupine.** Lassen's only yellow-flowered lupine. Flowers dull yellow. Leaves gray-green. Plant 1-3' tall. Common in dry forests, from 5000-7000'. **Plate 10.**

L. obtusilobus, **silver-leaved lupine.** Flowers bluish. Leaves silvery, hairy. Plant 6-16" tall. In moist-to-dry soils, from 6000-9000'. **Plate 11.** *L. sellulus*, **Torrey's lupine,** is similar, with hairy, dull-green leaves. Plant 2-8" tall. Common in dry, gravelly places, from 4000-8000'. *L. arbustus* ssp. *silvicola*, **crest lupine,** is similar, but with green leaves, and is the common blue-flowered lupine of moist-to-dry slopes. Plant 1-2' tall. From 5500-7500'.

L. polyphyllus ssp. *superbus*, **large-leave lupine.** Flowers pale violet or pale blu. Usually common along streams, from 400(8000'. **Plate 8.**

Trifolium sp., **clover.** These plants are usu ally small, with leaves composed of thre leaflets. Flowers pealike, in small, dens clusters. About a dozen species in meadow and forests, from 5000-8000'. **Plate 11.**

Liliaceae (Lily Family)

Calochortus Leichtlinii, **Leichtlin' mariposa tulip.** Petals ½-1½" long, white with purple spot above yellow base. Plan 6-16" tall. In dry, open places, from 4000 8000'. **Plate 12.**

C. macrocarpus, **sagebrush mariposa tulip** Flowers lavender, 2-4" wide. In sagebrus fields, from 4000-6000'. **Plate 3.**

C. nudus, **naked star tulip.** Petals 3, white t pale-lavender. Leaves grasslike. Plant 4-10" tall. In moist places, from 4000-7500'. **Plat 6.**

Erythronium purpurascens, **plain-leave fawn lily.** Flowers white, with yellov throats. Leaves long, waxy. Plant small, deli cate. In wet places, from 4000-8500'. **Plate 4.**

Lilium Kelleyanum, **little leopard lily** Flowers showy, yellow-orange to scarlet with purple spots. Lower leaves usually in incomplete whorl of 4-6 leaves. Plant 2-6 tall. In wet places, from 4000-8000'. **Plate 8.**

L. pardalinum, **leopard lily.** Flowers showy orange-to-red, with purple spots. Lowe leaves usually in whorls of 7 or more leaves. Plant 3-8' tall. In wet places, up to 6000'. **Plate 2.**

L. Washingtonianum, **Washington's lily.** Flowers white, spotted, 3-5" long. In brush and woods, from 4000-6000'. **Plate 3.**

Veratrum californicum, **California corn lily.** Flowers white. Leaves large, cornlike. Common, usually in meadows, up to 8000'. **Plate 8.**

Loasaceae (Loasa Family)

Mentzelia laevicaulis, **giant blazing star.** Flowers yellow, 4-6" wide. In dry, rocky places, up to 6000'. **Plate 2.**

Loranthaceae (Mistletoe Family)

Arceuthobium campylopodum, **western dwarf mistletoe.** Tiny, scaly parasite on branches of conifers. In woods and forests, up to 8500'. **Plate 1.**

Malvaceae (Mallow Family)

Sidalcea oregana ssp. *spicata*, **Oregon checker.** Flowers pink, inch-wide, in terminal cluster. Leaves deeply cleft into linear segments. In wet places, up to 7500'. **Plate 7.**

Nymphaceae (Water Lily Family)

Nuphar polysepalum, **yellow pond lily.** Flowers large, yellow. Leaves large, floating. In ponds and lakes, up to 7000'. **Plate 1.**

Onagraceae (Evening Primrose Family)

Epilobium obcordatum, **rock fringe.** Flowers pink-to-magenta, 4-petaled, each deeply cleft. Leaves of two kinds: short and long. Plants prostrate. In rock crevices, usually in subalpine places, from 6000-9200'. **Plate 15.**

Gayophytum Nuttallii, **Nuttall's gayophytum.** Flowers white-to-pink. 1/16-¼" wide. Plants small, delicate. In dry places, up to 9000'. **Plate 9.**

Orchidaceae (Orchid Family)

Corallorhiza maculata, **spotted coralroot.** Root parasite. Plant orange-to-red. In shady forests, up to 7500'. **Plate 1.**

Habenaria dilatata var. *leucostachys*, **Sierra rein orchid.** Flowers small, white, with projecting spur. In bogs and wet meadows, up to 8000'. **Plate 6.** *H. sparsiflora*, **green rein orchid**, is very similar, but with pale-green flowers.

Papaveraceae (Poppy Family)

Argemone munita ssp. *rotundata*, **prickly poppy.** Flowers large, white, with yellow center composed of 150-250 stamens. Leaves spiny, thistlelike. In very dry, open places, from 3500-6500'. **Plate 3.**

Polemoniaceae (Phlox Family)

Collomia grandiflora, **large-flowered collomia.** Flowers tubular, salmon-colored. In dry, rocky places, up to 8000'. **Plate 2.**

Ipomopsis aggregata, **scarlet gilia.** Flowers trumpetlike, inch-long, scarlet. Leaves skeletonlike. Plant 1-2½' tall. In moist-to-dry places, from 4000-8000'. **Plate 14.**

I. congesta var. *montana*, **ballhead ipomopsis.** Flowers white, tiny, in inch-size globe. Leaves few, deeply lobed. Plant small, prostrate. In rocky, often subalpine places, from 6500-10,400'. **Plate 15.**

Leptodactylon pungens ssp. *pulchriflorum*, **granite gilia.** Flowers funnel-like, white-to-violet. Leaves needlelike. Plant shrubby, 4-12" tall. In rocky places, from 5000-9000'. **Plate 13.**

Linanthus ciliatus, **whisker brush.** Flowers tubular, white-to-pink, with yellow throats. Plant ½-4" tall. Common in dry, open places, up to 8000'. **Plate 13.**

Phlox diffusa, **spreading phlox.** Flowers trumpetlike, fairly small, and white, pink or pale-blue. Leaves needlelike. Plant 2-12" tall. Common in gravelly or sometimes rocky places, from 3500-9000'. **Plate 13.**

Polemonium californicum, **California Jacob's ladder.** Flowers small, violet or pale-blue. Leaves with many pairs of leaflets. Plant low, spreading. On shady forest floors, from 6000-7500'. **Plate 9.**

P. pulcherrimum, **skunk-leaved polemonium.** Flowers white, with yellow centers. Leaves with many pairs of foul-smelling leaflets. Plant matted, 2-12" tall. In alpine places, from 9800-10,400'. **Plate 16.**

Polygonaceae (Buckwheat Family)

Eriogonum marifolium, **marum-leaved buckwheat.** Flowers tiny, in clusters of gold-to-rust. Leaves tiny, oval, gray-green. Plant prostrate. On dry, open slopes, from 6500-9200'. **Plate 15.**

E. nudum var. *oblongifolium*, **nude buckwheat.** Flowers tiny, in white clusters on leafless stems. Plant 1-2½' tall. In open places, up to 7000'. **Plate 12.**

E. pyrolifolium, **pyrola-leaved buckwheat.** Superficially very similar to the very common pussy paws, in the following family, but the buckwheat's leaves are wide and smooth. Plant prostrate. Usually on dry subalpine or alpine slopes, from 7500-10,400'. **Plate 15.**

E. umbellatum, **sulfur flower.** Flowers tiny, in yellow, ascending clusters. Plant 4-12" tall. Common in dry, open places, up to 9200'. **Plate 13.**

Oxyria digyna, **alpine sorrel.** Flowers tiny, brownish red. Leaves round to kidney-shaped. Plant 2-10" tall. In alpine and subalpine places, from 8500-10,400'. **Plate 16.**

Polygonum amphibium var. *stipulaceum*, **water smartweed.** Flowers pink, in thumb-sized clusters. In ponds and lakes, up to 7000'. **Plate 1.**

P. Davisiae, **Davis' knotweed.** Flowers tiny, white-to-green, clustered along spreading stems. Leaves dull-green. Plant 4-12" tall. In open, gravelly and rocky places, from 6500-9200'. **Plate 10.**

Rumex Acetosella, **sheep sorrel.** Flowers tiny, reddish yellow. Leaves arrowhead-shaped, with one large, pointed lobe and, at base of leaf, two smaller pointed lobes. In somewhat open places, up to 6500'. **Plate 3.**

Portulacaceae (Purslane Family)

Calyptridium umbellatum, **pussy paws.** Flowers tiny, pinkish white, in tufted clusters. Stems red. Plant 1-8" tall. Common in dry, gravelly places, from 2500-9000'. **Plate 12.**

Claytonia lanceolata var. *sessilifolia,* **western spring beauty.** Flowers white to pale-pink. Leaves usually only one pair. Plants 1-4" tall. In moist-to-wet places, from 7500-8500'. **Plate 4.**

Lewisia triphylla, **three-leaved lewisia.** Flowers white, with pink stripes. Leaves fleshy, usually 3. Plant 1-4" tall. In moist-to-wet places, from 5000-8000'. **Plate 4.**

Montia perfoliata, **miner's lettuce.** Flowers white, small. Edible leaves circle stem. In moist, shady places, up to 6500'. **Plate 3.**

Primulaceae (Primrose Family)

Dodecatheon alpinum ssp. *majus,* **alpine shooting star.** Flowers 4-petaled, with yellow at base of each. Common in wet places, from 4000-8000'. **Plate 5.**

Pyrolaceae (Wintergreen Family)

Chimaphila umbellata var. *occidentalis,* **western prince's pine.** Flowers drooping, white-to-pink. Leaves shiny, evergreen. In shady forests, from 2500-7000'. **Plate 9.**

Pterospora andromedea, **pinedrops.** Root parasite. Plant orange-to-rust, 1-3' tall. In forests, from 2500-7000'. **Plate 1.**

Pyrola picta, **white-veined wintergreen.** Flowers similar to those of western prince's pine, above. Leaves dark-green, with white veins. On shady forest floors, from 3000-8500'. **Plate 9.**

Sarcodes sanguinea, **snow plant.** Root parasite. Plant bright red, to 1' tall. In shady forests, from 4000-7000'. **Plate 1.**

Ranunculaceae (Buttercup Family)

Aconitum columbianum, **monk's hood.** Flowers purple to blue-violet, shaped like a monk's hood. In wet places, from 4000-7500'. **Plate 8.**

Aquilegia formosa, **crimson columbine.** Flowers nodding, composed of 5 united "petals," each with a red, upright spur and a yellow throat. In shady, wet places, from 4000-7500'. **Plate 7.**

Caltha Howellii, **marsh marigold.** Flowers white, with yellow centers. Leaves round to kidney-shaped. In bogs or marshes, from 4500-8000'. **Plate 4.**

Delphinium Nuttallianum, **Nuttall's larkspur.** Flowers spurred, blue-violet. Stem leaves usually composed of three lancelike leaflets. Usually common in meadows, from 5000-8000'. **Plate 5.**

Ranunculus alismaefolius var. *alismellus,* **dwarf plantain-leaved buttercup.** Flowers bright, shiny, waxy yellow, with 5 or 6 petals. In wet places, from 4500-7500'. **Plate 5.**

Rosaceae (Rose Family)

Fragaria platypetala, **broad-petaled strawberry.** Flowers white. Leaves of 3 leaflets. In moist, sandy places, from 4000-7000'. **Plate 9.**

Potentilla glandulosa, **sticky cinquefoil.** Flowers cream-to-yellow. Leaves composed of toothed leaflets. Plant 4-30" tall. In moist-to-dry places, up to 9200'. **Plate 10.**

Rubiaceae (Madder Family)

Galium Grayanum, **Gray's bedstraw.** Flowers greenish white, later forming very hairy seeds. Leaves ¼-½", in whorls of 4. Plants spreading. Stems 1-4" long. Usually on dry, subalpine slopes, from 7500-9200'. **Plate 15.**

Saxifragaceae (Saxifrage Family)

Peltiphyllum peltatum, **umbrella plant.** Leaves huge, up to 2' wide. In and along streams, up to 5000'. **Plate 1.**

Saxifraga aprica, **Sierra saxifrage.** Flowers white, in a small, terminal cluster. Plant 1-5" tall. Often in mossy or wet places, from 6000-8500'. **Plate 4.**

S. Tolmiei, **alpine saxifrage.** Flowers white, with yellow center, clustered on reddish flower stalk. Leaves basal, thick, fleshy. Plant 1-8" tall. In moist-to-rocky places, from 8000-10,000'. **Plate 16.** *S. punctata* spp. *arguta,* **brook saxifrage,** is similar, but with nonfleshy, roundish, toothed leaves. Plant ½-1½' tall. In wet places, from 6000-8000'.

Scrophulariaceae (Figwort Family)

Castilleja Applegatei, **Applegate's paintbrush.** Flowers scarlet, somewhat leaflike. Leaves dull-green, with wavy margins. Plant ½-2' tall. Common in dry, open places, from 2000-9000'. **Plate 14.** *C. miniata*, **giant red paintbrush**, is very similar, but leaves are bright green and have smooth margins. Plant 1-3' tall. Fairly common in dry-to-wet places, up to 8000.'

C. Payneae, **pumice paintbrush.** Flowers dull-orange, somewhat leaflike. Plant 4-8" tall. Fairly common in pumice or gravel, from 5500-9000'. **Plate 13.**

Mimulus guttatus, **common large monkey flower.** Flowers yellow, with red dots on throat. Plant 2-24" tall. Usually common along creeks or at springs, up to 8000'. **Plate 5.**

M. primuloides, **primrose monkey flower.** Flower yellow, one per stem. Leaves small, basal, usually with long, scattered hairs. Plant 1-4" tall. Common in open, wet places, from 4000-7500'. **Plate 5.**

M. Torreyi, **Torrey's monkey flower.** Flowers pink, with yellow throats. Plant 1-6" tall. In dry, open places, up to 7000'. **Plate 14.** This common plant is often found with an equally small, similar "monkey flower," *Collinsia Torreyi*, **Torrey's blue-eyed Mary.** Its flowers are 2-lipped, the upper lip white or pale yellow, the lower lip blue-violet. Up to 8000'.

Pedicularis densiflora, **Indian warrior.** Flowers dark red. Leaves green, reddening with age. Stems reddish. Plant 6-12" tall. Partial root parasite on woody shrubs. In woods and brush, up to 5000'. **Plate 1.**

P. groenlandica, **elephant heads.** Flowers pink-to-magenta, shaped like tiny elephant heads, clustered on tall stalk. Partial root parasite in very wet, open places, from 5500-8000'. **Plate 7.**

P. semibarbata, **dwarf lousewort.** Flowers dull-yellow. Leaves dull, dark-green. Very common on forest floors, from 5000-7500'. **Plate 9.**

Penstemon Davidsonii, **Davidson's penstemon.** Flowers inch-long, magenta-to-purple. Leaves small. Plant matted, in alpine and subalpine rocky places, from 8000-10,400'. **Plate 16.**

P. gracilentus, **slender penstemon.** Flowers mostly blue-violet, with pink to red-violet at base. Stem slender, usually solitary. Fairly common in dry, somewhat open places, from 4000-7000'. **Plate 11.**

P. neotericus, **derived penstemon.** Flowers mostly blue violet, with pink to red-violet at base. Stems many. Leaves dull-green, basal leaves with short stalks. Plant 1-2' tall. Fairly common in dry, open places, from 3500-7000'. **Plate 14.**

P. Newberryi, **mountain pride.** Flowers red, tubular. Leaves small, leathery. Plant bushy, ½-1½' tall. In bedrock cracks, on rocky slopes or even in pumice, from 5000-9200'. **Plate 14.**

P. oreocharis, **meadow penstemon.** Flowers tubular, ½" long, magenta-to-purple. In dry-to-wet meadows, from 4500-7500'. **Plate 7.**

P. speciosus, **showy penstemon.** Flowers mostly blue-violet, with pink to red-violet at base. Stems many. Leaves green, basal leaves with stems almost as long as leaf blade. Plant 1-2½' tall. In dry, open places, from 3500-8000'. **Plate 14.**

Verbascum Thapsus, **common mullein.** Flower stalk dense with small, yellow flowers. Mature plant 4-8' tall. In dry, open places, often roadsides, up to 7000'. **Plate 2.**

Veronica alpina var. *alterniflora*, **alpine brooklime.** Petals violet, with dark veins. Flowers tiny, 4-lobed, in small, terminal cluster. In or near water, from 6000-8000'. **Plate 5.**

V. americana, **American brooklime.** Flowers small, violet, 4-lobed, growing in paired clusters, each pair rising from a pair of leaves. In streams, ponds and lake margins, up to 7500'. **Plate 1.**

Umbelliferae (Carrot Family)
(Also known as Apiaceae)

Note: All species have tiny flowers in umbrellalike clusters. Some species of this carrot-and-parsley family are highly edible, but others, such as poison hemlock and water hemlock, are fatal. Some edible species resemble some poisonous species, therefore don't eat any of them!

Angelica Breweri, **Brewer's angelica.** Balls of white flowers in umbrellalike cluster. Leaves divided into many lancelike leaflets. Stems hollow. In meadows, woods and rocky slopes, from 3000-8000'. **Plate 8.**

Heracleum lanatum, **cow parsnip.** Flowers white. Leaves up to 2' wide, each composed of 3 maplelike leaflets. In moist-to-wet places, usually at edges of meadows, up to 7500'. **Plate 8.**

Ligusticum Grayi, **Gray's lovage.** Flowers white, clustered on long stalks. Leaves of several deeply toothed leaflets. Fairly common in moist places, from 4000-7500'. **Plate 6.**

Perideridia Parishii, **Parish's yampah.** Flowers white, in inch-size cluster. Leaves divided into 3 linear leaflets. Plant 1-3' tall. Usually common in meadows, up to 8000'. **Plate 6.** *P. Bolanderi,* **Bolander's yampah,** and *P. Gairdneri,* **Gairdner's yampah,** are similar, but with 5 or more leaflets per leaf. The first has small clusters merged into a large cluster; the second has small clusters, each on a long stem, so the clusters are separate, not touching.

Violaceae (Violet Family)

Viola Bakeri, **Baker's violet.** Flowers yellow. Leaves with smooth edge. Plant 1-4" tall. In moist-to-wet places, from 4500-8000'. **Plate 5.** *V. glabella,* **smooth yellow violet,** is similar, but its leaves are slightly toothed and plant is usually over 4" tall. In wet, shady places, up to 7000'.

V. Macloskeyi, **Macloskey's violet.** California's only native white-flowered violet. Plant usually 1-2" tall. In very wet places, from 3500-8000'. **Plate 4.**

V. nephrophylla, **northern bog violet.** Flowers blue-violet. Leaves heart-shaped. Plant 2-8" tall. In moist, shady spaces, up to 7000'. **Plate 5.** *V. adunca,* **western dog violet** is similar, but flowers are deep- to pale-violet and stems are creeping.

V. purpurea ssp. *dimorpha,* **mountain violet.** Flowers yellow. Leaves toothed. The only violet in dry, fairly open places. Common from 4500-9000'. **Plate 9.**

SHRUBS

Shrubs, though plentiful, are usually not in flower, and hence most visitors disregard them. This section covers the bulk of the shrubs growing in Lassen Park, Caribou Wilderness and Thousand Lakes Wilderness. Uncommon species are omitted, as are most of those growing below the park. Those growing in dry Hat Creek Valley can be identified along Chapter 18's Spatter Cone Nature Trail. Those growing in moist, cool,

low-elevation forests can be identified along Chapter 19's Burney Falls Nature Trail. Many of Lassen Park's shrubs can be seen along the Park Road (Chapter 8) and along the park's nature trails (Chapter 10). Along the park's other trails (Chapters 11-14), interesting trailside shrubs are mentioned in the route descriptions.

Because shrubs are generally not in flower, technical botanical keys are often useless. Hence the following list is based primarily on habitat. Under each habitat the plants are listed alphabetically by family. The habitats are:
1. Wet Meadows, Streams and Lakeshores
2. Fir Forests
3. Gravelly Flats and Slopes
4. Dry, Open Slopes
5. Moist, Rocky Slopes.
As you might expect, some plants overlap habitats.

1. Wet Meadows, Streams and Lakeshores

Betulaceae (Birch Family)

Alnus tenuifolia, **thinleaf alder.** Also known as mountain alder, this shrub is very common along streams and meadows. Its leaves are oval, toothed and 1-3" long.

Cornaceae (Dogwood Family)

Cornus stolonifera, **creek dogwood.** As its name implies, it grows along creeks, rarely elsewhere. Its leaves are paired, pointed, smooth margined and 2-4" long. Its branches are reddish. Photo on p. 205.

Ericaceae (Heath Family)

Kalmia polifolia var. *microphylla,* **bog kalmia.** This miniature shrub grows best on the park's higher boggy slopes. Its leaves are paired, narrow and ½-1" long. Flowers, when present, are rose-colored and showy, clustered atop a stem. Photo on p. 57.

Ledum glandulosum var. *californicum,* **Labrador tea.** Farily common at lakes and along creeks, this shrub is best identified by the turpentine odor of its leaves. The leaves are oblong and bluntly pointed, green above, yellow-green below and ½-1½" long. P. 57.

Phyllodoce Breweri, **red mountain heather.** Decked with needlelike leaves, this miniature shrub is the park's commonest wet-habitat heath, and it usually grows with the three other heaths. Like the kalmia, it has rose-colored, showy flowers that seem to atract mosquitoes—heaths and mosquitoes certainly go together. Photo on p. 57.

Vaccinium occidentale, **western blueberry.** This knee-high huckleberry grows in boggy meadows and along lakeshores. Its leaves are oval, pointed, whitish green and ½-1" long.

Rosaceae (Rose Family)

Amelanchier pallida, **pallid serviceberry.** Usually found along or near streams, this highly variable shrub has broad leaves ¾-1½" long and flattened along their end. The leaves are toothed on the sides and on the blunt end, but not near the base. P. 57.

Spiraea densiflora, **mountain spiraea.** Like the serviceberry, this shrub's leaves are toothed only along the upper half of the leaf, not near the base. The leaves are ¾-1½" long and half as wide. Flowers are very small, but form rose-colored, showy clusters. This shrub often associates with red mountain heather.

Salicaceae (Willow Family)

Salix Jepsonii, **Jepson's willow.** Leaves are usually 1-3" long, ½-1" wide, and usually wider beyond their midpoint. Plants grow in wet-to-damp meadows and slopes. P. 57.

S. Lemmonii, **Lemmon's willow.** This willow, growing in all kinds of wet environments, is easily the area's commonest willow. Leaves are 1-4" long and usually only ¼-½" wide.

S. Scouleriana, **Scouler's willow.** Growing to tree-size proportions, this willow tends to shun water and just barely fits into the wet-environments category. Like Jepson's willow, it has leaves that are wider beyond their midpoint. The trunk's bark is smooth and light-gray, almost like aspen bark.

Saxifragaceae (Saxifrage Family)

Ribes nevadense, **Sierra currant.** Growing along streams or in moist, shady woods, this rather delicate shrub is the commonest of the area's currants and gooseberries. Its leaves are 3- or 5-lobed and resemble small, blunt, maple leaves. Of the area's currants and gooseberries, this species is the only one that lacks *both* spiny leaves and hairy stems, though minor hairs are on the leaves' undersides. Photo on p. 204.

2. Fir Forests.

Ericaceae (Heath Family)

Arctostaphylos nevadensis, **pinemat man-**

zanita. This is the very common forest-floor plant that rarely gets over knee-high. Its leaves are small, pointed and tough. Its whitish-pink flowers, when present, are tiny, hanging and urn-shaped. Photo on p. 57.

Fagaceae (Oak Family)

Castanopsis sempervirens, **bush chinquapin.** Where fir forests are fairly open, this robust shrub can do well. Its leaves are leathery and oblong, dark green above and pale yellow-green below. The fruit is a very spiny ball about 1" in diameter. Photo on p. 57.

3. Gravelly Flats and Slopes.

Compositae (Sunflower Family)
(Also known as Asteraceae)

Haplopappus Bloomeri, **Bloomer's goldenbush.** This foot-high shrub is easily the commonest shrub of gravelly areas. It produces golden yellow sunflowers after early August, but usually goes unrecognized before then. Its leaves are about 1-2" long but only ⅛" wide. Photo on p. 57.

4. Dry, Open Slopes.

Ericaceae (Heath Family)

Arctostaphylos patula, **greenleaf manzanita.** Commonest just outside and below the park, this robust shrub makes a major incursion into the Manzanita Lake-Table Mountain area. It is also quite plentiful on southwest-facing slopes above Lee and Kelly camps, along the park's southern borderlands. The leaves are bright-green, leathery and round-to-oval. The bark is dark red and very smooth. Photo on p. 205.

Fagaceae (Oak Family)

Quercus vaccinifolia, **huckleberry oak.** Though extremely common at mid-elevations in the Sierra Nevada, this drab, waist-high oak barely makes it north far enough to enter the park. However, it does grow in local abundance on dry, rocky slopes above Drakesbad and above Warner Valley. Its dull leaves are leathery and oblong, about ½-1" long. Its acorns average ½" long.

Rhamnaceae (Buckthorn Family)

Ceanothus prostratus, **squaw carpet.** A dense mat, 1-4" high but up to 3 yards wide, this plant is unmistakable. Its shiny, dark-green leaves are hollylike. It sporadically appears, usually in gravelly or rocky places at the park's lower elevations. It does better in dry areas below the park. Photo on p. 57.

C. velutinus, **tobacco brush.** Often associated with greenleaf manzanitas but growing in fairly dry, diverse habitats up to 8000', this robust shrub is best recognized by its glossy, sticky, evergreen leaves. These are elliptical, 1-3" long, and finely toothed. When in bloom, this lilac is sensuously aromatic.

Rosaceae (Rose Family)

Holodiscus microphyllus var. *glabrescens,* **small-leaved cream bush.** This drab plant grows in Hat Creek Valley as well as on the Brokeoff Mountain summit. Its leaves are ½-1" long and are toothed only along the upper half of the leaf. Flowers are small, whitish and clustered. Plants are 1-4' tall.

5. Moist, Rocky Slopes.

Caprifoliaceae (Honeysuckle Family)

Sambucus caerulea, **blue elderberry.** This large shrub ranges from 6-20' tall and grows up to an elevation of 6000', barely entering the park. It is prominent at Battle Creek Campground, west of the park's headquarters. Each leaf is composed of 5-9 leaflets, each toothed, lancelike and 2-6" long. Flowers bloom atop stems in flat-topped clusters, these changing to clusters of blue berries. Photo on p. 177.

S. microbotrys, **red elderberry.** A miniature version of the above, this species gets only waist-high, if that, and it grows from 6500-8500'. Its flower clusters are domelike, changing to clusters of red berries. Photo on p. 101.

TREES

In Lassen Park, Caribou Wilderness and Thousand Lakes Wilderness, most of the trees are conifers. In the following key, the digger pine, growing in hot, dry areas, is the only conifer that doesn't reach these high elevations. Up here, the only broad-leaved trees are all members of the willow family: aspen, cottonwood, willow. Between 6000' and 3000', other broad-leaved trees appear: two oaks, an alder and a dogwood. In the key below, trees are listed by leaf characteristics. In the description that follows, the trees in each group are listed in order of ascending elevation.

Conifers: all evergreen in this area.
1. Pines: needles in bundles of 2-5, cones hanging (a. 2 needles, b. 3, c. 5).
2. True Firs: needles in rows along branches, cones upright.

3. False Fir and Hemlock: needles in rows, cones hanging.
4. Other Conifers: leaves scalelike.

Broad-leaved trees: all deciduous in this area.
5. Willow: leaves usually 3-6 times longer than wide.
6. Alder, Aspen, Cottonwood and Dogwood: leaves usually 1-2 times longer.
7. Oaks: leaves lobed.

1a. Pines with 2 needles.

Pinus contorta var. *Murrayana,* **lodgepole pine.** Needles 1-2½" long. Cones 1-2½" long. Bark thin and scaly. Tree 50-120' tall. Grows where ground water is plentiful, from about 5000-8000'.

1b. Pines with 3 needles.

P. Sabiniana, **Digger pine.** Needles gray-green, 8-12" long. Cones broad, 6-11" long. Trunk usually divided, foliage sparse. Tree 40-80' tall. Grows in foothills and in Hat Creek Valley up to 4500'.

P. ponderosa, **ponderosa pine.** Needles yellow-green, 5-10" long. Cones 3-5" long, with out-turned prickles. Bark yellow and platy in mature trees. Tree 150-200' tall. Grows on well-drained flats and gentle slopes, from 2000-6500'.

P. Jeffreyi, **Jeffrey pine.** Needles blue-green, 5-10" long. Cones 5-10" long, with in-turned prickles. Bark reddish brown, with butterscotch odor detected in bark furrows of mature trees. Tree 50-180' tall. Usually grows in drier places than ponderosa pine and usually on steeper slopes and at higher elevations, from 4000-8500'.

P. washoensis, **Washoe pine.** Needles gray-green, 4-6" long. Cones quite variable in size, usually under 5" long, with in-turned prickles. Bark similar to that of Jeffrey pine, but without butterscotch odor. Tree 80-180' tall, growing only in park's Butte Lake area at about 6000-6500'.

1c. Pines with 5 needles.

P. Lambertiana, **sugar pine.** Needles 3-4" long. Cones long and narrow, 10-16" long, growing at ends of long, graceful branches. Area's tallest tree, 150-240' tall. Usually grows on well-drained slopes, from 3000-6500'.

P. monticola, **western white pine.** Needles 2-4" long. Cones narrow, 4-8" long. Checkerboard pattern on bark of mature trees. Tree

Plate 1. Aquatic herbs (first four) and parasitic herbs (last five).
Top row, left to right: *Nuphar polysepalum* (Nymphaceae), *Polygonum amphibium* (Polygonaceae), *Peltiphylum peltatum* (Saxifragaceae). **Middle row:** *Veronica americana* (Scrophulariaceae), *Arceuthobium campylopodum* (Loranthaceae), *Corallorhiza maculata* (Orchidaceae). **Bottom row:** *Pterospora andromedea* and *Sarcodes sanguinea* (both Pyrolaceae), *Pedicularis densiflora* (Scrophulariaceae).

41

Plate 2. Herbs generally growing below 6000 feet; flowers yellow-to-scarlet.
Top row, left to right: *Silene californica* (Caryophyllaceae), *Eriophyllum lanatum* and *Helenium Bigelovii* (both Compositae). **Middle row:** *Madia elegans* and *Tragopogon dubius* (both Compositae), *Lilium pardalinum* (Liliaceae). **Bottom row:** *Mentzelia laevicaulis* (Loasaceae), *Collomia grandiflora* (Polemoniaceae), *Verbascum Thapsus* (Scrophulariaceae).

Plate 3. Herbs generally growing below 6000 feet: flowers white, white-and-yellow, blue, violet or purple.
Top row, left to right: *Chrysanthemum Leucanthemum, Cichorium Intybus* and *Cirsium vulgare* (all Compositae). **Middle row:** *Calystegia malacophylla* (Convolvulaceae), *Calochortus macrocarpus* and *Lilium Washingtonianum* (both Liliaceae). **Bottom row:** *Argemone munita* (Papaveraceae), *Rumex Acetosella* (Polygonaceae), *Montia perfoliata* (Portulacaceae).

Plate 4. Herbs generally growing in wet places; plants usually less than one foot tall; flowers white, pinkish-white, off-white, or white-and-yellow.

Top row, left to right: *Stellaria longipes* (Caryophyllaceae), *Gentiana Newberryi* (Gentianaceae), *Lotus oblongifolius* (Leguminosae). **Middle row:** *Erythronium purpurascens* (Liliaceae), *Claytonia lanceolata* and *Lewisia triphylla* (both Portulacaceae). **Bottom row:** *Caltha Howellii* (Ranunculaceae), *Saxifraga aprica* (Saxifragaceae), *Viola Macloskeyi* (Violaceae).

Plate 5. Herbs generally growing in wet places; plants usually less than one foot tall; flowers yellow, violet, red-violet or blue-violet.

Top row, left to right: *Gentiana simplex* (Gentianaceae), *Dodecatheon alpinum* (Primulaceae), *Delphinium Nuttallianum* (Ranunculaceae). **Middle row:** *Ranunculus alismaefolius* (Ranunculaceae), *Mimulus guttatus* and *M. primuloides* (both Scrophulariaceae). **Bottom row:** *Veronica alpina* (Scrophulariaceae), *Viola Bakeri* and *V. nephrophylla* (both Violaceae).

45

Plate 6. Herbs generally growing in wet places; plants usually ½-2½ feet tall; flowers white, greenish-white, pinkish-white or yellow.

Top row, left to right: *Achillea lanulosa, Arnica Chamissonis* and *Taraxacum officinale* (all Compositae). **Middle row:** *Cardamine Breweri* (Cruciferae), *Stachys rigida* (Labiatae), *Calochortus nudus* (Liliaceae). **Bottom row:** *Habenaria dilatata* (Orchidaceae), *Ligusticum Grayi* and *Perideridia Parishii* (both Umbelliferae).

Plate 7. Herbs generally growing in wet places; plants usually ½-2½ fet tall; flowers not whitish or all-yellow, but some yellow may be present.
Top row, left to right: *Hackelia floribunda* (Boraginaceae), *Erigeron peregrinus* (Compositae), *Dicentra formosa* (Fumariaceae). **Middle row:** *Sisyrinchium bellum* (Iridaceae), *Prunella vulgaris* (Labiatae), *Sidalcea oregana* (Malvaceae). **Bottom row:** *Aquilegia formosa* (Ranunculaceae), *Pedicularis groenlandica* and *Penstemon oreocharis* (both Scrophulariaceae).

47

Plate 8. Herbs generally growing in wet places; plants usually taller than 2½ feet at maturity.

Top row, left to right: *Cirsium Douglasii* and *Senecio triangularis* (both Compositae). *Corydalis Caseana* (Fumariaceae). **Middle row:** *Lupinus polyphyllus* (Leguminosae), *Lilium Kelleyanum* and *Veratrum californicum* (both Liliaceae). **Bottom row:** *Aconitum columbianum* (Ranunculaceae), *Angelica Breweri* and *Heracleum lanatum* (both Umbelliferae).

Plate 9. Small herbs generally growing in forest.
Top row, left to right: *Apocynum pumilum* (Apocynaceae), *Hieracium albiflorum* (Compositae), *Gayophytum Nuttallii* (Onagraceae). **Middle row:** *Polemonium californicum* (Polemoniaceae), *Chimaphila umbellata* and *Pyrola picta* (both Pyrolaceae). **Bottom row:** *Fragaria platypetala* (Rosaceae), *Pedicularis semibarbata* (Scrophulariaceae), *Viola purpurea* (Violaceae).

Plate 10. Herbs generally growing in forest; flowers off-white, greenish-white, creamy or yellow.

Top row, left to right: *Triteleia ixioides* (Amaryllidaceae), *Silene Lemmonii* (Caryophyllaceae), *Anaphalis margaritacea* (Compositae). **Middle row:** *Microseris nutans, Senecio aronicoides* and *Whitneya dealbata* (all Compositae). **Bottom row:** *Lupinus Andersonii* (Leguminosae), *Polygonum Davisiae* (Polygonaceae), *Potentilla glandulosa* (Rosaceae).

Plate 11. Herbs generally growing in forest; flowers pure white, yellow-orange, red, violet or blue.

Top row, left to right: *Allium campanulatum* and *Brodiaea hyacinthina* (both Amaryllidaceae), *Hackelia californica* (Boraginaceae). **Middle row:** *Stephanomeria lactucina* (Compositae), *Erysimum capitatum* (Cruciferae), *Phacelia mutabilis* (Hydrophyllaceae). **Bottom row:** *Lupinus obtusilobus* and *Trifolium* sp. (both Leguminosae), *Penstemon gracilentus* (Scrophulariaceae).

Plate 12. Herbs generally growing in dry, open places; flowers white or off-white.
Top row, left to right: *Arenaria Kingii* (Caryophyllaceae), *Chenopodium incognitum* (Chenopodiaceae), *Antennaria alpina* (Compositae). **Middle row:** *Brickellia Greenei* and *Cirsium foliosum* (both Compositae), *Monardella odoratissima* (Labiatae). **Bottom row:** *Calochortus Leichtlinii* (Liliaceae), *Eriogonum nudum* (Polygonaceae), *Calyptridium umbellatum* (Portulacaceae).

Plate 13. Herbs generally growing in dry, open places; flowers white and leaves needlelike, or flowers yellow or dull-orange and leaves not needlelike. Top row, left to right: *Balsamorhiza sagittata, Hieracium horridum* and *Senecio canus* (all Compositae). **Middle row:** *Wyethia mollis* (Compositae), *Leptodactylon pungens* and *Linanthus ciliatus* (both Polemoniaceae). **Bottom row:** *Phlox diffusa* (Polemoniaceae), *Eriogonum umbellatum* (Polygonaceae), *Castilleja Payneae* (Scrophulariaceae).

Plate 14. Herbs generally growing in dry, open places; flowers deep-pink, red, violet or blue.

Top row, left to right: *Dichelostemma congestum* (Amaryllidaceae), *Cycladenia humilis* (Apocynaceae), *Nama Lobbii* (Hydrophyllaceae). **Middle row:** *Ipomopsis aggregata* (Polemoniaceae), *Castilleja Applegatei* and *Mimulus Torreyi* (both Scrophulariaceae). **Bottom row:** *Penstemon neotericus, P. Newberryi* and *P. speciosus* (all Scrophulariaceae).

Plate 15. Herbs generally growing in dry, open, usually subalpine places.
Top row, left to right: *Silene Douglasii* (Caryophyllaceae), *Chaenactis nevadensis* and *Raillardella argentea* (both Compositae). **Middle row:** *Streptanthus tortuosus* (Cruciferae), *Epilobium obcordatum* (Onagraceae), *Ipomopsis congesta* (Polemoniaceae). **Bottom row:** *Eriogonum marifolium* and *E. pyrolifolium* (both Polygonaceae), *Galium Grayanum* (Rubiaceae).

Plate 16. Herbs generally growing in subalpine or alpine places.
Top row, left to right: *Senecio Fremontii* (Compositae), *Arabis platysperma* and *Cardamine bellidifolia* (both Cruciferae). **Middle row:** *Draba aureola* (Cruciferae), *Phacelia frigida* (Hydrophyllaceae), *Polemonium pulcherrimum* (Polemoniaceae). **Bottom row:** *Oxyria digyna* (Polygonaceae), *Saxifraga Tolmiei* (Saxifragaceae), *Penstemon Davidsonii* (Scrophulariaceae).

Common shrubs of Lassen Park. Top row, left to right: bog kalmia, Labrador tea, red mountain heather. Middle row: pinemat manzanita, pallid serviceberry, Jepson's willow. Bottom row: bush chinquapin, Bloomer's goldenbush, squaw carpet.

50-150' tall. Grows on well-drained slopes, from 5500-8500'.

P. albicaulis, **whitebark pine.** Needles stiff, 1½-3" long. Cones 1½-3" long. Bark thin and scaly, like that of lodgepole pine. Tree up to 50' tall, but a prostrate shrub at highest elevations. Grows from 8000-10,000'.

2. True Firs.

Abies concolor, **white fir.** Needles 1-2½" long, in 2 rows. Each needle with a half twist at base. Cones 3-5" long. Bark of mature tree gray-brown, deeply furrowed. Tree 150-230' tall. Grows on slopes with good soil, from 2500-6500'.

A. magnifica, **red fir.** Needles ¾-1½" long, curving up, densely covering branches. Cones 5-8" long. Bark of mature tree reddish brown, deeply furrowed. Tree 120-200' tall. Grows on slopes with good soil, from 5500-8500'.

3. False Fir and Hemlock.

Pseudotsuga Menziesii, **Douglas-fir.** Needles soft, about 1" long, and growing all around the branches. Cones 2-4" long, lightweight, with toothed bracts projecting from scales. Bark dull-brown, deeply furrowed. Tree 150-230' tall. Usually grows along with firs, from 2000-6000'.

Tsuga Mertensiana, **mountain hemlock.** Needles soft, about 1" long, and growing all around the branches. Cones 1-3" long, lightweight, without bracts. Bark purplish brown to reddish brown. Tree 25-100' tall. Grows in areas of deep snowpack, from 6500-9200'.

4. Other Conifers.

Calocedrus decurrens, **incense-cedar.** Leaves yellow-green, scalelike, about ⅛-¼" long, and growing in flat, horizontal sprays. Cones about 1" long, with only 2 fertile scales. Bark cinnamon-brown, fibrous. Tree 80-150' tall. Associates with white firs and ponderosa pines, growing from 2000-6500'.

Juniperus occidentalis, **western juniper.** Leaves gray-green, scalelike, about ⅛" long, growing on rounded branchlets. Cones berrylike, blue-black when mature, though covered with a whitish powder. Bark cinnamon-brown, shreddy. Tree 10-50' tall.

Rare in Lassen Park, with a few specimens i the Butte and Juniper lakes areas. Grows i dry, rocky places, from 3000-7500'.

5. Willow.

Salix lasiandra, **Pacific willow.** Leaves lon and narrow like those of Lemmon's willow but twice as large, about 6" long by 1" wid Bark deeply furrowed, unlike that c Scouler's willow, which is also often tre size. Tree 15-40' tall, with trunk up to 2½' i diameter. Best seen at Manzanita Lak Grows in wet places, up to 6500'.

6. Alder, Aspen, Cottonwood and Dogwood.

Alnus rhombifolia, **white alder.** Leaves ol long, toothed, 2-4" long. Cones browr ½-¾" long. Bark scaly, brown. Tree 30-10C tall. Grows in shady woods along stream up to 5000'. Photo on p. 204.

Cornus Nuttallii, **Pacific dogwood.** Leave oblong, not toothed, 2-5" long. Large white-petaled "flowers," the petals bein modified leaves. Bark quite smooth, gray brown to red-brown. Tree 10-50' tall, grow ing in shady, moist-to-wet places, from 2000-5000'.

Populus trichocarpa, **black cottonwood** Leaves toothed, 2-3" long, about half as wid as long. Bark gray-brown, furrowed. Tre 60-120' tall. Grows near water, up to 7000'. *P. tremuloides,* **aspen.** Leaves finely toothed 1-2" long, roundish with pointed tip; rustl in the wind. Bark thin, white. Tree 10-60 tall. Grows where ground water is abundant from 5000-7000'.

7. Oaks.

Quercus Garryana, **Oregon white oak** Leaves deeply lobed, 3-6" long, and usuall widest past midpoint. Lobes are rounded Acorns stubby, about 1" long. Bark light gray, scaly. Tree 20-60' tall. Grows in moist to-dry places, from 2500-4000'. Photo p. 204 *Q. Kelloggii,* **California black oak.** Leave deeply lobed, 3-8" long, and usually wides before midpoint. Lobes have points. Acorn 1-1½" long. Bark blackish brown, scaly. Tre 50-80' tall. Grows in moist-to-dry places from 2000-5500', almost entering Lasse Park near Manzanita Lake.

7 Zoology

Introduction

Most campers are still fast asleep as another summer dawn breaks over Manita Lake. The lake's bird population, however, has already been stirring and inging for two hours. A Brewer's blackbird alights on a willow branch projecting ut from the lake's northwest shore. In doing so, it unknowingly plays a crucial role n a chain of events as it dislodges a leafhopper, who had been happily sucking the uice of a willow leaf. Struggling in the lake's placid water, it sends ripples across he surface. These attract a water scorpion, which had been lurking among sedges ;rowing in shallow water beneath the willow branch. In an instant the water corpion lashes out at the hapless leafhopper, securing a tasty meal. But in doing so, t exposes itself to a fingerling trout, which had been drawn by the commotion, and he trout quickly dispatches the water scorpion. Lazily it swims to the lake's hallow southwest waters in search of more prey. Instead, it becomes the prey, as an dult common garter snake darts out from a cluster of pink, thumb-sized water martweeds (had the trout been mature and the snake immature, the feast would ave been the other way around). The trout, however, is not quickly downed, and in he struggle, the garter snake succumbs to a great blue heron, who consumes the nake, trout and all. But by now a fisherman is heading down the campground's rail to the lake, and the heron flies away without being seen. The fisherman reaches he lake, surveys its quiet waters, and thinks, "How peaceful; Nature sure is vonderful." Then he casts his line into the lake.

If you could talk with the animals that were consumed in the foregoing story, hey would not agree that Nature is "peaceful" or "wonderful." These terms, and)thers we often use to describe our feelings about Nature, are certainly biased. Rather, the old cliche holds true: Nature plays no favorites. *Every* organism is exposed to death from the moment of its conception. Very few organisms live to see naturity; infant and juvenile mortality is the rule rather than the exception. If anything, Nature is *not* wonderful, but rather a "jungle" where the fittest survive.

Still, being at the top of a food chain, we can enjoy Nature in the mountains, fo
we don't have to constantly look over our shoulders to see what beast is going to try
to eat us next. If you're not at the top of a food chain, you have to worry. The story
above describes one such food chain, which begins with a willow leaf and ends
with a great blue heron. Food chains are not isolated series, but rather are interlock
ing. The fingerling trout could have been eaten by a water shrew, a larger trout, or
the fisherman; its fate didn't lie with the garter snake. Likewise, every animal has an
assortment of species it can feed on and also an assortment of species that could
feed on it. Therefore, in the Manzanita Lake area, hundreds of species can be
directly or indirectly involved with one another, and the sum of these species
makes up a food net. With all these interrelated species maintaining checks and
balances, the natural environment in Lassen Park is quite stable, considerably more
so than a sterile urban environment.

Nature in the wilderness, while being quite stable, is not very efficient. The
leafhopper, sucking juices from the willow's leaf, used only 10-20% of the energy
present in the juice. The rest of the energy was lost as heat. Likewise, the water
scorpion used only 10-20% of the energy presented by the leafhopper, and so on. Of
the energy initially present in the willow's leaf, the heron, at the top of the food
chain, got to use only about 1/100 of 1% of it. Looked at another way, 5 tons (10,000
pounds) of willow leaves are required to add a pound to a heron. Obviously, if
you're at the top of the food chain, you're going to be few in number. Hence
animals, particularly predators high on their food chains, are quite scarce compared to plants. This is one reason why wildflowers are so much more easily
viewed than animals—there are so many more of them. Of course, almost all
animals shun humans, which makes them scarcer still. In Lassen Park, only a few
birds and mammals come up to us for handouts; we must work to see the other
species.

Invertebrates

Invertebrates, which are animals without
backbones, usually occupy the lower pos-
itions in a food web, and their numbers are
high. In a mountain meadow there can be
thousands of invertebrates in every square
yard: the invertebrate population in Dersch
Meadows could run into the billions. As in
other land environments, insects make up
the bulk of the species. They serve as con-
sumers and predators, and the latter could
probably keep the former in check without
the aid of birds. Insects are probably the most
important agents in the pollination of plants.
Pollinators range from hummingbird-sized
sphinx moths down to almost microscopic
beetles. Mosquitoes are important pollinators in our mountain environment, more
so than bees or flies, which are relatively
uncommon above 6000 feet. Insects also cull
forests of old and sickly trees and then re-

duce the fallen snags to humus, with the aid
of other invertebrates and of fungi and bac
teria. It appears that vertebrates, including
man, are unnecessary in any land environ
ment; rather, we are a superfluous "cream of
the crop" occupying the upper rungs of the
food web. But how different the Lassen land
scape would be without vertebrates; a fores
without birds would seem hauntingly mute

Fish

Fish are regarded as the lowest of the ver
tebrates, since all other land vertebrate
evolved from fishy ancestors. In the Lassen
area, the predominant kind of fish is trout
and the common species are rainbow, brown
and eastern brook. Only rainbow trout is na
tive to Lassen Park. The other trout were
intentionally introduced in the park, bu
chubs, suckers and dace were accidentally
introduced when they were used as live bait

Today, most lakes in the Lassen area outside the park are still planted with trout, often with hybrids. For information on fishing conditions, see Chapter 4.

Amphibians and Reptiles

Ancestral fish gave rise to ancestral amphibians about 380 million years ago, which in turn gave rise to ancestral reptiles about 340 million years ago, the time when the earliest forms of trees and ferns appeared. This time seems very remote, but in terms of earth history it is quite recent. If all of the earth's history could be compressed into one year, then amphibians would appear on December 1 and reptiles on December 4.

Amphibians and reptiles, like fish, are cold-blooded, and hence do rather poorly in mountain environments. In the park proper, only six species of amphibians and seven species of reptiles exist, but more are found lower down, such as near the park headquarters in the Mineral area, where red-legged frogs and western pond turtles exist.

Park and wilderness-area amphibians include the ensatina, rough-skinned newt, long-toed salamander, western toad, Pacific tree frog and foothill yellow-legged frog. Both the ensatina and the foothill yellow-legged frog barely make it up to mountain environments, and they are more common along Hat Creek and at Burney Falls State Park. Amphibians rarely stray far from water, so you can expect to find them in or around lakes and ponds, along creeks, in moist or wet meadows, and on moist floors of forests.

Park and wilderness-area reptiles include the sagebrush lizard, western skink, northern alligator lizard, rubber boa, California mountain king snake, common garter snake and western terrestrial garter snake. Lower down, particularly in Hat Creek Valley, you can also expect to see the western rattlesnake and its harmless, rattleless mimic, the gopher snake. The sagebrush lizard is very similar to the western fence lizard, or "blue belly," which is so common at low elevations. It prefers dry, sunny places, usually among rocks or brush. In contrast, the skink and the alligator lizard prefer woodlands and forests. The boa and mountain king snake also share this shadier environment. The latter is most common below 6000 feet,

outside the park. Garter snakes hunt frogs, tadpoles, small fish and salamanders, among other species. In the Sierra Nevada, where mountain yellow-legged frogs are abundant, so too are garter snakes, which along with trout are their main predators. But this frog is absent in the Lassen area, and the foothill species barely makes it into the park. Therefore, garter snakes tend to be considerably less abundant, at least around lakes. You're most likely to see them in meadows, where mice and invertebrates abound.

Birds

Birds appear to have evolved from a major group of dinosaurs about 130 million years ago. They are sketchily represented in the fossil record, perhaps because their delicate bones were rarely preserved. In terms of species, birds greatly outnumber other Lassen vertebrates. There are about 200 species in Lassen Park, Caribou Wilderness and Thousand Lakes Wilderness. Their nearest competitors, the mammals, have about one-fourth that number. Many of the bird species found up here are also found down in Hat Creek Valley and Burney Falls State Park, but down there, other bird species also appear. The following list of birds omits the species generally found only below 6000 feet. Furthermore, the list is restricted to species that are fairly common, at least during summer, or that merit comment. The birds are listed in the same order as on the park's checklist, which, like so many other checklists, uses the order in Peterson's *Field Guide to Western Birds*. If you've got a copy of that bird guide or another bird guide, you can familiarize yourself with the listed species before you come up to the park. Manzanita Lake, which is very accessible, is easily the best area for bird watching in the entire park.

In this list, a series of letters follows each bird. For example, in the first entry, these are c,c,u,i/l,m. This line of data, and others like it, is taken from the park's bird checklist. The first four letters indicate the abundance of the bird in four seasons: summer, fall, winter, spring. Summer is defined as June through August, fall is September through November, winter is December through February, and spring is March through May. In the example the bird is common in summer,

Common vertebrates of Lassen Park. Top row, left and right: the Steller's jay and Clark's nutcracker are both vociferous members of the crow family. Middle row: the Oregon junco is frequently seen; the mountain chickadee is frequently heard. Bottom row: the red-shafted flicker sometimes forages on the ground; the golden-mantled ground squirrel does so almost exclusively.

common in fall, uncommon in winter, and its status is unknown for spring. The letter or letters following the slash indicate the bird's habitat(s), with the most important one listed first. In this example the two habitats are lakes and marshes.

The list's abbreviations are as follows:

Abundance
c—common; almost certain to be seen or heard

u—uncommon; may be seen or heard

r—rare; unlikely to be seen or heard

x—extremely rare; not to be expected

—insufficient data; abundance unknown

Habitats
a—aerial

b—brushlands

c—cliffs, rocky areas, talus slopes, fell fields

f—forests

l—lake water

m—marshes, muddy shores, mudflats

o—open vegetated terrain, wet and dry meadows

r—riparian (creekside) vegetation

s—sand bars, lakeshores, rocky stream banks

A brief note or two accompanies each species. Refer to Peterson's guide or others for identification.

Pied-billed grebe, c,c,u,i/l,m. Similar in body shape to coots and sharing their habitats, Look for them among the coots at Manzanita Lake.

Great blue heron, u,u,r,i/m,o,l,r. Large, beautiful, shy birds that quickly take flight once they see you. Look for them at Snag Lake or at shallow lakes, ponds and marshes off the beaten track.

Canada goose, c,c,c,c/l,o,m. These geese frequent the park's larger, lower lakes, particularly in the fall.

Mallard, c,c,u,c/l,m. The park's commonest duck. To be expected below 7500 feet wherever there is standing water.

Common merganser, u,r,i,r/l. With long, narrow bills, these ducks are easy to identify. Try the less frequented lakes.

Red-tailed hawk, c,u,u,u/a,o. The park's largest and commonest hawk, easily distinguished from other large, soaring birds by its reddish brown tail.

Golden eagle, u,r,r,r/a,c,o. Shuns man, often alighting on remote summits. Soars above open lands.

Bald eagle, u,u,r,r/a,l. Prefers to soar above lakes and prefers fish to rodents.

Blue grouse, u,u,u,u/f.Strictly a forest dweller. Spends winters eating conifer needles and staghorn lichen—not an enviable menu.

Mountain quail, u,u,r,u/b. Quite common in dense brush, such as on Warner Valley slopes, but mainly in brush below the park.

American coot, c,c,r,r/l,m. A drab water bird. Abundant at Manzanita Lake.

Killdeer, u,r,i,u/s,o. Typically stays close to water. Often sings its name, "kill-deer." Recognized by its two dark bands across its chest.

Spotted sandpiper, c,u,i,i/s,m. Associates with killdeers, but more numerous. At many meadows and lakeshores.

California gull, u,u,i,i/l. If you see a gull in the park, it's probably a California gull. Similar, slightly smaller, ring-billed gulls are rare in these mountains.

Great horned owl, u,u,u,u/f,o,b,r. One of the joys of country living is to have one of these whoo-ing in your yard. Campground litter attracts mice, which in turn attract these owls. Look for them here at dusk or dawn.

Common nighthawk, c,u,i,u/a,o. An oversized "swallow" chasing aerial insects, sometimes doing so in small groups.

Rufous hummingbird, c,r,i,i/o,b,r. Wear a bright-red shirt or pack and these birds may seek you. Normally it is attracted to tubular flowers such as penstemons.

Calliope hummingbird, c,r,i,u/o,b,r. The park's smallest bird, this "hummer" keeps more to streams and meadows than does its larger cousin.

Northern flicker, c,c,c,c/f,r,b,o. (Formerly called red-shafted flicker.) Being a typical woodpecker, this bird flies by a series of flaps and glides, and each series of wing flaps flashes the vermilion color of its wings' undersides. This flashing flight makes it one of the park's most often sighted birds.

Pileated woodpecker, u,u,u,u/f. A crow-sized woodpecker with a red crest, this unmistakable bird is more common below the park, where oaks and conifers mingle.

Red-breasted sapsucker, c,u,i,u/r,f. Its presence is indicated by the horizontal rows of closely spaced holes it drills in the trunks of aspens, cottonwoods and larger alders and willows. Manzanita Lake is a fine place to look for this bird.

Hairy woodpecker, c,c,c,c/f,r. This woodpecker, with a white back and a broad, black eye stripe, frequents forests that are mostly below 7000 feet, particularly those below the park.

White-headed woodpecker, c,c,c,c/f. Having a white head, this woodpecker is easy to spot and identify. Look for it in forests of white firs, ponderosa pines and sugar pines.

Black-backed woodpecker, u,u,u,u/f. (Formerly called black-backed three-toed woodpecker.) The dominant woodpecker in forests of lodgepoles, red firs, western white pines and mountain hemlocks.

Western wood-peewee, c,u,i,u/f,r. An often overlooked, dusky, drab flycatcher. Look for it along edges of forests, meadows and lakes.

Olive-sided flycatcher, c,r,i,u/f. Prefers treetop perches, making it hard to spot, but sometimes found at lakes, such as Manzanita Lake.

Violet-green swallow, u,u,i,u/a,f,r,c. Very common in the Sierra Nevada and much of California, but not here. Seen at Manzanita Lake.

Tree swallow, c,u,i,c/a,r,f. The commonest Lassen-area swallow above 6000 feet.

Steller's jay, c,c,c,c/f. This bird and the following large, gray "jay" go out of their way to make their presence known. The Steller's jay frequents all the park's campgrounds and many of its backcountry campsites.

Clark's nutcracker, c,c,c,c/f,c,o. At about 7000-7500 feet, this bird replaces the Steller's jay. Very common along the Bumpass Hell Nature Trail and along the lower part of the Lassen Peak Trail.

Mountain chickadee, c,c,c,c/f. Heard by the author all summer long, but rarely seen. Listen for this tiny bird's song: fee'-bee-bee, or chick'-a-dee-dee-dee. Look on outer branches of conifers.

White-breasted nuthatch, c,c,c,c/f. Usually seen descending trunks of trees in search of insects and spiders. Prefers pine forests and oak woodlands.

Red-breasted nuthatch, c,c,c,c/f. A smaller version of the above, this nuthatch prefers fir forests.

Brown creeper, c,c,c,c/f. In contrast to nuthatches, the creeper spirals up the trunks of conifers.

American dipper, c,c,c,c/s,l. (Formerly called dipper or water ouzel.) This chunky, gray bird stalks insects, and sometimes small fish, along the bottoms of swift creeks and streams. Note its oversized feet and its bobbing, or dipping, habit.

Rock wren, u,u,i,r/c. Living up to its nam this wren dwells in rocky places. None of t park's five kinds of wrens is common.

American robin, c,c,u,c/o,r,f. This e tremely common, very adaptable thrush seen, usually in grassy places, from the par headquarters' lawn up to subalpine slopes

Hermit thrush, c,x,x,c/f,b. Well camo flaged, it looks like a fox sparrow but stands little taller. This forest-and-woodland-flo bird has the same mannerisms as its cousi the robin.

Mountain bluebird, u,u,r,u/o,f. Like flycatcher, it chases after flying insects. Pr fers higher forests and subalpine places. Yc may even see it on Lassen Peak's summit

Golden-crowned kinglet, c,c,r,c/f. Bare larger than a hummingbird, this extreme common bird is hard to see, for it usuall hunts insects in the upper branches of con fers, particularly firs. Hutton's vireo, whic closely resembles this bird, is found belo 5000 feet.

Ruby-crowned kinglet, u,u,i,u/f,b,r. Simil to the above, this bird feeds in lodgepol and sings a louder song.

Orange-crowned warbler, c,c,i,i/r,b,f. Loc for this small, drab, olive-green bird i creekside shrubs up to about 7500 feet. Ma zanita Lake, with all its shrubs, is a favorit spot.

Nashville warbler, c,c,i,i/f. This gray headed, yellowish bird frequents conifers a well as willows and alders.

Yellow warbler, c,u,i,u/r. Up in th mountains, if you see a "canary," you'r probably viewing a yellow warbler. It prefe willows, alders, aspens and cottonwoods.

Hermit warbler, c,u,i,c/f. Identified by it yellow head and gray body, this bird is nev ertheless hard to see, for it forages high up i conifers, particularly white firs and suga pines.

MacGillivray's warbler, c,c,i,u/b,r. Simil to the Nashville warbler but larger, this wa bler prefers brush in the wettest places, suc as a willow cluster in a boggy meadow.

Wilson's warbler, c,c,i,c/r. Similar to Mac Gillivray's warbler in habitat.

Red-winged blackbird, c,u,i,c/m,o. Ver common below the park, such as in lowe Hat Creek Valley. Seen at Manzanita Lake

Brewer's blackbird, c,c,x,c/r,m. The com mon blackbird around the park's meadow marshes and lakes.

Western tanager, c,u,i,u/f. Despite its stron

beak, this bird prefers succulent insects. Like flycatchers, it typically darts out after flying insects. Look for it in conifers, particularly lodgepoles at the edge of a lake or meadow or, at lower elevations, among oaks. You can't fail to recognize the bird, with its scarlet head, yellow body, and black wings, back and tail.

Evening grosbeak, u,u,r,u/f. These large finches aren't that common but, like other finches, they travel in groups, hunting for seeds among oaks, pines and firs.

Cassin's finch, c,u,i,u/f,o,b. Look for groups of these red-and-brown birds in forests, particularly in lodgepoles lining a meadow.

Rosy finch, r,r,r,r/c,o. (Formerly called gray-crowned rosy finch.) The only Lassen-area bird that actively exploits alpine environments, which aren't all that common. It must have done considerably better during the Ice Age.

Pine siskin, c,u,r,c/f,o,r. These small, brown-streaked birds generally forage among lodgepoles, and are best seen in those lining a meadow.

Dark-eyed junco, c,c,u,c/f,b,r. (Formerly called Oregon junco.) One of the commonest birds in the mountains, it is easily recognized by its black or gray cap and by its white outer tail feathers, noticed when it flies.

Chipping sparrow, c,u,i,u/f,o. Prefers brush in drier woodlands and forests.

White-crowned sparrow, u,u,i,u/o,b,r. Expect to see them around meadows, streams and lakes.

Fox sparrow, c,c,i,c/b. Mostly forages in dry, dense brush.

Lincoln's sparrow, c,u,i,i/r,o. Prefers shrubs along creeks or in and around boggy meadows.

Mammals

You'll never see most of the park's mammals, for most are secretive and usually nocturnal. Shrews, moles, mice and rats go about their business harvesting seeds, grasses, insects and other food sources. Predators, too, steer clear of man, so don't expect to see a weasel, marten, fox, coyote, bobcat or mountain lion, although they may be close by. During the day you are most likely to see chipmunks, golden-mantled ground squirrels and deer. Around dusk, up to six species of bats pursue flying insects, and a bear or

two may wander into a campground. All leave you alone if you don't antagonize them. Deer, marmots and beavers add to the joy of the Drakesbad area.

Some animals are quite abundant, but give only traces of their presence. Pocket gophers leave long strings of tailings known as "gopher ropes." Badgers excavate broad holes in the ground as they pursue gophers and other rodents. Porcupines eat bark off trees. Pikas leave piles of droppings on the rocks of the talus slopes they inhabit. And once you come to recognize bear droppings, you discover that bears are more prevalent than you thought. Despite their typically carnivore teeth, Lassen's black bears definitely prefer to eat vegetation, such as berries, mixed in with a healthy dash of insects and an occasional rodent. Perhaps in the distant past their ancestors ate a lot more flesh. In contrast, many rodents, which supposedly are herbivores, eat some meat. The deer mouse even kills and eats other mice.

Mice are the park's most abundant mammals, and they are most numerous in meadows. The mountain meadow mouse and the long-tailed meadow mouse rarely stray from meadows, but other species of mice are found there and elsewhere. Mice usually number a few dozen per acre, but can number in the hundreds. California moles tunnel in drier meadows, leaving their tailings on the surface as meadow mounds. Streamside vegetation, particularly alders and willows, also teems with rodent life. Aplodontia, western jumping mouse, shrew-mole, Trowbridge shrew and northern water shrew make their homes in this dense, nutrient-rich habitat. The water shrew is an avid swimmer, and like the dipper, this tiny mammal will hunt underwater, even in trout-inhabited lakes.

In drier places, Sierra pocket gophers plow through loose soil, consuming plants from below. If rocks or logs suitable for dens are around, then Sierra Nevada golden-mantled ground squirrels move in and forage on the surface. Yellow-bellied marmots also occupy drier habitats, particularly in the subalpine realm. Here they are joined by pikas, which are rat-sized members of the rabbit family. Chipmunks exploit a number of dry habitats. The lodgepole chipmunk is the commonest one in the park and, being acrobatic, it climbs shrubs and trees to get berries and seeds—in addition to foraging on the ground. The park's commonest tree squirrel is the chickaree, or Douglas squirrel, which is at home in all of the park's conifers. While weasels, red foxes, bobcats and badgers pursue the ground rodents, the marten pursues the tree squirrels, chasing them down among the treetops. The relatively uncommon northern flying squirrel, which loves to feed on lichens, escapes the marten by gliding from tree to tree.

Most of the park's mammals are rather permanent inhabitants, storing food for the winter or hibernating through it. The mule deer, however, makes seasonal migrations, avoiding the snow. The mountain lion, its primary predator, migrates with the herd. Most of the park's deer migrate up from the foothills, foraging on the new vegetation as snow retreats with every passing week. By late spring they reach the park, and they stay there until October, when they begin a reverse route down to their winter range. Indians also migrated, hunting the deer and harvesting the seeds, leaves, roots, tubers and berries of a great variety of plants. They were as much a part of the natural landscape as the plants and animals they utilized.

Modern man is every bit as dependent on plants and animals as his ancestors were. Unfortunately, we are annihilating species at an alarming level, destroying complex interrelationships that nature took millions of years to evolve. In doing so, we are undermining our own survival. If we are to survive as a species, we must learn to live within the framework of nature, as the Indians did.

8   Lassen Park Road Log

Introduction   The Lassen Park Road—a portion of Highway 89—traverses through some of the park's finest scenery, and it therefore gives the visitor a fine introduction to the park. With the following road log, the visitor can become acquainted with Lassen's more prominent landmarks plus some of its plants, animals and, particularly, its geologic history.

There are 67 roadside markers along the Lassen Park Road, the first one found at the park's southern boundary and the last one at the Manzanita Lake Entrance Station, near its northwestern boundary. This chapter covers a slightly longer stretch of Highway 89, starting at the highway's junction with Highway 36, 4.5 miles south of the park's southern boundary, and ending at the highway's junction with Highway 44, just outside the park. Chapter 9 continues the Highway 89 road log, starting at the latter junction and going north to a junction with Highway 299.

You can drive through Lassen Park in about an hour, but if you are using this road log, then plan on several hours. If you like a relaxed pace, want to do a little hiking or want to really look at the wildflowers, then allow a full day. The author took three.

A word of caution is necessary. A few roadside markers can be easy to miss—indeed, one or more may be missing altogether. In addition, turnouts aren't present at every marker, and where they are present, they usually accommodate only one to several cars. Therefore, drive slowly, and you'll have greater success at finding the markers and managing to squeeze into a parking space. Don't block the highway traffic. If there is no space to park, drive ahead to the nearest turnout and walk back. Also, if you miss a marker and want to turn around, do so on a safe stretch of highway, not on a blind curve.

Lassen Park Road Log

Miles north of Hwy. 36W jct.	Miles south of Hwy. 44W jct.	
0.0	34.1	From where **Highway 36 joins Highway 89**, they coincide for 22.5 miles east, then Highway 89 branches south along the west shore of Lake Almanor while Highway 36 continues through Chester, which is near

the lake's northwest shore. Childs Meadows Resort, Gurnsey Creek Campground and Fire Mountain Lodge lie east of your starting point and west of Highway 36/89's junction with Highway 32, and several more lodges lie along Highway 36/89 east of that junction. West from your starting point, Highway 36 descends 4.2 miles to Volcano Country, a privately run campground, then goes 0.2 mile farther to very complete Mineral Lodge. Westward, Highway 36 continues 41 miles to Red Bluff, first passing the Lassen Volcanic National Park headquarters in 0.7 mile, then Battle Creek Campground 1.2 miles after that.

Go 2.0 miles to

2.0/32.1   Road 29N22, branching west. This road first winds 1¼ miles to a junction with a primitive road that climbs over a low ridge to McGowan Lake, on private land. In 1¼ more miles, Road 29N22 crosses a lateral moraine and descends south along its west side, reaching a junction with Road 30N16 in ½ mile. This road descends 2.2 miles south to Highway 36, reaching it midway between Mineral Lodge and the 36/89 junction. In winter, you can make an easy, mostly downhill, 5.2-mile cross-country ski trip by following Road 29N22 west, then Road 30N16 south to Highway 36.

Go 1.7 miles to a view of

3.7/30.4   Bluff Falls, about 50 feet high, and at its peak discharge in June. Being largely spring-fed, the falls flow through most of the summer, the water spreading out at the base and supporting a broad thicket of thinleaf alders. This is your first good wildflower stop. Three of the taller species to look for are arrowhead butterweed, monk's hood and leopard lily. On dry slopes just outside the park you may also see the relatively uncommon Sierra morning glory. Both the morning glory and the leopard lily are at the top of their elevation range, the lily giving way in the park to little leopard lily, which is also called Kelley's lily. Corn lily, named for its cornlike leaves, is found here and in or by most of the park's wet meadows.

Go 0.8 mile to

4.5/29.6   Roadside marker 1, the south boundary of Lassen Volcanic National Park. Leave Lassen National Forest. The park's of-

ficial road log begins here. Before 1980, there was a small plaque commemorating Congressman John E. Raker, whose bill, signed by President Woodrow Wilson on August 9, 1916, established Lassen Volcanic National Park. The stone entrance marker, called the Raker Memorial, was built in 1931, the year your road was completed through the park.

Go 0.5 mile to

5.0/29.1   2, the Brokeoff Mountain Trail. This trail climbs 3.8 miles to the mountain's summit, which, at 9235 feet elevation, is high enough to support a few species of alpine plants. This summit, Mt. Diller, Eagle Peak and the upper half of Lassen Peak are the only places in the entire Lassen area to support such vegetation. The Brokeoff Mountain Trail begins around 6680 feet elevation, starting by a creek that flows through a thicket of thinleaf alders and Lemmon's willows. Like the Bluff Falls creek, this one supports a diverse array of water-loving wildflowers. Coyote mint dominates the dry slope by the trailhead and is accompanied in a few spots by leafy thistle, a spiny, prostrate sunflower.

All but one trail starting from the Lassen Park Road is described in Chapter 11, and the trails are described in the same order you will encounter them along this road log. The Bumpass Hell Nature Trail is described in Chapter 10.

The next 0.7 mile of road, almost to the ski area, is across debris of an enormous landslide. This may have occurred about 3300 years ago, and mature trees have long been growing on this site. Another major landslide in the near future is quite unlikely.

Go 0.4 mile to

5.4/28.7   3, the Southwest Entrance Station. The Park Service has been charging entrance fees since July 1, 1931, when the completed Park Road officially opened, and you pay here unless you have a Golden Eagle Passport. You can purchase one of these at the entrance station.

Immediately beyond the entrance station is a 250-car parking lot, which is usually quite empty in summer but can be overflowing on a winter weekend, when skiers flock to the area. The **Sulphur Works Walk-in Campground**, with 24 units, is along the parking lot's east edge.

From the north end of the campground a trail rambles 1.6 miles east to a view of Mill Creek Falls, a very interesting combination of three waterfalls. Totalling about 75 feet high, Mill Creek Falls ranks as the park's highest waterfall.

Go 0.2 mile to

5.6/28.5   4, Lassen Chalet. This ski lodge once was scheduled to be replaced by a much larger visitor center. Just north of the ski lodge you pass two ski lifts, which may be relocated in the 1990s and ultimately abandoned, perhaps by the turn of the century, after other ski park facilities are developed nearby but outside the park.

As you drive to the next stop, you pass by acres of open slopes, these dominated by mountain mule ears, which are large-leaved sunflowers that *en masse* fill the air with a subtle aroma.

Go 0.8 mile to

6.4/27.7   5, Sulphur Works, an active hydrothermal area. If you don't have the time to hike to Bumpass Hell, stop 17, hike the short, signed nature trail through the Sulphur Works. The parking lot here also serves as the starting point of a trail to Ridge Lake. This steep trail climbs up a linear landslide deposit that is bounded by two creeks—one immediately west of the Ridge Lake trail and one between this trail and the Sulphur Works nature trail.

In 1866 T.M. Boardman and Dr. Mathias Supan purchased the "Sulphur Works" and at first mined its sulfurous clay. Later, Dr. Supan's son, Milton, saw more profit by abandoning the mine and opening a resort. This resort remained in the Supan family until 1952, when the park, after a condemnation suit, acquired the property.

Go 0.3 mile to

6.7/27.4   6, elevation 7000 feet. Just past the elevation sign is a decapitated trunk of a large western white pine. Note the bark's checkerboard pattern, which is well developed on mature specimens. The western white pine is easily the commonest species of the park's three species of five-needled pines—the "white pines" group. The whitebark pine, with short needles and thin, scaly bark, grows mostly above 8500 feet. The sugar pine, with long cones hanging from the tips of long, slender branches,

grows mostly below 6000 feet, that is, only in the park's lowest areas.

Sunflowers dominate most of the terrain below you, particularly mountain mule ears and arrow-leaved balsamroot, but also lesser amounts of relatively inconspicuous Douglas sagebrush and mountain brickellbush.

Go 0.4 mile to

7.1/27.0   7, a Brokeoff Mountain viewpoint. Brokeoff Mountain, the 9235-foot-high peak to the west, is the park's second highest peak. Its nearly vertical north cliff gives one the impression that a northern part of the mountain broke away, hence the name "Brokeoff Mountain." The name, given by early settlers, stuck, unfortunately, perpetuating the misconception. Even the famous geologist, Howel Williams, working in the late 1920s and early 30s, believed the northern part of the mountain had been faulted down, though, he admitted, no proof could be offered. Today, there is still no evidence to indicate that any major faulting occurred. The mountain's steep north face, like deep Mill Creek canyon below you, can be attributed largely to the erosive action of glaciers working over a period of several hundred thousand years. The glaciers' task was made easier by the abundance of solfatarized volcanic rocks, that is, the highly decomposed rocks you saw around the Sulphur Works and more you'll see north of Diamond Peak. Brokeoff Mountain, Diamond Peak and other summits were once part of a large volcano, Mt. Tehama, which will be discussed at some of the stops on the way to Lassen Peak.

You are now driving around Diamond Peak, which is an accumulation of resistant volcanic rock that lay immediately east of Mt. Tehama's principal vent. However, the rock wasn't resistant enough to resist the pull of gravity. Perhaps initiated by a large earthquake, a major rockslide, about ⅓ mile wide, broke loose from the peak's south slope, east of your viewpoint. The slide crashed southeast down to East Sulphur Creek, below you. A smaller slide broke loose below your viewpoint and descended to West Sulphur Creek. Both slides are prehistoric in age, but a future slide cannot be ruled out.

At this stop and the next one you can examine wildflowers growing on the dry, sunny ridges and slopes descending from each stop. "Unrecognized pigweed" is a strange name for a strange "wildflower" that grows in abundance at each. Its tiny flowers lack petals. Although this gray-green plant belongs to the same plant family that includes beets and spinach, don't eat it; first, because that's illegal, and second, because its leaves are mildly poisonous. Look also for cream bush, with its seasonally abundant show of small, creamy flowers, and for alpine prickly currant, with spiny stems. When in bloom, the following wildflowers, spanning the colors of the rainbow, are very noticeable: California stickseed, with white "pinwheel" flowers; granite gilia, densely covered with pale, violet, tubular flowers; changeable phacelia, with violet tubular flowers; Douglas' wallflower, with yellow-orange, four-petalled flowers; Applegate's paintbrush and giant red paintbrush, both with scarlet, tubular flowers, the former with wavy leaves; scarlet gilia, with scarlet, trumpet-shaped flowers; and showy penstemon, with rosy blue, tubular flowers.

Go 0.6 mile to

7.7/26.4   8, Diamond Point. Here you have sweeping views both up and down Mill Creek canyon. Mt. Conard is the spreading mass breaking the skyline 1½ miles southeast of you. Once called Black Butte, its name was changed in 1948 to honor Arthur L. Conard, the organizer and president of the Lassen Park Development Association, which fought for the establishment of the park. The mountain is an eastern remnant of Mt. Tehama. To the right of the mountain, on the distant skyline, is the southernmost part of the Cascade Range. Southeast of that skyline, the Cascade Range gradually yields to the Sierra Nevada as granitic rocks begin to appear on the surface.

Watch for traffic if you want to examine the nearby cliff of volcanic rock. The rocks occur in layers, or beds, and the beds dip to the east, indicating that their source—the vent of ancient Mt. Tehama—was to their west. These are beds of tuffs and beds of breccias. Tuffs are nothing more than accumulations of small fragments of volcanic rock, typically 4 mm (1/6 inch) or less in diameter. Breccias are accumulations of fragments 32 mm (1¼ inches) or more. Lapilli, uncommon in the cliff, are accumulations of fragments 4-32 mm in diameter. A special kind of lapilli—cinders—is plentiful around basaltic cinder cones. All three types are expelled from volcanic vents during an eruption.

Go 0.3 mile to

8.0/26.1   9, a view of Lassen Peak. The Lassen Peak Trail switchbacks up the peak's right (southeast) edge. Eagle Peak stands just below and left of Lassen. Mt. Conard, which you've already seen, stands to the south-southeast. Eagle Peak can be reached by hiking west cross-country from the Lassen Peak Trail parking lot (stop 22), and Mt. Conard can be reached by an easy cross-country climb from a trail to Cold Boiling and Crumbaugh lakes (stop 30). The wildflowers at stop 9 are similar to those at the two previous stops.

A cistern lies across the road, should you want any water for yourself or your car's radiator. Watch for traffic.

Go 0.1 mile to

8.1/26.0   10, a view of Mt. Tehama's lava and ash, seen across the canyon. Because these layers dip to the east, the volcano's vent must have been to the west. By looking at the dips of Mt. Tehama's remaining layers of lava and ash, geologists can more or less reconstruct the size of this once-great volcano and the height and location of its summit. This peak was roughly 5 miles in diameter and about 11,000 feet in elevation, and its summit vent stood above the site of today's Sulphur Works. The volcano was about the size of today's Mt. Hood, in northern Oregon, and like it, Mt. Tehama had lava flows radiating from its lower slopes, covering a large section of the countryside.

Both Mts. Hood and Tehama are classified as stratovolcanoes, which are large volcanoes built up of alternating layers of flowing molten lava and layers of ash and blocks. You saw some layers at stop 9, and you see more across the canyon. Each layer represents a volcanic episode and, as you can see, Mt. Tehama had many. Its first eruptions began about 600,000 years ago. By 300,000 years ago it may have built up to its maximum height, and by 100,000 years ago it had been greatly eaten away by glaciers and was in its last eruptions. A product of the Ice Age, Mt. Tehama may have experienced glacial erosion early in its existence, and at ts maximum height it probably lacked the symmetry of a pre-1980 Mt. St. Helens, resembling instead Mts. Hood, Jefferson or Shasta. Over Mt. Tehama's history the peak erupted enough lava and ash to build up its summit 4000 feet above the surrounding landscape.

If you look down the steep slopes below, you should be able to see pond-sized Ink Lake, which is usually covered with a layer of algal scum. It is certainly not appealing. Several hot springs still seep along the floor of the canyon, and altered volcanic rocks lie around them.

Go 0.2 mile to

8.3/25.8 11, fallen boulders. Diamond Peak's summit pinnacles are unstable, as you can see from the nearby boulders. The large one you see on the skyline is one of several that could break loose at any moment—though they might stand for thousands of years. Perhaps your best chance of seeing a golden eagle will be in this vicinity, for these magnificent birds often visit the summit pinnacles.

You'll see one large boulder at the head of a boggy meadow. If you were to examine it (expect to get muddy shoes reaching it), you'd see that it appears to be made up of a lot of boulders cemented together. This boulder is a remnant of an *autobrecciated* lava flow, a flow that was still slowly moving as it was hardening. The result was that the flow, almost solid, broke into countless pieces due to the motion, but the flow's material was still "sticky" enough to bond the rocks together into a cohesive unit. Autobrecciated lava flows were extremely common in the northern Sierra Nevada.

The boggy meadow contains an assortment of small, water-loving plants including dwarf plantain-leaved buttercup, three-leaved lewisia, alpine shooting star and Baker's violet.

Go 1.0 mile to a

9.3/24.8 Scenic turnout. Here is one of the best views of Diamond Peak's pinnacle-studded summit. You also see Lassen Peak and, below, severely glaciated Little Hot Springs Valley. The terrain in your area is largely clothed in red firs and western white pines.

Go 0.3 mile to

9.6/24.5 12, another view of Diamond Peak. The peak may have been named for its summit pinnacles, which can appear diamond-shaped from some views, but the peak's name has also been ascribed to occasional quartz and calcite crystals found in the rock, though neither is diamondlike. Diamond Peak's minerals, like those of the rest of Mt. Tehama, are about two thirds feldspars, most of the remainder being split quite evenly between quartz, a glassy mineral, and several pyroxenes, which are dark, heavy minerals. There is a fair amount of calcium in some of the minerals, and when these weather, the calcium is carried in solution, sometimes being deposited nearby as calcite.

Your turnout is about 7770 feet in elevation, and here you are at the lower edge of the subalpine zone, as indicated by the appearance of a few droopy-topped mountain hemlocks among the many firs and pines.

On your drive up to the next marker you will pass some hydrothermally decomposed volcanic rocks, which are similar to those you saw at stop 5, the Sulphur Works. At present there is no significant hydrothermal activity in this higher location, although there certainly was some in the past. Such activity in the park appears to be waning, for at one time it was widespread but now it is confined to localized pockets. There are no turnouts along this stretch of past activity.

Go 0.8 mile to

10.4/23.7 13, the head of Little Hot Springs Valley. For perhaps 100,000 years, possibly longer, glaciers have descended Little Hot Springs Valley, deepening and widening it. At one time, Mt. Tehama towered about 3000 feet above your spot, but one or more glaciers, flowing down the southeast flank of the volcano, gradually cut back—up-canyon—into it. The rocks in the volcano's center had been largely altered by hydrothermal activity and hence were easily erodible. Glaciers cut into this material and "quickly"—perhaps over 100,000 years—carved away most of the volcano's core. Diamond Peak, composed of less altered volcanic rock, was less erodible and hence projects above the hydrothermal areas surrounding it.

This stop is another good one for botanizing. If you walk about ¼ mile down the road to the bend, you can see some roadside water-loving wildflowers that usually aren't seen lower down. Look for two orchids: the Sierra rein orchid and the green rein orchid. The former, with white flowers, stands out; the latter, with pale green, blends into the dense vegetation. Also look for brook saxifrage and marsh marigold. Jepson's willow, with inch-wide leaves, is found nearby. Pink, showy elephant heads tap their roots into those of adjacent herbs and shrubs and thus derive some of their nourishment through root parasitism. On some drier slopes near the road grow plants that you've seen below, such as coyote mint, changeable phacelia, leafy thistle and unrecognized pigweed. Arrow-leaved balsamroot grows in abundance on slopes below the road.

Go 0.3 mile to

10.7/23.4 14, Emerald Point, at about 8040 feet elevation. You can now consider yourself in the subalpine zone, for mountain hemlocks are quite common here and above. John Muir, the famous 19th century mountaineer, naturalist and conservationist, thought that mountain hemlocks were the most beautiful of California's conifers (conifers are cone-bearing, usually needle-leaved, evergreens). He also felt that some of the finest groves were on the southern slopes of Lassen Peak. Mountain hemlocks grow best in areas of heavy snow accumulation, and Muir realized the importance of a deep snowpack to the trees' survival: "When the first soft snow begins to fall, the flakes lodge in the leaves, weighing down the branches against the trunk. Then the axis bends yet lower and lower, until the slender top touches the ground, thus forming a fine ornamental arch. The snow still falls lavishly, and the whole tree is at length buried ... It is as though this were only Nature's method of putting her darlings to sleep instead of leaving them exposed to the biting storms of winter."

Young lodgepole pines, western white pines and red firs are also flexible enough to bend with the snow, though they are often deformed because of it, especially on steeper slopes. Mature trees growing on slopes often have curved trunks, due to snow having bent them in their early years. However, above the snow pack the trunk is usually straight unless it has been struck by lightning or attacked by insects.

At Emerald Point you have a fine view of the dark peaks that are remnants of Mt. Tehama. Mt. Conard, to the south, is a remnant of the volcano's east flank. At the foot of Mt. Conard, deep in Mill Creek canyon, are some of the volcano's oldest rocks, dated at about 600,000 years. Across from Mt. Conard stands the long ridge summit of Brokeoff Mountain, which is the volcano's highest remnant. North of that summit is Mt. Diller, which was a part of the volcano's northeast flank. Mt. Diller is named for Professor Joseph S. Diller, who did most of the basic geologic field work in the Lassen area, beginning in 1883 and still writing about the park's geology when he died in 1928. Professor Howel Williams continued the task, and in 1932 synthesized his work into an excellent, classic study on the park. It would be fitting if Williams, who died in 1980, were to be honored for his great contribution. Perhaps misnamed Brokeoff Mountain, which looks across to Mt. Diller, should be renamed Mt. Williams in honor of this great geologist and fine gentleman.

Pilot Pinnacle, west of you, is the fin on the ridge northeast of Mt. Diller, and it too is part of Mt. Tehama. Note how the strata—the layers of lava and ash—dip away from the glaciated canyon below you. If you mentally project the strata upward, you see that they meet in an area above and just west of Diamond Peak.

North of us is Ski Heil Peak, which is composed of a volcanic rock called dacite. This rock erupted atop a now buried vent, not from Mt. Tehama's summit vent. Eagle Peak, to the right, and massive Lassen Peak, to the right of both, are also dacite domes that erupted from local vents.

Go 0.1 mile to

10.8/23.3 15, Emerald Lake. Glaciers, descending from slopes above, gouged out a

Left: the Sulphur Works fumes away (stop 5). A steep-walled roadcut at Diamond Point reveals a part of Mt. Tehama's interior (stop 8). A golden eagle rests on a Diamond Peak pinnacle (stop 11). A glacial erratic, at the far end of the Bumpass Hell parking lot, rests at the brink of a cliff (stop 16).

basin to produce Emerald Lake and nearby Lake Helen. Snow often remains around these lakes until late July or early August. Around Emerald Lake look for dainty, ankle-high fawn lilies, with showy white-and-yellow flowers. Red mountain heather, a low, subalpine shrub, lines most of the lake's shore.

Until mid-July the Emerald Lake area usually has enough snow for winter sports, and above, near Lake Helen, the sports—mostly sliding down snow—sometimes continues into early August.

Go 0.3 mile to

11.1/23.0   16 and 17, a glacial erratic and the Bumpass Hell Nature Trail. A 10-foot-high glacial erratic, which is a boulder that was carried by a glacier, rests on the brink of a bedrock escarpment at the far end of the Bumpass Hell Nature Trail's parking lot. Note how the bedrock has been planed smooth by the glacier, creating a surface called glacial polish. From this spot you have another fine view of the peaks seen at Emerald Point. A small knoll near the erratic has dry, gravelly soils that support sun-loving vegetation such as buckwheat, granite gilia, mountain pride, coyote mint, mariposa tulip and cream bush. Pinemat manzanita grows beneath this area's conifers.

The start of the Bumpass Hell Nature Trail is near the entrance to the parking lot, and this trail is described in detail in Chapter 10. The trail's popularity can be judged by the size of the parking lot, and since it attracts a lot of people, it also attracts a few Clark's nutcrackers. These large, grayish members of the jay family are just as noisy as the Steller's jays that look for handouts lower down at the park's campgrounds and picnic areas.

Go 0.2 mile to

11.3/22.8   18, Lake Helen, elevation 8162 feet. This lake was named for Helen T. Brodt, who climbed Lassen Peak in 1864, the first woman known to have done so. Her ascent party, led by Major Pierson B. Reading, was the third known to have reached the summit.

Lake Helen lies in a high basin that accumulates more snow than most other areas of the park. The snowpack usually gets 10-20 feet thick by spring, and in some years it can have drifts more than 30 feet thick. This

depth, of course, accounts for the long-lasting snow patches, which may not entirely disappear until mid-August. Lake Helen, therefore, is a very cold lake, and being an impressive 110 feet deep, its temperature never gets above 50°F. The water near its bottom stays about 35-40°F year-round.

The snowfield by the section of road along the lake's south shore is a favorite among children. However, in August, protruding rocks may pose hazards.

Just east of the snowfield is a small outcrop of highly fractured dacite. Water seeping down its vertical cracks can feeze and expand, breaking the bedrock apart. A few plants, such as catchfly and Fremont's butterweed, take advantage of the cracks, sinking their roots into them and aiding in the breakdown of the rock.

Go 0.1 mile to

11.4/22.7   19, the Lake Helen Picnic Area, usually snowbound until August. In 1933, just two years after the Lassen Park Road and the Lassen Peak Trail were completed, the Shasta Historical Society placed a bronze plaque here in honor of Helen Tanner Brodt's Lassen ascent.

Lake Helen lies in a basin carved in dacite rock, while Emerald Lake, below, lies in one mostly carved in andesite rock that was once part of Mt. Tehama. The andesite weathers differently, usually breaking down to smaller pieces than does dacite. In weathering, andesite also releases more nutrients. Therefore, the Emerald Lake basin supports denser and more diverse vegetation than does the Lake Helen basin. The long-lasting snowfields at Lake Helen also contribute to the dearth of wildflowers.

Go 0.2 mile to

11.6/22.5   20, a road branching right. A snow-survey course extends from this road over to the picnic area. Snow samples are taken along this course in winter and spring to determine the depth and density of the snowpack. A foot of fresh snow weighs about 1/10 as much as a foot of water, but old, compacted snow may weigh half as much as an equal volume of water. By determining the volume of water in a snowpack, water planners can predict how much runoff water

California will receive, and they can act accordingly.

Go 0.4 mile to

12.0/22.1   21, a view of Lake Helen. Here you have another fine view of some of the remnants of Mt. Tehama: Brokeoff Mountain, Mt. Diller, Pilot Pinnacle and, below, Diamond Peak. A popular misconception was that in Mt. Tehama's latest stage, the mountain collapsed, much as Mt. Mazama exploded and then collapsed, giving rise to the crater of Crater Lake. However, evidence is lacking, and if there was a collapse after an eruption, it must have been minor. The deep canyon before you, lying where Mt. Tehama once stood, evolved largely through glacial erosion, which had been going on for quite some time. Certainly the cirque (a glacial basin) holding 110-foot-deep Lake Helen took thousands of years to carve, and Mt. Tehama had to be largely eroded away before a glacier could flow south through the basin and down Mill Creek canyon. The dacite bedrock in the Lake Helen basin is about ¼ million years old, so the basin, cut in this rock, has to be significantly younger.

The dacite bedrock above the road's east side contains an abundance of inclusions, as do some granitic rocks of the Sierra Nevada. Thse inclusions may have been the first bits of magma to solidify. But they could also be only volcanic rock that got incorporated in a younger magma. (Magma is molten, subsurface rock that becomes lava if it approaches or reaches the surface. If magma fails to reach the surface, it solidifies as granitic rock.)

Go 0.2 mile to

12.2/21.9   22, foot of Lassen Peak, which, at 10,457 feet, is the park's highest summit. The hugh parking lot reflects the popularity of the Lassen Peak Trail. This trail, the peak, its views, it geology and its flora are described in Chapter 11. Lassen Peak, composed of dacite lava like much of the surrounding area, is a plug dome like its smaller neighbor to the west, Eagle Peak. It may have built up to its present height in several years or less, this traumatic event having occurred perhaps about 11,000 years ago. Since it erupted at the center of a glacial ice cap, it must have had a devastating effect on the surrounding glaciers, essentially extinguishing them. The Lake Helen and Emerald Lake basins probably became glacier-free at this time and the lakes came into existence.

Lassen Peak was named for Peter Lassen, a Danish emigrant who was instrumental in bringing settlers into and through the area in the 1840s and 50s. He may have been the first Caucasian to climb the peak, though the first recorded ascent was by Grover K. Godfrey in 1851. The peak's name underwent several changes before "Lassen Peak" became official. Jedediah Smith, seeing it in 1827, called it and the adjacent mountains Mt. Joseph. Peter Lassen called this mass the Sister Buttes in the 1840s, a time when Lassen itself was known as Snow Butte. After Lassen's death in 1859, his name became attached to the peak and the land he loved. Lassen's Butte evolved to Mt. Lassen and finally, in 1915, to Lassen Peak.

Go 0.3 mile to

12.5/21.6   23, highest point of Lassen Park Road. When the Lassen Park Road was completed over this pass in 1931, the road's highest elevation was surveyed at 8512 feet. However, the road was later improved, lowering the pass to about 8500 feet. Snowstorms usually close the road in mid- or late October, and it is reopened, when possible, in time for the Memorial Day weekend, though in some years not until mid-June. This local area stays a winter wonderland through much of July.

Go 0.3 mile to

12.8/21.3   24, an open forest of whitebark pines. In the Lassen area and in the northern Sierra Nevada, this pine is the timberline species, growing higher than mountain hemlock. On Lassen Peak, the highest hemlock grows at about 9200 feet while the highest pine grows at about 10,000 feet. As mentioned at stop 14, hemlocks rely on a deep cover of snow to get safely through winter. The hardier whitebark pine faces the chilly blasts of winter at our mountain pass, but high on the peak the gale-force subzero winds are too much even for it. The tree adapts in its uppermost range by growing as a spreading shrub low enough to be covered by a couple of feet of snow. Branches growing above the snow cover are killed by winter's chill.

Go 0.3 mile to

13.1/21.0   25, a view of Lake Almanor. Distant Lake Almanor, a reservoir of the Pacific Gas and Electric Company, spreads across the flat floor of a graben. A graben differs from an ordinary valley in that it is a large, fault-bordered, downthrust block; streams play only a minor role in carving such a valley. There are a number of grabens east and north of the Lake Almanor graben.

Warner Valley lies closer to us. It too owes its existence in part to downfaulting, though glaciers and streams did most of the carving, and hence it is not a graben. Glaciers, when at their known maximum, extended down-canyon to within 2 miles of the western edge of Chester.

In 1863 William Brewer and Clarence King of the Whitney Survey came up the route you see. Big Meadows existed before Lake Almanor, and the team headed through it, then up Warner Valley to Boiling Springs Lake, which they reached on September 24. They also visited Steamboat Springs—Devils Kitchen to today's travelers. The next day they climbed up-canyon, perhaps passing within a few hundred yards of your viewpoint, then climbed Lassen Peak the following day.

Mt. Harkness is the highest peak on the left side of Warner Valley. A shield volcano, it erupted into existence fairly late in the Ice Age, perhaps 100-200,000 years ago. Small glaciers descended from its summit, though a contemporary glacier, flowing down Warner Valley, was up to 1200 feet thick. This volcano was named after Harvey W. Harkness, a president of the California Academy of Sciences, who visited Cinder Cone and local pioneers in 1874 and was able to verify that Cinder Cone had indeed erupted during the winter of 1850-51.

Go 0.6 mile to

13.7/20.4   26, Reading Peak and glacial moraines. Reading (pronounced "Redding") Peak is the prominent peak about one mile due east of your spot. It, like most of Lassen Park, has been glaciated more than once. From this peak, which is more of an east-west ridge than an isolated mountain, glaciers should have flowed *down* its north and south slopes. They didn't. They mainly flowed *past* its north and south slopes, though small glaciers high on the peak certainly contributed ice to the main flows. The evidence for the direction of ice flows is chiefly in the pattern of the area's glacial moraines, though linear scratches on bedrock also indicate direction of flow.

Glacial moraines are deposits of rocks and sediments that glaciers have carried, pushed or dragged along. Over thousands of years, glaciers can pile up a very impressive amount of rocks and sediments—some of the area's moraines are hundreds of feet thick. By studying the orientation and distribution of the moraines, one can determine the direction and extent of the glaciers during the last major glacial episode. Glaciers descending northeast past the north slopes of Reading Peak curved north down the Hat Creek drainage, flowing about 2 miles beyond the park's north boundary. Glaciers descending east past the south slopes of Reading Peak curved southeast down the Kings Creek and Warner Creek drainages, flowing about 4 miles beyond the park's south boundary.

The distribution of moraines also raises a question. If you were to fly over the Reading Peak area, you'd see huge moraines both north and south of the peak. The northern ones indicate that ice flowed northeast only about as far as the Park Road in the Dersch Meadows area. The southern ones indicate that ice flowed east only to the west margins of Corral Meadow and Flatiron Ridge. Why are these glacial moraines so voluminous and at the same time so short?

To the author's knowledge, no one has ever asked or answered this question. He speculates that these moraines, and the glaciers that produced them, are intimately linked to the eruption of Lassen Peak. Geologists who have studied the Lassen area have placed this eruption late in the Ice Age, roughly 11,000 years ago. Before then, an ice cap buried almost all the Lassen high country, and it sent its icy fingers—glaciers—out beyond the park, as noted above. When Lassen erupted through the ice cap, the volcano must have destroyed a significant chunk of it. The ice cap, the author believes, never fully recovered, and the glaciers retreated to less than half their former length. Lassen's eruption produced a superabundant source of loose rock—just look at the peak's extensive talus slopes today. The smaller glaciers, operating for 1000-2000 years, had no trouble transporting about ¼ billion tons of Lassen's dacite debris to their current locations—the moraines north and south of Reading Peak. Thus the eruption of Lassen Peak neatly explains the retreat of the glaciers and also accounts for the voluminousness of their moraines.

Go 0.5 mile to

14.2/19.9 27, trail to Terrace Lake and other destinations. Because you're still up in the subalpine zone, snow lasts into mid-July along the first part of this hemlock-lined trail. After the snow melts you can visit Terrace, Shadow and Cliff lakes and then return—all in an easy day hike. Or you can continue past Cliff Lake, descending along some of the thick moraines mentioned in the previous stop, then end your hike at stop 38 along the Park Road. Just a few minutes' walk from your trailhead, another trail branches from the lakes trail, this one descending, sometimes very steeply, down to stop 42 along the Park Road, which is the site of former Hat Lake.

Go 0.1 mile to

14.3/19.8 28, Reading Peak. Here, at about 8030 feet, you head briefly south, then leave the subalpine zone behind as you descend along the southwest flank of Reading Peak. Reading Peak is, like Lassen Peak, a volcanic dome, or plug dome. Because it is composed of dacite lava like Lassen, it is also known as a dacite dome. Unlike Lassen, it is not dome-shaped, for glaciers have been flowing past it for perhaps 100,000 years or more, trimming off its north and south flanks. During periods of maximum glaciation, the peak was almost completely buried under ice.

Formerly known as White Mountain, the name was changed to Reading Peak to commemorate Major Pierson B. Reading's pioneering role in the Lassen area. Reading was the first American citizen to settle in Shasta County. In 1844 he received a land grant from the Mexican government, a linear, 26,632-acre parcel that stretched along the Sacramento River. Today's settlements of Cottonwood, Anderson and, of course, Redding grew up in this land grant.

Go 1.0 mile to

15.3/18.8 29, a view of Upper Kings Creek Meadow. The Park Road has been descending along the top of a lateral moraine, which is a moraine that lies along the side of a glacier. At your vantage point you are about 400 feet above Upper Kings Creek Meadow, and the post-Lassen glacier flowing through it was at least this thick. The pre-Lassen glacier was about 500 feet thicker.

Seismic measurements indicate the meadow lies atop a basin that is buried under as much as 100 feet of sediments. A deep lake may once have existed here, but until someone drills a core down to the basin's floor, the depth and existence of such a lake will be matters of speculation. At least one shallow lake existed.

Basins such as this one are good places to look for clues to the park's geologic history. Volcanic rocks, containing radioactive elements, can be dated, and where we find such rocks deep in a basin, we know that all the sediments above it are younger, for they were deposited atop it. If these deposits are of a glacial nature, then we know the maximum age of the glacier. If another eruption spreads volcanic rocks on top of the glacial deposits, then we can determine the minimum age of the glacier, for it has to be older than the deposit on top of it. In the Sierra Nevada, geologists have spent decades looking for such dateable glacial sediments, but despite dozens of huge moraines and a fair amount of volcanic activity, no glacial sediment has been precisely dated, though a lot have a minimum or a maximum age. Lassen Park, with its very extensive volcanic activity, offers perhaps the best hunting ground to unravel the ages of glacial periods in California's mountains during the later part of the Ice Age. In 1980 the U.S. Geological Survey began dating volcanic rocks of the park and its surrounding area. The project will take years to complete, but it is bound to produce a wealth of information.

After your road switchbacks at the end of the lateral moraine, you pass two more turnouts that give you a view of Upper Kings Creek Meadow. As you descend to the headwaters of Kings Creek, in the upper part of the meadow, you have another turnout. Note that lodgepole pines are encroaching on the meadow, and they may ultimately convert it to a forest. However, lodgepole incursions are often temporary, for brief, wetter times can kill such a lodgepole stand, causing the flat to revert back to meadow.

Go 1.2 miles to

16.5/17.6 30, a road to Kings Creek Picnic

Area. A campground once existed where the day-use picnic area lies. However, a 1970 study by the U.S. Geological Survey indicated the site would be a dangerous one if Lassen Peak were to erupt again.

At the end of the ⅓-mile-long spur road, a trail takes off south to Cold Boiling and Crumbaugh lakes. A short trail also descends ⅓ mile along Kings Creek, ending where the creek crosses the Park Road near the next road stop. The section of creek along this trail and along the picnic area's spur road is a fine place for wildflower hunting, particularly in August, when wildflowers at lower elevations have mostly gone to seed. Dry, gravelly soils on slopes bordering the meadow support an abundant crop of silver-leaved lupines.

The lupines and other plants support a population of Sierra pocket gophers, who leave their calling cards in the form of "gopher ropes," which are linear tailings left by their burrowing activities when snow covered the ground. The gopher population, churning the soil, improves its condition much as earthworms do at lower elevations.

Go 0.5 mile to

17.0/17.1   31, Kings Creek, the midpoint between Highways 36 and 44. You are half-way through your road log. A glacier plowed across the terrain, heading southeast over the low divide, as is indicated by the direction of glacial striations on nearby bedrock. Upper Kings Creek, in contrast, meanders east through the upper meadow, then winds through a middle meadow to the lower meadow. If a future glacier descends through here again, it may likely trim a few feet off the divide, and then upper Kings Creek will empty south into the headwaters of Hot Springs Creek.

All the park's meadows are favorite haunts for deer; come early in the morning or late in the evening to see them (but they also prowl the campgrounds at night in search of food). Bird watchers, look for dippers along the creek's rapids and for spotted sandpipers along its lazy meanders.

Go 0.6 mile to

17.6/16.5   32, middle Kings Creek meadow. There is a small picnic area on the north side of the road immediately past the bridge. The park's tallest lupine, the large-leaved lupine, grows along the creek bank together with arrowhead butterweed, wandering daisy and a host of other water-loving plants.

This area sometimes overflows with cars, for the trail to Kings Creek Falls, starting just east of the bridge, is a popular one. Visit the falls between 10 a.m. and noon for the best photographs. During most of the day the falls are generally in the shade. The 1.2-mile hike to the falls takes about ½ hour—longer if you are captivated by the beauty and music of the Kings Creek Cascades, which you pass along the way.

Go 0.3 mile to

17.9/16.2   33, dwarf mistletoe. The western dwarf mistletoe and, to a much lesser extent, the American dwarf mistletoe parasitize the park's conifers. Look for the western dwarf mistletoe in nearby red firs with brown branches. The mistletoes cause the branches to swell, and they eventually kill the branches, though not the tree if it is healthy. The mistletoes are easiest to spot on branches that are swollen but still having green needles. The brownish, scaly, needle-sized parasites blend in well with dead needles.

Go 1.0 mile to

18.9/15.2   34, a view of the Kings Creek drainage basin. Mt. Harkness, to the left of Lake Almanor, is, at 8045 feet, the most prominent peak in the Kings Creek drainage basin. It is the only peak in Lassen Park that still has a fire lookout station manned during the summer. Saddle Mountain, below and to the left of it, stands 5 miles east of us and hides the park's largest, deepest lake, Juniper Lake. Its origin is largely due to Mt. Harkness erupting on the scene, damming a valley.

Corral Meadow, only 2 miles east of us, lies below Saddle Mountain. The last glacier flowing down the Kings Creek drainage advanced almost to the meadow and dumped sediments into it. Your road's viewpoint is on a moraine left by a glacier that originated in a cirque about ¾ mile away, high on Reading Peak.

Other views include a north-south line of peaks near the park's eastern border, beyond which lies adjacent, lake-blessed Caribou Wilderness. In the northeast, Prospect Peak, at 8338 feet, is the highest peak in the park east of your viewpoint.

Go 0.8 mile to

19.7/14.4 35, elevation 7000 feet, in a red-fir forest. The park averages about 7000 feet elevation but ranges from 5300 feet near Kelly Camp to 10,457 feet on the summit of Lassen Peak. Most of the park's terrain lies between 6000 and 8000 feet, which is the approximate vertical span of the red-fir forest. Red firs dominate the forest, though western white pines certainly abound. Mountain hemlocks grow in the snowier, usually higher sections, lodgepole pines in the wetter sections and Jeffrey pines in the drier sections. Wildflowers are usually scarce. The only plant growing in significant numbers on the forest floor is the lowly pinemat manzanita.

On October 12, 1962, a storm with gusts of wind exceeding 100 mph blew down a lot of trees in some places, such as here. Red firs suffered the greatest casualties. But then, blowdowns, like lightning fires, are a part of nature, and forest trees have experienced such events for millions of years.

Go 0.6 mile to

20.3/13.8 Lupine Picnic Area. Here you see Christine's lupine, with pale-yellow flowers, gray-green leaves and sometimes reddish-green stems. A variety of Anderson's lupine, this lupine is common only in Lassen Park and the adjacent lands. The park's five other species of lupines have bluish flowers.

Go 0.7 mile to

21.0/13.1 36 south, Summit Lake Campground's southern sites. A trail at the end of these campsites descends 2½ miles to Corral Meadow, a popular camping area for backpackers.

Divide Lake would be a better name for Summit Lake, for it lies on a flat divide, and ground water seeping from it flows into two river systems. Water seeps north into East Fork Hat Creek, eventually reaching the Pit River, and water seeps south into Summit Creek, evenutally reaching the Feather River. Summit Lake receives perhaps too much use by swimmers and fishermen, and the water is somewhat polluted (largely due to the campground's proximity) and relatively low in trout.

Go 0.1 mile to

21.1/13.0 36 north, Summit Lake Campground's northern sites. Due to heavy snowfall in the area, the Summit Lake Campground usually doesn't open until mid-June. Snow patches often remain on the ground until the Fourth of July or later. Once open, the campground is extremely popular and the sites are usually all taken even during the week.

From the northeast corner of Summit Lake a trail climbs east, giving rise in just under one mile to a trail to the Cluster Lakes and another one to the Twin Lakes. By making a loop hike along these two trails, you can visit about a dozen lakes in about 11 miles of hiking—a moderate day hike or an easy overnight backpack hike.

About 70 yards beyond the campground entrance, a closed road heads west from the Park Road and quickly branches, the right branch leading to Summit Lake Horse Corral, for equestrian campers.

Go 0.3 mile to

21.4/12.7 37, Summit Lake Ranger Station. If you plan to camp overnight in the park's backcountry, you'll need a wilderness permit. Get one here. A hikers's parking lot lies just beyond the ranger station, and from the lot a trail heads 0.4 mile over to the northeast shore of Summit Lake.

Go 0.1 mile to

21.5/12.6 38, a trail climbing southwest up to Cliff, Shadow and Terrace lakes. Although the climb isn't all that bad, you'd do better to start at marker 27 on the Park Road and descend along the trail to marker 38.

Go 1.2 miles to

22.7/11.4 39, Dersch Meadows, with East Fork Hat Creek flowing through them. The Dersch family, who settled north of Lassen Park in 1861, grazed sheep in these meadows until the 1880s. By the turn of the century, stockmen were running tens of thousands of sheep during the summer in the park's mountain meadows, severely overgrazing them. However, after Lassen National Forest was created in 1905, grazing was increasingly restricted and, after the creation of the national park, it was eventually banned. Today, Dersch Meadows is a fine place to look

for wildflowers, though you'll often end up with wet or muddy shoes if you do some serious botanizing. July is the best month for wildflowers—and for mosquitoes—so be prepared.

Go 0.3 mile to

23.0/11.1   40, a forest in transition. Here you'll see some young red firs and a lot more young lodgepole pines. When a piece of land is cleared, say by fire, blowdown or logging, conifers bordering the area reseed it. In your location the principal competitors are lodgepole pines and red firs. Lodgepole pines do better in open areas and become dominant, as is happening here. But as they grow and provide more shade, they tip the advantage in favor of red firs, which eventually grow above them and shade them out. Such a transition from one species to another is called *succession*. As the forest changes in composition from one tree to another, so too do its shrubs and wildflowers and, to a lesser extent, its animals. The species that ultimately dominate an area together make up the *climax association*.

Go 0.6 mile to

23.6/10.5   41, the Nobles Trail parking area, just past a closed road descending northwest. Today it is used by hikers heading down to Hat Creek or over to Badger Flat, but for pioneers it was the most efficient emigrant route across northeastern California down to the northern Sacramento Valley. William H. Nobles, a prospector, discovered this natural route in 1851, when he was returning to his native Minnesota. He realized it was shorter than and superior to Peter Lassen's route of 1847, and convinced others to back construction of a road in 1852. The completion of the Transcontinental Railroad in 1869 brought about the demise of this emigrant route and others like it.

Your turnout, with your first good view of Lassen Peak since stop 31, is along the southeast boundary of a giant mudflow, and you won't leave it until stop 50, after you bridge Lost Creek.

Go 0.2 mile to

23.8/10.3   42, Hat Lake site. Hat Lake had a brief history, coming into existence on May 19, 1915, when a wall of mud rumbled down Lassen's northeast slope, damming up Hat Creek with logs and debris. Incoming sediments immediately began to reduce the size of the lake, halving it to about 10 acres by 1930, to 1 acre by 1950 and to a wide creek by 1980.

An uncomfortably steep trail climbs up to Paradise Meadow and then beyond to a junction with a trail from Terrace Lake. United as one, they briefly climb to stop 27 on the Park Road. Rangers lead wildflower hikes up to Paradise Meadow as well as to Crescent Crater, which is the large cone to the right of Lassen Peak. Its slopes support one of the most diverse assemblages of wildflowers in the park. The crater may have originated after a dacite dome had a tremendous eruption, blowing away much of the dome. The age of the dome is still uncertain, but it may be roughly equal to Lassen Peak in age. Geologists disagree.

Go 0.4 mile to

24.2/9.9   43, a view of Hat Mountain, standing 2½ miles to the east. Although it is a forested version of the park's famous Cinder Cone, it is not, technically speaking, a cinder cone, for it is composed largely of lava flows. It may be less than 11,000 years old, for its smooth form gives no indication of glacial erosion. Before that approximate date, the lava plateau supporting the cone lay under an ice cap hundreds of feet deep. The plateau was substantially eroded but Hat Mountain appears to have been unscathed.

Go 70 yards to

24.2/9.9   44, the Devastated Area. Memorial Day 1914 was a day Lassen's early settlers would long remember. At about 5 p.m. on that day, May 30, Lassen Peak awoke from its long sleep, blasting a 25-by-40-foot crater out of its summit. By the end of March 1915, the peak had erupted about 150 times, and its summit crater had been enlarged to about 1000 feet across. The eruptions were *phreatic* explosions of old rocks and ash. Such explosions are caused by the percola-

---

Left: Reading Peak and Upper Kings Creek Meadow (stop 31). Gopher ropes among lupines and knotweeds (stop 30). Parents watch as children scramble about on Hot Rock (stop 48). Lassen Peak and Crescent Crater (right), viewed from the Devastated Area parking lot (stop 44).

tion of ground water down to or close to the volcano's magma (subsurface lava), which converts it to superheated steam. No lava reached the surface in these eruptions, so the eruptions were cold and snow was not melted by falling ash.

In the Lassen area the winds usually blow northeast, and a disproportionally large amount of ash accumulated in Lassen Peak's mildly glaciated northeast bowl. Somewhat protected from the wind, this bowl also builds up a deep snowfield, as deep as 40 feet. Storm after storm brought in new snow, and about every other day, Lassen erupted and deposited a new layer of ash on the fresh snow. By mid-May 1915, a huge accumulation of snow and ash lay in Lassen's northeast bowl—the one you see from your viewpoint. The stage was set for a catastrophe.

About 9 p.m. on the evening of May 19, 1915, inhabitants noticed a glow atop the peak—lava had appeared on the mountaintop (it may have appeared inside the crater a day or two earlier, but bad weather had obscured the peak). This lava welled up to the rim of the crater, and its heat generated several small mudflows down the peak's north and northwest slopes. Some lava spilled southwest 1000 feet down the peak's western slope, creating a mudflow of moderate proportions. But when some lava spilled onto the peak's upper northeast slope, it melted the deep snowfield and generated a devastating mudflow greater than anyone back then would have imagined. A wall of mud literally rumbled downslope, fortunately waking the few settlers in the valleys below. It was also fortunate that the tremendous accumulation of ash caused the mudflow to flow slowly, more like wet concrete than a flood of water. The flow moved only several miles an hour, slowly enough for Elmer Sorahan to run down to his neighbors and wake them. No lives were lost.

When daylight broke on the morning of the 20th, some of the settlers returned and viewed their devastated area. The flow had buried luxuriant meadows under mud, rock and snags. The flow got up to 18 feet deep in at least one place, judging by the mud remaining on a standing tree. Almost every tree in the mudflow's path was lost, and the thousands of trees broken away littered the landscape. The flow had breached Emigrant

Pass—the low, broad divide you're standing on—and sent a wall of mud north, averaging ⅓ mile wide and 10-20 feet thick, 4 miles down Hat Creek before significantly diminishing in volume over another 3 miles. The flow northwest down the Lost Creek drainage was similar in volume.

But the worst was yet to come. At about 4:30 p.m. on May 22, Lassen Peak produced its largest explosion—the 174th recorded. It sent an ash cloud 30,000 feet into the air, the ash darkening the sky as far east as northwestern Nevada. Almost simultaneously, it blasted superheated air northeast downslope, totally leveling the forest in an area 1 mile wide by 3 miles long. This "Hot Blast" which created the "Devastated Area" caused trees to be blown over like matchsticks, all the prone trees pointing away from the source of the blast. The blast was hot enough to scorch the timber and start at least one small fire.

Today the Devastated Area, shown on your book's topographic map, doesn't appear very devastated, for reforestation is well underway. Aspens, which propagate mostly from roots and seldom from seeds, were among the first trees to appear, for their roots and lower stems had survived the mudflow. You'll see many of these white-barked trees over the next mile, though encroaching lodgepole pines eventually may shade them out. Jeffrey pines grow in areas with less ground water. Remember that all these trees you see have grown since 1915 or later.

After the May 22 eruption, volcanic activity declined, though heavy eruptions occurred sporadically through the end of the year. Only four such eruptions occurred in 1916, from late October through mid-November. Many more eruptions occurred from January through June 1917, but then the activity apparently ceased—though the volcano smoked and steamed on and off until February 1921.

Go 0.7 mile to

24.9/9.2 45, Raker Peak. (The road's shoulder is soft, so be careful not to get stuck.) The peak originally lay outside the park, but was incorporated in 1929, when the park was enlarged by 39 square miles. The peak's name was then changed from Divide Peak to Raker Peak, named for Congressman John E. Raker, the park's staunch supporter, who had died in 1926.

Like Prospect Peak, Mt. Harkness and Sifford Mountain inside the park and West Prospect Peak, Badger Mountain and Table Mountain along its northern boundary, Raker Peak is a shield volcano. And, like all but Badger and Table mountains, it has a cinder cone atop it. However, what you see is a large, steep-walled dacite dome, which erupted onto the volcano's southwest flank. The wall of cliffs is due to erosion by a major glacier that followed our road's route northwest past the peak. The glacier was about 800 feet thick in this vicinity, or, in other words, as thick as the cliffs are high. Such a thickness exerts a force on the glacier's base of about 23 *tons* per square *foot*.

Go 0.3 mile to

25.2/8.9 46, Old Boundary Spring. When the park was created in 1916, part of its northern boundary lay only 0.4 mile north of this spring. From the road's southwest side a path drops 25 yards to the still-flowing, chilly spring. Look for the common large monkey flower, with yellow, inch-long, tubular flowers.

Go 0.4 mile to a

25.6/8.5 Closed Road. This junction is about 100 yards south of the park's original north boundary.

Go 0.2 mile to

25.8/8.3 47, a forest of Jeffrey pines, lodgepole pines and aspens. Most of the trees to the west grew up after the 1915 mudflow, though the large Jeffrey pine opposite the roadside marker is obviously older. In the park, Jeffrey pines reach maturity in about 200-300 years and lodgepoles in about 100-200 years. Higher up, where the growing season is shorter, red firs take about 250-400 years and mountain hemlocks, growing even higher, take about 300-500 years. The Jeffrey pine can usually be distinguished from its look-alike cousin, the ponderosa pine, by the butterscotch odor you smell if you stick your nose in a bark furrow of a mature specimen. A mature ponderosa pine smells more like resin.

Go 0.4 mile to

26.2/7.9 48, Hot Rock. This is one of many hot rocks from Lassen's summit area that were transported down here in the May 19, 1915 mudflow. This one lies about 4½ miles from its source. When Benjamin Loomis and others visited this area on the 22nd, only hours before the "Hot Blast," they noted water still boiling around some of the larger rocks. One rock had even been hot enough to ignite wood lying beside it. When the Loomis party viewed Lassen Peak from these hot rocks, not a tree blocked their view, unlike the many that do today.

The hot rock at this stop is one of the largest, about 300 tons, if you assume half of it is buried. This is a fair assumption, since the rock would have settled on the valley's buried floor after the mud had ceased to flow. The floor here lies under about 5-10 feet of mud. This rock, composed of dacite lava with white feldspar crystals, is a part of the lava flow that spilled northeast onto the snow-and-ash field. This lava could have been as hot as 1650°F (900°C) when molten, so it is no wonder that the larger hot rocks stayed hot for days.

Go 0.4 mile to

26.6/7.5 49, Lost Creek bridge. The 1915 mudflow was the last of a series of sediments to pass through this area. Roughly 900 A.D., give or take a hundred years, a series of four pyroclastic flows swept down through this area. A pyroclastic flow is similar to Lassen's May 22nd "Hot Blast," except that a great deal of volcanic material accompanies the gas. Such horizontally directed blasts, composed of a mixture of extremely hot, incandescent fine ash, coarser rock fragments and hot gases, are called *nuees ardentes* (pronounced "new-ay' ar'-dawn," French for "burning clouds"). They can travel downslope at 200 miles per hour and hence are far more threatening than slowly moving mudflows. These pyroclastic flows were the first products of a series of eruptions that foreshadowed the extrustion of several dacite domes, the Chaos Crags.

Chaos Crags aren't the only cluster of dacite domes you'll see in this area. A 1200-foot-high forested peak, standing due west of you, is but one of a cluster of several that your road will take 5 miles to drive around. These domes may be 12,000-20,000 years old, for the last glacier to pass through here had to squeeze between them and Raker

Peak. The glacial ice at your spot was at least 600 feet thick.

Go 0.1 mile to

26.7/7.4 50, west boundary of the May 1915 mudflow. The mudflow continued several miles down this canyon. Trees in the canyon were broken from their roots, and some stumps still remain buried today. We know the date of their destruction: May 1915. Similarly, trees were destroyed by the four pyroclastic flows mentioned at the previous stop. Geologists look for remnants of such trees, for these, like other "recently" buried organic matter, contain small amounts of radioactive carbon 14. By measuring the amount of carbon 14 left in such samples, geologists determined the approximate date when the trees were destroyed by the pyroclastic flows.

From stops 41 through 50, the Park road has more or less taken the route of the old Nobles Trail, which was used by emigrants to California in the 1850s and '60s. Like the area's meadows, it lies under a sea of mud. In about 250 yards this historic wagon road branches right and then parallels the mudflow down-canyon. This route is now a service road, closed to motor vehicles but not to hikers or equestrians. Since it is viewless and waterless, it has few takers.

Go 0.6 mile to

27.3/6.8 51, Lost Creek Diversion Flume, also called the Sunflower Flume and Canal, seen just below the road. This was built in 1904-07 by the Shasta Power Company, which planned to supply water to a small hydroelectric plant. However, the flume was difficult to maintain and supplied very little water, and it was abandoned when the May 1915 mudflow ruined its intake.

You are now in a shady forest dominated by white firs growing on fertile slopes that are part of a large glacial moraine. Jeffrey pines, which were codominant with lodgepole pines in the level mudflow area, are now subordinate, and lodgepole pines are virtually absent. As the open forest in the mudflow area matures and provides more shade, white firs will invade it, although, the firs are unlikely to achieve dominance, due to different environmental conditions in that area.

Go 0.1 mile to

27.4/6.7 52, a crossing of the diversion flume, which is now on your left. The next roadside marker is on the left and on a curve with little room for stopping, so you might read the next passage first and then drive through the area.

Go 0.8 mile to

28.2/5.9 53, a burned area. Fires are part of the natural scene and plants adapted to them long ago. When an area such as this one is burned, the resulting open space is usually first invaded—at this elevation—by greenleaf manzanitas, tobacco brush and other shrubs, which you'll soon see. Jeffrey pines and sugar pines are likely to follow, shading out some of the shrubs. As shade increases, white firs invade and prosper, shading out virtually all of the shrubs. Given enough time, the firs also shade out the pines, for pine seedlings need sunny ground to get established. But then, another fire, a strong wind, a volcanic eruption or a disease may open the forest once again and another plant succession will begin.

Go 0.5 mile to

28.7/5.4 54, sugar pine. At 5630 feet elevation, this specimen is near the upper end of its range. In the Lassen area the tree is usually found between 3000 and 6000 feet elevation, and therefore it grows mostly below and outside the park. The sugar pine is easily the largest of the park's three species of white pines, which were mentioned back at stop 6. The sugar pine's cones are the largest of any pine's, 10-16 inches long. The Atsugewi, or "Hat Creek" Indians, visited this part of the park from about June through October and ate the pine's white, sweet resin as candy. In quantities, however, it acts as a laxative.

Go 0.2 mile to

28.9/5.2 55, Lost Creek Organization Campground. Groups wishing to use this rarely full campground must make reservations in advance.

Go 0.2 mile to

29.1/5.0 Crags Campground. This campground was developed after Manzanita Lake Campground was temporarily closed in

1974. Lost Creek and Crags campgrounds, lacking views or nearby lakes, are the least-used campgrounds in the park.

Go 0.1 mile to

29.2/4.9 56, ponderosa pine. In addition to three species of white pines, Lassen Park has three species of yellow pines, these with needles in bundles of three. Only the ponderosa and Jeffrey pines are common. The Washoe pine, which grows only in a few isolated areas in northeastern California, is found in the park only in the Butte Lake area.

Your linear stretch of road is paralleling a fault, which lies immediately southwest (left) of the road. Because erosion occurs faster along faulted, fractured rocks than along bedrock, a former stream cut a gully along the fault. Today the flow is entirely subterranean, and the ponderosa pine, standing where a creek ought to flow, is probably tapping this water source.

Go 0.3 mile to

29.5/4.6 57, an open forest. The linear gully just below you runs along the previously mentioned fault. The bedrock on your side of the gully has been lifted up with respect to the bedrock on the opposite side. Tens of thousands of years ago, before the faulting occurred, ground water from seasonal snowfields seeped east to this general locality, nourishing a fine forest. But with faulting, the ground water seeped southeast along the fault and our land uplifted east of the fault was deprived of this source. The slopes east and above you extend only a short way to a nearby ridge, so there is very little surface for rain and snow to collect on and eventually flow down. Compounding the drought situation, these low slopes lie in a "rain shadow," created by Table Mountain, to the west, which stands about 1000 feet above the low slopes and robs them of a lot of precipitation. Consequently, the forest here is quite open and dry, composed mainly of white firs and ponderosa pines. There are also a few sugar pines and incense-cedars, both species doing well on open slopes. Shrubs such as greenleaf manzanita, Bloomer's goldenbush and tobacco brush also do well here.

The next roadside marker is on a blind curve with little room for safe parking, so you might read the next passage first and then drive through the area.

Go 0.2 mile to

29.7/4.4 58, a Table Mountain fault. As the road curves through the gully, it crosses the previously mentioned fault, which slices northwest through the lower northeast slopes of Table Mountain. Two more similarly oriented faults slice through the mountain, one on each side of its main summit.

Lassen Park lies at the highly active crossroads of three geologic provinces. It lies along the western edge of the Great Basin, which is composed of hundreds of northwest-oriented, fault-generated mountains and valleys. The park also lies near the southern end of the Cascades and close to the northern end of the Sierra Nevada.

Go 0.5 mile to

30.2/3.9 59, shield volcanoes. As you climb these brushy slopes, you have eastward views of brushy Badger Mountain and two peaks behind it, West Prospect Peak to its left and Prospect Peak to its right. Like Table Mountain, all are shield volcanoes, which are volcanoes with low-angle slopes. The Prospect Peaks have slopes of a lower angle because their lavas, being basaltic, are more fluid than the andesitic lavas of Table and Badger mountains.

Badger Mountain's west slope is being reforested by the U.S. Forest Service. A huge fire, similar to one on Table Mountain, ravaged Badger Mountain and upper Hat Creek Valley in the last century. In such very large burn areas, brush can grow so dense that pines can't get established, and the area can still be a brush land a century after the burn. The same is true for large areas of clearcut logging; one cannot strip the land of conifers and expect a forest to spring back in a few decades.

The shrubs on your fire-ravaged slopes are mainly greenleaf manzanita, with its smooth, dark red bark, and tobacco brush, with its glossy leaves and seasonal sprays of aromatic flowers. Bitter cherry, with small, narrow leaves, is found in lesser amounts.

Go 0.4 mile to

30.6/3.5 Sunflower Flat, with a large turnout on the left. Here a bronze plaque, placed in 1931 when the Park Road was completed, marks the route of the old Nobles Trail, first used by emigrants in 1852. Sunflower Flat supposedly got its name because of an abundance of mountain mule ears, which are large-leaved sunflowers that produce a curious aroma. None were seen in 1980, though there was a smattering of Bloomer's goldenbush, a low, late-blooming shrub in the sunflower family.

Go 0.2 mile to

30.8/3.3   60, Nobles Pass. Ill-defined Nobles Pass lies almost a mile up the Nobles Trail. The trail climbs about 50 feet higher than it had to, going through a low gap about 200 yards north of a slightly lower gap. Nobles Trail is, nevertheless, an amazingly easy, fairly direct route, unlike most other pioneer trails across California's mountains. Could you have scouted such a route? William Nobles, a gold miner, was either a very keen scout or a very lucky man. In 1851, when he treked east on this virgin route, no map existed to show the area's streams and mountains, yet he seems to have made all the right decisions to find his way through it. In 1975 the park's section of the Nobles Trail was recorded in the National Register of Historic Places.

Go 0.4 mile to

31.2/2.9   61, white fir. White firs may exceed 200 feet in height, but few in the country reach the sheer bulk of this 170-foot-high specimen. Its trunk is about 7 feet in diameter. It may have been a seedling when Chaos Jumbles, which you are about to cross, catastrophically broke loose from Chaos Crags a few hundred years ago.

Go 0.1 mile to

31.3/2.8   62, the eastern edge of Chaos Jumbles. These deposits are the result of a series of three or more rockfall-avalanches that probably occurred in rapid succession back about 1670 A.D. It seems that hot molten rock beneath the northwest base of Chaos Crags got close enough to the surface to superheat the ground water and produce a stream explosion that triggered the rockfall-avalanches. Rocks altered by superhot water are found in the source area, indicating that the area had been "steaming away" for some time. When the supposed

blast occurred, millions of tons of rocks came crashing down, compressing a layer of air, so it is believed, which then acted as a suitable lubricant for the mass to rush downslope at speeds of 100-200 miles per hour. These rockfall-avalanches moved with such great momentum that they climbed as much as 400 feet up the slopes of Table Mountain. By the end of the last rockfall-avalanche, which may have been only minutes after the first, about 200 million cubic yards of debris lay strewn across the landscape. In a way, the event might have been similar to the May 18, 1980, collapse of the north side of Mt. St. Helens, but without the accompanying eruption and ash cloud, for Chaos Jumbles rocks were cool or cold when they came to rest. No evidence of fire exists.

Also at this stop you'll see a sign:

WARNING

ROCK AVALANCHE HAZARD
NEXT 2.3 MILES

NO STOPPING OR PARKING
NEXT 2.3 MILES

Since you won't be able to stop at posts 63 through 66, you should read this book's following information about them in advance.

Go 0.6 mile to

31.9/2.2   63, Chaos Jumbles—post removed. The gray, lifeless mountain mass to the southeast is Chaos Crags, a series of four or more plug domes. The formation of these domes was preceded by violent volcanic activity that may have occurred sporadically over some years. These eruptions of very hot ash and rock were then followed by the extrusion of dacite lava, which, being thick and pasty, accumulated on the spot rather than flowing far from the vents. Each dome may have taken only months or, at most, several years to form, the earliest one having formed about 900 A.D. It is not known whether all the domes formed around this date or whether some formed centuries later.

As you drive toward the center of Chaos Jumbles, you'll note that the trees are smaller and fewer than those closer to the edge. Some specimens are, nevertheless, just as old as the oldest ones at the edge, but they are growing more slowly in harsher soil-and-water conditions. In any devastated area, the edges are the first to show significant vegetation, since the edges are closest to plants bearing seeds.

Go 1.0 mile to

32.9/1.2 Manzanita Lake Campground road. The Chaos Crags Trail begins at a bend 200 yards up this road, and the trail allows close inspection of both Chaos Crags and Chaos Jumbles. About ⅓ mile beyond the trail you reach the Manzanita Lake Picnic Area, to the right, and the campground's entrance station, immediately ahead. You can launch nonmotorized boats at the lake's picnic area. Between this road and the museum, just ahead, a man-made creek diverts water from Manzanita Creek into Reflection Lake.

Go 0.1 mile to

33.0/1.1 64, Loomis Museum, now closed. In 1926, Benjamin Loomis, an early settler who probably took more photographs of Lassen Peak in eruption than anyone else, bought 40 acres of private land in the Manzanita-Reflection lakes area. The following year he and his wife financed the construction of the Mae Loomis Memorial Museum, dedicated to the memory of their only child. In 1929 they donated the museum and the 40 acres of land to the park. The museum is a splendid rock structure and certainly deserves to be preserved, if not reopened. It is recorded in the National Register of Historic Places.

Go 0.1 mile to

33.1/1.0 65, Reflection Lake, with no parking available. This lake formed in a large depression within Chaos Jumbles. Two other nearby ponds, hidden from the road, had a similar origin. Ground water flows beneath Chaos Jumbles and surfaces at all these depressions, forming bodies of water. Likewise, Manzanita Lake, ahead, probably receives more water from ground water than from Manzanita Creek. About 100 yards past marker 65, a man-made creek diverts water from Reflection Lake down to adjacent Manzanita Lake. In early morning and late after-

Paradise Meadow, a struggle to reach, is a typical, mosquito-plagued subalpine meadow.

noon, when the water is still, both Reflection and Manzanita lakes present mirrored views of Lassen Peak and Chaos Crags.

Go 0.2 mile to

33.3/0.8 66, Manzanita Lake, elevation 5847 feet. At the next stop you can park your car and walk along the lake's shoreline trail. This lake came into origin when the Chaos Crags rockfall-avalanches swept through here and came to a stop about ¾ mile west of the Highway 44/89 junction—the end of this road log. The deposits dammed Manzanita Creek, thereby giving rise to Manzanita Lake. The rumply surface along the north shore of the lake is the southern edge of Chaos Jumbles. In May 1915, some small mudflows poured down Lassen Peak into Manzanita Creek, and tons of sediments ended up in the lake. A large, future mudflow or rockfall-avalanche could eradicate the lake and/or form a new lake.

Go 0.2 mile to

33.5/0.6 67, Manzanita Lake Entrance Station. The park's official road log ends here. You'll find the lake's shoreline trail beginning only a few yards from the station. If you walk along it, you'll note a low dam on the lake's west shore. This raised the lake's level by only several feet. The Northern California Power Company had hoped to raise the level even higher, but the porosity of the volcanic sediments making up this earthfill dam caused it to "leak like a sieve." Today, a dense root network of mature alders and willows growing on the dam prevents it from eroding and greatly reduces seepage.

Go 0.4 mile to a

33.9/0.2 road branching left. Many Park and Forest Service employees live in temporary quarters along this road. The Manzanita Lake area is in a state of flux. Over the next

decade or two, a new visitor center will be built together with new living quarters, museum, campground, trails and other features. These, hopefully, will be in localities that are less exposed to future rockfall-avalanches, though no one can predict if, when or where one will occur.

Go 0.1 mile to

34.0/0.1 Visitor Center, about 100 yards east of the park's western boundary. From the center's parking lot a very short nature trail loops around the local vegetation. To your west lies a 2-mile-long stretch of shrubbery known as Manzanita Meadows, composed primarily of greenleaf manzanitas. In 1966 a large section of it was bulldozed and planted with ponderosa, Jeffrey and sugar pine seedlings. A dozen years later the manzanita was dense as ever. The plantation on Badger Mountain, mentioned back at stop 59, has suffered the same fate. Reforestation can be very expensive.

But should we destroy the manzanitas? Manzanita leaves are prime deer forage, and Manzanita Meadows is prime fawning ground for some of the park's deer. There are two subspecies of mule deer in the Lassen area, the Rocky Mountain mule deer, with a tip of black on an otherwise white tail, and the black-tailed deer, with an essentially black tail. The "Black tails" are more common, and they migrate east up to the park in the springtime. Indians used to follow the deer to the uplands, hunting them and gathering the developing tubers, leaves and seeds along the way.

Go 0.1 mile to a junction where

34.1/0.0 Highway 44, from the west, joins northbound Highway 89. The next chapter describes Highway 89 north down Hat Creek Valley to Highway 299, in the Burney Falls area.

9 Hat Creek Valley Road Log

Introduction   This chapter's road log begins where the previous chapter's road log left off, namely, at the Highway 89 junction with Highway 44, which is immediately beyond Lassen Park's northwest boundary. Unlike the Highway 89 road log through Lassen Park, the one through Hat Creek Valley is unofficial. It further differs in that the park's road log deals primarily with the interpretation of natural features, whereas this chapter's road log deals primarily with roads, campgrounds, picnic grounds, trails and other manmade features. Interpretation of the scenery is substantially less. No wildflowers are mentioned, so consult the botany chapter if you see some interesting plants.

This Hat Creek Valley Road Log starts north from a highway junction outside of Hat Creek Valley Recreation Area. The 35.1-mile log ends at the Highway 299 intersection, from where the traveler can then drive to McArthur-Burney Falls Memorial State Park or to the towns of Burney or Fall River Mills, all three being just a few minutes' drive away. This log, though written with motorists in mind, is an excellent one for bicyclists. Indeed, the route is probably one of California's finest bicycle routes, receiving high marks for scenery, logistics and road condition.

Hat Creek Valley Road Log

Miles north of Hwy. 44 jct.	Miles south of Hwy. 299 intersection	From where Highway 44 joins Highway 89, they coincide for 13.4 miles, and then Highway 44 climbs east shortly north of
0.0	35.1	Old Station. To the west of your starting point, Highway 44 descends 45 miles to

Interstate 5 in Redding. If you're driving east from Redding up Highway 44, you'll encounter the following features: After about 27½ miles you'll pass through

89

A large spatter cone (mile 11.9/23.2). Big Spring supports lush aquatic vegetation (mile 9.7/25.4). Entrance to Subway Cave (mile 13.7/21.4).

Shingletown, your last chance for gas, food and supplies until Hat Creek Resort, at mile 0.4/24.7 of this chapter's road log. About 3 miles beyond "central" Shingletown you pass a rest area, to your left, then in 1.2 miles pass the Mt. Lassen KOA campground, to your right. After 6.9 more miles your road curves sharply left through Viola, a proverbial town that you'll completely miss if you blink your eyes. A paved road branches right here, passing homesites and then becoming a graded road as it climbs to USFS Road 17, their junction being 3.6 miles from Highway 44.

From the curve in Viola, Highway 44 winds 5.4 miles to a junction with Road 17, on which you can drive 21.7 miles south to Highway 36, Road 17 ending at 36 1.1 miles west of Lassen Park headquarters. Road 17 provides access to Deep Hole, Blue Lake Canyon and Heart Lake, all described in the last part of Chapter 15. Just 1.1 miles past the Road 17 junction, Highway 44 reaches the Highway 89 junction, which is the starting point of this chapter's road log.

Go 1.3 miles to

1.3/33.8   Eskimo Hill Summit, at an elevation of 5933 feet. On your left (west) is a parking area with a rest room, both of them mainly for winter recreationists coming up here for fun in the snow.

Go 2.7 miles to

4.0/31.1   USFS Roads 16 and 32N13. Road 16, starting west, is the main road leading to the southern trailheads of Thousand Lakes Wilderness (see Chapter 17). If you start along this road you'll immediately encounter Ashpan Snobmobile Park, the starting point of about 25 miles of posted routes for snowmobilers.

Road 32N13 goes southeast to Lost Creek, crossing it 2.8 miles from Highway 89, and only 100 yards from Lassen Park's northern boundary. The road then winds 3.5 miles over to a junction with the Emigrant Ford Road, which, during the 1950s, had a campground where the road ended at Hat Creek. Road 32N13 then descends 1.2 miles to Road 32N12, this junction being immediately east of Lost Creek.

Go 4.1 miles to

8.1/27.0   USFS Road 32N12, branching left (southeast) and going 0.8 mile to road 32N13, which was mentioned in the previous stop. Road 32N13 begins a southward climb from the east side of the Lost Creek bridge and begins a northward descent from the west side of this bridge. Lost Creek joins Hat Creek just north of the bridge, the latter then flowing past Big Pine Campground and reaching Highway 89 by Big Spring. Road 32N13 parallels the creek, going 1.3 miles down to the campground. This stretch of road between the Lost Creek bridge and Big Pine Campground constitutes the Twin Bridges Dispersed Recreation Area, a primitive campground. Possible campsites are found on both banks of Hat Creek.

Just 0.2 mile beyond the Lost Creek bridge, Road 32N12 crosses the Hat Creek bridge, the second of the "Twin Bridges." The road then continues 1.5 miles southeast to the Plantation Loop Road, which is no longer a loop road, for it climbs south just 0.4 mile to the northeast base of Badger Mountain. Park here if you want to follow the **Pacific Crest Trail** south into Lassen Park, the trail starting along an abandoned part of the loop road. This trail is described in Chapter 18.

At the loop-road junction you are 2½ miles southeast from Highway 89, and if you were to continue 9¼ miles along the graded road, you would reach the fire-lookout station atop West Prospect Peak. During the summer, it is usually open from 8 a.m. to 5 p.m. daily. This summit provides you with the best views of upper Hat Creek Valley. From your high point you look north directly along the faulted east edge of the valley—the Hat Creek Rim escarpment. To the northwest lie Potato and Little Potato buttes, both active at times in the last several thousand years and producing localized lava flows. The large lava flow spreading across the floor of Hat Creek Valley originated at the Spatter Cones (see mile 11.9/23.2). Sugarloaf Peak, a sporadically active lava cone, is the youthful peak growing along the west side of down-faulted Hat Creek Valley. The high peaks about 8 miles west of Sugarloaf Peak are part of a rim of an extinct Ice Age volcano, and today the remnants of this volcano make up the bulk of Thousand Lakes Wilderness (see Chapter 17). Just 2¼ miles to your southeast, Prospect Peak stands slightly higher than West Prospect Peak, and it provides better views of the Lassen Park backcountry (see Chapter 14). A quite recent cinder cone and lava flow lie between the two peaks.

If you don't drive 9¼ miles up to the fire-lookout station, but rather drive only the first 4 ⅓ miles toward it, you'll reach a creek, crossing it immediately north of where its two branches unite. This spot is the "trailhead" closest to Badger Flat, Soap Lake and the Cluster Lakes. Badger Flat is just 0.4 mile up the right branch of the creek, and at it you can either head east on the Nobles Trail, which is a closed road that goes to Soap Lake and beyond, or else head south up a trail to the Cluster Lakes. Both routes are described in Chapter 11. Remember, regardless of where you enter Lassen Park, you'll need a wilderness permit if you stay in its backcountry overnight (see Chapter 3).

Go 0.2 mile to

8.3/26.8 Vista Point, a large turnout on the highway's east side. Signs identify the point's views, which include Lassen Peak, Sugarloaf Peak, Hat Creek Rim, Hat Creek Valley and the Potato Buttes. In 1980 the views of the valley and the buttes were being consumed by rapidly growing pines of the adjacent Deer Hollow-Badger Mountain Plantation. The Deer Hollow Trail, about 150 yards long, takes you through the western edge of this plantation, with signs explaining the reforestation of this area, a process that began in 1961.

Go 0.5 mile to

8.8/26.3 Big Pine Campground road, which winds ½ mile east to the campground's entrance. This campground and the Twin Bridges primitive campground, along the road south from it, both provide camp space when the overly popular Highway 89 campgrounds of Hat Creek Valley are packed full—usually from the Fourth of July through Labor Day.

Go 0.7 mile to

9.5/25.6 Logan Lake road, branching northwest from a curve in Highway 89. If you drive about 2¼ miles up this road—most of it across private land—you'll approach the north shore of seasonal Logan Lake. The lake lies in a down-faulted basin, and, 2¼ miles from the highway, you'll be parked along a

major, southeast trending fault that rivals th Hat Creek Rim fault system in length.

Less than 100 yards after the Logan Lak road leaves Highway 89, it gives rise to Roa 33N16, branching west (left). This fine roa goes 7⅓ miles over to USFS Road 16, mee ing it 4¾ miles from that road's junctio with Highway 89 (at mile 4.0/31.1). If yo drive 4 miles west on Road 33N 16, you pas between two cinder cones, these being pa of a dozen cones that extend in a line fro Bear Wallow Butte north 6½ miles to Eil Butte. All may have been active in the la 20,000 years. About one mile before yo road reaches Road 16, it skirts along th southern base of Devils Rock Garden, whic is a huge lava flow that may be less than 100 years old. It originated from one or mor vents along the line of cinder cones.

Go 0.2 mile to

9.7/25.4 Big Spring, found just before th highway curves from east to northeast. B Spring flows year-round, pouring water int Hat Creek. During fall and winter this larg spring often contributes more water to Ha Creek than Hat Creek itself brings to the spo Big Spring, with gushing, pure water, is fine spot for a picnic.

Go 0.7 mile to

10.4/24.7 Hat Creek Resort, with a store cabins, gas pumps and the Old Station Pos Office, all immediately north of a bridge ove Hat Creek. This resort appeals to fishermen who can almost cast a line from their cabi door.

Go 1.5 miles to

11.9/23.2 Hat Creek Campground and th Spatter Cone Nature Trail. The larg campground is situated between the high way and Hat Creek, and many campers fis along its bank. On the east side of the high way is the campground's sewage-dispos station, and from its south edge the relativel short nature trail climbs to 17 spatter cone See Chapter 18 for a description of feature seen from the trail's numbered posts.

Go 0.2 mile to

12.1/23.0 Old Station Picnic Groun which is a pleasant, creekside day-use are immediately   north   of   Hat   Cree Campground.

Go 0.7 mile to

12.8/22.3 Uncle Runts Place, in "downtown" Old Station. It serves good meals at fair prices and is a magnet for long-distance Pacific Crest Trail hikers. During July you're almost certain to see a few, each having some pretty tall tales to tell.

Go 0.5 mile to

13.3/21.8 Sandy Picnic Ground, which is immediately north of a gas station and immediately south of Highway 44. For travelers driving east on Highway 44, the gas station will be the last one until Susanville or Westwood, both located along Highway 36. See the next entry.

Go 0.1 mile to the

13.4/21.7 Highway 44/Highway 89 junction. Highway 44, which has coincided with Highway 89 for the last 13.4 miles, now branches east, going 28 miles to a junction with Lassen County Road A21, then another 18 miles to a junction with Highway 36. On Highway 36 you have a 6-mile drive east to Susanville, with gas, food, supplies and services. Road A21 goes 18 miles south to Highway 36, crosses it, and continues one mile into Westwood, a small lumber town with less of everything. See Chapter 16 for an in-depth account of this area's roads and trails.

Two points of interest lie closer to the 44/89 junction. The closer one is a trailhead parking area for the **Pacific Crest Trail**. You reach it by driving 2.9 miles on Highway 44, climbing to the edge of a forest and forking left on Road 33N21. Just 0.2 mile north on this road you'll see the trailhead parking area, on your left. See Chapter 18 for a description of the Pacific Crest Trail north from the trailhead.

Precisely 11.0 miles east from Highway 89, Highway 44 reaches a junction with Road 32N21, this road climbing 6.5 miles to Lassen Park's large, fairly popular Butte Lake Campground (see Chapter 14).

Go 0.3 mile to

13.7/21.4 Subway Cave and Cave Campground. If you have time for only one scenic stop, make it Subway Cave, located by a picnic area 0.2 mile east of Highway 89. Bring a lantern or a flashlight. See Chapter 18 for detailed information on the cave, its trails and the area's natural history.

Cave Campground, like Hat Creek Campground 1.8 miles south of it, is large and extremely popular. Use Big Pine Campground (mile 8.8/26.3) if both are full. Off the highway, Big Pine Campground is a lot quieter.

If you walk west across Cave Campground, you'll reach a bridge over Hat Creek. From this bridge the enjoyable Hat Creek Trail descends 3.8 miles to Bridge Campground (mile 17.4/17.7) The next three road stops provide access to this fine fishermen's trail, which is described in Chapter 18.

Go 0.5 mile to

14.2/20.9 Sugarloaf Picnic Ground, on the west bank of Hat Creek and lying near the east base of Sugarloaf Peak, a potentially active volcano. This picnic ground is a fine spot to observe the Hat Creek Rim escarpment, which has been faulted up with respect to the floor of Hat Creek Valley. A group of faults exist along the valley's west slopes, as you'll see at mile 29.1/6.0. The dry, scrubby lava flow covering the floor of the valley originated at the Spatter Cones (mile 11.9/23.2) and is believed to be on the order of 1000-2000 years old.

Go 0.8 mile to a

15.0/20.1 road branching west. From the end of this very short road a bridge takes you over Hat Creek to the adjacent Hat Creek Trail.

Go 1.7 miles to

16.7/18.4 Rocky Campground. This tiny campground is almost always full during summer. It lies along one of the nicest parts of Hat Creek and has a bridge across it to the Hat Creek Trail.

Go 0.6 mile to a

17.3/17.8 road branching east. This road narrows to a trail about midway across Hat Creek Valley, and the road and trail are part of the Hat Creek Valley Loop, a system of trails described in Chapter 18.

Go 0.1 mile to a

17.4/17.7 bridge across Hat Creek. The entrance to **Bridge Picnic Ground** is immediately north of the creek and the

Hat Creek Radio Astronomy Observatory's 85-foot-diameter radio telescope (mile 24.5/10.6). bridge provides access from Rocky Campground to the Hat Creek Trail (mile 16.7/18.4). Thousan of trout can be seen at the Crystal Lake State Fish Hatchery (mile 35.1/0.0). Shallow Baum Lake, ne to the fish hatchery, is stocked with trout (mile 35.1/0.0).

entrance to midsized **Bridge Campground** is immediately north of that entrance. The Hat Creek Trail, descending from Cave Campground, ends along the east perimeter of Bridge Campground, close to Hat Creek.

Go 3.9 miles to

21.3/13.8   USFS Road 33N25, climbing west from a bend in the highway. This road leads up to the **Tamarack Trailhead,** a popular starting point for hikers going into Thousand Lakes Wilderness (see Chapter 17).

Go 1.2 miles to

22.5/12.6   Honn Campground, which is another small, popular campground along Hat Creek.

Go 1.8 miles to

24.3/10.8   Hat Creek Ranger Station, which is the only place in Hat Creek Valley where you can get wilderness permits for Thousand Lakes Wilderness or Caribou Wilderness. See Chapter 3 for more information on wilderness permits.

Go 0.2 mile to the south end of a

24.5/10.6   loop road, starting northeast. This road loops back to Highway 89, but first it gives rise to a private drive to the **Hat Creek Hereford Ranch Campground,** then to USFS Road 22, which leads you to the **Hat Creek Radio Astronomy Observatory.**

From a store and gas station at the loop junction, drive ¼ mile to the Hat Creek Hereford Ranch. The campground is on this cattle ranch, and it has more conveniences that the USFS campgrounds. It has hot showers, a laundry room and a trout pond. Also, its sites are far enough away from Highway 89 that traffic noise is not bothersome. In contrast, each of the highway's USFS campgrounds has at least several sites that are within a stone's throw of the highway, Cave Campground being the worst. Lumber trucks, roaring down the highway before the break of dawn, will awaken you to this fact.

To reach the Hat Creek Radio Astronomy Observatory, leave the highway and drive 1.4 miles along the loop road to its junction with USFS Road 22. If you're driving south on the loop road, you'll reach this junction in 0.9 mile. East on Road 22, you'll reach the observatory's entrance in about 1.8 miles, then drive south ¾ mile to the observatory's office. Operated by the University of California, this observatory is open to the public on weekdays, usually from 9 a.m.-4 p.m. Berkeley's Radio Astronomy Lab selected Hat Creek Valley because of its relative isolation from manmade radio waves. A buildup of homes in the valley's lower north end could put an end to the interesting research being done at this facility. Read their visitor's information sheet for facts about their radio telescopes and about their research.

From the observatory's entrance, Road 22 goes east about ½ mile before turning north to switchback up the faulted escarpment of Murken Bench. About 4¼ miles beyond the entrance, the road crosses the **Pacific Crest Trail** about 100 yards before heading through a shallow pass on the Hat Creek Rim.

Go 1.7 miles to the north end of a

26.2/8.9   loop road, starting east. As mentioned in the previous entry, this road goes 0.9 mile to a junction with Road 22. The **Hat Creek Playhouse,** on Highway 89, is about 100 yards south of this junction.

Go 0.1 mile to

26.3/8.8   Hat Creek Post Office, with adjacent cafe and general store.

Go 1.7 miles to a

28.0/7.1   road branching west. Once the site of Boundary Campground, it is now a day-use area that attracts fishermen.

Go 1.1 miles to a

29.1/6.0   road branching southwest. From this junction you can look south straight along a major fault. The fault cuts between Brown Butte, to the east, and Dudgen Butte, to the west. Brown Butte has been raised hundreds of feet relative to Dudgen Butte. This fault continues south-southeast, finally disappearing under Sugarloaf Peak, which probably owes its origin to a conduit along this fault. The fault may continue southeast under the Spatter Cones and beyond them to the Prospect Peaks.

Just ½ mile west of this fault is another one. This is the same fault that crosses Highway 89 around mile 9.5/25.6. It cuts south right through Dudgen Butte, raising its east half about 200 feet above its west half. To the north, the fault is unseen, traversing under valley sediments and crossing Highway 89 about ½ mile south of your next stop, Cassel Road.

Faulting and volcanism usually go hand in hand, and from your junction you also get a view in the east of very youthful Cinder Butte. Its summit is but one of at least seven vents that lie along the same fault that cuts along the base of the Murken Bench escarpment. Like the Spatter Cone vents of upper (southern) Hat Creek Valley, the Cinder Butte vents have buried the valley floor under basaltic lava, this outpouring definitely having occurred in the last several thousand years, if not in the last thousand. From your junction you also see 7863-foot-high Burney Mountain, a young volcano rising in the southwest. The area covered by this guidebook may be the most active volcanic area in the conterminous United States, and to build homes in this area, particularly in Hat Creek Valley, makes about as much sense as building a ski resort on the north slope of Washington's Mt. St. Helens.

Go 1.2 miles to

30.3/4.8   Cassel Road, branching northeast. This road goes 1.9 miles to Rising River, then 1.3 miles more to tiny Cassel, on the Cassel-Fall River Mills Road. Much if not most of the water flowing north down Hat Creek Valley does so underground, surfacing along a 2-mile-long swath along the base of a Cinder Butte lava flow. Unfortunately, this extremely interesting hydrological phenomenon is on private property and therefore off limits.

From the road junction in Cassel, you can follow the Cassel-Fall River Mills Road one mile west, then one mile north, to a road that heads 1.2 miles east to the **Crystal Lake State Fish Hatchery**. This is described in the next entry.

East from the Cassel junction, the Cassel Fall River Mills Road climbs 3.0 miles to crossing of the **Pacific Crest Trail**, this crossing being about 2 miles before the road passes between two quite recent cinder cones that are being eaten away for commercial use.

Go 4.8 miles past homes
and ranches to the

35.1/0.0   Highway 89/Highway 299 junction. Your road log ends here. Ahead on Highway 89 you'll reach the entrance to McArthur-Burney Falls Memorial State Park in 5.8 miles (see Chapter 19).

On Highway 299 you can head southwest 1½ miles to Johnson Park, then 3½ miles beyond it to central Burney, which probably ranks above Chester and Susanville in number and diversity of services available. Or you can head northeast toward Fall River Mills and McArthur, both with considerably fewer services. If you start in that direction you'll reach the Cassel-Fall River Mills Road in 2.2 miles. By taking that road south 2.4 miles, then another road east 1.2 miles, you'll arrive at the entrance to Crystal Lake State Fish Hatchery.

The fish hatchery, located along Hat Creek near the south end of Baum Lake, supplies trout of all species and hybrids to various places from the northern Sierra Nevada to the Oregon border. Hat Creek gets a lion's share of the trout. From Big Spring north to the site of former Boundary Campground this creek is stocked with trout—particularly near the campgrounds—once or twice a week. No wonder, then, that the Highway 89 campgrounds attract so many fishermen. Though you can't fish at the hatchery, you can fish at nearby Baum Lake. This you reach by branching north on a spur road you meet 100 yards before the fishery entrance.

10 Lassen Park's Nature Trails

Introduction Lassen Volcanic National Park has three major nature trails, each requiring several hours if you really want to do it right—half that time if you're in a hurry. These trails are the Bumpass Hell, Boiling Springs Lake and Cinder Cone nature trails. If you plan to be in Lassen Park for a day or less, try to fit one of these into your schedule. The Bumpass Hell Nature Trail, which starts high on the Lassen Park Road, is the most popular of the three, and it rivals the Lassen Peak Trail in popularity. The fourth trail—at least in 1980—is the Indian Ways Nature Trail, which is located behind the Visitors Center, near the park's northwest corner. Since this trail may be moved or abandoned in a few years, it is not described in this book.

There are two other "nature trails" in the park that are described in the following chapter. These are the Sulphur Works Trail and the Lassen Peak Trail. Unlike this chapter's four nature trails, neither has numbered posts. (The posts' numbers correspond to those found in the park's trail pamphlets and in the following trail descriptions. Occasionally a post is missing, but this does not present a real problem.) The Sulphur Works Trail does have signs that explain the area's geothermal features, and the Lassen Peak Trail does have a pamphlet that contains information about the peak and its plant and animal life. North of the park you'll find three more nature trails: the Spatter Cone Nature Trail and the Subway Cave Trail, both in Chapter 18, and the Burney Falls Nature Trail, in Chapter 19.

With the park's nature-trail pamphlets in hand, the author hiked this chapter's nature trails, making corrections and additions as well as identifying and photographing trailside wildflowers. The area's more common wildflowers appear on plates in the botany chapter. The author hopes that with these plates, plus the text that accompanies them, visitors will be able to identify most of the flowers they'll see.

Bumpass Hell Nature Trail

Trailhead Post 17 on Lassen Park Road, 5.7 miles above the Southwest Entrance Station and 1.1 miles below the Lassen Peak Trail parking lot.

Distances 1.0 mile (1.6 km) to Bumpass Hell viewpoint
1.4 miles (2.3 km) to Bumpass Hell
2.8 miles (4.6 km) round trip

Trail description Almost every summer day hundreds of visitors take this trail, which usually becomes essentially snow-free in mid- or late July. Allow 3 hours for a leisurely hike, and consider bringing water since usually there is no drinking water along the route. Please help keep this popular trail clean by bringing back any refuse you might have to a trash barrel near the start of the trail. Traversing along the northeast edge of an Ice Age volcano, Mt. Tehama, this trail takes you to the park's most active hydrothermal area. Along the trail you'll see evidence of some of the forces that have shaped this landscape and you'll see that a dynamic interplay of forces still persists.

1 Glaciers had cut deep into Mt. Tehama, eradicating most of it by the time Lassen Peak made its appearance. Lassen may have erupted 11,000 years ago. Lassen's formation began as dacite lava squeezed out onto the surface. This lava was so thick and pasty that it domed up into a mass about ½ mile high rather than flowing downslope, as basaltic or andesitic lava would have done. Dacite domes are known to grow as much as 100 feet in a single day, though the average rate is somewhat less. Lassen Peak grew to its present size in perhaps just a few years, becoming one of the largest plug domes in the world, if not the largest.

2 A glacier, which is a flowing body of ice usually hundreds of feet thick, descended south from a pre-Lassen crest and left its imprint on these rocks. Whenever you see polished bedrock with straight, parallel grooves (glacial striations), you can be quite sure that a glacier has passed by. Also look for crescentic gouges, another sign of glaciers. Watch for more glacial evidence ahead.

3 Mt. Tehama, a stratovolcano similar in height, shape and bulk to northern Oregon's Mt. Hood, once covered all the nearby land you see. From Mt. Conard, on your left, it extended west to Brokeoff Mountain, the largest remnant, then north to Mt. Diller and Pilot Pinnacle and east past our location. Its summit, about 11,000 feet in elevation, probably centered over today's Sulphur Works. Tehama's birth began about 600,000 years ago; then flows and eruption debris built it up to its maximum height by perhaps about 300,000 years ago. As with today's Cascade Range volcanoes, Tehama was inactive most of the time, and since it was born in the Ice Age, glaciers probably flowed down its slopes from its early days onward. Thus its destruction began almost as soon as it was born. In its last eruptive days its flanks were already deeply cut by glacial canyons.

4 You know you are high in the mountains when you see a whitebark pine. You can recognize this tree by its scaly bark and i short needles that grow in groups of fiv Only a few specimens live "down" here 8200 feet; they are usually found higher, ar they are the only trees that can survive tl strong, subfreezing winds that whip pa Lassen Peak in winter. High-elevatic habitats aren't that old, geologically spea ing, and the ancestral whitebark pines, lil other ancestral mountain species, had evolve to successfully adapt to such habitat

5 Here we have an anomaly, Lake Hele filling a 110-foot-deep basin scooped out unquestionably—by a southward-flowir glacier (the glacial striations point soutl ward). Yet above Lake Helen is the ui glaciated south flank of Lassen Peak. Whei did the glacier come from? Had it come fror Mt. Tehama, whose summit stood southwe of us, the striations would be northeas oriented. As you can see, they aren't. In add tion, one would have to explain why tl glacier flowed northeast over this bedroc and then northeast up over the currentl existing crest at the base of Lassen Peak. Th answer seems to be that one or more glacie descended south from one or more dome that preceded Lassen Peak. When Lasse erupted, it buried the evidence of a previou dome, but we do know that dacite domes lil it were formed long ago. Indeed, there is cluster of pre-Lassen domes at the south bas of the peak and more along its northwe base. The dacite bedrock you see along th part of the trail has been radiometricall dated at about 250,000 years old. Althoug glaciers may have developed on these pr Lassen domes, they could not flow south a long as Mt. Tehama, several miles to th southwest, towered above them. As long a that stratovolcano existed, it probably sent glacier or two northeast downslope, perhap overriding the domes. Only after backwarc cutting glaciers on Tehama's south flank ha cut through most of the volcano would dome-originated glacier have been able t flow south unimpeded. This switch in th glacial regime—from glaciers radiating ou from one point to glaciers flowing from sev eral locations—may have taken place in th last 100,000 years.

6 The boulder sitting across the canyo just to the left of the parking area demor strates the power of a glacier. This *glacic erratic* was carried south along in the ic low, and left perched on the ridge when the ice melted. Look at it when you return. It is composed of andesite. Had it been an erratic carried northeast by a Mt. Tehama glacier, it would be, like that mountain, composed of andesite. Near this post, watch for mountain pride (Newberry's penstemon), growing out of cracks in rocks. When in bloom, it produces a cluster of tubular inch-long, crimson flowers.

7 Lake Helen has no surface outlet. Rather, its water seeps through the ground, emerging lower down in a spring that, with several others, gives rise to East Sulphur Creek. Chinquapin, with smooth, leathery leaves, and cream bush, with dull, toothed leaves, are two common shrubs found nearby.

8 As lava cools it contracts, and this contraction creates joints—a system of parallel cracks in the lava. Water then seeps into these cracks, freezes, expands, and pries loose blocks of rock that tumble down and accumulate, forming talus slopes. These bouldery slopes may look forbidding to us, but to the pika, a relative of rabbits, they make an ideal home. Listen for the harsh, high-pitched call of these "tailless," small-eared, rat-sized mammals. In their bouldery dens, pikas dry lupines and other plants in "haystacks" before storing them for winter food. In this vicinity the commonest lupine is the silver-leaved lupine, whose silvery hairs may reduce the amount of ultraviolet radiation reaching the leaf surface. They may also help reduce water loss and prevent frostbite on chilly summer nights. If the hairs' only function were to provide protection from ultraviolet radiation, which increases with altitude, then one would expect all of Lassen Peak's summit plants to be densely hairy. Most are not.

9 To the northwest you can see where the dark-brown andesite of former Mt. Tehama gives way to gray dacite of later domes. Brokeoff Mountain, Mt. Diller and pointed Pilot Pinnacle are remnants of Mt. Tehama, as is Diamond Peak, 1¼ miles to the southwest. East of Pilot Pinnacle you see flat-topped Ski Heil Peak and larger, rounded Eagle Peak, both dacite domes like Lassen Peak.

10 If you hike the park's trails before late July, you'll note that the Bumpass Hell Nature Trail is about the last one to break free of snow. It is therefore no surprise that we find mountain hemlocks locally dominating in this area, for hemlock seems to be the only tree that relishes—and even prolongs—deep, long-lasting snowpacks. Notice how the trees tend to grow in clusters. This behavior causes snow to pile around and over them. Then, in early summer, these clusters shade the nearby snow, causing it to linger weeks after nearby barren slopes have become snow-free. The tree, it appears, would rather surround itself with snow than be exposed to the subfreezing winds that can occur in winter or spring. In winter the blowing winds can easily drop the effective temperature to -50°F and below. At these elevations it does not pay to be a tall, sturdy tree. It is better to bend with the wind and to be buried as much as possible under the relatively warm snow.

You can walk a few yards out to a nearby viewpoint, where you may see a sign about Mt. Tehama. In 1985 the sign said the volcano collapsed about 10,000 years ago—a statement that is folk history and definitely not true. See page 21 and road stops 3 and 5 for a more accurate geologic portrayal.

11 Pinemat manzanita, usually knee-high or less, is a plant of the heath family that is typically found in fir forests. But it does well in rocky, subalpine areas too, for it avoids most of the chilling winds by hugging the ground. Then, too, its waxy leaves help conserve water that would be otherwise evaporated by strong winds. Its berries provide important food for local birds and mammals, who in turn help propagate the shrubs by passing the seeds out of their digestive systems. The animals' feces provides some plant nutrients, and it certainly retains moisture better than rocky soil.

12 These dead trees were struck by lightning. Lightning storms are frequent near timberline, but because the vegetation is sparse, fires rarely spread far.

13 On a clear day you can see the Coast Ranges, to the west, and the Sierra Nevada, to the south and southeast. Your trail is in the southern end of the Cascade Range, which extends north all the way to the Mt. Garibaldi area of southern British Columbia. The major rocks of these three ranges differ in composition, method of formation and time of formation.

The rocks you see in the Cascade Range are overwhelmingly volcanic. Indeed, in the area covered by this book, they are entirely volcanic—at least on the surface. Other rock types are buried beneath the surface. The volcanic rocks were produced by eruptions and flows from both volcanoes and fissures, the former greatly predominating in the Lassen area. An example of a fissure eruption is the Hat Creek Valley basalt flow (see the Spatter Cone Nature Trail in Chapter 18). The Cascade's rocks are geologically young, mostly less than 40 million years old. In the Lassen area, most are less than 5 million years old.

The Coast Range rocks are composed mostly of marine sediments that are generally 70-150 million years old. These sediments, deposited in shallow water in the eastern part of the Coast Ranges area and in a deep trench in the west, were later uplifted and compressed, and the result was the folded, faulted rocks one sees in the ranges today. The trench developed, and the shallow basin behind it, when one large, eastward-moving section of the earth's crust dived east beneath another large section. The diving section encountered increasing temperatures and pressures and eventually melted, and some of the resulting molten rock—called magma—rose up through the earth's crust. The magma that reached the surface erupted as lava; the magma that solidified beneath the surface became granitic rock. In the Sierra Nevada, weathering and erosion, operating over tens of millions of years, have stripped away most of the overlying rock, exposing large areas of granitic bedrock. At present, the closest granitic rocks are found about 30 miles south and east of our trail, and these exposures represent the northernmost part of the Sierra Nevada.

14   Your nose probably tells you before your eyes that you are approaching Bumpass Hell, a steaming, fuming hydrothermal area. Molten or nearly molten volcanic rock lies beneath the surface, perhaps several miles down. Bumpass Hell was named after Kendall Vanhook Bumpass, who discovered it and later lost a leg as a result of burns suffered in 1865 when his leg broke through the crust into a boiling mudpot. **Don't let this happen to you.** The crust can and does break away. **Heed all warning signs and stay on established trails.**

16   Three types of lava are visible here. That which forms the rugged wall on the far side of Bumpass Hell is *dacite*, the same material that composes Lassen Peak. Stiff and pasty

when molten, it tends to flow very little, solidifying in place as a plug dome.

Mt. Harkness stands on the left skyline. I is a shield volcano with a small cinder con on top. Its low, spreading shape, like that of prone Roman shield, is due to the highl fluid nature of the *basalt* that flowed quit far from its summit. The Hawaiian Island are the tops of a series of large shield vol canoes.

Ancient Mt. Tehama, which extended eas to the ground you stand on, was composed c *andesite*, which is intermediate between da cite and basalt in characteristics. Tehama was created by eruptions from a magma chamber, which was several miles below th earth's surface and which periodically sen up magma that erupted to gradually build u the volcano. The contents of such chamber can change with time. They often start out a basalt, change to andesite, then later to da cite or even rhyolite. Tehama, however, re mained essentially andesitic throughou most of its history, though it gave rise t dacite domes along its perimeter.

For your safety the trail has been rerouted Consequently you jump from post 16 to pos 21. If you were to branch left onto the ol trail on Bumpass Hell's western slopes you'd encounter posts 17 through 20. You however, keep right, descend east acros often-snow-patched slopes, then reach second junction near the bottom of your des cent. The old trail, with posts 20 through 17 climbs west from here. Turn right and cross nearby creek. From its east bank a little-use trail, described in the next chapter, con tinues eastward to Cold Boiling Lake an other destinations. You'll find posts 21 to 3 along the boardwalk maze.

21   Change is constant in Bumpass Hell an many features now differ from the way the were when K.V. Bumpass first viewed then in the 1860s. Some of the changes have bee sudden, but most have been the result o slower but persistent processes.

At a fork in the boardwalk, continu straight ahead for posts 22 to 26; posts 27 t 31 are off to the left.

22   A magma chamber several miles belov the surface may be sending up feeders tha give rise to the hydrothermal activity foun at Bumpass Hell, Devils Kitchen, Drake' Springs, Boiling Springs Lake and Termina Geyser. These thermal features are, interest ingly enough, more or less along a line that trends east-southeast from Bumpass Hell. While no surface fault has been discovered that runs continuously along this "line," the line may nevertheless represent a subsurface fracture or weakness in the earth's upper crust. The steam produced at these hydrothermal areas is more the result of ground water percolating down to the hot magma feeders than of steam given off by the feeders. Thus in late summer, after the snow has melted and the amount of ground water has decreased, the hydrothermal activity decreases noticeably.

Fumes are present in the steam. One ubiquitous odor—that of rotten eggs—is due to hydrogen sulfide, which is a combinaton of sulfur and hydrogen that forms when oxygen is scarce or absent. In the presence of oxygen, hydrogen sulfide is converted to sulfuric acid. The amount of hydrogen sulfide in the fumes is very small, about ½ of 1%. Discounting steam, about 95% of the fumes is carbon dioxide, an odorless gas. Nitrogen and hydrogen, both odorless, make up about 3½% and 1% respectively.

23 Sulfuric acid is responsible for the extensive decomposition of volcanic rock

Bumpass Hell, one of its mud pots, and a red elderberry (described on page 40).

found in Bumpass Hell and other hydro-thermal areas. In the pools you see, such as the one near you, the acid is very dilute, due to the abundance of water. In such pools the acid is too weak to totally decompose the volcanic rock. Instead, intermediate products are formed. The rock's feldspar crystals are broken down to mostly kaolin and alunite, while its quartz crystals are broken down to opal. Kaolin, a white clay, is essentially composed of aluminum, silicon, hydrogen and oxygen. Alunite is more complex, containing also potassium and sulfur, and it can be white, grayish-white, or yellowish-white. Opal, which is essentially quartz with water, is quite variable in color, ranging from colorless to white, gray or brown.

24   Outside the pools the sulfuric acid can become quite concentrated. Then, complete decomposition occurs, and both kaolin and alunite are broken down to opal and similar compounds. The whitish material in the mound before you is a nonprecious form of opal.

25   This former pool is an example of the continual changes in an active hydrothermal area. While this pool has dried up, others in Bumpass Hell have enlarged and new ones have formed.

26   East Pyrite Pool boils violently in spite of the cool stream usually flowing into it. The black scum and bubbles on the surface contain tiny crystals of pyrite, or fool's gold. This compound is formed when iron from decomposed volcanic rock reacts with sulfur from the magma's rising fumes. When existing as visible crystals, fool's gold, with its brassy-yellow color and metallic luster, superficially resembles gold, whence its name. Other iron compounds cause red, yellow and tan colors in Bumpass Hell.

The trail ends here. Do not go beyond this point because the thin crust will not support your weight. Serious injuries could occur if you should come in contact with the steam and boiling water under the fragile surface. To continue along the nature trail, go back to the fork and start north up it. The boardwalk forks at post 29; post 27 is at the extreme left, 31 at the extreme right.

27   Mud pots are an intermediate type of hydrothermal feature between hot springs, which have a plentiful supply of water, and fumaroles, which are quite dry. As ground water diminishes later on in the season, the mud becomes less fluid and the bubbling more violent. The mud pots then become mud volcanoes, throwing mud high enough to build up a rim.

28   In 1947 West Pyrite Pool was enlarged by about 800 square feet, essentially doubling in size when a large portion of the surrounding crust collapsed—the largest sudden change in topography ever recorded in Bumpass Hell.

29   Acid, steam, rain and frost will continue to attack these rounded boulders until they too are reduced to a clay or powder.

30   Yellow sulfur crystals often form on surfaces covered by thin sheets of thermal waters or where hydrogen sulfide hisses from holes in the ground.

31   Tremendous amounts of energy are released in dramatic form by the "Big Boiler." The flow of energy in nature is continuous, and everything in nature, living or not, is tied to it. Big Boiler can reach temperatures greater than the boiling point for this altitude, which is about 198°F (92°C). It is one of the world's hottest fumaroles, with temperatures up to 320°F (160°C). The pool temperatures average about 185-196°F (85-91°C). As in a pressure cooker, pressurized steam underground is heated well above the boiling point.

Post 31 is the last numbered stop on the Bumpass Hell Nature Trail. But, as mentioned earlier in this description, posts 17 to 20 are along an old stretch of trail that you'll find immediately west of the creek that drains Bumpass Hell. You'll encounter these in reverse order.

20   See if you can distinguish between the andesite rocks to the west and the dacite rocks to the north and east.

19   As long as ground temperatures are normal, some plants can survive quite close to a fumarole or a hot pool. In this area of wet ground you'll see red mountain heather and, less commonly, bog kalmia, both water-loving relatives of the pinemat manzanita you saw earlier. Both have pinkish flowers, but the heather has small, needlelike leaves while the kalmia has larger, broader leaves. Also present are some sedges and rushes.

18   Violent, roaring, hot steam spews from the "Steam Engine," one of the more active fumaroles of Bumpass Hell.

17   No stake here in 1980. The park pamphlet mentions features already discussed above.

Boiling Springs Lake Nature Trail

Trailhead In the park's Drakesbad area. From the north end of Chester, a recreation-oriented community, follow Feather River Drive west out of town. You fork left in ⅔ mile, then continue 5½ miles to a second junction, where you fork right. Follow the road 10.1 miles up to the trailhead's short spur road, which branches left just past the Warner Valley Campground. Just before the campground the main road gets steep, so don't attempt to pull a large trailer up it.

Distances 0.9 mile (1.4 km) to Boiling Springs Lake
2.3 miles (3.6 km) round trip

Trail description Like the preceding nature trail, the Boiling Springs Lake Nature Trail takes you to an active hydrothermal area. This trail, however, has several advantages: fewer people, a longer hiking season, more wildflowers and warmer weather. Because it is lower, this trail is warmer and it becomes mostly snow-free in mid-June. Visit it from late June through mid-July if you're interested in wildflowers. Allow two hours to leisurely hike this trail, but add an hour or two if you're looking at the wildflowers. If the day is hot, bring water, for none is available after you cross the bridge, early in the hike. Please help keep this popular trail clean by bringing back any refuse you might have and depositing it in the trash barrel at the start of the trail.

1 Most of the trees in this picnic area are lodgepole pines. This pine has a specific scientific name of *contorta*, which means twisted, referring to its twisted needles. The needles occur in bundles of two; other Lassen Park pines usually have needles in bundles of three or five. Lodgepole needles typically persist for 6-8 years before dropping off. Likewise, the cones may persist for several years before dropping.

2 At the base of this dead lodgepole are the remains of a colony of large red ants. The collection of twigs and pine needles represents a shelter-building project of a well-developed social system. Look for horsetail by the base of this tree.

3 Hot Springs Creek, which you'll soon bridge, is fed partly by natural thermal water from Boiling Springs Lake, Devils Kitchen and a few hot springs along the trial. However, most of the water comes from a stream

above Devils Kitchen and from cold springs along the sides of Warner Valley, so the creek's summer temperature is usually about 50 to 55°F. Farther down the valley this creek joins with Kings Creek to form Warner Creek. Watch for the dipper, a small, chunky, bobbing gray bird that feeds in the fast-flowing water.

In the Drakesbad area, as well as in most of the park below 7500 feet elevation, you'll see mountain alders growing along creeks, by springs and in or around meadows. At lower elevations this shrub is replaced by the white alder, a small tree. Before late July you can expect to see the following hydrophilic (water-loving) wildflowers—and others—in this creekside environment. White or creamy flowers: Brewer's bittercress, white brodiaea, corn lily, Gray's lovage, long-stalked starwort, swamp thistle, naked star tulip, yarrow. Yellow flowers: sticky cinquefoil, common dandelion, common large monkey flower. Pink flowers: Oregon checker. Red-violet flowers: California blue-eyed grass, meadow penstemon. Blue-violet flowers: alpine brookline, large-leaved lupine.

4 Beavers have been active in Warner Valley and the Drakesbad area. Their home is usually a pile of sticks and mud in a pool behind a dam that they build across a stream. The best place to look for beavers is at nearby Dream Lake (see Chapter 12).

Cross the large bridge over Hot Springs Creek. This is your last source of drinking water.

5 White fir is one of the most common trees along this trail. The needles grow singly rather than in groups, as they do on almost all pines. The large white fir behind these two young ones is more than 14 feet in circumference, one of the largest you'll see in this area. True fir cones grow upright and fall apart at maturity while still attached to branchlets. You may see a few entire or partly eaten cones on the ground, cones cut down by chickarees (Douglas squirrels).

6 The exposed slope becomes dry and barren in late summer, but it is rich with flowers through early July, most of the flowers being those of Parish's yampah, a relative of carrots and parsley. The grayish bare exposure facing you on the opposite slope is composed of mineral deposits from hot springs, some of which are still active. You will see a small hot spring at post 8.

7 Parts of Lassen's landscape have been uplifted, dropped or laterally offset by faults, none of them major. Faults fracture the bedrock, and these rocks are more susceptible to weathering and erosion than unfractured ones. If hot springs arise on faults, as they are likely to do, the weathering and erosion are all the more intense. Thus gullies often develop along faults, and they can grow in time into canyons. In your area one fault extends from Devils Kitchen east along Hot Springs Creek to Warner Valley. A second fault extends from the creek southeast up a gully to Boiling Springs Lake, then one mile beyond it to Terminal Geyser. These and other faults probably played some part in the origin and/or development of your valley, of Kings Creek canyon, northeast of you, and of spacious, flat Warner Valley, up which you drove.

These troughs, however, probably owe much if not most of their size to large glaciers that plowed down them several times during the latter part of the Ice Age. The last major glacier to enter Warner Valley was about 1500 feet thick, and ice this thick exerts about 44 tons per square foot. No wonder, then, that glaciers can transform shallow, narrow canyons into deep, broad canyons. Major glaciers existed in the Lassen area as recently as about 10,000 years ago. Since then, streams here have eroded very little, contrary to what others have believed. Note how deep Hot Springs Creek, which you just crossed, has cut into the valley floor since glaciers left it—only 10-20 feet.

8 Several natural hot springs feed this miniature stream that supplies water to the steaming thermal pool at Drakesbad Guest Ranch. The pool is for guests only, and reservations are often made several years in advance, because demand far exceeds available accommodations. The water averages about 125°F (52°C) where it reaches the surface, but probably is superheated to as much as 500°F (260°C) a mile or so beneath the earth's surface, where it is close to molten rocks.

In the 1880s Edward R. Drake settled in this area and gradually acquired 400 acres of land that extended west up to Devils Kitchen. A loner, Drake didn't encourage

tourism, as did Alex Sifford, who purchased the property in 1900. Sifford developed a small resort and promoted the thermal waters for a health spa, or bad. The Sifford family operated this friendly resort until 1958 when the government finally purchased the property and added it to the park. The Siffords, in contrast with the Lees and the Kellys in Warner Valley, supported the Park Service in its early, trying days. Because of this, the Park Service in 1972 renamed Red Mountain, 2 miles south of Drakesbad, changing it to Sifford Mountain in honor of Alex Sifford.

9 This large incense-cedar is 22½ feet in circumference. The reddish bark looks somewhat like that of the Sierra's giant sequoia, but these don't grow here even though they could (see page 25, next-to-last paragraph). Incense-cedars, like pines, firs, hemlocks and sequoias, are conifers, and you'll see this specimen's small, two-lipped cones lying about on the ground. Large strips of incense-cedar bark were used by Indians to build conical shelters. These trees are the primary trees used in the manufacture of pencils. But they aren't logged for lumber because their wood is highly susceptible to fungal rot, particularly by the fungus *Polyporus amarus*. The tree is very susceptible to fire, but then, it is one of the first trees to establish in an area that has been leveled by fire.

From the junction your trail climbs left. The trial to the right leads to others that go to Drakesbad, Dream Lake and Devils Kitchen. In 20 often muddy yards you reach a second junction. Your trail climbs left while the trail to the right leads to others that go to Drake Lake and Devils Kitchen. The latter is a fascinating area of violently steaming fumaroles, hot springs and boiling mud pots at the head of Warner Valley.

10 The broad-leaved shrub here is Scouler's willow. Most species of willows grow best in wet meadows or along streams and lakeshores. This one, however, prefers dry places along meadow edges or in open woods. Its leaves, like those of the moisture-loving Jepson's willow, are widest past their midpoints and are rather blunt at their tips. In contrast, the park's four other willows have leaves that are widest near their bases and taper narrowly to their tips.

11 The stream bed near the trail is Boiling Springs Lake's overflow channel. It usually dries by mid-July, exposing whitish mineral deposits derived from the lake. Many miniature plants cover Lassen's varied terrain. Called "belly plants" by some botanists because you almost have to lie on your stomach to examine them, these wildflowers go unnoticed by most of the park's visitors. A common one here is whisker brush, a needle-leaved plant often less than one inch tall. Three other small, delicate, water-shunning plants you may see are gayophytum, with tiny white flowers, Torrey's collinsia, with blue-and-white-lipped flowers, and Torrey's monkey flower, with yellow-centered pink flowers.

12 Red-fir needles are shorter, more curved and in denser clusters than are white-fir needles. They are also not as flat as white-fir needles, nor do they have the conspicuous half twist at their bases. The red fir's upright cones are usually 5-8 inches tall while those of white firs are about 3 to 5 inches. Both trees are extensively cut for lumber, both in the Sierra and in the southern Cascades.

13 Evidences of old fires may be seen in many places in the forest. Long, dry summers cause the forest litter to become extremely flammable. Much of the park south and east of Lassen Peak is scanned by a fire lookout who operates the lookout station atop Mt. Harkness in mid- and late summer. Fires started by careless hikers and campers are reported and extinguished as soon as possible by firefighting crews. Lightning fires, however, have been a natural process in forests for millions of years, and these are allowed to burn if they don't pose any threat to visitors or to extensive stands of timber.

14 Large Jeffrey pines, like the one above you, have probably withstood many fires in their lifetimes, which can range up to 500 years or more. Under natural conditions, a fire burns any section of a forest about once every 10 years. Such fires are small, and they usually burn shrubs and litter, rarely mature trees. Conifer seedlings seem to have a much higher survival rate in freshly burned ground than in littered ground. If you stick your nose in a deep furrow in the bark of a Jeffrey pine, you'll detect a butterscotch odor, which is usually lacking in a similar species, the ponderosa pine. Another distinguishing characteristic—one of several—is cone size: Jeffrey's are 5-10 inches long, ponderosa's are 3-5 inches. While pine cones

and fir cones are somewhat similar, those of pines hang from branches while those of firs grow upright on them. You'll see young firs nearby. Note that the white fir has yellow-green needles, but the red fir has silver-green needles, hence its name "silvertip."

15 The branched, chartreuse-colored growths on tree trunks are staghorn lichens. The lichen is a specialized combination of a fungus and an alga growing together for the mutual benefit of each. The green alga uses sunlight and moisture to provide food for the lichen while the fungus provides support and holds the mass together. The lichen does not harm the tree, and it grows on dead snags just as well. Note that staghorn lichens appear on trunks several feet above the ground, this lower limit approximately representing the top of the average winter snowpack.

Other species of lichens, some living hundreds of years, grow on barren rocks, spreading radially as they do. By knowing their growth rates, scientists can estimate how long these lichens have been present, which is useful information when you're trying to determine the frequency of rockfalls in an avalanche-prone area.

16 If you're hiking through forest lands below 7000 feet in Lassen Park or in the lands adjoining it, you're not very likely to see a black bear. However, once you learn to recognize their droppings, you'll see that they really do get around. But being timid and often being active at night, they generally stay out of sight. Or at least, they used to. Increasingly, Lassen's campgrounds are being raided by bears who have discovered this new source of food and, as the "word" gets spread around, more bears can be expected to turn up at campgrounds. If you stay in one, store your food in your vehicle's trunk, not on a campground table.

In the deep forest near this post you may see two small shade-loving plants: the white-veined wintergreen, with veined, oval leaves, and the spotted coralroot, a red-orange orchid. The coralroot derives its energy needs by parasitizing soil fungi rather than by relying on sunlight. The wintergreen gets part of its energy needs from sunlight and part from soil fungi. Neither species is common, so don't pick them. After all, every plant and animal in the park is protected for the enjoyment of future visitors. Like the wintergreen, the dwarf lousewort hedges its bets by deriving energy both from sunlight and from root fungi of trees and shrubs, which it parasitizes. This drab, prostrate plant of sunny forests is very common, but it is seldom seen by visitors due to its dull leaves, pale flowers and small size.

From the junction your trail climbs right; a horse trail to Terminal Geyser climbs left.

17 In national parks, snags and logs are usually left in place, for they provide food and/or shelter for mammals, birds, insects and other invertebrates. Here you'll see logs that were invaded by bark beetles, as evidenced by the "engravings" they've left. In a weakened tree, bark beetles bore through the bark to the cambium, the tree's thin layer of living cells that produces the heartwood and the bark. In a healthy tree, this layer produces enough sticky resin to literally drown out bark-beetle attacks. But once in the cambium, a successful female bark beetle bores a tunnel, laying eggs along it. The resulting larvae then bore tunnels of their own away from the main tunnel, consuming cambial cells in their path. This further weakens, if not kills, an already weakened tree. These beetles also attack fallen trees. In lodgepole pines, seen in great numbers in the park's red-fir belt, needleminer moth larvae bore through the pines' needles, thereby weakening these trees and setting the stage for a bark-beetle invasion. But the beetles and the moths have as much right to existence as do the stately trees, though we'd much prefer the latter. Nature plays no favorites: indeed,

Lassen and Reading peaks, in the distance, break the forested skyline above Boiling Springs Lake.

"she" is very cruel. One may feel at peace or may experience great inspiration while walking through a quiet, solemn forest, but then one is usually unaware of the silent death and destruction continually occurring around him. The typical life experience of a plant or animal is death at an early age. Plants rarely make it past the seed stage, and most that do so die before they can reproduce. Animals fare little better, most of them dying before adulthood. What we see, then, in the forest—or in any ecosystem, for that matter—are the lucky survivors, who are indeed a privileged few.

18 In this dense stand of fairly young white firs, only the most vigorous trees will survive. The weaker ones will eventually be crowded out in their struggle to obtain enough sunlight to survive. Some will die as they become shaded by faster growing ones. But then, these trees have already shaded out most of the shrubs that first invaded this once-open area. Competition is unrelenting, and usually only the fittest survive.

On larger firs you may have noticed that the large upright cones grow on the uppermost branches. These are the female cones. Like pines, firs also have small, hard-to-see male cones that hang from lower branches. Why the segregation of sexes? Well, this positioning of female and male cones makes self-pollination rather difficult, since pollen can't fall up to the female cones. Cross-pollination, however, is favored, for winds can blow the pollen from one fir to the next. This is an advantage. Self-pollination, or inbreeding, greatly increases the chances that recessive genetic traits—usually detrimental or even lethal—will be expressed. Cross-pollination, on the other hand, usually guarantees that a recessive gene —say, from a pollen grain—will be linked with a dominant gene from a seed, and this latter gene will prevent the recessive trait from developing. But more important, interbreeding produces more traits than does inbreeding, and the more diverse a given population is, the better chance it has to evolve to meet new environmental or biological challenges. Inbreeding to create a pure "master race" only hastens a population toward extinction.

19 When a tree such as this white fir is bent over by winter snow, some of the side branches may replace a weakened or dead top. When a top is completely broken off or killed, one and sometimes two side branches will turn upward, as on the small tree on the other side of the trail. The struggle to survive is a strong and necessary one.

20 Look closely at the cross section of this fallen Jeffrey-pine trunk. The concentric growth rings show the age of the tree. The faster and softer growth is during the spring. The slower and harder growth is during the summer and fall. The harder growths decay more slowly, so they protrude beyond the softer growths. The living and growing part of the tree trunk is the cambium, a thin layer immediately under the bark. The inside of a living tree as well as the outer layers of its bark are dead. As the tree expands through growth, the bark splits and cracks, each tree species forming its own characteristic bark pattern.

The low shrubs here, usually less than a foot tall, are pinemat manzanitas. In Spanish, "manzanita" means "little apple," and all manzanita species produce small, applelike berries that are relished by birds and mammals. These are preceded in early or mid-July by white, urn-shaped flowers. Late in summer the shrubs' red bark peels off in thin, papery curls, the peeling due to expansion caused by growth of new cambium and bark beneath it.

In this dry soil you may see the dwarf plants mentioned at post 11 plus some larger ones that are still small by human standards. Three of them are: Torrey's lupine, with bluish-white pea-shaped flowers; nodding microseris, with yellow sunflowers that nod before they blossom upright; and pretty face, a monocot with yellow flowers arranged in an open, umbrellalike group.

22 You are walking up the lower north slope of Sifford Mountain, formerly called Red Mountain. This volcano came into existence late in the Ice Age, perhaps about 60,000 years ago, as it built its way skyward in a series of eruptions. Though its base measures about 3 miles across, its summit stands only 800-1300 feet above the rolling surface it built upon. Lassen Peak, in contrast, is about 2 miles across and rises 1600-2900 feet above its base. The difference between the two is due to the nature of their lavas. Lassen Peak lava is dacite, a volcanic rock rich in silica and poor in iron-and-magnesium-bearing dark minerals. This composition results in thick, pasty lava that flows very little, and it often builds up a steep-sided plug dome, such as Lassen Peak.

Sifford Mountain lava, on the other hand, is poor in silica but rich in dark minerals, and when molten it is much more fluid. Hence, the flows travel farther outward and are thinner. The resulting volcano, Sifford Mountain, is low and broad, and is called a shield volcano because it resembles a flat-lying Roman shield. The park has three other shield volcanoes: Raker Peak (described at post 45 in the Lassen Park Road Log), Mt. Harkness (described in Chapter 13's Mt. Harkness hike), and Prospect Peak (described at post 28 in the next nature trail).

After Sifford Mountain formed, it was somewhat eroded by small glaciers that descended its flanks and by larger ones that descended east through the Drakesbad area. Hikers adept at cross-country navigation may want to climb to Sifford's north slope to examine its glaciated, collapsed lava tubes, then climb to its summit to view the surrounding landscape as well as to investigate the remains of its eroded cinder cone.

23 You are about to enter the Boiling Springs Lake hydrothermal area. The odor of rotten eggs is due to hydrogen sulfide produced from sulfur in oxygen-poor rising gases. Listen for the thumping of the bubbling mud pots. Just ahead, your trail crosses the lake's outlet stream, which is usually dry by mid-July. It then continues around the lake and returns you back to this junction.

Please be careful! The mud pots, steaming fumaroles and boiling pools are dangerously hot. Crust near the edges of these may be thin and slippery. Avoid serious burns by staying on the trail.

24 These pits are dried-up mud pots that have ceased much of their activity, although some steam may still be visible. The underground "plumbing" may have been partly sealed off by the slumping of clay and other products of the decomposition of lava. Then, as pressures built up, new channels may have opened and steam may have escaped from other vents.

The next station is straight ahead near the edge of the lake. Do not approach too closely!

25 By a large sugar pine you'll see Boiling Springs Lake, which is about 120°F (49°C) by mid-May and about 125°F (52°C) during much of the summer. In the dead of winter it may be about 110°F (43°C), which is still

scalding hot. The hot pools by its shore average 190-201°F (88-94°C), the higher figure being the boiling point of water at this elevation. Lying along a young fault, the lake is heated by steam and fumes rising through underground vents and fissures. On cool days you may see water vapor rising from the lake. During summer the lake level drops more than a foot. The exposed mud around the edge of the lake then dries and, being rich in clay, it contracts, forming cracks. The lake is about 630 feet long and its shoreline perimeter is about 2000 feet.

Return to post 24 and start a walk around the lake.

26 The yellow-tan color, normal to the lake, is due to clay, opal and iron-oxide particles suspended in the water. See posts 22-26 of the Bumpass Hell Nature Trail for the processes and chemistry involved in transforming solid volcanic rocks into these substances. The green color seen in shallow water and in wet mud is due to algae—microscopic plants that have adapted to the hot-water environment.

When wet, these clay banks are very slippery.

27 White, crusty salts, sometimes seen on the surface, are related to alum and have an astringent sweet-sour taste. Mosses grow well here, which seems surprising, since the ground becomes very parched by midsummer.

28 This is one of the few places in the park where you can see huckleberry oak, which is probably the commonest shrub in the Sierra Nevada. This shrub has huckleberrylike leaves that are evergreen and drought-resistant. Late in the summer, look for acorns, which are relished by various birds and mammals.

29 The noisy, steaming fumarole across the lake is the most consistently active hydrothermal area in the vicinity. You may see sizzling "frying pan" activity in the stream delta just this side of the fumarole. Steam escaping from small vents in shallow pools sounds like eggs frying and smells like eggs rotting—due to hydrogen-sulfide gas. Escaping gases you *don't* smell are carbon dioxide, nitrogen and hydrogen.

30 Pileated woodpeckers occasionally build nests nearby in high, hollowed-out parts of trees. These crow-sized woodpeckers, the largest in California, chip away bark on snags and logs to reach beetle larvae and carpenter ants.

31 The gully at the end of the lake runs southeast along a fault. Down it runs a seasonal creeklet that is the lake's only inlet stream. It typically dries up in early summer. Do not cross the gully here but rather take the trail across it farther upstream.

32 The swollen appearance of the branchlets of these young red firs is caused by western dwarf mistletoe. This small, scaly, golden-colored parasite does not have broad leaves like the common mistletoe used at Christmas time. Seeds, sometimes left on branches by birds, sprout and grow into the tree. This parasitic growth prevents the flow of nutrients, causing the swelling and weakening of the branch. Look for the dwarf mistletoe on swollen branches having green needles.

33 The trail climbing southeast (right) goes 1.5 miles to a view of Terminal Geyser, which is a small hydrothermal area with a violently steaming fumarole. Another trail branches south from the Terminal Geyser trail and goes 1.0 mile over to Little Willow Lake, short on willows but long on mosquitoes. These pests die off by late summer as the shallow lake dries up to become a wet meadow.

34 Here is a fine view of Lassen Peak. With binoculars you may be able to spot the trail

zigzagging up the left side of the 10,457-foot mountain. It is a type of volcano known as a plug dome, as is Reading Peak, the long ridge to the right of Lassen, and Bumpass Mountain, the skyline knob just left of Lassen.

35 The attractive, tall incense-cedar to the right is over 18 feet in circumference. On your way back to the trailhead you may see low shrubs with spine-tipped branches. These are known as snow bush or mountain whitethorn ceanothus, and deer browse their leaves despite the thorns.

36 To catch another glimpse of mud pots, turn left here and descend to post 37. The main trail descends to a junction by post 16.

37 A mud pot is a type of hot spring consisting of a shallow pit or cavity filled with hot, generally boiling mud. Depending on the amount of water present, the mud may have any degree of consistency up to a thick mush or mortar. The mud is thinnest when snowmelt drains into this basin, and it can dry solid when the ground is parched in mid- or late summer. Steam and gases from underground fissures come up in large bubbles through the thick mud. As the bubbles break, mud is splattered in all directions to form a rim around the vent.

38 The mud consists mostly of clay and opal colored by iron oxides and sulfur.

39 Follow the trail down to post 23.

Cinder Cone Nature Trail

Trailhead At the Butte Lake Ranger Station near Butte Lake, in northeast Lassen Park. To reach it from the west, take Highway 44/89 north to a junction just north of Old Station, in Hat Creek Valley. Highway 89 continues north down the valley, but you take Highway 44 east 11.0 miles to Road 32N21, climbing south. If you are coming from the east, take County Road A21 north from Westwood or Highway 44 west from Susanville. From the junction where the two paved roads meet, you take Highway 44 west 16.8 miles to Road 32N21. This road climbs 2.4 easy miles to the Butte Creek Campground, then 4.1 steeper miles to Butte Lake's Ranger Station and Campground.

Distances 1.4 miles (2.3 km) to north base of Cinder Cone
5.0 miles (8.1 km) round trip

Trail description Stark black chunks of lava, volcanic bombs, vast cinder and ash fields and lava-scorched tree snags provide a setting for the climax feature of this nature trail, 700-foot-high Cinder Cone. This self-guiding trail leads you through a devastated landscape of recent volcanic activity. History and dramatic geologic events are combined as you follow the route of early pioneers working their way west to the Sacramento Valley. Along the way you pass through a pine forest to the edge of a massive lava flow and then up the slope of Cinder

Cone to the rim for a panoramic view of lakes, forests, and mountains. Below you are Fantastic Lava Beds, Painted Dunes, and Snag and Butte lakes, and in the distance Lassen Peak dominates the horizon.

The complete round trip takes about 3 or 4 hours. If you don't want to make the entire trip, then at least hike a little over one mile to a view of Cinder Cone. The nature-trail hike is usually a warm one and water is essentially absent. Therefore, unless you are starting early in the morning, plan to carry water. Unless you wear calf-high boots, you're almost certain to get pebbles in your shoes, a minor nuisance. The trail begins in front of the ranger station and descends 150 yards southeast to the northwest tip of Butte Lake.

1 You might have noticed that the ground in the Butte Lake area is covered with cinders. Cinders are fragments of scoria ranging from 4 to 32 mm (1/6 to 1¼") in diameter. (Scoria is vesicular lava that has been explosively ejected from a volcanic vent.) Particles smaller than 4 mm are ash, and those larger than 32 mm are bombs. Ash, cinders and bombs have a common origin, for all have been blown into the atmosphere by an explosive volcanic eruption. The smaller the particles, the farther they can travel from their source. The main *cinder* source in this area is Cinder Cone, about 1½ miles to the southwest. This cone erupted violently at least three times, scattering dark-gray volcanic debris over about 30 square miles of neighboring terrain. Lassen Peak violently erupted in May 1915, and some of the debris fell in the Butte Lake area, coating it with a thin veneer of beige ash and cinders. Fairfield Peak, Crater Butte and Hat Mountain are all relatively close cinder cones that may have been active from 5000 to 50,000 years ago, but they are quite certainly extinct now. Likewise, the cone atop nearby Prospect Peak may have erupted during that period. That cone is the only one close enough to shower the area with cinders, but along your nature trail, Prospect's cinders have been buried by the more recent, voluminous cinders of Cinder Cone.

2 From this spot you can see the northwest arm of Butte Lake and part of Fantastic Lava Beds, composed of four or more lava flows. Butte Lake, occupying a glaciated, faulted basin, was decreased in size when the lava advanced northeast into the western part of the lake.

3 From about late July through mid-August the shallow west point of Butte Lake turns pink with water smartweed, a member of the buckwheat family. Most buckwheats, however, prefer dry, harsh environments, as you'll see on Cinder Cone.

You now start southwest along a narrow road that is closed to motor vehicles. This is part of an old emigrant trail William H. Nobles established in 1852 as a shorter alternative to Peter Lassen's 1847 trail. It left the Lassen Trail in northwest Nevada and headed southwest to Susanville, keeping north of Nevada's Pyramid Lake and eastern California's Honey Lake. Beyond Susanville, which developed a few years later, the Nobles Trail gradually curved northwest up to Poison Lake, then climbed south, as you did, up to Butte Lake. On this book's topographic map you can see parts of this trail wandering westward across the park. Nobles Trail finally ended at Mt. Shasta City, far from the Mother Lode gold fields, and hence it was less popular than routes to the south.

4 Until the early 1970s you could drive along Nobles Trail from Hat Lake north and then east to Badger Flat. Now, however, the trail is closed to motor vehicles, which makes exploring it a more peaceful experience for modern-day "pioneers." See Chapter 11 for the trail's route description.

5 One of the common trees around Butte Lake and throughout most of the park is the lodgepole pine. Its needles are short and grow in groups of two. The cones typically remain on the branches for several years. The bark is thin and scaly like that of a whitebark pine, which has needles in groups of five. The lodgepole gets its name from its narrow, straight trunks, which are excellent for cabin logs and for telegraph poles. In the 19th century this tree was also called a tamarack.

6 In the Butte Lake area you'll see three similar species of yellow pines: the ponderosa pine, the Jeffrey pine and the rare Washoe pine. In this locality the ponderosa pine is near its upper elevation limit; westward it grows down to about 2000 feet elevation. Its needles are bright yellow-green and 5-10 inches long. Its cones are 3-5 inches long. In mature trees the bark is platy and dull yellow. Its sap has a resinous color.

The Jeffrey pine is the commonest yellow pine in Lassen Park, growing well in drier habitats. Its needles are dull blue-green and 5-10 inches long. Its cones are also 5-10 inches long. The bark is red-brown and usually has somewhat vertical furrows. Its sap has a butterscotch odor.

The Washoe pine occurs in small, isolated groves in northeastern California, one of these being the Butte Lake area—Lassen Park's only specimens. Its needles are gray-green and 4-6 inches long. Its cones are 4-5 inches long. The bark is similar to that of a Jeffrey pine, but lacks a butterscotch odor.

Now that I've given you some of these pines' more distinguishing characteristics, I must confess that even a professional botanist (which I am not) can't always distinguish among these three trees when they all grow together. This is because individuals of each species can be quite variable in form. The only certain way to identify them is by chemical analysis of their resin (sap). The specimen at post 6 is presumed to be a Jeffrey pine.

Douglas squirrels, also known as chickarees, attack the pine's cones, which like those of many other pine species, take two years to mature. The squirrels chew the cones apart to get at the seeds. Piles of chewed cone scales may be seen at the bases of trees or on a favorite log.

7 Despite injuries caused by lightning, insects, disease, wind and snow, trees are often able to recover and continue growing. When a tree is bent over by snow or some other force, tree-produced chemicals called auxins stimulate growth on the under side of the trunk. This causes the under side to grow faster than the upper side, and the tree tends to right itself.

8 Fantastic Lava Beds consist of a kind of volcanic rock that is either andesite or basaltic andesite in composition. In the past this rock was called basalt, but geologic terminology has changed. The lava was a thick, pasty, slowly flowing mass that was red-hot inside to the tune of about 2100°F (about 1150°C). As the lava slowly advanced, its crust cooled and hardened all the while and was twisted and broken into the blocky mass you see here. Lavas with such blocky textures are known as aa (pronounced ah-ah), a Hawaiian term.

9 Look at the lava closely. You may see white, glassy bits of quartz. These are interesting, since quartz-crystal formation is uncommon in this kind of volcanic rock. The quartz probably got here because of a mixing between two magmas. (Magma is subterra-

nean, molten rock that erupts as lava, ash, cinders and/or bombs if it reaches the earth's surface.) Basaltic magma worked up through the earth's crust and encountered a different magma, one that was rich in quartz. This quartz, along with some other materials, was incorporated into the basaltic magma, altering its composition to andesite or basaltic andesite. Crystals that formed in one kind of rock but were later incorporated into another kind are called xenocrysts ("foreign crystals"). Thus the rocks of Fantastic Lava Beds are technically known as quartz-xenocryst basaltic andesite.

The trail climbing right goes to the Butte Lake Campground Amphitheater. Check the park's Summer Activities Schedule for campfire talks given at this small outdoor amphitheater.

10 Either lightning or heat from the latest lava flow may have started fires that scorched these trees. If a tree is not killed by fire, its cambium, just under the bark, starts to grow over the wound. All but the inner layer of bark is composed of dead cells, as is the heartwood beneath the cambium. The bark protects the cambium, the wood provides support, water and nutrients, and the cambium generates new wood and bark. If a fire scar is small, new bark will grow completely over it. If it is large, then insects and fungi can invade the cambium and sometimes kill the tree. Note the holes drilled by wood-boring insects.

11 From here, descend a 150-yard spur trail to Cold Spring, a pocket of cold water among lava blocks at the base of the lava flow.

12 The surface of Cold Spring marks the ground-water level. The spring usually has water well into August, but as the water table lowers in late summer, the pool may become dry. Look and listen for pikas. These small, short-eared members of the rabbit family live among the flow's boulders and gather nearby grasses and sedges for winter food.

Return to post 11 and continue southwest.

13 An old trail to Prospect Peak leads off to the right, climbing about 2200 feet in 3¼ miles to the site of an old fire lookout station.

14 Trees felled by wind, lightning or other causes slowly decay and return to the soil. Carpenter ants, termites, beetles and fungi all do their part. The insects chew the wood into tiny particles while building their tunnels. Fungi live in the dead wood and slowly decompose the tree.

15 Bark beetles, also known as engraver beetles, chew tunnels just under the bark of weak or freshly killed trees and leave intricate patterns in the wood (see post 17 of the preceding nature hike). In contrast, boring beetles, also known as long-horned beetles, produce larvae that tunnel deep within the trunk of the tree. These black-headed grubs can get to be over 2 inches long and deliver quite a bite (they do, after all, chew wood for a living). Woodpeckers, nevertheless, find these large grubs and the smaller bark-beetle larvae quite appealing. The most common woodpecker along this trail—and probably in the whole park—is the red-shafted flicker, which flashes pale red-orange as it flaps its wings in flight.

16 The whitish, fluffy material cropping out at the edge of the lava flow is diatomaceous earth, the remains of countless numbers of one-celled algae called diatoms. These grow in oceans, lakes, ponds, springs, and even in wet soil. Unlike some other algae that produce shells of calcium-carbonate (which can accumulate to form chalk deposits), diatoms produce shells of silicon dioxide—the same chemical compound that makes up quartz crystals. The diatoms' shells accumulated here and along Butte Lake's northwest arm when a lava flow advancing northeast into the lake scraped along the lake's bottom, pushing these lake-bottom deposits to their present locations.

17 Fantastic Lava Beds are composed of lavas from at least four different eruptions, the first one occurring about 1567 A.D. and the last one occurring in the winter of 1850-51. Although the latest lava generally flowed northeast down the center of the beds, it did spill out to the Nobles Trail in several places, including a ¼-mile stretch here. Some of the trees growing along this stretch back in 1851 were probably killed by the heat of the lava. Dead snags along the edge of the flow may be remnants of these trees.

18 Notice that there are great quantities of pine cones under the trees but very few seedlings. The porous cinders, about a foot or two deep, and the dry summer weather both pose great problems for newly germinated seedlings.

Along your trail you may see pinedrops, which are single-stemmed plants that get up to be about 2 feet tall in this area. They are easy to recognize since their stems are orange to brownish-red. Lacking the green pigment chlorophyll, they cannot produce carbohydrates by photosynthesis. Instead they parasitize soil fungi, robbing them of their nutrients. A close relative of the pinedrops—the stout, bright-red snow plant—has soil fungi of its own and together they have a fairly good working relationship. The fungi "rob" the snow plant of some of its carbohydrates, but then, they also provide some water and important nutrients that enable the snow plant to produce these carbohydrates in the first place. We may think of fungi as only pesky primitive plants that destroy trees, but a forest may not be able to survive without them. The snow plant is found in shadier forests, especially ones with fir trees.

19 The beautifully symmetrical Cinder Cone, straight ahead, rises 700 feet above its base. It was formed by explosive eruptions that threw volcanic ash, cinders and bombs out from a central vent. Much of the material fell around the vent, building up the cone. Its shape is essentially undisturbed by water erosion because even in the heaviest rainfall, water quickly sinks into the porous cinders instead of flowing downslope.

20 Ash and cinders can be blown out of a crater by the explosive force of steam and other gases. Such particles are usually cold to the touch. But if molten lava is very close to the surface, the ash and cinders in contact with the lava can be red-hot, even molten. Then the resulting eruption appears fiery, but the ash and cinders are not on fire nor do they burn.

21 The exposed tree root crossing the trail here is protected by layers of bark just as the trunk is. While roots are growing underground they do not normally develop such thick bark layers. Why are these roots exposed?

22 This Jeffery pine and others nearby were toppled by gale-force winds of a severe storm on October 12, 1962. The depression left where this tree was standing may persist for tens of years before wind and gravity obliterate all trace of it. Winds blew down trees in various parts of the park, especially in one 20-acre red-fir stand about ½ mile northeast of Rainbow Lake. The pines you see along your trail were particularly susceptible to blowdown because they have shallow root systems that extend through loose pumice and soil. Notice that winds have exposed the shallow roots of some other trees in this vicinity.

Just beyond post 22 the nature trail branches left, leaving the Nobles Trial.

23 Even though the shape of Cinder Cone is relatively undisturbed by heavy rainfall, its surface can be marred by unattractive footprints, which may remain for months or years. Help preserve the beauty and character of this photogenic cone and its adjacent cinder fields by staying strictly on the trail.

24 Tiny particles of light-colored rock here are pumice blown by the wind from Lassen Peak during its 1914-1915 eruptions. In the great eruption of May 22, 1915, some volcanic ash was carried as far as Reno, Nevada, about 113 miles from the peak. Pumice is a

The steep Cinder Cone Nature Trail, a view back down it, and a view of the cone's crater and rim. Beyond the rim stands Lassen Peak (far right), rounded Fairfield Peak (center), flat-topped Crater Butte (left of Fairfield Peak), and twin-peaked Saddle Mountain (far left).

light, frothy-glass lava containing many gaseous bubbles. The frothy nature of the pumice, coupled with its water-tight bubbles, enables it to float on water. It is erupted from volcanoes producing dacite or rhyolite; scoria is erupted from those producing basalt or andesite. Cinder Cone, being basaltic in nature, did not produce pumice.

25 The slopes of Cinder Cone are about 35° in steepness. This is the approximate angle of repose for cinders, meaning that loose cinders cannot stay in place on cinder slopes steeper than this. You might have noticed that the blocks at the edge of Fantastic Lava Beds have a slightly steeper angle of repose, about 40°. This is because the blocks, being angular, can wedge together and hence are less likely to roll. Your trail ahead is steep, as trails go, about 23° (the angle of repose for some hikers?). The energy you'll expend walking up its loose cinders will make the trail seem even steeper.

26 Large, rounded boulders at the base of the cone are called volcanic bombs. They were blown out of the vent in the center of the cone and rolled down the slope while still hot but already hardened.

27 Lassen Peak is visible in the distance over the shoulder of Cinder Cone. You are looking at the peak's northeast slope, which was devastated in May 1915 by a huge mudflow and a "great hot blast." Cinder Cone never gave off a great hot blast as Lassen did, for its basaltic lava is about 50% silica (silicon dioxide) compared to 65% for Lassen's dacitic lava, and that increase of only 15% makes it surprisingly more explosive. One geologist found a 6-inch-diameter piece of pumice atop Prospect Peak, it having been blown about 10 miles northeast in Lassen's hot blast. Lassen had about 170 eruptions before the great blast of May 22, these eruptions being *phreatic* in nature, that is, due to percolating ground water. The water seeped down close to the volcano's rising magma and then, being converted to steam, it exerted strong pressure that blew away the overlying rocks. The rocks and associated debris were too cool to melt Lassen's snow. Today, patches of snow remain on the upper slopes of the peak all summer.

28 Prospect Peak is the rounded shield, or Hawaiian-type, volcano directly to the right of the trail, northwest of you. It was built late in the Ice Age by layer after layer of basalt flows that are almost identical in composi-

tion to those of Fantastic Lava Beds. Th eruptions were relatively mild, like those o many Hawaiian volcanoes, and each flov averaged perhaps 25 feet in thickness. Bein relatively fluid, the lavas flowed about : miles from the central vent, and they built u a cone averaging only 10° in steepness. Suc low angle "shield" volcanoes get their nam from their resemblance to a Roman shield. / 600-foot-high cinder cone, formed after th Ice Age (that is, in the last 10,000 years), sit atop Prospect Peak, indicating that its fina activity was more explosive. However, ear lier in its history, Prospect Peak may hav had previous cinder cones, each one de stroyed by following lava flows and perhap to some extent by glaciation. The dens growth of trees on the peak's slopes show that it has been inactive for perhaps 1000 2000 years or more.

Your route goes right, counterclockwise, t the opposite side of the main rim.

29 The elevation here is about 6900 feet You are standing on the largest of four crate rims, each perhaps representing a differen eruption. Along this trail you see only thre of the four rims: the main rim, the lowe center rim, and part of an outer rim, a few fee below this post. John Hittell's 1885 *Hand-Book of Pacific Coast Travel* mentions tha two miners saw a volcano that "threw up fire to a terrible height." They and others prob ably witnessed Cinder Cone's winter 1850-51 eruption, which may have built up the center rim as well as produced the well-documented lava flow you'll see on your descent. Geologists have identified two othe ash-and-cinder eruptions, one dated abou 1567 A.D. and another dated about 166€ A.D., the dates determined by tree-ring analysis.

Before leaving post 29 note the vegetatior that has managed to take hold since the las eruption. Lodgepole pines and Scouler's willows seem to be doing best, but a few Jeffery pines are succeeding too. How their seeds got inside the cone is a mystery. Perhaps strong winds blew in pine seeds from trees on the slopes of Prospect Peak, but this doesn't explain how the willows' seeds go there. Unintentional transport by birds may be the answer.

30 Here, just above part of the old, outer rim, you have a fine panoramic view. Scanning clockwise, you first see unimpressive Ash Butte, on the east-southeast skyline. To the right are two neighboring summits, Red Cinder and Red Cinder Cone. These are but 3 of about 80 cinder cones found east of Butte and Snag lakes, south of Highway 44 and west of County Road A21. Mt. Hoffman rises from the east shore of Snag Lake while Mt. Harkness, well beyond it, stands on the far skyline. Saddle Mountain is the distant, flat-topped peak west of Mt. Harkness and Snag Lake, while Crater Butte is the flat-topped cinder cone west of Saddle Mountain. Another cone, Fairfield Peak, stands in full view, just 2½ miles to our southwest. Lassen Peak lords over a high-ridge skyline, with Reading Peak to the left of Lassen, Crescent Crater at Lassen's right base, and Chaos Crags to the right. All these peaks are composed of dacite. Hat Mountain, another cinder cone, lies in the midground between Reading and Lassen peaks. For much better views of these and other Lassen Park features, climb either Prospect or Lassen peaks. From both you can see north to the Crater Lake rim in southern Oregon—on a clear morning.

Note the barren depression about ½ mile southwest from the base of Cinder Cone. Early-season drainage from Twin Lakes and Rainbow Lake temporarily ponds up at the west base of Painted Dunes, soon seeping underground. What happens to it? As ground water it flows northeast beneath Painted Dunes and Fantastic Lava Beds, then reappears in Butte Lake. Snag Lake too drains beneath Fantastic Lava Beds to Butte Lake. Horseshoe Lake once emptied into Butte Lake via Grassy Creek, but a Cinder Cone lava flow, perhaps occurring about 1720 A.D., blocked Grassy Creek's lodgepole-lined northern course and thereby created Snag Lake. Lakes formed in this manner are called coulee lakes. Snag Lake got its name from the trees killed by this flooding, some snags being still standing in the 1800s when pioneers first saw the lake.
31 Looking directly down the outside slope of Cinder Cone, you can see the source of the rough, black lava flow of the winter of 1850-51. You can trace its path toward Snag Lake, then off to the left toward Butte Lake.

From here, take the trail behind you to the center rim and look into the deep crater; a very steep trail descends to its moonscape bottom.

32 The vent or vents from which all these

cinders were blown have been covered with cinders and other material falling and sliding back into the central crater. Such materials blown out of a volcanic vent are called pyroclastic materials. From about 1567 to 1851 there have been at least three cinder-cone eruptions and at least four lava flows. Cinder Cone may never erupt again, but then, it may continue erupting through coming millenia to build another Prospect Peak.

Continue counterclockwise along the inner rim then take a short trail northwest to the outer rim, along which you can walk 80 yards west down to post 29 and return the way you came. The nature trail climbs east to the cone's highest point.

33 Here is an excellent view of most of Fantastic Lava Beds. Note Butte Lake, at the beds' far end. This lake's east shore is very straight, for it lies along a fault. Downfaulting may have created a shallow lake basin, though glaciers certainly passed through the area, gouging out sediments and soft rock as they continued northward almost down to Butte Creek Campground. Near the end of the Ice Age, glaciers covered the rolling terrain of northeast Lassen Park with several hundred feet of ice. The glacier ice at Butte Lake was about 800 feet thick, while at Badger Flat, 5 miles west of Cinder Cone, it was about 100 feet thick.

The nature trail now descends to the south base of Cinder Cone, then circles clockwise along its base back to post 22.

34. You are viewing the main part of well-named Painted Dunes. Just after the Painted Dunes lava flow had spread out and when it was still very, very hot, Cinder Cone erupted, spraying cinders for miles around. Some of these cinders landed on the still hot lava and consequently they were oxidized and thereby colored by this intense heat. It is this oxidized layer of cinders that makes Painted Dunes so colorful. Note the cinder-coated flow immediately north of Painted Dunes. This may be Cinder Cone's oldest lava flow. Since it is older than the Painted Dunes flow—maybe only by days or weeks—it had cooled sufficiently so that cinders falling on it were not oxidized and consequently they retained their drab color. The main lava flow, making up the bulk of Fantastic Lava Beds, and the winter 1850-51 flow both came *after* Cinder Cone's big eruption, so they lack cinders and retain a very fresh appearance.
35 Few plants can grow under the hot, dry

conditions of this exposed southeast slope. But you still may see several species of wildflowers, each a perennial that sends a taproot deep into the cinders. Annuals seem too delicate to pioneer such a moonscape. Sulfur flower, a buckwheat like Butte Lake's water smartweed, maintains a low profile except when it sends up stalks with dense clusters of tiny yellow flowers. Nude buckwheat, in contrast, grows erect, but has few leaves and these are at its base, not on its naked stem. By reducing leaf surface, it reduces water loss. Its flower clusters are creamy white. Pioneer rock cress adds a dash of pink to the bleak landscape when it flowers, but these soon give way to long, upright mustard-seed pods. Mountain pride (Newberry's penstemon) usually grows out of bedrock cracks but it seems to do well in these loose cinders. Here it appears more as a low, densely leaved shrub than as a wildflower. Its small, leathery leaves are well suited for this harsh environment. Its tubular, crimson flowers are insect-pollinated, the insects haphazardly carried here by the winds. The plant's compact form promotes retention of wind-blown sand and organic matter, thereby building up a primitive soil that is ripe for colonization by less hardy plants.

36   Take your time on this descent. Even more than on the ascent, you are likely to get pebbles in your shoes. Empty them at post 37 or, if you can wait, at post 40. You probably won't get any more pebbles past post 40.

37   Pines but not firs are slowly invading cinder-covered Painted Dunes, but few can be seen growing in the rough, blocky lava flows. If no more eruptions occur, a lodgepole-pine/red-fir forest will ultimately develop, perhaps in 1000-2000 years.

38   Just below you is the source of the winter 1850-51 basalt flow. A narrow trail descends to the flow's vent, post 39. You can bypass it and continue straight ahead to post 40, found beside a double-trunked Jeffrey pine.

39   Reaching back in the "cave" you can feel cold air. In early summer you may even see ice. Such ice caves are common in lava flows where protected pockets stay cold due to lack of air circulation. Flows erupt from the base of a cinder cone more often than from its summit. Those that erupt from its summit easily tear a deep gash through the cone's loose cinders, as happened on the east flank of Hat Mountain.

40   You are now at the edge of Painted Dunes. Sit on a volcanic bomb and empty your shoes. Ahead, please stay on the trail to avoid marking the cinder fields with footprints.

41   Note the abundance of volcanic bombs at the base of the cone. Most of them are gradually falling apart due to chemical weathering and due to expansion caused by freezing of water that accumulates in cracks. Heating by the sun has little effect, if any, in decomposing these rocks.

42   The trail west along the base of Painted Dunes soon curves south and splits, one trail climbing southeast over to Snag Lake, another climbing southwest up to Rainbow Lake. The Snag Lake trail is the more interesting and popular trail, and Snag Lake has better swimming. Neither lake is stocked with trout.

The nature trail continues to the right, climbing north to the Nobles Trail.

43   These are called breadcrust bombs because of their characteristic surface patterns. Homemade bread that has been lightly cut before baking to allow steam to escape will come out of the oven with a similar pattern.

At the Nobles Trail turn right and hike northeast up it.

44   You are back on Nobles' Old Emigrant Trail. Can you imagine the difficulties the wagon trains had in crossing these fields of loose cinders? Along even rougher parts of the trail, people have found broken wagon parts and discarded utensils.

Follow the trail back to Butte Lake.

11 Lassen Park Trails: Trails starting from Lassen Park Road

Introduction Because the Lassen Park Road climbs from 5850 feet at Manzanita Lake to about 8500 feet at its high point, and because this road has about one dozen trailheads located along it, any hiker driving up this road is certain to find one or more trails to suit his or her fancy. Mountaintops, flowery meadows, crashing cascades, sulfurous fumaroles, placid lakes, silent flats—these features and more await the hiker eager to explore this chapter's trails. The following synopsis gives you an idea of what to expect.

If you are driving north from the park's southwest boundary, your first trail will be a moderately difficult one to Brokeoff Mountain, which has summit views rivaling those of Lassen Peak. Next, a trail goes from Sulphur Works Walk-in Campground over to Mill Creek Falls, the park's highest waterfall. Just up the road at the Sulphur Works you can take a very short self-guiding trail around some steaming fumaroles or take a longer one steeply up to Ridge Lake. Higher up, hundreds of people a day make the easy trek over to Bumpass Hell, the park's most active hydrothermal area, while others make the pilgrimage to the craggy summit of Lassen Peak.

Shortly beyond the Lassen Peak trailhead the road begins to descend, and you can take a trail down to subalpine Terrace, Shadow and Cliff lakes or, from Kings Creek Picnic Area, a short trail over to Cold Boiling Lake's effervescent springs. For wildflower lovers, a stroll down Kings Creek provides fruitful rewards. From Lower Kings Meadow, many hike to another popular attraction: the cascades and falls of Kings Creek. Three trails radiate from the Summit Lake area: one south toward Drakesbad, one east to the park's lake-studded backcountry and one west up to Cliff, Shadow and Terrace lakes. As you approach Hat Creek, you'll meet the Nobles Trail, a little-used, historic route good for those who shun crowds. At the Hat Creek bridge, a trail descending from the Terrace Lake area and Paradise Meadow comes to an end. In a warm, lower-elevation forest the Park Road twice crosses the Nobles Trail, an old pioneer route. Finally, in the Manzanita Lake area you'll find four trails: one popular trail around Manzanita Lake, one up Manzanita Creek to fields of wildflowers, one to Crags Lake at the foot of threatening Chaos Crags and, again, the Nobles Trail.

Brokeoff Mountain Trail

Trailhead Post 2 on Lassen Park Road, 0.5 mile north of park's south border and 0.4 mile south of Southwest Entrance Station.

Distances 1.5 miles (2.5 km) to Forest Lake
2.7 miles (4.3 km) to south ridge
3.5 miles (5.6 km) to west ridge
3.8 miles (6.1 km) to summit

Trail description Brokeoff Mountain provides summit views second only to those from Lassen Peak. Brokeoff, however, lacks the crowds, though a dozen hikers on its tiny summit does seem a bit too much. The Brokeoff summit is the highest remaining part of Mt. Tehama, an extinct volcano that once rose about 4000 feet above this hike's trailhead. Brokeoff, like Lassen, hosts alpine vegetation at and near its summit; no other peaks reached by trail in this book rise to this vegetation zone. If you plan to spend more than an hour at the summit, consider bringing water and, for protection from increased ultraviolet radiation, a hat and/or dark glasses.

You'll conveniently find water in a splashing creek by the trailhead. From July to early August, both creekside and dry-slope wildflowers abound, delaying inquisitive botanists on their upward trek. The trail immediately jogs south and cuts through a wide stretch of interwoven alders whose abundance is proportional to the abundance of surface and near-surface water. In early season expect to get your feet wet.

Beyond the alder thicket the trail climbs briefly west, turns northwest and fords two creeklets before climbing a brief ½ mile to a slope above a dwindling pond. At it, amateur botanists can expect to add a few more species to their day's list. In another brief ½ mile we recross one of our creeklets and veer momentarily south. Here, where the trail increases its gradient, hikers bound for Forest Lake should leave the trail and follow the creeklet 200 yards north to the shallow, log-strewn lake. Swimming and fishing are nonexistent, but wildflowers—and with them, mosquitoes—abound. Incidentally, the lake plus the creek our trail has been following more or less make up the southwest edge of a 3300-year-old landslide that slipped from the steep slopes above the lake. The slide, which is inactive at present, extends downslope to the Lassen Park Road and beyond.

The Brokeoff Mountain Trail now climbs steadily for over a mile to surmount the mountain's brushy south ridge. Now with essentially uninterrupted views along the remaining trail, we have good reason to stop and rest as the air becomes increasingly rarefied. After a brief hike north toward the summit, we leave the ridge, dominated by pinemat manzanitas and cream bushes, and traverse northwest up a gravelly slope dominated by Davis' knotweeds. Squatting for a closer look, one may find tiny Gray's bedstraw nestled among them. These and other species appear in the botany chapter's subalpine and alpine wildflower plates.

Well within the subalpine zone, we complete our northwest climb to a switchback by the peak's west ridge. Here you can walk a few yards north to the actual ridge itself and get an impressive view of the intimidating, almost vertical face of Brokeoff Mountain. Out on this windswept ridge, alpine and subalpine plants hug the ground in sterile soil among loose rocks. And loose they are, from pebbles to large blocks, so watch your step: a slip off the ridge could be fatal.

Fortunately, the remaining trail is anything but treacherous—unless a thunderstorm is approaching; then, get back down into forest cover as quickly as you can. A saddle marks the midpoint of the remaining ⅓-mile climb, and from it we have more views of the mountain's north face. The best views, however, are from the small summit at trail's end, for here we can take in a 360° panorama. Starting from Brokeoff, a sinuous ridge—capped by Mt. Diller, Pilot Pinnacle, Ski Heil Peak and Eagle Peak—winds northeast to domineering Lassen Peak. That peak erupted in 1914, destroying a newly built fire lookout on its summit, so in the same year a replacement lookout, now gone, was built atop Brokeoff.

Our summit—Brokeoff Mountain—is, like Mt. Diller to the northeast, a remnant of a large volcano, Mt. Tehama. Mt. Diller's glaciated flanks expose layers of lava that came from the volcano's 11,000-foot summit, which was centered roughly over today's Sulphur Works. Because Mt. Tehama was a child of the Ice Age, it was almost continually attacked by glaciers. Though it began to form about 600,000 years ago, it may not have reached its maximum height and extent until about 300,000 years ago, but by then the glaciers had already made significant inroads into its flanks. And once the glaciers cut deep into the volcano, they were able to cut down all the faster, since they had reached those regions that had been decomposed by the sulfurous solutions and gases. If you look at your summit's north face, you should be able to identify its solfatarized andesite lavas, which are pale brown or yellowish brown. These stand out from the nonsolfatarized lavas, which are black and fresh-looking. For more on Mt. Tehama, see the geology chapter and the first part of the Lassen Park Road Log (Chapter 8).

Mill Creek Falls and Conard Meadows

Trailhead Sulphur Works Walk-in Campground, which is immediately past the park's Southwest Entrance Station.

Distances 0.3 mile (0.5 km) to West Sulphur Creek
1.6 miles (2.6 km) to Mill Creek Falls view
1.7 miles (2.8 km) to East Sulphur Creek
1.8 miles (2.9 km) to Mill Creek Falls brink
2.3 miles (3.7 km) to Conard Meadows
2.9 miles (4.7 km) to Conard Lake
3.5 miles (5.6 km) to Crumbaugh Lake
4.4 miles (7.1 km) to Cold Boiling Lake
5.1 miles (8.2 km) to Kings Creek Picnic Area

Trail Description Although this lightly used trail goes all the way to Kings Creek Picnic Area, few take it past Mill Creek Falls. Wildflower lovers may be interested in Conard Meadows, but destinations beyond that are most easily reached from the picnic area, mentioned later in this chapter.

Our route starts at the campground's north end and drops to a footbridge across West Sulphur Creek. At this crossing you are at the same elevation as the falls' viewpoint, but the trail unnecessarily drops and climbs, insuring you'll get plenty of exercise as you lose and gain 300 vertical feet both going and returning. The falls' viewpoint is precariously close to the brink of the creek's canyon wall, so watch your footing. Mill Creek Falls, about 75 feet high, is the park's tallest fall. It is, nevertheless, a dwarf when compared to Burney Falls (Chapter 19). However, what makes Mill Creek Falls interesting is that is is really three falls. East Sulphur Creek and Bumpass Hell's creek, each draining a hot-springs area, unite as they plunge about 25-30 feet into a pool, which in turn spills over, tossing water 50 feet to the canyon floor. When the runoff is at its maximum, usually from mid-June through mid-July, the volume is so great that the two upper falls, only a few feet apart, merge into one. Then, you'll hear the thundering falls well before you reach the viewpoint.

In early season you may be unable to cross East Sulphur Creek to get at the brink of the falls. This is probably for the better, since the brink is dangerous enough even in mid- and late summer. The rocks in the canyon just below the fall are among the oldest andesite rocks erupted from Mt. Tehama (see previous hike, last paragraph). They date back about ½ million years and, when Mt. Tehama was at its highest, this area you're hiking in lay under about 4000 feet of volcanic rock.

If you return the way you came, note that the firs by West and East Sulphur creeks are mostly red firs, while those on the drier slopes between the two creeks are mostly white firs. The red firs definitely prefer more water.

If you continue onward, be careful when you cross Bumpass Hell's creek, for you cross it close to the brink of the waterfall. From the creek the trail climbs all too steeply to the lower end of Conard Meadows, a beautiful wildflower garden from mid-July through early August. The climb beyond its creek is nicely graded, and midway to spreading Crumbaugh Lake you'll see Conard Lake—a large pond—about 200 yards downslope. Ironically, camping is allowed at Conard Lake, which lacks sites, but not at Crumbaugh Lake, which has them. See the "Cold Boiling and Crumbaugh Lakes" hike, which originates at Kings Creek Picnic Area, for trail information beyond Conard Lake.

Sulphur Works: An Active Hydrothermal Area

Trailhead Post 5 on Lassen Park Road, 1.0 mile north of the Southwest Entrance Station.

Distance 0.1 mile (0.2 km) for entire walk

Trail description This very short loop trail, situated between two branches of West Sulphur Creek, is a self-guiding nature trail that has several signs to interpret the surroundings. With fumaroles steaming, mudpots bubbling and hydrogen-sulfide gas permeating the air, it's a wonder that vegetation grows in the area. But it does. Just after you start the trail, you'll see low pinemat manzanitas and spiny-seeded chinquapins, both shrubs common constituants of fir forests. Labrador teas, as usual, are close to water, and are easily identified by the turpentine odor of their leaves. The firs in this vicinity are red firs, and associated with them, as usual, are western white pines.

You are walking through an area that one geologist, Howel Williams, thought to be the central vent of an Ice Age volcano, Mt. Tehama. About 300,000 years ago, when the volcano may have reached a maximum height of 11,000 feet, Lassen Peak and other prominent peaks of today were nonexistent, and the volcano reigned as a solitary landmark much as Mt. Hood, an equal-sized volcano in northern Oregon, does today.

The andesitic rocks of the Sulphur Works are being decomposed by hot, acidic water which, at this elevation of about 7000 feet, boils at about 195°F (90°C). But underground, the acidic water is under pressure and can build up to superheated temperatures, making it very corrosive. No wonder then that the andesite is readily broken down to easily erodable residues. Kaolin and opal are the commonest products.

Today's steaming activity has been referred to as the last dying gasps of the ancient volcano, but it would be better viewed as a sign of still active volcanism. One cannot discount a new eruption anywhere in the Lassen area. The kind of steaming activity is related to the amount of ground water available. Hot pools exist when it is plentiful, but as the water diminishes, the pools evolve to mudpots, which in turn evolve to "dry" vents—fumaroles.

The most obvious odor emitted by the steaming activity is that of rotten eggs, the odor being due to hydrogen sulfide. Fortunately, the gases in the air aren't strong enough to pose a hazard. For more information about hydrothermal activity, see the previous chapter's Bumpass Hell Nature Trail, posts 21 to 31.

Ridge Lake

Trailhead Sulphur Works parking lot, 1. mile north of the Southwest Entrance Station

Distance 1.0 mile (1.6 km) to Ridge Lake

Trail description If you like trails that are short and very steep, this one, with an average grade of 20%, is for you. Although you're allowed to camp near the lake, you probably won't want to carry a backpack up to it. This hike is best suited for dayhikers.

Rather than build a trail switchbacking up slopes to Ridge Lake, the trail crew built one up a narrow, descending ridge confined between two close-lying creeklets. This ridge is, incidentally, an old landslide that stabilized centuries ago. While you stop to catch your breath, you can identify some of the more common wildflowers along the route, such as coyote mint and California butterweed. A more exciting find is the delicate Sierra onion and, in rocky areas near the lake, the solitary-flowered silky raillardella. After you've climbed about 0.7 mile, the creek on your left ends at a spring—a seepage from Ridge Lake. In like manner, the creek on your right ends at a spring, except in early season when melting snowbanks cause the lake to overflow.

When you reach the lake, you'll see it is almost cleft in two by a narrow, waist-deep neck. The larger, eastern part is deep enough for swimming but, at almost 8000 feet elevation, it never warms up sufficiently to make swimming very pleasant.

Although the trail ends at the lake, you can make an easy ⅓-mile climb—no steeper than your trail—up slopes to the crest. Your views from a small crest summit are rewarding, for you can gaze down the two glaciated canyons that begin at the crest. You can also look across to the nearly vertical north face of Brokeoff Mountain and the less steep slopes of Mt. Diller, both showing northwest-dipping lava flows. Both peaks are remnants of Mt. Tehama, an 11,000-foot-high Ice Age olcano that towered 4000 feet above your ailhead and sent its glaciers radiating out cross most of the western half of Lassen ark.

Bumpass Hell and Cold Boiling Lake

Trailhead Post 17 on Lassen Park Road, 5.7 miles above the Southwest Entrance Station and 1.1 miles below the Lassen Peak Trail parking lot.

Distances 1.0 mile (1.6 km) to Bumpass Hell viewpoint

1.4 miles (2.3 km) to Bumpass Hell

3.1 miles (5.0 km) to Cold Boiling Lake

3.8 miles (6.1 km) to Crumbaugh Lake

3.9 miles (6.2 km) to Kings Creek Picnic Area

5.7 miles (9.2 km) to Mill Creek Falls

7.5 miles (12.1 km) to Sulphur Works Walk-in Campground

Trail description Until late July, expect a fair amount of snow along the first mile or so of trail. But even with a lot of snow, the trail to Bumpass Hell is quite easy to follow—just follow the footprints. For between the Fourth of July and Labor Day, the Bumpass Hell Nature Trail is very popular, and on many days more than 100 visitors trek 1.4 miles to Bumpass Hell, then trek back. Few care to hike beyond Bumpass Hell, though the trail from it is one of the park's best-graded trails. If you've arranged for someone to meet you at Kings Creek Picnic Area or at Sulphur Works Walk-in Campground, then your hike will be downhill most of the way.

From a small bridge across Bumpass Hell's outlet creek, your trail climbs ¼ mile east to a saddle above Bumpass Hell, providing you with a last view of this churning cauldron. Ahead you see Saddle Mountain due east of you and taller Mt. Harkness, to its right, both peaks situated along the northwest rim of deep, glaciated Warner Valley. In the distance, Lake Almanor spreads miles over fertile land once known as Big Meadows.

Your trail then descends south toward Mt. Conrad, giving you the opportunity to examine its northern slopes and its north ridge,

which provides a natural cross-country route up to its summit. Views change as your trail angles northeast, descending ¼ mile to a creeklet that provides excellent water well into August. Sipping the water of this wildflower-adorned creeklet, you can leisurely explore the lands below you, with shallow Crumbaugh Lake definitely catching your eye. Next, your trail slants down across a steep outcrop of glaciated lava, which has some large, overhanging sections that will speed you on your way to safer footing by a second creeklet. Put on your mosquito repellent here, for the Cold Boiling Lake environs, a few minutes' walk ahead, is mosquito heaven well into August.

After a ½-mile moderate descent from the second creeklet, you arc around the spongy-shored lake, which is more of an oversized pond than a lake. If you feel like wading through mud, you can walk out to the cold, bubbling springs, just south of the lake, that give the lake its name. Cold Boiling Lake's springs may be boiling hot deep down within the earth's crust, but the water is certainly cool by the time it reaches the surface. Just beyond the springs you come to a trail junction, from where you can head out to Kings Creek Picnic Area, a 15-minute walk, or down to Sulphur Works Walk-in Campground, a mostly descending 2-hour hike.

Lassen Peak Trail

Trailhead Lassen Peak parking lot, 6¾ miles above the Southwest Entrance Station and ¼ mile below Lassen Park Road's highest point.

Distance 2.3 miles (3.7 km) to summit

Trail description The Lassen Peak Trail rivals the nearby Bumpass Hell Nature Trail in popularity. On one summer day, the author met about 400 hikers on the trail, and this was on a week day, not on a weekend! I hope you will meet fewer, but Lassen Peak is a magnet attracting hikers of all ages (one 3½-year-old made it to the summit unaided). For your comfort, carry water, bring a windbreaker and suntan lotion, wear dark glasses and/or a hat: the summit is windy, the summit snowfield bright and the ultraviolet radiation strong. And take note: restrooms are installed only after the snow

elts, by late July or early August, so use the cilities down at the parking lot. Further- ore, don't attempt to climb the peak if the eather is threatening, for not far beyond the art there is no place to hide from lightning. nless you are well acclimated, you will nd yourself often short of breath, so rest ten. The trail begins at 8450 feet elevation, the air is thin, and by the time you reach e summit it is considerably thinner, the air eing about ⅓ less thick than it is at sea level. he Lassen Peak Trail, completed along with e Lassen Park Road in 1931, stays very ose to a steep 15% grade over most of its ngth, and this steepness, combined with e thin air, makes the trail seem consid- rably longer than it actually is. Also, snow ften lingers on parts of the trail well into ugust, and this too can add to your climb- g effort. Some returning hikers are temp- d to slide down snowfields to speed up eir descent, but iced-over surfaces speed eir descent far more than they can safely andle.

Davis' knotweeds and scattered whitebark ines dominate the area as we start north to a witchback. From it you can look west up a ully, the start of a 2-mile cross-country oute to small, soggy-shored Soda Lake, of nterest to naturalists but not to swimmers or ishermen. Beyond the switchback you limb to a grove of mountain hemlocks that ypically harbors snow patches. Your climb s only moderate for the next ¼ mile, but rom the next switchback the grade becomes teep, and it stays steep all the way to the ummit area, reached about 40 switchbacks ater.

After about 3 of these switchbacks you nter the alpine realm. Here, at about 9200 eet elevation and about one mile up the trail, ou see the last of the mountain hemlocks, hese existing in dwarfed forms due to severe vinters. Cream bushes, knotweeds, jewel lowers, ferns and a few other species also re at the top of their limits, but silver-leaved upines flourish locally, soon not to be seen bove. Too, Davidson's penstemon puts in n appearance, among the first of more than dozen alpine species you may see. Look for remont's butterweed, a sunflower that

grows among rocks in small numbers from 8000 feet elevation all the way to the top. Notice how it and several other species shrink in height and bulk with increasing elevation, existing on Lassen's summit as miniature plants. (Photos of most of these wildflowers appear on the subalpine and al- pine wildflower plates in the botany chap- ter.)

The great majority of hikers, however, are not interested in wildflowers, but rather will be wondering "How much farther to the top?" Sign posts count off each half mile. Stop and rest often, for the views of the sur- rounding countryside below you are indeed spectacular. Try to visulaize Mt. Tehama, an 11,000-foot-high volcano, whose summit once stood about 2 miles south-southwest of you. Today you see only parts of its flank, the largest part being prominent Brokeoff Mountain, about 4 miles to the southwest. Mt. Diller, the long, sloping ridge north of Brokeoff, is another remnant, and between the two, large glaciers from Mt. Tehama's upper slopes flowed northeast. Glaciers, gnawing into Tehama's flanks for several hundred thousand years, brought about its demise, and then smaller glaciers formed on the remaining ridges. One such glacier de- scended south from the Lassen Peak area, scraping out a basin now filled by large, or- bicular, 110-foot-deep Lake Helen. Then, perhaps 11,000 years ago, dacite lava erupted at this site, destroying the glacier and building up Lassen Peak in just a matter of years (see Chapter 10's Bumpass Hell Na- ture Trail, posts 1 to 6).

Your views momentarily disappear as your trail climbs through a small alcove. At about 10,000 feet elevation and only ⅓ mile from the broad summit area, it is an excel- lent, wind-free place to rest. Because it provides shelter from the hostile elements, this alcove supports a relatively abundant amount of plants. Here you'll find the park's highest sedges, and nearby you'll see some very stunted whitebark pines, also the park's highest. Above them, you are certainly in a bona fide alpine realm.

A large boulder marks your successful ar- rival at Lassen's broad summit area, and

_eft: Lassen Peak, viewed from Brokeoff Mountain's summit. Mill Creek Falls is composed of two :onvergent streams plunging into a common pool that spills over to the base of the gorge. Ridge ᴌake, with a narrow, shallow "waist," separates into two lakes late in the summer of dry years. ᴀttractive Crumbaugh Lake, bottom, receives relatively few visitors.

golden-mantled ground squirrels may scurry up to you to demand an "entrance fee." This squirrel population probably dates back to the mid- and late 1930s, when hikers first began coming up in droves, giving handouts to the friendly rodents. The Park Service, however, discourages both feeding and handling them.

The summit area's high point is perfectly obvious, though the route up to it may not be so. Just follow the footprints, often across snow, to the high point's north slope. Sitting on the rocky, pointed top, you have a 360° view of the Lassen area landscape. On a clear day you can see north well into southern Oregon and south to the San Francisco Bay Area. In 1913 a fire-lookout station was built on this very spot, providing someone with the very enviable job of surveyihg the countryside as well as watching glorious sunrises and sunsets (today, the trail and the summit area are closed to camping, but with an early start you can witness a sunrise). The station, however, was short-lived, for Lassen began erupting in May 1914, totally destroying the lookout by October. In May 1915 it erupted the summit lava you see, followed by a major explosion that destroyed several square miles of forest to the northeast (see Chapter 8's Lassen Park Road Log, posts 44 to 50). If you look across the summit area, you'll see the dark 1915 lava flow, spilling both southwest and northeast down the peak's uppermost slopes. A pre-1914 crater lies buried under the western part of this flow; the flow itself came from a crater more centrally located. Today you'll see a crater on the flow's north edge, developed after the tremendous May 22, 1915 explosion. To its northwest lies yet another crater, this one blown out in 1917, the last year of significant volcanic activity. The peak steamed actively for several years after that, diminishing over the years to nothing by the early 1940s.

One of the best descriptions of Lassen's summit views is that by William H. Brewer, a notable botanist who was on the peak's second recorded ascent, back in September 1863. The first recorded ascent was by a miner, Grover Godfrey, back in 1851, but Peter Lassen, after whom Lassen Peak, Park, Forest and County are named, may have climbed it earlier. The third party known to have ascended the peak did so in August 1864, and it included the first woman to

reach the top, Helen Brodt, after whom La Helen was named.

Over four weeks, Brewer and his Whitn Survey companions journeyed from Sacr mento northward through Grass Valle Quincy, Big Meadows (today's Lake A manor) and Warner Valley, then made a ba camp perhaps near Lake Helen. The climbed the peak in bad weather on Septer ber 26, then repeated the ascent in bett weather on September 29. With a brig moon two days past its full, they arose at 1: a.m., ate breakfast, and by 2:45 a.m. were their way. Brewer and his small par reached the summit between 4:30 and 5: a.m., just as the eastern horizon was begi ning to glow red with anticipation of su rise. Brewer's words:

"As we gaze in rapture, the sun comes the scene, and as it rises, its disk flattened atmospheric refraction, it gilds the peaks o after another, and at this moment the field view is wider than at any time later in t day. The Marysville [Sutter] Buttes rise fro the vapory plain [Sacramento Valley], i lands in a distant ocean of smoke, while f beyond appear the dim outlines of Mou Diablo and Mount Hamilton, the latter 2 [217] miles distant.

"North of the Bay of San Francisco t Coast Range is clear and distinct, from Na north to the Salmon Mountains near t Klamath River. Mount St. Helena, Mount S John, Yallo-balley [Yolla Bolly], Bull Chump [Bully Choop Mountain], and all i other prominent peaks are in distinct vie rising in altitude as we look north.

"But rising high above all is the conic shadow of the peak we are on, projected the air, a distinct form of cobalt blue on ground of lighter haze, its top as sharp an its outlines as well defined as are those of t peak itself—a gigantic spectral mountai projected so high in the air that it seems f higher than the original mountain itself— but, as the sun rises, the mountain sinks int the valley, and, like a ghost, fades away at t sight of the sun.

"The snows of the Salmon Mountair [specifically, the Trinity Alps] glitter in th morning sun, a hundred miles distant. Bu the great feature is the sublime form Mount Shasta towering above its neighbo ing mountains—truly a monarch of the hill It has received some snow in the late storm and the snow line is as sharply defined an level as if the surface of an ocean had cut it against the mountain side."

(With this book's map, you can identify ozens of features in and near Lassen Peak.) Brewer recognized the volcanic nature of the Lassen countryside, but he probably was naware that it contained examples of all our types of the world's volcanoes. Mt. hasta is the prime example of a *composite olcano*, or stratovolcano, though Sugarloaf eak and Burney Mountain, both west of Hat reek Valley, appear to be stratovolcanoes in he making. Lassen Peak and Chaos Crags are excellent examples of *volcanic domes*, also nown as plug domes. Prospect Peak, Mt. [arkness, Sifford Mountain and Raker Peak re the park's four *shield volcanoes*, while inder Cone and Hat Mountain are two of its ore prominent *cinder cones*.

Take time to explore Lassen's fascinating ummit area or to enjoy its perennial snow-eld. On your descent, keep to the trail. hortcutting destroys the trail (your tax dol-rs to repair it) and sliding down iced-over nowfields can lead to serious injuries.

Terrace, Shadow and Cliff Lakes

Trailhead Post 27 on Lassen Park Road, 2.0 niles east of Lassen Peak Trail parking lot nd 6.8 miles southwest from Summit Lake Campground.

Distances   0.5 mile (0.8 km) to Terrace Lake
0.8 mile (1.2 km) to Shadow Lake
1.6 miles (2.6 km) to Paradise Meadow
1.7 miles (2.7 km) to Cliff Lake
2.9 miles (4.6 km) to Hat Creek trailhead (post 42)
3.7 miles (6.0 km) to Dersch Meadows trailhead (post 38)
3.9 miles (6.2 km) to Summit Lake Ranger Station (post 37)

Trail description   Lying in the shadow of Reading Peak, Terrace, Shadow and Cliff Lakes remain trimmed with snow through mid-July. Before then, your descent to Ter-ace Lake may be one big snow slide. You tart at just over 8000 feet elevation in a sub-alpine forest locally dominated by mountain nemlocks. In several minutes you reach a rail junction and must decide which route o travel. Terrace Lake is ⅓ mile to the east

and Shadow Lake is immediately east of it. These are perhaps the two most popular des-tinations of this lightly used trail. Because these two are so close to the park road, camp-ing at them is prohibited. Likewise, it is pro-hibited at Cliff Lake, which lies off the beaten track. The author highly recommends all three. Shallow, rockbound Terrace Lake has a sublime beauty about it. Shadow Lake, with its great depth, displays an azure-blue color worthy of a precious gem. Cliff Lake, with its tree-studded island and nearby mas-sive cliffs, looks like a transplant from Lake Tahoe's Desolation Wilderness. Beyond the Cliff Lake junction, you descend 2.2 miles northeast to Dersch Meadows, most of the descent being along the crests of glacial moraines. For the significance of these fresh looking, young moraines, see Chapter 8's Lassen Park Road Log, post 26.

If you choose the Hat Creek option, be pre-pared for a knee-knocking descent. Plan to have someone meet you at the Hat Creek trailhead, for you won't want to hike back up this overly steep trail. The route begins eas-ily enough, if you're descending it, with pleasant views of Lassen's massive east flank revealed over the first mile. Note the rock-walled, glacier-carved canyon at the foot of the peak. This was cut by a glacier or a series of glaciers prior to Lassen's eruption onto the scene. About 1½ miles from your trailhead you cross incipient Hat Creek, originating in Paradise Meadow 160 yards south of you. When you visit it, you become "paradise" for a myriad of mosquitoes looking for a feast. Botanists, however, will find it a flowery treat in late July and early August.

From the creek crossing, the trail plunges northward alongside the creek, relinquish-ing its maddening gradient after ¾ mile. You then have a soothing descent to the site of Hat Lake, which once beautifully mirrored Lassen Peak. The lake had a brief history, coming into existence on May 19, 1915, when a wall of mud rumbled down Lassen's northeast slope, damming up Hat Creek. In-coming sediments immediately began de-creasing the size of the lake, reducing it to about 10 acres by 1930, to 1 acre by 1950, and to a wide creek by 1980. This is an incredibly fast sedimentation rate, but then there was an abundance of loose sediments. Some gla-cial lakes in the High Sierra are about as large today as they were when glaciers left them about 10,000 years ago.

Cold Boiling and Crumbaugh Lakes

Trailhead   Kings Creek Picnic Area, at the end of a ⅓-mile-long spur road. This spur road is 4¼ miles east of the Lassen Peak Trail parking lot and 4½ miles southwest of the Summit Lake Campground.

Distances   0.8 mile (1.3 km) to Cold Boiling Lake

1.5 miles (2.4 km) to Crumbaugh Lake

2.4 miles (3.8 km) to Twin Meadows

2.5 miles (4.0 km) to Bumpass Hell

3.3 miles (5.3 km) to Mill Creek Falls

5.1 miles (8.2 km) to Sulphur Works Walk-in Campground

Trail description   From near the end of the picnic area, a trail climbs southwest over a broad, low ridge, reaching a meadow-edge junction in ½ mile. This stretch can have trailside snow through mid-July, but by early August wildflowers are blooming, silver-leaved lupines easily being the most numerous species. From the junction, a southbound, seldom-used trail makes a leisurely 2-mile descent to Twin Meadows—an excellent hike for those who love walking through a silent forest. The trail once continued beyond the meadows, heading southwest down North Arm Rice Creek and then climbing northeast to Drake Lake. Those attempting this route will meet stiff resistance from groves of alders, and they'd do better to just head east cross-country, more or less contouring over toward that lake. Excellent map-interpretation skills are a must to successfully reach the lake.

The bulk of the hikers, who aren't that many, head west ¼ mile over to a second junction, this one just south of Cold Boiling Lake. You'll find its "boiling" springs bubbling away just a stone's throw from the junction. Prepare for muddy feet if you attempt to wade through a mire out to them. Perhaps a mile or two below the earth's surface, the springs' waters are boiling, but they are certainly cool at the surface.

If you're climbing up to Bumpass Hell, circle counterclockwise around Cold Boil-

ing Lake, fighting off mosquitoes along t[h] stretch. A better choice is to make a leisure ¾-mile descent to shallow, spreading Cru baugh Lake. As you start this descent y may notice the whitish, decomposed roc of this area. These are opal, which read forms in areas of hot-springs activity. We c therefore infer that in the not-too-dista past, Cold Boiling Lake was steaming aw just as Boiling Springs Lake (Chapter 1 does today. Just before the trail crosses t outlet creek, a spur trail forks over to Cru baugh Lake's northeast arm. The main tr enters flat meadowland and plows throu sedges and grasses to a wildflower display the wetter soils above the lake's west sho Camping is not allowed here (or at Cold Bo ing Lake), which is unfortunate since t forested south shore has several suitab sites.

Leaving that shore, you start a traver across shady slopes, spotting Conard La within a half mile's walk. When you see you can leave the trail for a cross-coun route south up a ridge to Mt. Conard's su mit. The trail from the Conard Lake ar down to Mill Creek Falls and Sulphur Wor Walk-in Campground is described in the verse direction in this chapter's second hik

Upper Kings Creek

Trailhead   Same as for preceding hike.

Distance   0.3 mile (0.5 km) to Lassen Pa Road

Trail description   From the Kings Cre Picnic Area turnaround, a trail paralle Kings Creek ¼ mile southeast, as both ru along the northwest base of a low glaci moraine. Where the moraine dies out, bo the creek and trail bend east-northeast a promptly reach Lassen Park Road. Alo this brief trail, note the contrast between w creek-bank vegetation and dry, morain vegetation. Monkey flowers, elephant head marsh marigolds and other water-lovi plants grow only a few feet away fro water-shunning silver-leaved lupines a Davis' knotweeds. Also investigate t wildflowers along the spur road leading the picnic area, particularly where the ro crosses the creek.

Kings Creek Falls and Sifford Lake

Trailhead Post 32 on Lassen Park Road, 5½ miles east of the Lassen Peak Trail parking lot and 3½ miles southwest from Summit Lake Campground

Distances 0.7 mile (1.1 km) to Kings Creek Cascades

1.2 miles (1.9 km) to Kings Creek Falls via foot trail

1.5 miles (2.4 km) to Kings Creek Falls via horse trail

1.8 miles (2.8 km) to Bench Lake

2.2 miles (3.5 km) to Sifford Lake

4.1 miles (6.6 km) to Corral Meadow

4.6 miles (7.4 km) to Warner Valley C.G. via ridge trail

4.7 miles (7.6 km) to Warner Valley C.G. via Bench Lake

5.0 miles (8.0 km) to Summit Lake's south campground

5.2 miles (8.4 km) for Kings Creek Falls-Bench Lake-Sifford Lake loop

6.4 miles (10.4 km) to Warner Valley C.G. via Corral Meadow

Trail description As you can tell from the foregoing list of destinations, a good variety of routes are possible. Undoubtedly the most popular hike is the foot trail down to Kings Creek Falls. A good number of hikers make a loop, first down to Kings Creek Falls, then over to Sifford Lake via Bench Lake, and finally northwest back to the trailhead. You can make this loop in the other direction, but then, if you reach Kings Creek Falls much later than noon, it will be in the shade and will photograph poorly. Also, you then have to climb up the steep, scenic cascades foot trail or take the easier, less scenic horse trail alternate. Expect abundant snow patches until mid-July.

The number of cars parked at or near the trailhead gives you an idea of how many other hikers to expect. The trail parallels Kings Creek eastward, approaching but never reaching the creek's north bank. Hemlock Lake lies hidden over a low ridge to the south, lined with red firs as well as mountain hemlocks. Labrador tea is also present, almost guaranteeing an abundant crop of mosquitoes. Nevertheless, the lake can offer a refreshing swim throughout most of August. It is best reached by starting cross-country from the *west* end of the Kings Creek trailhead bridge.

On the trail, you reach a fork after a ½-mile stroll from the trailhead. The right branch crosses a narrow part of Lower Kings Creek Meadow over to a nearby ford or bridging of Kings Creek. Sometimes a log may be present; if not, jump or wade. Most hikers turn left, across a low ridge and descend briefly to a junction just before the brink of Kings Creek Cascades. A foot path descends steeply alongside the cascades, a second footpath goes about 170 yards out to a viewpoint, and a horse trail, providing distant views similar to those from the viewpoint, descends ½ mile to the base of the cascades. Check out the center trail first, for along it you get a very good overview of Kings Creek Cascades crashing down the narrow gorge. As you look east across the forested slopes of Flatiron Ridge, you see Mt. Harkness standing most prominently on the horizon. Saddle Mountain flanks it to the left, while farther away, a ridge topped by Red Cinder Cone approximately marks the eastern border of Lassen Park. From the west end of level Flatiron Ridge, forested slopes rise up toward us. These gentle slopes are in fact an enormous amount of glacial debris left perhaps about 9-11,000 years ago. See Lassen Park Road Log, post 26, for an elaboration on these and other glacial moraines.

The footpath down along Kings Creek Cascades is steep, and the scenery is pleasantly distracting, so be careful because you really do have to watch your step. After a dozen or so minor falls, the cascades conclude with a large one, near which you meet the horse trail. You now descend a pleasant ¼ mile to a junction and continue 100 yards beyond it to the brink of Kings Creek Falls. The falls are about 50 feet high, so a slip over the brink would certainly be fatal. Don't get too close to the edge. Many hikers like to scramble down to the base of the falls, but only a rocky, steep *de facto* route exists, not an official trail, so be careful if you descend the potentially loose, slippery rocks. Photographers take note: the falls are in shade in early morning and during most of the afternoon, so plan to visit the falls between 10 a.m. and noon.

Devastated Area, viewed from summit of Lassen Peak. Chilly Cliff Lake, with a vegetated island, too cold for comfortable swimming, unlike warm Sifford Lake, bottom left. Kings Creek Falls is sunlight only a few hours each day.

Very few hikers continue on the trail beᵗ ond Kings Creek Falls. This trail climbs ᵗver two low ridges, then descends steeply ᵗlong the headwaters of the west fork of ᵗings Creek. Wildflowers are locally abunᵗlant, particularly along creeks from late July ᵗhrough mid-August. About 2.0 miles beᵗ ond the falls and immediately before crossᵗng the west fork, you can find an acceptable ᵗampsite that makes a pleasing alternative to ᵗverly popular Corral Meadow, about 0.9 ᵗnile to the southeast. From the campsite, ᵗummit Lake's south campground is about ᵗ.8 miles away.

If you are bound for Bench Lake and Sifᵗord Lake, backtrack 100 yards from Kings ᵗreek Falls to a junction and immediately ᵗross the creek. Your trail then climbs briefly ᵗo the base of a long cliff with an extensive ᵗalus slope. The talus has been accumulating ᵗver the last 10,000 years, which gives you ᵗn idea of how fast the cliff is being broken ᵗlown. You'll see two caves near the base of ᵗhe cliff, the larger one recessing about 15 ᵗeet. About 0.6 mile from the junction your ᵗrail tops a low spot in the lateral moraine ᵗhat dams chest-deep Bench Lake. Perhaps ᵗhe lake loses a fair amount of water through ᵗlacial sediments, for by Labor Day the lake ᵗs barely more than a mudhole. Slightly ᵗmaller, though deeper, Sifford Lake is much ᵗetter.

With that lake in mind, you descend a ᵗully between two moraines, reaching anᵗother trail in 0.4 mile. This one follows a dry ᵗlateral-moraine crest 1.6 miles east down to ᵗhe Pacific Crest Trail, which you can then ᵗake either 1.0 mile down to Warner Valley ᵗampground or 1.4 miles over Flatiron ᵗidge to Corral Meadow. Instead, you'll ᵗprobably make a curving ⅓-mile climb up to ᵗ small flat with silver-leaved lupines, then ᵗbranch south and go just under ½ mile to Sifford Lake. The lake is small and mostly shallow, but still deep enough for swimming. Because it lies in fairly open terrain, it can become snow-free by mid-June and warm up to a decent temperature by early July. From mid-July through late August it stays in the mid or upper 60s, ranking as one of the park's warmest lakes.

When you return to the main trail, you have a mostly leisurely 1¼-mile climb northwest up to the Lower Kings Creek Meadow trail junction. Along this ascent, look for glacial evidence: moraines (loose,

often linear piles or rocks and debris), erratics (large, glacier-carried rocks), striations (scratch marks on bedrock), chattermarks (gouges in bedrock) and polish (smooth surfaces on bedrock). From the junction you walk ½ mile back to your trailhead.

Summit Lake to Corral Meadow

Trailhead At the southeast end of Summit Lake's south campground. Since no parking is available at the trailhead, you'll have to park by the lake's south-shore picnic area if you are dayhiking or by the Summit Lake Ranger Station if you are backpacking. These sites add 0.3 mile (0.5 km) and 1.1 miles (1.7 km) respectively, each way, to the following destinations.

Distances 2.5 miles (4.0 km) to Corral Meadow
4.8 miles (7.8 km) to Warner Valley Campground
6.7 miles (10.8 km) to Swan Lake
7.3 miles (11.7 km) to Lower Twin Lake
7.8 miles (12.6 km) to Horseshoe Lake Ranger Station
9.2 miles (14.8 km) to Juniper Lake Ranger Station

Trail description Dropping 700 feet to Corral Meadow in 2.5 miles, this trail provides the easiest route to the spacious, popular campsites along the west margin of Corral Meadow. Climbing back up your trail is another matter. Several minutes after you start hiking down the trail, you'll cross a spring-fed creeklet and in a few yards spy a huge western white pine, one of the park's largest. These pines plus lodgepoles and red firs shade your moderate descent. After 1⅔ miles you reach a junction from where you could head briefly upstream to a campsite by two confluent creeks. Most hikers go 240 yards downstream, passing a small campsite immediately before bridging the west fork of Kings Creek. You parallel this creek, usually at a distance, down to Corral Meadow's spacious campsites beside Kings Creek. Consult Chapter 12's northbound Pacific Crest Trail for the route from Warner Valley Campground up Grassy Swale to Swan and Lower Twin lakes.

Summit Lake to Echo, Twin, Rainbow and Snag Lakes

Trailhead   At the east end of Summit Lake's north campground. If you are dayhiking, you can park in the campground's adjacent day-use parking area. If you are backpacking, you'll have to park by the Summit Lake Ranger Station trailhead. If so, add 0.4 mile (0.6 km) each way, to the following destinations. This short additional stretch, unfortunately, is through a mosquito-plagued bog.

Distances   1.8 miles (2.9 km) to Echo Lake
3.2 miles ((5.1 km) to Upper Twin Lake
3.7 miles (5.9 km) to Lower Twin Lake
4.1 miles (6.6 km) to Pacific Crest Trail at southeast shore of Lower Twin Lake
4.2 miles (6.8 km) to Pacific Crest Trail at north shore
4.9 miles (7.9 km) to Rainbow Lake
7.4 miles (11.9 km) to Snag Lake
8.5 miles (13.7 km) to Cinder Cone summit
9.8 miles (15.8 km) to Butte Lake Ranger Station
12.8 miles ((20.6 km) for Twin Lakes-Grassy Swale-Summit Creek loop

Trail description   The park's finest collection of lakes is best reached from Summit Lake's north campground. You can either head down to seven Cluster Lakes, described in the following hike, or can head down to Lower Twin Lake and branch out from there. Both route plans start uphill from moraine-dammed Summit Lake. Divide Lake would be a better name: perched atop a broad divide, Summit Lake contributes water to both East Fork Hat Creek and Summit Creek. The contribution is all ground water except when spring snowmelt water seeping into the lake causes it to overflow down the Summit Creek channel.

Summit Lake's north-shore trail barely starts east before it is joined by the trail from the ranger station. It then goes a brief spell to the lake's northeast finger, from where a trail

branches south to the lake's amphitheat and south campground. Now you start moderate climb east, first up a gully and the up a ridge. Where you switchback on it yc have your first good view of Lassen Pea due west, and Crescent Crater, on its nor flank. Among pinemat manzanita in an ope forest, you climb shortly to a plateau an reach a junction, 1.0 mile from the trailhea The next hike branches left toward the Clu ter Lakes; this hike branches right, crosse this glaciated lava flow, and then descenc to the north tip of fairly deep Echo Lake. C all the lakes mentioned in this and the fo lowing hike, Echo is the only one wher camping is prohibited. This lake, like th Twin Lakes below it, displays a good fores lake *ecotone*, that is, a transition zone be tween forest plants and lake plants. Pinem; manzanitas, characteristic of well-draine forest slopes, give way to red mountai heathers only a few feet from the shore These in turn give way to a narrow band c shoreline species, notably wester; blueberry, primrose monkey flower an; moss. Sedges grow along the shoreline an; advance into the shallow water. Ecotone can also exist on a much broader scale, a; say, a red-fir forest merges into a white-fi forest.

Echo Lake is a goal worthy in itself, bu most hikers descend to the Twin Lakes be fore heading back. Doing this, we climb ou of the depression holding Echo Lake, the; drop east, passing a meadow and a stagnan pond before heading north through a smal; flat-floored valley. The lava flows expose; on the valley's steep sides yield to a shallow linear lakelet, from which we drop rathe; steeply down more lava flows to the wes corner of Upper Twin Lake. Look fo: campsites along its west, south and eas; shores but not along the north shore, whic; the trail skirts. Steep slopes above its shore and others above the west shore of Lowe: Twin Lake, make camping impractical.

Flowing until about late July, Uppe: Twin's rollicking outlet creek drops about 4(feet to the southwest corner of Lower Twin Here you'll find a shoreline trail that make; an 0.4-mile traverse over to the Pacific Cres: Trial and the lake's east-shore campsites The main trail, however, hugs Lower Twin': west shore, the trail being crowded by stee; slopes and semistable talus. After ½ mile th trail heads east across the lodgepole-lined north shore to the southern end of an old road, which is now part of the Pacific Crest Trail. Through most of July you'll see a long reflection pond extending several hundred yards north from Lower Twin Lake, but it dries up soon after the lake's outlet creek ceases to flow.

Now at the Pacific Crest Trail, you have a choice of options: 1) head ⅓ mile north on the road, then fork northwest over to the Cluster Lakes (described in the following hike); 2) head 3.0 miles north down the road to the Nobles Trail, then 1.0 mile northwest on it to Soap Lake (described in this chapter's Nobles Trail hike); 3) head south on the Pacific Crest Trail to Swan Lake, Grassy Swale or Corral Meadow (described in Chapter 12's northbound Pacific Crest Trail hike); or 4) head over to Rainbow Lake and make some more decisions there.

With this last goal in mind, start south on the Pacific Crest Trail, which narrows from a jeep road to a horse path before you reach the Rainbow Lake trail. You'll find lodgepole-shaded campsites along Lower Twin's east shore both north and south of this junction. Expect vociferous Steller jays and, before late July, voracious mosquitoes. Lower Twin Lake, being relatively shallow, offers pleasant swimming by mid- or late July.

The ½-mile climb up to Rainbow Lake is a pleasant, well-graded one, and from where the trail begins a short descent to the lake's west corner, you could start a 650-foot climb to the summit of Fairfield Peak. You'll find a fairly large campsite by Rainbow Lake's west corner and several more along its east shore. The lake is even shallower than the Twin Lakes, and it offers fine swimming until the wind whips up, usually in mid-afternoon.

From the northeast shore a trail heads northeast 2⅔ miles over to the base of Cinder Cone, this trail being described in Chapter 14.

Another trail, 2.0 miles long, first climbs briefly southeast to a crest, then drops east to a nearby gully before traversing across rolling open terrain. The soil on it is deep and loose, and walking across it is about as tedious as walking along a sandy beach. Everywhere, Bloomer's goldenbush is attempting to stabilize the soil, for this late-blooming sunflower does very well on dry, gravelly flats. As you begin a steep descent

toward Snag Lake, you may encounter two species of gravel-loving wildflowers: cycladenia, with tubular, rose-colored flowers and broad, smooth-edged leaves, and Lobb's nama, with tubular, magenta flowers and narrower, shallowly toothed leaves. Such plants give way to water-loving ones when you cross a creeklet about ¼ mile before a trail junction. The brightly colored, nodding flowers of the crimson columbine are perhaps the most eye-catching.

When you reach Snag Lake's west-shore trail, you can take it ½ mile north to a couple of campsites or continue on your trail, which quickly fades away, out to sites on a peninsula. This west-shore peninsula and the east-shore point opposite it are both part of a recessional moraine, that is, a moraine left at the front of a glacier as it sporadically retreated southward up-canyon. From Snag Lake, either backtrack up your steep route or head over to Cinder Cone and then southwest back up to Rainbow Lake.

Summit Lake to Cluster Lakes

Trailhead Same as for preceding hike.

Distances 3.3 miles (5.3 km) to Little Bear Lake
3.5 miles (5.7 km) to to Big Bear Lake
4.3 miles (6.9 km) to Cluster Lake
4.4 miles (7.1 km) to Silver Lake
4.7 miles (7.6 km) to northernmost Cluster lake
4.9 miles (7.9 km) to Feather Lake
6.6 miles (10.6 km) to Lower Twin Lake
6.8 miles (11.0 km) to Badger Flat
7.2 miles (11.6 km) to Upper Twin Lake
8.8 miles (14.2 km) to Echo Lake
10.8 miles (17.3 km) for entire loop

Trail description As in the preceding hike, climb east, first up a gully and then up a ridge to a junction 1¼ miles from Summit Lake's north-shore campground. The preceding hike goes right here, but this hike goes left, eventually circling clockwise around to this junction. Of course, you can go counterclockwise and visit Echo Lake first, but they you'll have a fairly substantial climb south from Little Bear Lake—not the way to end a hike.

Heading toward Little Bear Lake, we make a gradual climb for ¼ mile, then climb moderately for an equal distance. We top the climb on a rumpled plateau of old lava flows, and here one can start an almost level cross-country route northwest to Hat Mountain, whose eastern base lies about ½ mile away. This cone differs from the park's more famous Cinder Cone in that it is composed mostly of lava flows, not cinders, and these flows are andesite, not basalt.

If you don't visit Hat Mountain, continue northward on the trail, dropping in about ½ mile to a pleasing lakelet. You can camp east of the lakelet or on one of the small flat areas above the lake. Being quite shallow, this lakelet is one of the park's warmest swimming holes. Another ½-mile leg takes us across the rest of the plateau and then, just before a tiny pond, we start a moderate-to-steep descent. Our trail descends a ridge that separates two small, glaciated canyons, then eases its gradient as it approaches shallow Little Bear Lake. It too is a good swimming hole, but the lodgepole-rimmed lake attracts too many mosquitoes until early or mid-August. Campsites are absent, due to lack of level ground. However, two exist near the northeast shore of Big Bear Lake, about 150 feet lower than Little Bear Lake. Though larger, Big Bear Lake also is a shallow lake, and you can wade far out into it.

Beyond Big Bear Lake we have a pleasant ½-mile stroll down to a junction, where our route angles right. You can of course go left and reach the southwest shore of Cluster Lake in about 200 yards. You'll find two or more good campsites by the lake's north end. The northernmost Cluster lake is attractive only until early July, when our trail north to the Bear Lakes is still mottled with snow. By mid-July the northernmost lake drops about one foot and its very shallow western arm disappears entirely, reducing the lake's area by one third. Before mid-July the mosquitoes are very numerous at this lake and all the Cluster Lakes, making them undesirable for most hikers. If you were to continue beyond the northernmost lake, you would cross its ephemeral outlet creek about 0.9 mile be-

yond the last trail junction, recross the creek in a little over ½ mile, and then make an easy, rolling descent for 1.2 miles through a white-fir/lodgepole-pine forest to the Nobles Trail in eastern Badger Flat. Pale-yellow-flowered Christine's lupines grow in abundance, though in places large-leaved mountain mule ears give them stiff competition. See the hike following the next one for information on Nobles' pioneer route.

Back at the junction among the Cluster Lakes, our circular route starts east, quickly crossing Silver Lake's outlet creek, which lasts about as long as snow remains in the vicinity. Shallow Silver Lake, the largest of the Cluster Lakes, has several campsites, but please use only those that are at least 100 feet away from shore and from trail. In the early morning, sunlit Lassen Peak reflects brightly in this lake's dark, placid water.

A low drainage divide separates Silver Lake from Feather Lake, the latter being perhaps the nicest of all the Cluster Lakes. The triangular lake 200 yards north of it is pleasant too, for though it is shallow, it probably has the fewest mosquitoes of any of the Cluster Lakes—an important consideration before late July. By early August all the Cluster Lakes (and the Twin Lakes, ahead) drop about a foot or so, and then a narrow yellow ring of tiny primrose monkey flowers circles each lake. Crest lupines, with their pale blue-violet flowers, are plentiful along our southeast traverse away from the Cluster Lakes. We pass two chest-deep ponds, and in August may notice a few stephanomerias, dainty, narrow-leaved sunflowers having composite flowers made up of 5-12 magenta-colored "petals," each petal being technically a whole flower.

Precisely 1.0 mile beyond Feather Lake we cross Twin Lakes' seasonal creek, which presents a beautiful, diverse wildflower display in mid-July, as usual, at the height of mosquito season. After climbing about 250 yards beyond the creek, we reach an old road, now a section of the Mexico-to-Canada Pacific Crest Trail. On a not-too-scenic section of this often-scenic trail, we traverse ⅓ mile south to the north shore of Lower Twin Lake. Here we branch west along the lake's north shore and take a trail 4.3 miles back to our trailhead—the reverse route of part of this chapter's previous hike.

Dersch Meadows to Cliff Lake

Trailhead   Post 38 on Lassen Park Road, about 0.1 mile west of Summit Lake Ranger Station. If you park at the hikers' lot near the ranger station, add 0.2 mile to the following destinations.

Distances   2.4 miles (3.9 km) to Cliff Lake
2.8 miles (4.5 km) to Shadow Lake
3.2 miles (5.2 km) to Terrace Lake
3.7 miles (6.0 km) to post 27 on Lassen Park Road

Trail description   The shortest route to these three lakes is to take this trail from its upper end, post 27, as described earlier in this chapter. However, until mid- or late July, snow can be a problem from post 27 down to Shadow Lake, and then the route from post 38 may be more desirable. Camping is prohibited at all three lakes.

The trail begins along the southern part of Dersch Meadows, which is a nearly level area of glacier-stream sediments laid down as recently as 9,000 years ago. In a few minutes you start climbing up one of many northeast-descending ridges, each one a glacial moraine. Glaciers flowed mostly northeast past Reading Peak rather than north from it, as one might first expect. For more information on the significance of the moraines you are climbing southwest on, see Chapter 8's Lassen Park Road Log, post 26. For more information on Mt. Tehama, see Chapter 10's Bumpass Hell Nature Trail, posts 1-3.

For almost 2 miles your trail climbs southwest, usually at a moderate grade, and in several places you can stop and enjoy the views north and east of the well-forested Lassen parklands. Symmetrical Hat Mountain is the prominent flat-topped hill seen down-trail. Views disappear and the trail levels before you cross Cliff Lake's outlet creek, about 2.0 miles from your trailhead. You then skirt past the north edge of a boggy meadow, reaching a junction about ¼ mile beyond the creek crossing. Here a lightly used trail strikes south 0.2 mile through a dense forest to cliff-bound, picturesque Cliff Lake, complete with a small island covered by shrubs and conifers.

Though shallow, the lake is one of the park's coldest, for snow patches tarry long around its southern shore.

West from the Cliff Lake spur trail the main trail climbs briefly to a bench, on which you'll immediately see a pond on your right and soon cross a pond-fed creeklet ahead. A short but moderate-to-steep trail stretch follows, taking you up the moraine that hides Shadow Lake. Being exceptionally deep for its size, this lake too is one of the park's coldest, as is beautiful Terrace Lake, just beyond it, whose basin harbors long-lasting snow patches. A moderate-to-steep ½-mile climb from Terrace Lake gets you to post 27 on the Lassen Park Road.

Nobles Trail to Badger Flat and beyond

Trailhead   The start of a closed road along Lassen Park Road, this junction being 0.2 mile northeast of the Park Road's bridge across West Fork Hat Creek. Park at the highway turnout just west of the closed road.

Distances   3.1 miles (4.9 km) to Hat Creek ford
4.1 miles (6.6 km) to Hat Creek horse camp
6.1 miles (9.9 km) to Badger Flat
7.8 miles (12.6 km) to Soap Lake
8.4 miles (13.6 km) to Cluster Lake
9.0 miles (14.5 km) to Silver Lake
13.4 miles (21.6 km) to Cinder Cone, northwest base
14.9 miles (24.0 km) to Butte Lake Ranger Station

Trail description   Most of Nobles' pioneer wagon road through Lassen Park still exists today, and all of it is closed to visitors' motor vehicles. A seldom used three-link section from Manzanita Lake to Lost Creek is described in the hike after the next one, but the bulk of the route, about 14.9 miles, is described here in this hike. This dry, almost lakeless route also receives very little use and therefore is a good one for hikers who perfer solitude over scenery. William H. Nobles, a prospector, discovered this natural route in 1851 when he was returning to his native Minnesota. Realizing it was shorter than and superior to Peter Lassen's pioneer

Top: rockbound Terrace Lake and large, deep Shadow Lake. Middle: Big Bear Lake and Silver La[ke] both shallow and ringed with lodgepoles. Bottom: hiker taking a lunch break beneath a shady bl[ue] cottonwood at Snag Lake's northwest shore.

route of 1847, he decided to secure financial backing to turn his on-paper route into a wagon road. The first emigrants to use it came in late summer 1852, followed by thousands of others until the completion of the transcontinental railroad on May 10, 1869. The route never achieved the popularity of other, more southern routes that led to California's gold fields and/or to western Nevada's silver fields.

Our road descends the Hat Creek drainage, just as a May 19, 1915 mudflow from Lassen Peak did. That mudflow, averaging about ¼-½ mile wide and about 10-20 feet thick, poured down the drainage, obliterating every tree in its way. Consequently, almost all the trees you'll see in the first 4 miles are post-1915 in age. Typically at this elevation, most of the trees are lodgepole pines, for these do very well in pioneering new ground. In time, firs should dominate the route.

After a moderate descent just under ½ mile long, we bridge West Fork Hat Creek, our last permanent trailside water until we ford Hat Creek in 2.6 more miles. Our road north now is almost level, and it stays that way alongmost of the east base of Raker Peak. Up to that base, the predominant roadside shrub is Bloomer's goldenbush, a low, uninteresting bush that most hikers overlook—until late August, that is. Then, it blossoms forth in golden sunflowers, locally painting fields of yellow across the landscape.

Along Raker Peak's east base, a few aspens and Jeffrey pines add diversity to the lodgepole forest, as do Christine's lupine, slender penstemon, coyote mint, pumice paintbrush and catchfly. Near the north end of the east base, the road begins to drop, and it continues to do so for a mile down to Hat Creek, which you ford about ¼ mile below a spur road to the right to some park cabins. Viewless camping is fine in this vicinity on either side of the creek. Keeping your feet dry at the crossing is a real trick until late August, unless you are fortunate enough to find a fallen log.

Once on the east bank, you traverse 0.9 mile north, staying within earshot of the creek but seldom within sight of it. At the end of your nearly level traverse, an old road heads 300 yards west to a fairly large campsite by Hat Creek. The 1915 Lassen

Peak mudflow swept across this site, then continued more than 2½ miles down Hat Creek, stopping in the vicinity of Emigrant Ford, about 9½ miles from the flow's source. The creekside campsite bears the dubious distinction of being the only one in the Lassen Park backcountry at which you can legally camp with horses. You'll see a small horse corral just north-northwest of this road's-end campsite, and from it a horse trail rollercoasters ⅓ mile northeast across glacial moraines to the Pacific Crest Trail.

From the campsite-road junction, we reach the Pacific Coast Trail in a like distance, climbing moderately up the Nobles Trail to some large Jeffrey pines on a small flat. Leaving trail junction and flat behind, we make an equally short climb to the southern base of fault-and-logging-scarred Badger Mountain. This shield volcano, lying just outside the park, was extensively clearcut, but Lassen Park's dense forest hides this unattractive sight from our view.

After about one mile of essentially level walking, we pass a shallow pond just north of the trail. Abundant grasses make visiting ducks vulnerable to predators, such as coyotes, for the grass easily frustrates their attempts to flee. On the other hand, long-legged great blue herons, hunting in the pond for frogs and garter snakes, effortlessly take off at the first sign of danger. You could camp by the pond and use its water in an emergency, but a much better site lies not far ahead. Eastward, you'll quickly come to a saddle from which an old spur trail veers right, dropping 275 yards south to a good campsite near the spring-fed, boggy west end of Badger Flat. In this wet meadow you can expect to find the pink-flowered Oregon checker, the off-white-flowered Newberry's gentian and the dark-blue-violet-flowered hikers' gentian, all fairly uncommon.

Beyond the old spur trail, the Nobles Trail, which also doubles as the Pacific Crest Trail over a 4.5-mile stretch, drops gently to the east end of Badger Flat. Here, by the east bank of a creek that flows through mid-July, a trail, mentioned in the previous hike, begins a 2.6-mile climb to a junction in the hub of the Cluster Lakes area. Our route, still an old road, climbs to a low saddle, then descends to a usually dry creek, encountered about ½ mile past the trail junction. Now skirting along the base of unseen Prospect

Peak, we parallel the creek briefly eastward until its bed fades into obliviion, then we gradually arc southeast over to a meadow harboring extremely shallow Soap Lake. For pioneers, who typically were struggling west along here in late summer, this lake must have been a welcome sight. Being shallow and rather low in elevation, this lake provides acceptably warm swimming even in early July, when most of Lassen Park's lakes still have snow nearby. You won't find any more trailside water until you reach either Lower Twin Lake or Butte Lake.

Precisely 1.0 mile past Soap Lake your road splits, and an old fire road—the Pacific Crest Trail—climbs 3.0 easy miles south to the north shore of Lower Twin Lake while the Nobles Trail traverses 4.3 often sandy miles east to the Butte Lake Ranger Station. The former route is entirely dry except before late June, when you'll cross the trickling Twin Lakes creek, about 0.9 mile along your route. The latter route, continuing its traverse along the base of Prospect Peak, is entirely dry after the snow melts in late spring. The route goes 2.3 miles to the first of three trail junctions near the northwest base of Cinder Cone. Look for mats of squaw carpet along this seldom-used stretch of trail. From the Cinder Cone onward, you are likely to meet up with several dozen hikers. See the Cinder Cone Nature Trail (Chapter 10) for a detailed interpretation of the geology and biology of the Butte Lake-Cinder Cone area.

Paradise Meadow

Trailhead   Post 42 near Lassen Park Road's bridge across West Fork Hat Creek.
Distances   1.4 miles (2.3 km) to Paradise Meadow
2.9 miles (4.6 km) to post 27 on Lassen Park Road

Trail description   No one in his right mind intentionally hikes up this steep trail to its end, for the trail is far easier when hiked in the opposite direction. Nevertheless, determined botanists may find the steep climb to Paradise Meadow worth the effort. The trail's steepness plus the meadow's mosquitoes dampen other people's enthusiasm. The wildflowers should be at their best in early August, about a week or two after those in Dersch Meadows, along the Park Road, have peaked.

Nobles Trail from Manzanita Lake to Lost Creek

Trailhead   Near Manzanita Lake Entrance Station
Distances   0.6 mile (1.0 km) to Summertown site
2.1 miles (3.4 km) to Nobles Pass
3.2 miles (5.2 km) to first crossing of Lassen Park Road
4.4 miles (7.1 km) to second crossing of Lassen Park Road
6.3 miles (10.1 km) to trail's end near Lost Creek

Trail description   Except for Blue Lake Trail, probably no other maintained park trail receives so little use. The reasons are obvious: lack of views and lack of water. History buffs and diehard nature lovers are perhaps the only ones willing to explore this route.

The route starts north along a service road beginning immediately east of the entrance station, and you follow it to its obvious end at the site of Summertown. From it the narrower Nobles Trail strikes east up a gully that separates Table Mountain from Chaos Jumbles, which is a huge rockfall-avalanche that broke loose from Chaos Crags around 1670 A.D. About ½ mile along this stretch of trail, sharp-eyed naturalists may spy two good-sized Douglas-firs, among the few to be seen in the park and certainly living among strange bedfellows—Jeffrey, lodgepole and a few sugar pines. A few white firs quickly appear as we progress eastward. Our gully deadends about a mile past Summertown and our trail switchbacks up around this problem before climbing easily over to ill-defined Nobles Pass. The open Jeffrey-pine forest now becomes a shadier forest of increasing white firs as we descend moderately to touch the Lassen Park Road, then cross it 0.3 mile later. You'll find the second stretch of the Nobles Trail beginning about 45 yards down the road.

The second stretch, just 1.2 miles long, starts among white firs but quickly reaches brushy slopes dominated by greenleaf manzanita and tobacco brush, both attempting to overgrow the trail. You re-enter forest just before reaching a shady flat and, near an ephemeral creeklet, you may be fortunate enough to see tiny, ankle-high western prince's pines, evergreen members of the wintergreen family. You now walk an almost level ½ mile through a mature forest of white firs and Jeffrey, ponderosa and sugar pines.

When you come to the Park Road, about 0.1 mile southeast of Lost Creek Organization Campground, walk southeast about 200 yards to the resumption of the Nobles Trail. This last stretch, about 1.8 miles along a closed, gravelly and/or sandy service road, is the least inviting. It climbs just over one mile to a spur road down to Lost Creek, then continues for about ¾ mile to where its tread is obliterated by the Lassen Park Road, this point being about ¼ mile north of the road's bridge across Lost Creek.

Chaos Crags Trail

Trailhead In Manzanita Lake area. From the Manzanita Lake Entrance Station drive ½ mile east to the Manzanita Lake Campground road and take it 200 yards to a bend where the road curves across Manzanita Creek. The trailhead is ⅓ mile before the campground's entrance station.

Distance 2.2 miles (3.5 km) to Crags Lake

Trail description Starting up Manzanita Creek, the Chaos Crags Trail passes through a noble forest of mature Jeffrey pines. To your left are the boarded cabins of Manzanita Lake Lodge, closed in 1974 because of an identified rockfall-avalanche threat from Chaos Crags. White firs, greenleaf manzanitas and tobacco brush appear before we cross a low glacial moraine and lose sight of Manzanita Creek. This moraine was left by a glacier perhaps 10,000 to 15,000 years ago, evidently just before Lassen Peak arose. As we traverse north through a shady forest, we cross low, rolling moraines that are much older, probably around 50,000 years old.

Along our shady traverse going ⅓ mile north from Manzanita Creek, a creeklet and then a spring provide fresh drinking water. Take advantage of them, for the water of Crags Lake leaves a lot to be desired. Past the spring our trail bends east and climbs along the forested south edge of Chaos Jumbles. After ½ mile, the trail's gradient steepens, climbing ¼ mile to a switchback that directs our efforts southwest. From where the trail

switchbacks east again, a spur trail goes a few yards out to a viewpoint—a good rest stop—and from here you can survey the lands to the west.

With less than ½ mile of trail to ascend, you now climb moderately through an open forest with a pleasing balance of conifers and evergreen shrubs. Red firs, western white pines, chinquapins and pinemat manzanitas are now common, and lodgepole pines appear just before you reach a ridge above Chaos Crater, the pit that holds dimunitive Crags Lake. From the ridge you get your best views of the steep, intimidating talus slopes of Chaos Crags and of relatively flat-topped Table Mountain, which is about 2 miles to the northwest. Three northwest-trending faults strike across Table Mountain: one on the west side of its east summit, one just east of the summit, and one at the east base of the mountain. The rocks on the east side of each fault have been uplifted with respect to those on the west side. Standing 12 miles from you, above and to the right of Table Mountain's east summit, are the clustered peaks of Thousand Lakes Wilderness, notably Magee, Crater and Fredonyer peaks. These, like Lassen Park's Brokeoff Mountain and Mt. Diller, are parts of the rim of an old 9000-foot-high volcano that has been largely dissected by glaciers.

Much closer to you lies Chaos Jumbles, a series of rockfall-avalanches that broke loose from Chaos Crags about 1670 A.D., each crashing swiftly downslope to lap against the lower slopes of Table Mountain. Lily Pond and Reflection Lake developed in large hollows in this debris, and Manzanita Lake was dammed behind the Jumbles' south edge. The Jumbles extend about ¾ mile west of the Highways 44/89 junction and about 3½ miles from the source area by Chaos Crater. Each flow, averaging better than 100 miles per hour, took only 2 minutes to traverse this distance. See Chapter 8's Lassen Park Road Log, posts 62 and 63 for more information on Chaos Jumbles and Chaos Crags.

Before you start a short, steep descent to murky Crags Lake, you might search for two relatively uncommon wildflowers sometimes seen growing along your rocky edge. They are ballhead ipomopsis, a small, prostrate plant with a globe of white miniature flowers, and shaggy hawkweed, an equally small, though rather upright, plant with hairy leaves and tiny yellow sunflowers. On unstable slopes above the "lake" you'll see the usual assortment of talus-slope wildflowers such as coyote mint, Davis' knotweed, silver-leaved lupine, pumice paintbrush, granite gilia, and one or more species of buckwheat.

With minor rockfalls occurring almost daily on the very steep slopes above Crags Lake, it is no wonder that from 1950 to 1980 the size of Crags Lake has been cut in half. At this rate the shallow lake could entirely disappear by or just after the turn of the century.

Manzanita Creek Trail

Trailhead   At the beginning of Manzanita Lake Campground's southernmost loop, Loop F. The campground's road begins from Lassen Park Road ½ mile east of the Manzanita Lake Entrance Station. Since no parking space is available at the trailhead, walk from your campsite or else park near the camp's store, about 0.4 mile down the road.
Distances   2.2 miles (3.5 km) to Manzanita Creek
3.5 miles (5.6 km) to trail's end
Trail description   This lighly used route dates back to summer 1925, when Benjamin Loomis and others built this narrow road up to the base of Crescent Cliff, then built a 2-mile foot trail that climbed over 3000 feet to the summit of Lassen Peak. This trail, averaging about 30% in grade, was twice as steep as today's Lassen Peak Trail, and it fell into disuse in the 1930s after that trail was completed. Today the old road serves as a fire road and as a hiking path. Lacking views and lakes, this route appeals to those who like exercise, solitude or wildflowers.

The narrow road climbs 160 yards to a broad trail, ⅔ mile long, that starts west before curving north along the campground's west edge as it gently descends to the south tip of Manzanita Lake. For about the first ⅓ mile your road, the Manzanita Creek Trail, climbs moderately through an extensive, dense cover of greenleaf manzanitas, gradually being replaced with Jeffrey pines and white firs by the time your trail crosses to the west side of a steep-sided gully. Your route switchbacks out of this gully, then climbs

moderately for 0.4 mile before the grade slackens. You now have a pleasant ½-mile climb to a notch in a ridge—a glacial moraine—which extends down-canyon almost to the Lassen Park Road. The glacier that left this ridge disappeared perhaps just before Lassen Peak erupted onto the scene, possibly about 11,000 years ago.

Beyond the notch you have an equally pleasant ¼-mile climb over to the road's bridging of Manzanita Creek. Gravel-loving wildflowers blossom in the dry soils along this open-forest stretch, the commonest ones being silver-leaved lupine, coyote mint, slender penstemon and pumice paintbrush. Locally, scarlet gilia will certainly catch your eye, while plain, dainty King's sandwort usually goes unnoticed. In shadier spots, white hawkweed, pinedrops and white-veined wintergreen may get your attention.

The vegetation momentarily shifts to water-loving species as we cross Manzanita Creek, then resumes its typical forest-understory species. Red firs are common, and on specimens with swollen branches you can expect to find drab western dwarf-mistletoes growing on the swellings. Look on the branches still having green needles if you want to see these miniature, scalelike parasites.

About 2.9 miles from the trailhead we reach our first meadow, roughly at 6900 feet elevation. We then hike past, close to, or through meadow vegetation until the trail becomes completely inundated by wildflowers in a large meadow below the northeast face of Loomis Peak. You should see several robust species of meadow wildflowers, corn lilies being by far the most common. Also look for large-leaved lupine, monk's hood, arrowhead butterweed, many-flowered stickseed and cow parsnip. Species thigh-high or less are too numerous to mention, but consult the wildflower photographs in the botany chapter to identify many of them. In the upper reaches of the meadow—say, at the base of Crescent Cliff—you may find the park's only good sized monkey flower with pink flowers, Lewis' monkey flower. Somewhat common in the High Sierra and very common in the Cascades of Oregon and Washington, this knee-high species is a rare find in the Lassen area.

A fair number of hikers, starting from Lassen Peak Trail's trailhead, head west cross-country over to boggy-shored Soda Lake, then traverse north to the saddle at the foot of Vulcans Castle. From it they drop north into the meadows of upper Manzanita Creek—our route. This route is an excellent one for scenery and for wildflowers, for in early August you should be able to see 50 or more easily identifiable species in bloom. Snow can hamper your efforts before mid-July. Should you take this route, be forewarned, for you can easily descend Blue Lake Canyon by mistake, ending up far away from your intended destination, Manzanita Lake Campground.

Top: Lassen Peak, viewed from a portion of Hat Creek terrain that was buried in a May 1915 mudflow. All the trees in view—lodgepoles—have grown since that date. Middle: Chaos Jumbles, Table Mountain and, above it, summits of Thousand Lakes Wilderness. Bottom: Chaos Crags and snowy Lassen Peak, viewed from Reflection Lake.

Manzanita Lake

Trailhead The Manzanita Lake Picnic Area is the best of several starting points, since it has a large parking lot, shoreline picnic tables and nearby rest rooms. This parking lot is along the lake's southeast shore, and you'll find it immediately to the right of and below the entrance to the Manzanita Lake Campground. The campground road leaves Lassen Park Road ½ mile east of the Manzanita Lake Entrance Station, which is another possible starting point.

Distance 1.5 miles (2.4 km) for entire loop

Trail description You can start this loop in either direction from the picnic area, from the entrance station, or from a campground trail ending at the lake's southernmost tip. The trail hugs the shoreline except for a ⅓-mile stretch north from the picnic area. This begins at the north end of the picnic area's parking lot, and from it you start north on a broad trail that once was a road. In about 90 yards you'll reach a grove of Pacific willows, the park's largest specimens. Turn right and go north another 90 yards to a bridge over Manzanita Creek, then turn left and go west 130 yards on an abandoned road to where the shoreline trail branches left from it. This route is more obvious in the clockwise direction.

In addition to Pacific willows, which are giants in the willow family, you'll also see large specimens of Scouler's willows, recognized by their smooth bark. The common, shrubby willow growing here and in most wet places in the park is Lemmon's willow. Another willow-family member is the black cottonwood, which has deeply furrowed bark like the Pacific willow, but has rather broad leaves. Mountain alders complete the complement of deciduous, water-loving shrubs and trees. Juxtaposed against such vegetation is an open, west-shore Jeffrey-pine forest with a few white firs and sugar

pines and much green manzanita and tobacco brush. A white-fir/lodgepole-pine forest prevails along the east and southeast shores.

This combination of vegetation groups coupled with shady, sunny, marshy and lake environments, makes the Manzanita Lake area extremely rich in habitats. In fact, of the nine habitats listed at the start of Chapter 7's bird checklist, only one habitat—cliffs, etc.—is missing. The Manzanita Lake area is the park's best area for birders. On any summer day you can expect to see about three dozen common species in, above or near the lake.

Manzanita Lake came into existence about 1670 A.D. when Chaos Jumbles broke loose from Chaos Crags and dammed Manzanita Creek. Thus a new habitat—still water—was formed, and several aquatic plants somehow managed to get established in this habitat. In midsummer the most prominent species is water smartweed, which sprouts thumb-sized clusters of tiny pink flowers, particularly in the shallow water of the lake's east end. (This plant has been mistakenly called lady's thumb, a nonnative, low-elevation plant not found in the Lassen area.) Spiked water-milfoil is another common, though reclusive, lake "wildflower." Its flowers are inconspicuous, but the plant is recognized by its hairlike leaves, which grow in whorls on rising, underwater stems.

Manzanita Lake's volume was substantially increased after the addition of a low dam in 1912. However, mudslides generated by Lassen Peak's 1915 eruptions brought tons of sediments into the lake, substantially reducing its volume. Trout have been introduced into the lake and today it is one of a few park lakes that are still stocked. Swimmers find the lake's water relatively cold considering the shallowness of the lake and its relatively low elevation. However, the lake apparently gets a lot of its water from cold groundwater seeping into it.

12 Lassen Park Trails: Drakesbad Area

Introduction The Drakesbad area is a compact one; you could cover all its trails in four easy day hikes. This would not include the trail from Warner Valley to Mt. Harkness—this chapter's first hike—which really doesn't fit well into either Chapter 12 or Chapter 13. The Drakesbad area trails, though sometimes steep, are relatively short, and they tend to create an aura of unhurriedness. Due to the area's relatively low elevation, its summer days are quite warm, and this heat too discourages strenuous activity. Visitors at the park-owned Drakesbad Guest Ranch bask in the sun or soak in its thermal pool—which unfortunately is open to guests only. But campers and day visitors can also experience this area's ambience of tranquility, particularly in the early morning or in the evening. Then, watch the beavers in Dream Lake; stroll through the meadows and observe the grazing deer and busy marmots; listen to the chorus of Hot Springs Creek and the birds feeding in its nearby foliage.

The trails divide into six hikes, the last one open-ended and continuing, literally, for hundreds of miles. The first, from Warner Valley to Mt. Harkness, is justifiably the least popular. It is not recommended, and it is included here simply because it exists. The peak's summit is more easily attained from Juniper Lake Campground (see the next chapter's first hike). The second hike includes the Boiling Springs Lake Nature Trail, which is the Drakesbad area's most popular hike. It also describes the trails to Terminal Geyser and Little Willow Lake. The third makes a loop to Devils Kitchen, which, like Boiling Springs Lake, has an assortment of hydrothermal activity that bubbles, steams, hisses, belches and thumps away. These two hydrothermal areas resemble the considerably more popular Bumpass Hell area, but each has its own special attractions. A fourth hike goes up a very steep trail to Drake Lake, which is a swimming hole that leaves hikers with mixed feelings. Fish are absent, so leave your pole at camp. The fifth hike climbs to Sifford Lake and to Kings Creek Cascades and Falls. Sifford Lake is the area's only good swimming lake, and it is more easily reached from the Lassen Park Road (see Chapter 11). Finally, the last hike, along the Pacific Crest Trail, climbs north from the Warner Valley Campground, and it offers you a variety of side trails; you are limited only by your time and imagination. Botanists will find this last trail particularly rewarding if they hike it in July.

Mt. Harkness
from Warner Valley

Trailhead   From the north part of Chester, head west out of town on Feather River Drive. In ⅔ mile your paved road branches left and you continue on it for almost 5½ miles to a junction from where your road angles north while a road ahead goes to Domingo Spring Campground. Drive 10 miles north to Warner Valley Campground. Northbound, you cross Warner Creek after 3.0 miles, then in 3.4 more miles, at a bend along a shady stretch, you reach this hike's trailhead. It is easily missed. Your road's pavement gives way to a graded surface at a prominent road fork, 0.8 mile up-canyon. Use that fork as a reference point if you go too far.

Distances   2.8 miles (4.5 km) to south tip of Juniper Lake
4.0 miles (6.4 km) to Mt. Harkness summit

Trail description   As stated in this chapter's introduction, this little-used trail is not recommended. This overly steep trail is used mainly by private landowners in Warner Valley and residents in the Lake Almanor area who ride horses up it, sparing them the effort. Your net elevation gain is about 2775 feet along this trail versus 1235 along the shorter trail from Juniper Lake Campground (first hike of the next chapter). In the park, no other trail climbs as much. Even in late spring, when the Juniper Lake road is still snowed in, the author finds hiking up that road preferable to this steep, often bushy trail. The trail's few pluses are: fair views of Lassen Peak, a grove of Scouler's willows (these more easily seen on the nature trail at post 10), and an appreciation for how high Mt. Harkness, a volcano, stands above a faulted, severely glaciated valley.

Boiling Springs Lake,
Terminal Geyser and
Little Willow Lake

Trailhead   See first hike's trailhead for directions to Warner Valley Campground. Just past the campground's western limit, turn left on a short spur road that goes over to a picnic area with a trailhead.

Distances   0.9 mile (1.4 km) to Boiling Springs Lake
2.3 miles (3.6 km) for entire nature trail, round trip
2.8 miles (4.5 km) to Terminal Geyser
3.4 miles (5.5 km) to Little Willow Lake

Trail description   See Chapter 10's self-guiding Boiling Springs Lake Nature Trail for a detailed description of the first part of this hike. In short, the trail starts west along the north bank of Hot Springs Creek, soon bridges it, then continues up the south bank to two junctions, one immediately beyond the other. From the first a trail leads to other trails going to Drakesbad Guest Ranch, Dream Lake and Devils Kitchen. From the second a trail leads to other trails going to Drake Lake and Devils Kitchen. Just before these junctions you'll pass above the resort's hot pool, which is strictly for guests only. Other facilities are open to the public, though meals are sometimes unavailable; make reservations in advance.

The nature trail then climbs ¼ mile to a junction, from which you have a choice of two equal-length routes to Boiling Springs Lake, Terminal Geyser and Little Willow Lake. If you're on horseback you should take the eastern (left) route. Hikers can choose either. The author prefers the western route, the one the nature trail follows. This trail climbs above the lake, crosses a usually dry inlet channel, then immediately reaches a junction. The nature trail heads north down to Boiling Springs Lake's northeast side, but if you're heading to Terminal Geyser or Little Willow Lake, you start southeast up through a stately fir-and-pine forest, climbing for just over ¾ mile before topping a crest and descending a bit over ½ mile to a reunion with the eastern trail.

If you take the eastern trail, you climb ¼ mile to the nature trail, which you meet above the north shore of Boiling Springs Lake. You walk but a few yards up the nature trail before forking left and taking a horse trail that ascends a southeast-climbing ridge for almost a mile before crossing over an east-west ridge and descending almost ½ mile to a junction with the western trail.

Along this descent you'll pass through several acres of mountain mule ears, these leafy sunflowers producing a pleasant, subtle aroma. A fairly recent fault runs between the eastern and western trails, extending From Drakesbad southeast up a gully to Boiling Springs Lake, then up a longer gully to the east-west ridge and finally down to Terminal Geyser and beyond.

Just 25 yards past the reunion of the two trails, we reach another junction. Continue downslope for Terminal Geyser; veer right for Little Willow Lake. You reach a road going to Terminal Geyser after a ¼-mile descent. Midway along this descent you'll meet a spur trail that goes east to a nearby overlook of the Terminal Geyser bowl, but the geyser is better viewed from below. Therefore, follow the road north 180 yards to the roaring geyser, at road's end. Continually churning out steam, it is technically a fumarole, not a geyser. Observe it with caution. On the broad area at road's end you'll see a capped well, drilled in 1978 by Phillips Petroleum Company, which was doing geothermal exploration. Tapping the underground steam for power would have led to the geyser's demise, so in 1980 the Park Service condemned this bit of private inholding.

Where your trail ended at the road you might have noticed that it continued downslope from the road's opposite side. This rarely-used segment descends 0.7 mile to the northern edge of Willow Lake meadow. The park boundary is not much farther, and private land lies immediately beyond it.

The trail to Little Willow Lake is a 1.0-mile segment of the Pacific Crest Trail. This trail, stretching from the Mexican border to the Canadian border, is usually well graded. But rather than contour from the junction over to the lake, the trail was built over a ridge, giving you about 200 feet to climb, both going and coming. One hopes the segment will someday be rerouted. Little Willow Lake is deficient in willows, but through July is replete with mosquitoes. The lake is better described as a wet marsh, and by late summer the lake dries up altogether. The lake's muddy basin tends to fascinate only diehard naturalists, and here one could do a serious study on the impact of nonnative vegetation on native fauna and flora.

Devils Kitchen and Dream Lake

Trailhead See the first hike's trailhead for directions to Warner Valley Campground. Just past the campground's western limit, turn left on a short spur road that goes over to a picnic area with a trailhead.

Distances 0.7 mile (1.1 km) to Dream Lake
2.3 miles (3.8 km) to Devils Kitchen via north trail
2.9 miles (4.7 km) to Devils Kitchen via south trail
5.3 miles (8.5 km) for Devils Kitchen loop

Trail description First we go just over ⅓ mile along the first part of the Boiling Springs Lake Nature Trail, passing its first nine trailside posts. Consult Chapter 10 for a detailed explanation of the features seen at each post. Just past a view of the Drakesbad Guest Ranch hot pool (for guests only), we meet a junction. The north-trail route begins here, branching right. If you take this hike's described loop, you'll return on the south-trail route, which comes in at a junction only 20 yards up the nature trail.

Branching right, we wander down to the bank of Hot Springs Creek, where the trail splits into a footpath left and a horse trail right, both reuniting at a bridge over the creek. From the other side of the creek, two trails strike northeast to the park-owned complex of Drakesbad Guest Ranch. The right trail goes to the central building, with the resort's office; the left goes to the resort's stables. Hikers starting at the resort can subtract 0.4 mile (0.6 km) from this hike's first two distances, 0.1 mile (0.2 km) from its third, and 0.5 mile (0.8 km) from its last.

You now start west through a beautiful meadow that often has deer grazing in it in the early morning and in the evening. About 175 yards from the resort junction you'll see a tread that strikes 40 yards south to a bridge, up which you can then continue 140 yards to man-made, beaver-maintained Dream Lake. The best chances for seeing beaver are in the early morning or in the evening. This small, shallow, artificial lake is trout-stocked. Being spring-fed, the lake is not as warm as one would expect, given its size and its relatively low elevation. Nevertheless, it is an acceptable swimming hole, particularly for

hikers denied the use of the resort's hot pool. As one can quickly discover, Hot Springs Creek is very c-c-cold, usually in the low 50s.

From the Dream Lake spur trail, the north Devils Kitchen trail continues through the Drakesbad meadow. You'll see marmot burrows along this open traverse and perhaps see the chubby rodents themselves. The marmots either burrow into high spots in the meadow or else under logs—very atypical marmot dwelling sites. Marmots usually make their burrows in rock piles, such as talus slopes, but here in this meadow there are none. Our trail at last bends right, climbing a few feet to higher ground, then traversing ¼ mile to a junction with the south trail, our return route. West, our forested route climbs almost a mile to the edge of Devils Kitchen, passing a small meadow just before reaching the hydrothermal area. The trail then makes a short descent to a trail fork. Here you can go either way, for the trail makes a loop and will return you to this spot. Stay on the trail, for some parts of Devils Kitchen can be quite dangerous. You could be severely burned if you broke through a section of thin crust that had boiling water beneath it.

Unlike Boiling Springs Lake, Bumpass Hell or the Sulphur Works, Devils Kitchen has a substantial stream flowing right through its middle, Hot Springs Creek taking advantage of the soft, easily erodible, decayed rock. This icy stream cascades into the basin, leaving it at its east end only a few degrees warmer. Unlike other hydrothermal areas, Devils Kitchen has a considerable amount of vegetation growing in its basin. Among the vegetation you'll see incense-cedars together with Labrador teas, an unusual combination. Here, around 6450 feet elevation, the tree is at the top of its elevation range, while the shrub is at the bottom of its range. You can recognize the "cedar" (not a true cedar) by its scale-like leaves (there's a large specimen at post nine of the nature trail). You can recognize the tea by its small, shiny leaves, which, if you rub between your fingers, will give them a strong turpentine odor. On your loop trail through Devils Kitchen, you'll see fumaroles and mud pots.

For an understanding of hydrothermal activity, read numbers 22-31 of the Bumpass Hell Nature Trail and numbers 24-29 of the Boiling Springs Lake Nature Trail.

After your tour through the area, return to the trail junction, branch right, and strike south across forested terrain. You'll jump across an alder-lined creek about 130 yards before coming to wider Hot Springs Creek, lined with alders and aspens. Look for a nearby log to cross on, or be prepared to get wet feet or backtrack to the north-trail route.

From the creek the south-trail route climbs to a junction with a steep, 0.9-mile trail to the north end of Drake Lake. The following hike describes this route as well as the scenery we'll see along our south-trail route back to our starting point. Briefly, our trail goes east for a little over one mile, curving down the usually dry Boiling Springs Lake outlet creek and then almost immediately reaching a junction with the nature trail. You descend it 20 yards to another junction, and if you came from the resort you veer left, but if you came from the start of the nature trail you veer right.

Drake Lake

Trailhead See the first hike's trailhead for directions to Warner Valley Campground. Just past the campground's western limit, turn left on a short spur road that goes over to a picnic area with a trailhead.

Distances 2.3 miles (3.7 km) to Drake Lake
4.1 miles (6.6 km) to park boundary

Trail description Drake Lake, about 4 feet deep on the Fourth of July and about half that by Labor Day, leaves something to be desired—more depth. Before mid-August, however, it can be suitable for those who want a warm, oversized wading pond. Too shallow to sustain trout, the lake is barren, though if one is interested in water fleas—almost microscopic branchiopods—the lake has about 100 million of them. These tiny, reddish crustaceans feed on even smaller, truly microscopic life forms, filtering out

Left: Mt. Harkness above the Drakesbad meadow. Barren slopes in Devils Kitchen. A capped well near Terminal Geyser. A cautious deer, lower left, in a meadow by Drakesbad Guest Ranch.

protozoans, algae and even bacteria from the lake water they ingest. Evidently, there are a lot of these protists in the water. So the lake has a questionable attraction, and the trail to it is certainly overly steep. So who visits it? Usually uninformed hikers, who are looking forward to a trout dinner, and horseback riders from the resort, who are letting their beasts of burden do all the work. For a more attractive lake, take the next hike up to Sifford Lake.

If you're not deterred by the preceding paragraph or are taking the first part of the Drake Lake trail over toward Devils Kitchen, then read on. As in the previous hike we go a little over ⅓ mile along the first part of the Boiling Springs Lake Nature trail, passing its first nine trailside posts, mentioned under that trail's description in Chapter 10. We reach a junction, climb left 20 yards to a second junction, and then branch right, leaving the nature trail. Folks coming from the Drakesbad Guest Ranch head southwest 0.1 mile to a junction by a bridge, then cross the bridge and take one of two soon-uniting trails over to the nature trail and head up it 20 yards.

In less than a minute we cross Boiling Springs Lake's usually dry creek bed, then climb up alongside it, at one point almost touching the nature trail on the opposite bank. The trail's gradient then eases as it climbs southwest to the first of many spring-fed creeklets we'll see. Most, however, are fed by springs just below the trail, not above it, which is fortunate, for otherwise we'd have to do a lot of plowing through alder groves. Where you cross the first creeklet, look for Sierra corydalis, a spreading, water-loving plant that superficially resembles a large lupine. But if you look closely at its erect rows of pale-pink flowers, you'll see that they resemble those of larkspurs and, like those wildflowers, are members of the buttercup family.

You pass a few giant aspens before crossing a smaller creeklet, then your trail rolls through a shady white-fir forest, providing you with occasional views of the spring-fed Drakesbad meadow below. After a ⅔-mile traverse, you reach a junction from which a trail departs north for Hot Springs Creek and Devils Kitchen, the latter being 1½ miles from the junction.

Folks bent on Drake Lake continue west soon to start a steep, open climb—one that you won't want to make on a hot afternoon. Midway up the trail you have opportunities to scan the countryside as you rest along the trail's switchbacks. But the steep section really isn't all that long, and as you re-enter forest cover, your trail's grade slackens. The lodgepole-rimmed lake is now about ¼ mile distant, and you reach it in minutes. The trail continues around the lake's west shore, then beyond it over an amorphous pass to die out just beyond the park's boundary. Campsites along the lake are few and small. It would be nice if trail would be built west from this lake over to Twin Meadows, enabling backpackers to make a loop to Crumbaugh and Sifford lakes, as they once could when an old, abandoned trail went up Rice Creek. At present, the trail beyond the lake (and some would say the trail up to it) is not worth taking.

Sifford Lake and Kings Creek Falls

Trailhead   See the first hike's trailhead for directions to Warner Valley Campground

Distances   3.0 miles (4.8 km) to Bench Lake
3.3 miles (5.4 km) to Sifford Lake
3.7 miles (5.9 km) to Kings Creek Falls
4.9 miles (7.8 km) to Lassen Park Road via Bench Lake and Kings Creek Falls
5.5 miles (8.8 km) to Lassen Park Road via Sifford Lake and ridge trail
9.4 miles (15.1 km) for Bench Lake-Kings Creek Falls Sifford Lake loop

Trail description   Sifford Lake, Bench Lake, Kings Creek Falls and Kings Creek Cascades lie closer to the Lassen Park Road than to Drakesbad. Therefore, if you're concerned about the shortest route with the least elevation change, take the trail starting from the Park Road (see Chapter 11). That hike requires only half the energy this one does.

This hike begins in the northeast corner of the Warner Valley Campground, which is your last opportunity for water until you reach Bench Lake, Sifford Lake or Kings

Creek. The climb can be hot and sunny if you get a late start. Our trail no sooner begins than it crosses a creeklet fed by a spring that flows from the base of the canyon wall we are about to climb. The trail soon switchbacks and then makes a very well-graded ascent northwest across lava flows. We get increasingly better views of the Drakesbad area until we enter a fir forest and shortly arrive at a junction.

One mile from the trailhead, we leave the northbound Pacific Crest Trail and branch left for a 1.6-mile climb, the trail staying mostly on or close to the crest of a lateral moraine left by a larger Warner Valley glacier. See Chapter 8's Lassen Park Road Log, post 26, for the significance of the glacial deposits in this upper Kings Creek drainage. Though our westward climb is always close to the brink of the Hot Springs Creek canyon, we get surprisingly few views, due to a dense stand of white and red firs. Westward, the firs yield to Jeffrey pines and to a lot of shrubs, particularly greenleaf manzanitas and tobacco brush.

Just beyond an open knoll, we make a slight descent to a junction in a shallow bowl. From it a trail forks right to Bench Lake, Kings Creek Falls and Kings Creek Cascades, while the main trail continues ahead ⅓ mile to a spur trail that goes over to warm, pleasing Sifford Lake, a good swimming hole. If you want to visit all these features, start first toward disappointing Bench Lake and plan to visit the falls between 10 a.m. and noon, when they are bathed in sunlight. Then climb up past Kings Creek Cascades to Lower Kings Creek Meadow and descend the main trail to the Sifford Lake cutoff. In the afternoon the lake offers excellent swimming—as well as your last drink. See Chapter 11's "Kings Creek Falls and Sifford Lake" hike for details.

Pacific Crest Trail, Drakesbad north to Lower Twin Lake

Trailhead See the first hike's trailhead for directions to Warner Valley Campground.
Distances 2.4 miles (3.8 km) to Corral Meadow

4.8 miles (7.8 km) to Summit Lake's south campground
6.7 miles (10.8 km) to Swan Lake
7.2 miles (11.6 km) to Lower Twin Lake
7.7 miles (12.4 km) to Rainbow Lake
7.8 miles (12.5 km) to Horseshoe Lake Ranger Station
11.6 miles (18.6 km) to Soap Lake
13.2 miles (21.3 km) to Badger Flat
15.3 miles (24.7 km) to park's north boundary

Trail description The Pacific Crest Trail, extending from the Mexican border to the Canadian border, slices through Lassen Park. This chapter's "PCT" hike goes only to Lower Twin Lake, just 7.2 miles of the trail's approximate 2600 miles. Few park visitors would want to hike farther than the lake from the Drakesbad trailhead; those who do should consult Chapter 11 ("Nobles Trail to Badger Flat and beyond") for the park's northern PCT, Chapter 18 for PCT segments north of the park, and Chapter 15 for PCT segments south of Drakesbad.

The northbound Pacific Crest Trail begins in the northeast corner of the Warner Valley Campground, crossing a spring-fed creeklet in less than 40 yards. The trail soon switchbacks and then makes a very well-graded ascent northwest across lava flows, one thick flow forming a prominent band of nearly vertical cliffs. We started in a forest of white firs, Jeffrey pines, incense-cedars and sugar pines, and when we re-enter forest higher up, the two last species are no longer with us.

Until that re-entry, we have some fair views of the Drakesbad area, and we pass some drought-resistant vascular plants. Among the most persistent are two penstemons: mountain pride, with crimson-colored flowers, and derived penstemon, with bluish flowers. The tiny, very common Torrey's monkey flower makes a brief display with its pink flowers, as does the fork-toothed ookow, with tight clusters of blue-violet flowers. These four species have tubular flowers. Dry, rocky habitats also suit many ferns, though we tend to think these vascular plants love only shade and moisture. Along your dry ascent you may see

Sierra cliff-brake, Indian's dream (another cliff-brake), imbricate sword fern (a dwarf variety of the shade-loving lowland species) and Eaton's shield fern (also known as rock sword-fern). Shrubs you may see are snow bush, which is never common anywhere in its range, and huckleberry oak, which is the dominant shrub of the Sierra's mid-elevations. In Lassen Park, however, it is rare, being restricted to the sunny slopes of Hot Springs Creek canyon and of Warner Valley.

We gradually leave the cliff escarpment and ease into a fir forest, shortly arriving at a junction. The trail branching left gives way to others climbing to Bench Lake, Sifford Lake, Kings Creek Falls and the Lassen Park Road (see previous hike). As we continue upward, white firs disappear, red firs become dominant, and western white pines join them. Our trail crosses the western part of Flatiron Ridge, which is composed of relatively flat layers of lava flows topped with glacial sediments. The lava flows in turn lie atop some of the park's oldest rocks, these being about 1 to 2 million years old.

From the crest of a moraine we wander down the gullied north slopes of Flatiron Ridge, and arrive at a trail junction at the outskirts of Corral Meadow. Here, a trail takes off down Kings Creek, crossing it in 2.0 miles, then leaving the park 1.4 miles later. This infrequently used trail is definitely worth taking to the creek crossing, for you get some pretty impressive views of the Kings Creek gorge. Immediately before the ford you'll traverse a broad, flat steam terrace with a good campsite. Kings Creek can be cold, deep and swift in its June runoff, making a ford of it quite dangerous. But you wouldn't want to continue down-canyon anyway, for the trail is poorly maintained. Beyond the park boundary it tends to die out, reaching a road—one of several in the area—in about 200 yards.

This hike's route, the Pacific Crest Trail, leaves the lower Kings Creek trail and quickly crosses two seasonal creeks. In the second one, which is the more persistent of the two, you may see American brooklimes, veronicas having violet-colored flowers. Whereas most veronicas grow close to water,

this species actually grows in it. About ¼ mile past the last junction we arrive at another junction in the midst of a plethora of campsites. Perhaps no other area in the Lassen Park backcountry receives such heavy use, not even the official backcounty campground by the Horseshoe Lake Ranger Station. Summit Lake is only about 2½ miles away along the trail climbing left from the junction.

From the spacious west-bank campsites our trail crosses to the east bank of Kings Creek—definitely a wet ford. But in 1980 there was a log bridge about 35 yards upstream, providing a dry crossing. From that log you then headed down to the trail's resumption—though a misleading de facto trail continues upstream, leading hikers astray. The trail goes a bit over 100 yards to the confluence where Grassy Swale and Summit creeks become Kings Creek. You can find an additional campsite in this vicinity. Immediately above the confluence, Grassy Swale creek noisily cascades 30 feet down into a small, shallow pool, which in turn spills into a deeper one—this one a cozy, if chilly, swimming hole.

In July the stretch of trail from Corral Meadow northeast through Grassy Swale rivals or surpasses Grassy Creek and the Cluster Lakes in mosquito density. If you're not interested in wildflowers, you'll want to hurry through this area as quickly as possible. Long pants and long-sleeved shirts are a definite asset. But if flowers interest you, you'll find dozens of species ranging from miniature plants, such as Macloskey's violet, primrose monkey flower and round-leaved sundew, up to robust ones, such as arrowhead butterweed, many flowered stickseed and large-leaved lupine. Consult the botany chapter for photographs and characteristics of many of the plants you'll see along this stretch.

From Corral Meadow our trail makes an initial climb, then wanders through a variable red-fir forest, arriving after one mile at a small, wet meadow—an excellent hunting ground for smaller wildflowers, such as those just mentioned. We loop around its south border and then, about ⅓ mile beyond it, we log-cross or boulder-hop Grassy Swale

Left, above: Lower Twin Lake. Below: sedges (left) and rushes (right) make up a lot of the "grasses" seen in Grassy Swale.

creek. Here is another good spot for botanizing, with a good number of average-sized
wildflowers present, such as common dandelion, wandering daisy and Gray's lovage.
Also nearby are two of the park's less common shrubs, Jepson's willow and the quite
rare purple-flowered honeysuckle.

More wildflower treats lie ahead, for
though we stay close to the creek for the next
⅓ mile, we're just far enough above its bank
to be on dry, gravelly soil. A different set of
flowers thrives in this soil, such as whitneya,
California butterweed and white hawkweed—all sunflowers. The creekside large-
leaved lupine gives way to Christine's and
silver-leaved lupines, while honeysuckle
yields to pallid serviceberry. In forest shade
you'll see one of the park's better displays of
spreading Jacob's ladder, while in drier,
sunnier spots you'll see many Davis' knotweeds. Here, around 6400 feet, the knotweeds are at the lower, wetter shadier limits
of their range, these plants of the buckwheat
family typically growing in higher, sunnier
spots.

After the ⅓-mile traverse, we return to
mosquitoland, a marshy meadow, lined with
western blueberries, that extends for several
hundred yards. In early or mid-July you may
be fortunate enought to see it blushing in
elephant heads, almost turning the meadow
pink. Like other members of their genus,
these colorful louseworts derive some of
their nourishment by parasitizing root fungi
of adjacent grasses, sedges and wildflowers.
In this very wet environment also look for
alpine shooting star and two orchids, Sierra
rein orchid and green rein orchid.

Almost ½ mile past the marshy Grassy
Swale creek meadow, we come to a junction
from which a trail strikes a boggy tread
across the swale before continuing 0.6 mile
up the swale to another junction. From that
junction one trail climbs 0.8 mile north up to
our route, the Pacific Crest Trail, while another, eastbound, takes you 1.4 nearly effortless miles over to the northwest arm of
Horseshoe Lake. Our PCT continues ⅓ mile
up the northwest bank of Grassy Swale creek
before leaving it for a moderate, one-mile
climb to meet the previously mentioned
trail.

Now follow the description in the
"Horseshoe-Snag-Swan Lakes Loop," found
in Chapter 13. You first hike to Swan Lake
and then to Lower Twin Lake, covering
1.2 miles to arrive at the start of a trail to
Rainbow Lake on the east shore of Lower
Twin Lake. The PCT continues along Lower
Twin's east shore to a north-end trail junction, to which a trail from Summit Lake
descends—see Chapter 11's "Summit Lake
to Echo, Twin, Rainbow and Snag Lakes."
The PCT, now an old, closed road, goes ⅓
mile down the Twin Lakes' drainage to another junction, this one with a trail leading to
the Cluster Lakes—see Chapter 11's "Summit Lake to Cluster Lakes." The old road then
goes 2.6 easy-but-dry miles through a
lodgepole forest whose gravelly floor often
presents colorful displays of spreading
phlox. You then meet and walk west on another old road, this one a pioneer route. To
complete the PCT through the park, follow
this road, which is described in Chapter 11's
"Nobles Trail to Badger Flat and beyond."

13 Lassen Park Trails: Juniper Lake Area

Introduction   The park's least crowded camping, fishing and hiking area is its southeastern part, centered around Juniper Lake, which is the park's largest and deepest lake. A small campground, rarely full, attests to this area's lack of popularity. This lack of people is not surprising, for although the scenery equals that of any other part of the Lassen backcountry, its trailheads are the hardest to reach. To find them, however, is simple. Leave Highway 36 in the north end of Chester and head ⅔ mile west on Feather River Drive to a fork. Angle right here and take the road all the way to Juniper Lake. The first 5.3 miles are fine, but then the pavement ends, and the next 7.8 miles to the Juniper Lake Ranger Station have a few rough spots; it certainly is not your first-class graded road. It is both longer and rougher than the graded roads up to Drakesbad and to Butte Lake. But this annoyance has its advantages, for it preserves the unspoiled park wilderness for the few who are willing to make the effort to get to it.

   This chapter begins with a climb to the area's most prominent peak, Mt. Harkness, which is usually the first hike that those new to this area want to take. Next comes a loop around Juniper Lake which, though easy, is amazingly hilly for a "shoreline" trail. A longer loop trail follows, encompassing Juniper, Indian and Horseshoe lakes—each very different. All three loop trails are short enough to be comfortably done as day hikes; indeed, you can't camp legally at the first two. The same applies to the two next hikes—both very short—one to Crystal Lake and one to Inspiration Point. In contrast, the three last hikes are best done as backpack trips, so that you have time to thoroughly experience the wilderness. Each, however, is short enough that hikers in good condition can do them as day hikes without too much effort. The first, the Horseshoe-Swan-Snag lakes loop, is one of the park's best, and it visits five lakes before ascending Grassy Creek and heading back to the trailhead. The Cameron Meadow-Grassy Creek hike is the shortest loop that hikers can make from any trailhead in this area. Finally, the last hike heads to Jakey Lake and beyond to lightly used tarns and the park's deepest backcountry.

Mt. Harkness

Trailhead   Take the Feather River Road ⅔
mile west out of Chester, fork right and drive
11.0 miles up to the Juniper Lake
Campground entrance, on your left. Drive
0.2 mile down the campground road, to
where it bends from southeast to southwest.
There is no trailhead parking, but most hikers walk to the trailhead from their campsite.

Distances   1.9 miles (3.1 km) to summit
5.5 miles (8.9 km) for Mt.
Harkness-Juniper Lake loop

Trail description   Snow patches typically
last through early July on the mountain's
upper slopes, providing an early-season
water source. After that, you'll have to carry
your own water, for none is available at the
fire lookout. Because the summit is
windswept and open, don't climb to it if a
lightning storm is threatening. Your first
mile of trail is a moderate climb through a
viewless forest of red firs, western white
pines and lodgepole pines. Mountain hemlocks then appear and your climb soon
steepens as you approach more-open slopes,
which begin at about 7500 feet elevation,
roughly 700 feet above your trailhead.

Now you'll see a prominent cliff of gray
rock to your left, a ridge of similar rock to
your right, and slopes of rubbly red cinders
ahead. The gray rock outcrops are composed
of lava flows that barely flowed from the
summit during the mountain's later history.
After these flows either erosion and/or a new
eruption removed the summit area and a
cinder cone developed in its place, probably
during or just after the last glaciation. During
this last icy period, small glaciers descended
outward from Mt. Harkness, particularly on
its north side, and they mildly eroded the
mountain. Most of these small glaciers then
united with a large ice cap that spilled south
from the ridge north of Juniper Lake, the ice
flowing partly into Warner Valley but mostly
down the Benner Creek drainage—along
which you drove up to Juniper Lake.

From the base of the cinder cone up to the
fire lookout along its rim, we have 500 feet to
climb. We start west, climbing steeply
through a hemlock grove to a nearby volcanic ridge, from which we have a fine view
of the cinder cone. Its northern third has
been removed by various erosive processes,

leaving a conspicuous bowl. Our trail climbs
130 yards up the west rim of the bowl to a
trail junction. If you're taking the recommended loop route, you'll descend on the
trail to your right, the loop route being 1.8
miles longer than if you return the way you
came.

Clark's nutcrackers announce their
presence in the few remaining western
whitebark pines as we climb gravelly slopes
decked with silver-leaved lupine and
Bloomer's goldenbush. In ⅓ mile we reach
the summit, and beside the lookout you'll
see more herbs and shrubs, two worth not-
ing. Here you'll see the cycladenia growing
in clusters, this low plant recognized by its
broad, smooth-edged leaves and its somewhat fleshy stems. In July it produces tubular, rose-colored flowers. The common shrub
here is the small-leaved cream bush, sometimes referred to as cliff spray or rock
spiraea. The latter is incorrect, for rock
spiraea (*Petrophytum*) is another member of
the rose family that grows only on limestone
rocks and cliffs of the southern Sierra and in
the Great Basin ranges. Cream bush
(*Holodiscus*) is a rose that produces small
creamy flowers, usually from mid-July to
early August. Oddly enough, no trees grow
along the rim of the mountain's cinder cone
even though the rim is 300 feet lower than
the wooded rim of Prospect Peak's cinder
cone. This may be due to very porous
pumice, and if so, then the cone could be
quite young—say, a few thousand years
old—rather than 20-30,000 years old, as is
usally proposed.

But you've climbed to the summit to look
at the views, not the pumice. While not so
spectacular as those from Prospect Peak,
Brokeoff Mountain or Lassen Peak, they are
nevertheless worth the hiking effort—which
is, after all, somewhat less than that required
at the other three peaks. With Lassen Peak
serving as your reference point, you can
identify most of the park's features. The
long, sometimes snowy ridge extending
south from Lassen Peak is composed mostly
of part of the northwest flank of Mt. Tehama,
an Ice Age volcano since eroded away by
glaciers. Its highest remnant is Brokeoff
Mountain, the apex at the south end of the
ridge, while the high point just north of it is
Mt. Diller.

Scanning clockwise from Lassen Peak, you see relatively close Saddle Mountain, sloping down into Warner Valley as does our mountain. In the distance, Chaos Crags stand above and mostly left of Saddle Mountain. Flat Moutain is the conspicuous, flat-topped cinder cone breaking the horizon just right of the mountain, while above and beyond the west shore of Juniper Lake, Fairfield Peak, another cinder cone, does the same. Rising just right and behind it is West Prospect Peak, joined to slightly higher Prospect Peak. At its base, famous Cinder Cone barely peeks over the ridge above the north corner of Juniper Lake.

Mt. Hoffman, with steep, southwest-facing slopes, breaks the skyline just east of the lake, while east of this peak stand two higher ones, Red Cinder Cone and Red Cinder, the eastern boundary of Lassen Park running between them. You'll recognize Bonte Peak, 2 miles east-northeast of our summit, by its finlike appearance, for southward-flowing glaciers have removed most of the mass of this mountain. In time, younger Mt. Harkness may take on a similar appearance if we have future glaciations. Black Cinder Rock is the high point immediately behind Bonte Peak, and its stands on a ridge in western Caribou Wilderness that runs 3 miles north to Red Cinder. North and South Caribou, the wilderness' two domineering peaks, are the two distant peaks behind Black Cinder Rock.

To the south and southeast lie long ridges—mostly glacial moraines—extending down toward Lake Almanor. The last glacier to flow south between Mt. Harkness and Bonte Peak was about 500 feet thick where it passed between them. Glaciers of an earlier episode were even thicker, and these descended to the outskirts of western Chester. Blue Lake, to the south, is trapped among glacial deposits, as is the seasonal lake just beyond it.

After soaking up all these views, descend back to the junction. The 1⅓-mile-long trail west down to glacial moraines near the south end of Juniper Lake is sometimes steep and often rocky. It justifiably receives considerably less use, though it does present some fair views. Watch your step on this descent, then head east on a shoreline trail back to camp. This trail is described, westward, in the following hike.

Juniper Lake Loop

Trailhead Anywhere along the Juniper Lake road (see this chapter's "Introduction" for driving directions to Juniper Lake). Most people hiking around or partly around Juniper Lake will start west from the end of the Juniper Lake Campground, so the following distances are measured from that point.

Distances 1.8 miles (2.9 km) to trail climbing east to Mt. Harkness
2.2 miles (3.6 km) to ford of Juniper Lake's outlet creek
3.3 miles (5.3 km) to start of summer-homes road
4.5 miles (7.3 km) to Juniper Lake Ranger Station
6.4 miles (10.3 km) for entire loop

Trail description The route is plainly obvious: walk around the lake. However, some parts are better than others, and so a little elaboration is appropriate. Different shorelines provide different views. Lassen Peak, for example, is seen only in the vicinity of the campground, and photographers should try to capture it early in the morning, when it reflects in the lake's still water. Saddle Moutain is the spreading mass to the left of Lassen Peak. When viewed from the lake's outlet forebay, Mt. Hoffman is the unimpressive, asymmetrical mountain nudging its summit directly above Inspiration Point. This "point" is composed of two small knolls on an almost level, forested ridge above the north shore of Juniper Lake. The point is definitely worth climbing—see the "Inspiration Point" hike later in this chapter. The best views of Mt. Harkness are at the Juniper Lake Ranger Station and vicinity, for from here you can readily identify the cinder cone that makes up upper part of the mountain.

Until rather late in the Ice Age, roughly 200,000 years ago, Mt. Harkness and Juniper Lake did not exist. There was instead a basin which during cold times supported an ice cap hundreds of feet deep, sending icy tongues south and southwest into Warner Valley and southeast down the Benner Creek drainage. In warmer interglacial times the basin was ice-free, and a creek drained south through it, then southwest down to Warner Valley, as the lake's outlet creek does today. But as Mt. Harkness began to build skyward, it dammed the southern part of the basin and ensuing flows gradually ponded up the lake until today it is an impressive 235 feet deep. The deepest spot is at the "p" in the words "Juniper Lake," on this book's topo map.

A total of 3.3 miles of trail and 3.1 miles of road encircle the lake, the trail extending from the west end of the campground clockwise over to the summer-homes road, along the lake's northwest shore. Except along that road, you have relatively easy access to any point along the lake's shore. Along that road a few private inholdings still remain, but perhaps some day a public trail will totally circle the lake.

Most hikers wouldn't find the summer-homes area all that interesting if they were to hike through it. Campers often walk on the trail along the lake's southeast shore, going as far as the lake's shallow forebay, which separates from the lake in late summer after the water level drops about 2 feet. Then, one can cut straight across to the glacial moraine on the opposite shore, shaving about ¾ mile off the loop's distance. The author's favorite spot is a bedrock point that juts out along the lake's southwest shore, about 0.4 mile north of the lake's forebay. It provides panoramas from Mt. Harkness north to Mt. Hoffman and has one fairly respectable diving rock—a feature uncommon to most lakes in volcanic areas.

Juniper Lake-Horseshoe Lake Loop

Trailhead   At west end of campground, as in preceding hike.

Distances   1.4 miles (2.3 km) to Horseshoe Lake's outlet creek via closed road
2.2 miles (3.6 km) to ford of Juniper Lake's outlet creek
3.5 miles (5.6 km) to Indian Lake
4.9 miles (7.9 km) to Horseshoe Lake R.S. via trail
6.2 miles (10.0 km) to Juniper Lake R.S. via Indian and Horseshoe lakes
8.1 miles (13.0 km) for Juniper Lake-Horseshoe Lake loop

Trail description   If you're interested in the shortest route to Horseshoe Lake, start at the

Juniper Lake Ranger Station, taking a close road. This climbs west, ascending 200 fee before descending more than 400 feet to trail junction before the Horseshoe Lak Ranger Station, seen just ahead. The lake' main camping area, equipped with table and outhouse, is between the ranger statio and the lake's east shore. The route de scribed in this hike takes a much longer trail one that skirts along the southeast shore o Juniper Lake, then climbs past Indian Lak before dropping to the Horsehoe Lak environs. It then returns via the closed road

With elevations ranging from a low o 6570 feet at Horseshoe Lake to a high of 711(feet at the saddle above Indian Lake, th route stays almost entirely within the red-fi belt. Most of the trees you'll see along you route are either red firs, western white pine: or lodgepole pines. The primary forest-floo vegetation is mostly lupines, grasses anc sedges early along the hike, and pinema manzanita later on. You should be able t distinguish between the two commo knee-high species of lupines. Christine' lupine has pale-yellow flowers, drab-greer leaves and reddish-green stems, and it pre fers dry, fairly sunny areas. Crest lupine ha: pale-blue flowers, green leaves and greer stems, and it prefers moister, somewha shady areas.

The trail undulates along Juniper Lake' southeast shore, requiring a bit more effor than a lazy stroll. The first ¾ mile of trai generally heads west toward Saddl Mountain, but then the route turns south west. At about that point you are opposit the lake's deepest spot, which lies about 23! feet below the water surface. In ¼ mile you trail bends even more to the south, and i skirts along the lakeshore for ⅓ mile to forebay on the south side of a glacia moraine. For most of the summer the waist deep forebay is connected to the lake prope by a knee-deep strait, but after the lake' level drops by that amount, you can wall over to the moraine.

Our trail continues ½ mile south to a junc tion. From here a rocky, fairly steep trai climbs 1⅓ miles east to a junction, and then a short trail continues ⅓ mile to the lookou station atop Mt. Harkness (see this chapter' first hike). Also from our junction, anothe trail starts southwest, tops a low moraine ir 15 yards and then descends 2⅓ miles to the or of Warner Valley (see Chapter 12, first ke). At our junction we turn right, crossing oraines two, three and four before reaching niper Lake's outlet creek, almost ½ mile stant. This creek usually begins to dry up early or mid-July. At the creek's west bank trail (the previous hike) climbs north, ossing a fifth moraine—the one above the ke's forebay. These moraines were evi-ntly left near the close of the last glacial eriod, when a glacier retreated northward, ccasionally pausing in its retreat and umping sediments that we see today as oraines. The forebay moraine is the oungest of the five.

From the west bank we climb northwest a trail bound for Indian and Horseshoe kes. Near the start we reach some bedrock utcrops with shallow soils, and the vegeta-on reflects this changed condition. You ay see some white firs and an occasional ffrey pine, but pinemat manzanitas locally redominate. Surprisingly, moisture-loving dgepole pines also do well here, this spe-es being extremely adaptable. Small, rought-loving wildflowers include least-owered monkey flower, alpine everlasting, orrey's collinsia, nodding microseris, ussy paws and mountain violet. All are irly common, especially the last two, ough by late July the violet has usually one to seed and is easily overlooked.

In about ½ mile our easy trail passes above nearby pond, to the right, then in another ½ ile, just after we descend past a stagnant ond, we get our first glimpse of Indian ake. You could drop to it here, but several inutes ahead you'll meet a spur trail de-cending 200 yards to this shallow lake. amping is legal at this lake and at the maller, semiclear lake northeast of it—if ou can find a level site more than 100 feet rom water. Both are better suited for day se, with the best swimming area (fewest nosquitoes) located near a rocky point on ndian Lake's north shore.

From the Indian Lake spur-trail junction ou have only 0.3 mile to climb to a shallow addle, beyond which you swap views of Mt. larkness and Bonte Peak for ones of Lassen eak and Crater Butte. Your trail soon be-omes steep, and you too often have to watch our footing rather than catch occasional iews of Horseshoe Lake, which is largely idden by the forest's trees. You'll not want to hike back up this steep route. Where the trail approaches the lake's southeast corner, you can head 50 yards out to the shore. Here you'll see yellow pond lilies, which also grow to the west and in other locations along the lake's margin. They tend to indicate that the lake is shallow, which is only half true—literally. For basically, the northern half of the lake is shallow, mostly less than 10 feet deep, but the southern half is quite deep, about 75 feet in its eastern sector (see "Horseshoe-Swan-Snag Lakes Loop," later in this chapter).

The trail swings over to the lake's east shore, and as you approach the lake's outlet you may see two or more paths climbing east over a low ridge to a closed road. Odds are you won't find the most efficient way over to that road, but you certainly won't get lost. A backcountry campground lies along the ridge, with sites for large groups to the south and sites for small groups to the north. The Horseshoe Lake Ranger Station lies im-mediately east of the campground's north end, and the closed road ends near the sta-tion's door. To complete your loop, climb east up the moderately steep road, then de-scend on a lesser grade to its end at a junction with the Juniper Lake road, immediately west of the Juniper Lake Ranger Station. If you've left a vehicle at the trailhead parking lot immediately east of the station, you'll save yourself about 2 miles of walking back to the lake's campground.

Crystal Lake

Trailhead At a bend in the road 0.3 mile northwest beyond the entrance to the Juniper Lake Campground (see this chapter's "Introduction" for driving directions to Juniper Lake).

Distance 0.4 mile (0.7 km) to Crystal Lake

Trail description The distances given at the trailhead sign (same as the above) are correct. Most hikers, however, would swear that the trail is at least ½ mile long. It's the trail's grade, averaging between 15-20%, that exhausts hikers. Nevertheless, most make it to the lake in about 15 minutes; hot-shots in under 10. Just before you reach the lake you may see a matted ceanothus that sprouts clusters of tiny lavender flowers in early and mid-July. This ankle-high evergreen shrub, the squaw carpet, normally grows best at 3000-6500 feet in the Lassen area, so here, at about 7200 feet, it is growing at its upper elevation limit.

Crystal Lake is one of the park's most beautiful lakes, for it doesn't have the usual monotonous ring of dense lodgepoles around it. Instead, it has an open, pleasing assortment of lodgepoles, red firs and western white pines, and even a few mountain hemlocks, growing on a highly variable topography holding the lake. Hemlocks are usually found above 7500 feet, and when they occur down at that elevation, it is usually on a north-facing slope. The lake basin is on a south-facing slope. However, this area's topography is so variable that it produces quite variable microenvironments. Hence we see, for example, squaw carpet and mountain hemlock growing in totally different environments only about 100 yards apart, both growing beyond their normal elevation limits.

From a low knoll just west of the lake's outlet, you get unobstructed views of Juniper Lake, Mt. Harkness and Lassen Peak. But most of the lake's visitors come not for the views, but rather for fishing or swimming. Both Juniper and Crystal Lake have trout— two of the few in the park that do—but large, deep Juniper Lake is usually too cold for pleasant swimming. Crystal Lake, with mid-summer temperatures ranging from the mid-60s to the low 70s, makes up for Juniper's deficiency. No camping is allowed at Crystal; do that at Juniper. On your way back down, take in the views near the top of the trail, then watch your step descending to the trailhead.

Trail description The trail gives you a mi ute or two of easy walking before you beg climbing moderately-to-steeply up to a lo ridge. On it you briefly climb northwe above the dense red-fir forest to the top of low knoll, Inspiration Point. A *de facto* tra continues to a second, slightly lower kno with similar views. White firs and Jeffr pines grow up here, which normally gro below the red firs and western white pin you passed on your ascent. However, th temperatures up here are warmer than dow at the lake, and the winters are less sever You may see mountain pride growing out cracks in the knolls' bedrock. This crimso flowered penstemon is quite uncommon i the park, though very common in the Sier Nevada.

Considering the lowness of the two knoll the views are indeed remarkable. From th second knoll, you get a clear view of Sna Lake, the Fantastic Lava Beds and Cind Cone behind them, and of Prospect and We Prospect peaks behind them. Lassen Pea pokes up through the trees to the west, whi Mt. Harkness and Juniper Lake poke throug to the south. An unbroken sea of forest lies the northeast, bounded on the north by M Hoffman and Red Cinder Cone and on th east by a ridge extending south from Re Cinder. The park's eastern boundary li about ⅔ mile west of the ridge.

During the last period of glaciation, La sen Park and Caribou Wilderness, east of were buried under hundreds of feet of ic The Red Cinder-Red Cinder Cone area wa one source of ice accumulation, from whic ice slowly flowed outward in all direction The Inspiration Point Ridge, low as it is, wa another source, its ice flowing north to Sna Lake and beyond, and south to Juniper Lak and beyond.

Inspiration Point

Trailhead About 30 yards east of the Juniper Lake Ranger Station's trailhead parking lot (see this chapter's "Introduction" for driving directions to the ranger station).

Distance 0.7 mile (1.1 km) to Inspiration Point

Horseshoe-Swan-Snag Lakes Loop

Trailhead At the Juniper Lake Ranger Sta tion (see this chapter's "Introduction" fc driving directions to it).

Right: a Mt. Harkness panorama—Lassen Peak at left, the Prospect Peaks right of center, an Juniper Lake between these peaks and a snow patch. Juniper Lake mirrors Saddle Mountain an Lassen Peak at dawn and dusk, viewed from the lake's campground. Bottom view of the lake is fror its southwest shore.

Distances   1.4 miles (2.3 km) to Horseshoe
Lake
4.8 miles (7.7 km) to Swan Lake
5.3 miles (8.5 km) to Lower Twin
Lake
6.2 miles (10.0 km) to Rainbow
Lake
8.6 miles (13.8 km) to Snag Lake
12.6 miles (20.3 km) for loop via
Cameron Meadow
12.9 miles (20.8 km) for loop via
Grassy Creek

Trail description   To sample the heart of
Lassen Park's backcountry, take this loop
trip. The loop is not very long, though it does
have its share of ups and downs, the ups
mainly along the last 3 miles. If you return
via Grassy Creek, you'll backtrack along your
loop's first 1.4 miles. If you return via Cameron Meadow, a shorter but definitely steeper
route, you'll return on the trail descending to
just west of the ranger station.

You start out by taking a closed road that
climbs west, first gently and then
moderately, up to a low spot on a spreading
crest. You then lose twice the elevation
you've gained, leveling off as you approach
the Horseshoe Lake Ranger Station. Just before it, you'll meet a trail on your left, which
goes 130 yards southwest to an abandoned
road. This road immediately forks, the
northwest fork climbing over a low ridge to
Horseshoe Lake. Campsites with tables
abound on the low ridge, the northern sites
used by small hiking parties, the southern
sites by large groups.

Among Lemmon's willows, which is the
park's commonest willow, we bridge Grassy
Creek, doing so just beyond the ranger station, and we meet the Grassy Creek trail. The
Grassy Creek return route, which is the author's preferred return route, climbs up the
creek's west bank to this spot. We head upstream to the nearby outlet of Horseshoe
Lake, which, with a view of Lassen Peak, is a
fine setting for a lunch or rest stop.

There is a small peninsula on the lake's
northeast shore, and as our trail climbs a bit
up toward it, we get a view southwest across
Horseshoe Lake. The view, though pleasing,
seems ordinary enough, lacking any
significance. Oh, but if we could drain the
lake, what a revelation we would have! From
your spot, mentally draw a line southwest to
the north (right) shore of the lake's south-

western arm. This line separates a shallo
lake bottom, to the right, from a much deep
one, to the left. North of the line the la
averages about 10 feet or less, having on
one moderately deep spot—about 20 feet-
near the west end of the lake's northwe
arm. This deeper spot is unexpected sin
yellow pond lilies, which grow only in sha
low water, are found nearby. The lake
northern half is so shallow that from the t
of our adjacent peninsula, you can almo
wade half way across this large lake.

But the lake's south half is also intriguin
It can be subdivided into two basins: th
southwest arm and the larger area east of i
The lake bottom drops to about 40 feet in th
arm and to about 75 feet in the eastern basi
The lake thus has three basins: 20, 40 and 7
feet deep. And what is the significance
this? Most of Lassen's smaller lakes are a
largely glacial in origin: glaciers typical
scoured out shallow hollows in the lan
scape, and each filled with water (und
proper conditions) after the glaciers disa
peared. But Lassen's larger lakes, such a
Juniper, Snag and Butte, owe more of the
origin to vulcanism than to glaciatio
Horseshoe Lake is a prime example, for eru
tions led to the creation of the three lak
basins, which were perhaps connected t
gether after a glacier, flowing north from th
ridge you see above the lake, modified th
area before disappearing.

Two more observations about the lake a
worth mentioning. First, on the map you
see a long meadow extending west and the
north from the lake's southwest arm. Man
have stated that any meadow like this or
was once a shallow part of a lake, forme
immediately after a glacier retreated, bu
that since then it was gradually filled wit
sediments, transforming it first to a swam
and then to a meadow. This happens if an
only if there is an active transportation
sediments into it. (Crags Lake and Hat Lak
are two good examples; the former has a
most been buried by repeated rockfalls, th
latter has been completely buried under ir
coming, stream-borne sediments) But fc
Horseshoe Lake and others like it, no activ
stream brings sediments into it. Horsehc
Lake's meadow probably dates back to abor
the time when the dying glacier was in i
last stage, bleeding sediment-laden stream
into the area, covering what might have bee

shallow arm with relatively even layer of ediments. But since then, very little sediment has entered the lake. In the last 10,000 r so years, the lake may have grown only everal feet shallower, due to organic debris nd volcanic ash falls collecting on the bottom.

Which brings us to a second observation: if o glaciers invade this area in the distant uture—which seems very unlikely—the ake will gradually fill in, and the shallow ake bottom opposite our peninsula will become a meadow. Then, there will be a small ake in today's 20-foot-deep basin and a large ne in the 40- and 75-foot basins. Eventually e small lake would go, then the large one ould divide into two lakes, the western one lling in before the eastern one. At last it ould all be meadow, soon to be replaced by fine forest. The elapsed time for such a cenario? At least 100,000 years, if not several times that. But this is pure fantasy, for e Lassen area is one of California's most active volcanic areas; so much has changed in e *last* 100,000 years that you wouldn't recgnize the area if you could go that far back n time. The area's most prominent features, uch as Lassen Peak, Prospect Peak, Mt. Iarkness and Chaos Crags, had yet to make heir appearances, and the same is true of ozens of minor features.

But pondering over dying lakes and ominus volcanoes won't get us to our next destiation, so we cross over the lake's northwest eninsula to start a traverse along the lake's orth shore. Then temptation rears its head, or the north half of the lake is a very attractve, if oversized, swimming hole. Here, the ake's pebbly bottom drops off quickly before eveling at about 10-15 feet. There are no ocks, snags or other submerged obstacles to vorry about, and no wade through 100 yards f lake-bottom ooze. And the lake's midsection, being less than 5 feet deep in places, ffectively keeps out cold water from the ake's deep, southern half.

At last beyond Horseshoe Lake, we face an lmost level hike, which is convenient before late July, since mosquitoes in this flatand can be quite fierce and we'll then want o hurry along. Five seasonal ponds—three mall ones, a large one and a triangular ne—mark our progress to a low, gravelly livide, which we reach just past the last ond. We now leave the Grassy Creek drain-

age for the Grassy Swale drainage, both in July being exceptionally fine zones for botanizing if one can stand the onslaught of mosquitoes.

Two more mosquito ponds greet us just past the divide, and as we scurry west along the base of Crater Butte, a mildly glaciated cinder cone, we quickly hit a junction with the Pacific Crest Trail, on the north bank of Grassy Swale creek. We branch right, cross the creek's often-dry bed, then make a concerted effort up a steep, but gradually easing, trail. After rising above the hum of mosquitoes, you may feel safe enough to pause and admire the mosaic of flowers splashed across the slopes. Among others, you'll see Applegate's paintbrush, Christine's lupine, California stickseed, coyote mint and mountain violet. On gentler slopes ahead, silver-leaved lupine and pumice paintbrush seasonally monopolize the open, gravelly forest floor.

The trail levels just before a junction with the Pacific Crest Trail, and if you want to climb nearby Crater Butte, which rises 500 feet above you, then do it from here. Allow about an hour, round trip. This cinder cone is—like its northern neighbor, Fairfield Peak—more lava flow than cinders, and both probably originated during the last episode of glaciation.

We meet the Pacific Crest Trail 6.2 miles north of its Warner Valley Campground trailhead and 9.1 miles southwest of its exit from the park, near Badger Mountain. We'll stay on this tri-state trail only 1.2 miles. After about 250 yards of northward progress, we crest a low divide and enter the Butte Creek drainage. You'll quickly note Swan Lake, a short distance below you. If you plan to camp at this typical backcounty lake, leave the trail here and look for a site above its south shore or ones on its east-shore bench. Our trail almost touches the lake at its northwest corner, then immediately crosses its barely discernible outlet creek before dropping ½ mile to a junction on the southeast shore of lodgepole-fringed Lower Twin Lake. Westward, a 4¼-mile route skirts along the lake's south shore, then climbs past Upper Twin and Echo lakes to Summit Lake's north campground. On a ¼-mile stretch, we start east, immediately passing a campsite before curving north to an east-shore junction. The Pacific Crest Trail continues onward to the Canadian border, but we decline the invitation and instead make an easy climb east to crescentic Rainbow Lake. Just before the trail drops to the lake's west shore, you can leave the tread for a 650-foot climb north to the summit of Fairfield Peak.

Fairfield Peak may be largely responsible for ponding up Rainbow Lake, not unlike the Horseshoe Lake origin, mentioned earlier. Most of the lake is bordered by slopes of varying degree, and this makes campsites few. Nevertheless, you'll see a good-sized one near the west shore and several small ones, with filtered views of Lassen Peak, near the southeast shore. From the north shore a trail climbs northeast over a low divide, going 2⅔ miles to the west base of Cinder Cone, then another 2 miles to the Butte Lake Campground and Ranger Station.

Our loop route, however, climbs briefly southeast to a crest, then drops west to a nearby gully before traversing across rolling, open terrain. The soil on it is deep and loose, so walking across it is about as tedious as walking along a sandy beach. Everywhere, Bloomer's goldenbush is attempting to stabilize the soil, for this late-blooming sunflower does very well on dry, gravelly flats. As you begin a steep descent toward Snag Lake, you may encounter two species of gravel-loving wildflowers: cycladenia, with tubular rose flowers and broad, smooth-edged leaves, and Lobb's nama, with tubular magenta flowers and narrower, shallowly toothed leaves. Such plants give way to water-loving plants when you cross a creeklet about ¼ mile before a trail junction.

When you reach Snag Lake's west-shore trail, you could take it ½ mile north to several campsites, but better ones are found if you continue straight ahead, on your trail, which quickly fades away. Look for sites out on the lake's peninsula, which is part of a moraine left by a glacier as it sporadically retreated south. Here, the lake's water is quite shallow—usually about 5-10 feet deep—and therefore quite warm. Our loop continues south, the trail approaching the tip of Snag Lake before climbing gently to a junction.

If you choose the shorter Cameron Meadow route, you branch left here and head ¼ mile over to a sturdy bridge across lively Grassy Creek, a fine resting spot. No far beyond it you branch right and moderately climb one mile up to Cameron Meadow, skirt along its west edge, then climb, usually gently, for ½ mile to another junction. Jakey Lake is an easy 1⅔ miles up the east-climbing trail (see this chapter's last hike). You quickly ascend along a tributary of Jakey Lake creek, then make an unforgiving 500-foot climb to a spreading, rocky bench. At its south end you top a narrow ridge then drop ½ mile to your original trailhead.

If you choose the Grassy Creek route, you climb 2⅓ miles of easy-to-moderate trail up to Horseshoe Lake, then retrace your steps back along the closed road leading to your trailhead. Both options are described in detail in the following hike, a loop that goes from your trailhead to Snag Lake via Cameron Meadow, then returns to it via Grassy Creek, Horseshoe Lake and the closed road.

Cameron Meadow- Grassy Creek Loop

Trailhead   Same as for preceding hike.
Distances   3.2 miles (5.1 km) to Grassy Creek bridge and to southeast shore of Snag Lake
              4.2 miles (6.8 km) to peninsula on west shore of Snag Lake
              5.2 miles (8.4 km) for loop via shortcut trail
              5.8 miles (9.3 km) to Horseshoe Lake via Grassy Creek bridge
              7.2 miles (11.6 km) for entire loop without side trips to Snag Lake
              9.8 miles (15.8 km) to Juniper Lake Ranger Station via Cameron Meadow and Butte Lake—and also via Grassy Creek, west shore of Snag Lake and base of Cinder Cone

---

Right: A sea of trees, viewed from Inspiration Point, makes up Lassen Park's eastern backcountry Lassen Peak nudges above trees, viewed from outlet of Horseshoe Lake. A lodgepole pine, with scaly bark, gets its roots wet at Crystal Lake. Inspiration Point, bottom, gives you a view of Mt Harkness and Juniper Lake.

Trail description The shortest, easiest
route to Snag Lake starts from the Juniper
Lake Ranger Station, climbs 240 feet in ½
mile to a crest, then descends 2.7 miles to the
lake's southeast shore. However, to return
back up this route is another matter, for you
then climb about 1000 feet—some of it very
steep and exhausting. Therefore it is better to
return via Grassy Creek, a slightly longer
route, since the trail up it has a gradient
ranging from gentle to moderate. And that is
the route taken along this Cameron
Meadow-Grassy Creek loop.

Our route begins on a closed road that
leaves the Juniper Lake road immediately
west of the Juniper Lake Ranger Station.
We'll be returning on this closed road, but
for now we walk up it only 50 yards before
branching right on a trail that climbs 0.5 mile
to a crest saddle. Along this moderate ascent
we climb through Lassen's predominant forest type, composed of red firs, western white
pines and lodgepole pines along with an understory dominated by pinemat manzanita.
These species obscure a view from the crest,
so we drop just a bit to a rumpled bench and
head north across it to a brink. Here we get
tree-filtered views of Prospect Peak, Cinder
Cone, Fantastic Lava Beds and Snag Lake.
Now comes a grueling descent, which can be
splotched with snow as late as mid-July.
After a knee-knocking ½-mile descent, we
reach an easier grade as we approach and
then descend 75 yards down a tributary of
Jakey Lake creek. In early season you may get
wet feet. From a small meadow by the creeklet's northeast bank, a trail climbs gently
eastward, arriving at Jakey Lake in just over
1½ miles (see the following hike).

We continue north, arriving at Jakey Lake
creek in about 110 yards. This is a good spot
to get a drink, take a break, and perhaps
identify stream-bank flowers. The corn lily,
which is the most common species in wet,
open, mountain environments, is of course
present, as is the large-leaved lupine, the
park's only water-loving lupine. Marsh
marigold grows in the wettest soils, while in
slightly drier soils grow plantain-leaved buttercup, bud saxifrage and western spring
beauty, the last two barely ankle high. Here,
and ahead in Cameron Meadow, you may be
fortunate enough to see up to five species of
violets—all the park's species other than the
water-shunning mountain violet.

Cameron Meadow lies an easy ½-mi
walk away, and midway to it we reach
junction with a shortcut trail that rambles 1
miles west to a junction with the Grass
Creek trail. This junction is 1.0 mile belo
Horseshoe Lake's outlet. (On this shortcu
trail, you go about 175 yards to a boulderho
across Jakey Lake creek, then ⅓ mile across
low, broad ridge to the south end of a ver
wet meadow—more good hunting for vic
lets, saxifrages and other species here. Wit
muddy boots (wet feet, if you're unlucky
you plod along the meadow's edge, perhap
too incensed with the mire to note the vege
tation. But it is worth observing. For exam
ple, along the sloping meadow's southwes
edge, the species tend to be zoned: corn lilie
closest to you, then marsh marigolds, the
willows, and finally grasses and sedges. Be
yond the meadow you make a snaking, roll
ing ⅔-mile traverse west, crossing tw
minor ridges before arriving at a junctio
above Grassy Creek. From here, an obviou
but definitely abandoned horse trail begins
climb up the east bank of Grassy Creek. Th
shortcut trail makes a short, steep drop t
Grassy Creek, which you jump across t
reach the trail up which our loop route re
turns.)

On that loop we gently descend north t
Cameron Meadow, reaching a cabin site at it
west edge in several minutes. Through July
shallow lakelet fills the meadow's northwes
corner, and the rest of the meadow isn'
much drier; in other words—mosquit
heaven. But that is a problem mountai
botanists always seem to face, since the in
sects usually peak at the height of the flower
ing season. This is not surprising for, amon
other reasons, mosquitoes are important pol
linators.

"Boggy" is the word for the next stretch o
trail, as we plow past corn lilies, alders
willows and lodgepoles, crossing Jakey Lak
creek after 100 yards and recrossing it 10(
yards later. We then proceed north to
snowmelt pond at the northeast edge of
low, nearby ridge, then start a 15-minute
moderate descent along glacial sediments t
a junction above unseen Snag Lake.

To reach the southeast shore of that lake
descend ¼ mile northeast. Campsites, how
ever, are better on the lake's west shore: the
are larger and more abundant, and they catch
the sun's early-morning rays. Therefore, i

you're planning to camp at the lake, continue along the loop route, which traverses southwest to a sizeable bridge over profuse Grassy Creek. Like other creek crossings, this one is a fine area for botanizing, and you should be able to add several species to your list that were not seen higher up on Jakey Lake creek.

From the bridge, the trail makes an irrational ¼-mile arc over to a junction with the Grassy Creek-west shore Snag Lake trail. The only possible merit of this unnecessary arc is that you approach the south shore of Snag Lake, near which you could camp. But this end of the lake is so shallow that acres of lake surface disappear when the lake drops a couple of feet in late summer. It's better to head ⅔ mile north to a trail intersection near the lake's southwest shore. From the intersection, a fairly steep trail climbs west to Rainbow Lake and also starts northeast. It dies out just short of Snag Lake, but you can continue northeast along the shore to fine sites on the lake's peninsula. Like the lake's northeast lobe, the water from the peninsula southward is mostly a shallow 5-10 feet deep, making midsummer swimming a real joy.

From the junction past the bridge, our loop trail climbs south, reaching the bank of Grassy Creek in about ½ mile. If you're hiking up this trail in July, be prepared for a wildflower feast. You'll see dozens of species—far too many to enumerate—but you should be able to identify many of them by consulting the botany chapter. Until you reach the creek, your southbound route climbs up moist-to-dry forest soils characterized by spreading phlox, coyote mint, dwarf lousewort, California stickseed and California butterweed. Along the creek's bank and through its adjacent meadows, the vegetation shifts. Look for corn lily, marsh marigold, alpine shooting star, Nuttall's larkspur, crimson columbine, wandering daisy, common dandelion, yarrow and many, many others. If you're lucky along this trail, you'll see all of the park's stickseeds (three species) and all of its violets (six species), plus many representatives of the figwort and buttercup families.

You leave this wildflower wonderland at a junction just before Horseshoe Lake. Take a minute to walk west to the lake and its view of Lassen Peak (see the early part of the preceding hike for observations on this lake).

Then cross Grassy Creek and climb a short trail that joins a closed road immediately past the Horseshoe Lake Ranger Station. You now have a moderately forested, usually dry, 1⅓-mile climb east over a ridge to your trailhead.

Jakey Lake and Red Cinder Cone

Trailhead Same as for the two preceding hikes.

Distances 2.9 miles (4.7 km) to Jakey Lake
5.7 miles (9.2 km) to Red Cinder-Red Cinder Cone saddle
8.8 miles (14.1 km) to Widow Lake
10.5 miles (16.8 km) to south shore of Butte Lake
12.7 miles (20.4 km) to Butte Lake Ranger Station

Trail description The second paragraph of the preceding hike describes the first 1⅓ miles of route down to a junction in a small meadow. From that meadow we take a trail eastward, staying fairly close to Jakey Lake creek at first as we climb just over ½ mile to the northwest edge of a swampy area with a knee-deep lakelet. This lakelet is one of several dozen in this area that formed after a glacier left the area. Although part of the glacier had its source high on the slopes to the south of us, its main source was around the Red Cinder Cone area. The glacier mostly flowed clockwise from that area, descending past the sites of Jakey Lake, Cameron Meadow, Snag Lake and Butte Lake, and finally terminating by today's Butte Creek Campground. The abundance of lakes and ponds assures the hiker of an abundance of mosquitoes, at least through late July. Thousands of frogs live in our swampy area, feasting on the mosquitoes that are feasting on us.

About 0.2 mile beyond the swamp we pass one of the park's largest western white pines, a two-trunked specimen (probably two individuals), the larger one being 6 feet in diameter. We are now close to Jakey Lake creek again, having left it just before the swamp, and we parallel it ⅔ mile up-canyon, usually on a gentle grade, to the west end of the lake. Jakey Lake, being shallow, is good for swimming in early and mid-August, after most of the mosquitoes have disappeared. Except for a site near the lake's outlet, campsites are essentially lacking, though you can always find one if you're resourceful.

The trail east barely stays above the lake as it traverses the shore. Just after we cross the lake's seasonal inlet creek, we turn southward for an easy climb to a nearby lakelet, which has a rocky west-shore peninsula, a good drying place after a dip in this warm swimming hole. In early summer tiny wildflowers flourish along this seasonally wet trail stretch, flowers such as western spring beauty and long-horned steershead. The latter is scarecely an inch tall, the former, about several inches. Later on in the season, as this area's bodies of water begin to drop, the equally small primrose monkey flower forms a ring of yellow around some of their perimeters.

From the lakelet our trail swings counterclockwise to a second one, this one shriveling to a shallow pond by the time mosquitoes abate. But just ahead is a good lakelet with an unseen, curved lake lying immediately east of it. You'll find flat ground near these two swimming holes, and hence could set up camp. Since leaving Jakey Lake, all the ponds and lakelets we've seen have been on our right, but soon we meet a triangular lakelet on our left, this one with semiclear water and minimal camping and swimming opportunities. Beyond it our trail very soon cuts through a seasonal, linear pond, then in about 45 yards cuts throughth the seasonal western arm of a lakelet. The lakelet, though abounding with snags, does have some swimming and camping potential. Its water, at least, is usually drinkable. This is more than can be said of a pond you see to the left, a few minutes' hike past the lakelet.

Beyond the pond our route is dry to the Red Cinder-Red Cinder Cone saddle. The first ½ mile is easy, but then we gear down for a steep climb to gain 300 feet in elevation, the trail almost leveling out as it passes a low, open knoll, to our left. If you have your heart set on climbing Red Cinder Cone, start your climb here, not at the saddle, and scramble up the knoll, then traverse northwest from it to a rocky bench with sweeping, but disappointing, views. Better ones are had from the twin summits of Red Cinder Cone, particularly from the northern one, but the best views are from Red Cinder. The battle up its slopes, however, makes its summit attractive only to the most fanatical peak baggers. See Chapter 14's last hike for a description of the features to be see from there and for a trail description to Widow and Butte lakes.

14 Lassen Park Trails: Butte Lake Area

Introduction In five hikes this chapter covers the trails of northeastern Lassen Park. The first hike, a very short one, goes to Bathtub Lake and its adjacent twin, both lakes providing the area's warmest and safest swimming. The second hike, a moderately strenuous one, climbs to the summit of Prospect Peak. The summit is lower than Brokeoff Mountain's summit (Chapter 11, first hike), but the views are equally impressive, and the effort required to attain them is considerably less. Prospect Peak, however, lacks the alpine wildflowers found on Brokeoff Mountain. Two of the last three hikes visit Snag Lake. The first visits the west shore of Snag Lake via Cinder Cone, with an optional loop to Rainbow Lake thrown in. The second visits the east shore of Snag Lake via Butte Lake. A third hike takes you to Widow Lake, but you can continue onward to Red Cinder Cone, then drop to Jakey Lake, Cameron Meadow and Snag Lake's southeast shore. However, all these features except Widow Lake are more easily reached from Juniper Lake (see Chapter 13).

Butte Lake's four trailheads are very close to one another and hence are mentioned here rather than duplicating this information at the start of each hike. For Prospect Peak, Cinder Cone and the west shore of Snag Lake, start either at the Butte Lake Ranger Station or at the westernmost tip of Butte Lake. If you start at the latter, you'll have to leave your car in a large parking area by Butte Lake's northwest-shore picnic area. From the east end of this parking area, a foot trail starts east for the east shore of Butte Lake, for the east shore of Snag Lake, and for Widow and Jakey lakes. From the lot's north side, a horse trail climbs to Bathtub Lake and Butte Lake's outlet. To reach the Butte Lake area, take Highway 44/89 north to a junction that is just north of Old Station, both in Hat Creek Valley. Highway 89 continues north down the valley, but you take Highway 44 east 11.0 miles to Road 32N21, climbing south. If you are coming from the east, take County Road A21 north from Westwood or Highway 44 west from Susanville. From the junction where these two paved roads meet, take Highway 44 west 16.8 miles to Road 32N21. This road climbs 2.4 easy miles to Butte Creek Campground, then 4.1 steeper miles to the Butte Lake Ranger Station and Campground.

Bathtub Lake

Trailhead See this chapter's Introduction.

Distances 0.4 mile (0.6 km) to Bathtub Lake or to its adjacent lake
1.4 miles (2.3 km) to Butte Lake's outlet

Trail description From the north side of the Butte Lake parking lot, your forest-shaded route, a horse trail, climbs ⅓ mile to a junction, from which a short trail descends east to a nearby lake. In about 65 yards an equally short trail descends north to Bathtub Lake. Camping is forbidden at both lakes. The horse trail descends to a flat a bit east of this lake, and from it equestrians can then walk a minute west over to the lake's east shore. From the flat, the horse trail climbs north over a low divide, then swings east to Butte Creek, crossing it and climbing moderately south ½ mile up to Butte Lake's outlet.

Both Bathtub Lake and its nearby twin offer relatively warm swimming, particularly from mid-July through mid-August, when the water temperature gets into the high 60s and sometimes into the low 70s. Bathtub Lake is barely deep enough for swimming, but its more popular twin, though shallow, is significantly better. However, in this lake, watch out for submerged logs and lake-bottom rocks. Take time to investigate the reddish bedrocks above the north and northwest shores of this lake. Their upper surfaces exhibit some of the best glacial polish in the park. Glacial striations on the polish indicate that the last glacier passing through here flowed north. During the last major glacial advance, the glacier was about 700-800 feet thick in this vicinity, and it extended north downslope to Butte Creek Campground.

Prospect Peak

Trailhead   See this chapter's Introduction.

Distance   3.3 miles (5.2 km) to summit

Trail description   Most park visitors climb Prospect Peak for its views, but the trail up to the summit also presents interesting, changing patterns of vegetation. You start in a yellow-pine forest, climb through a red-fir belt, and end in an open, subalpine forest.

Your trail begins directly in front of the Butte Lake Ranger Station, and for the first 0.4 mile, your level route is along the self-guiding Cinder Cone Nature Trail (see Chapter 10). From that trail's post 13, at about 6100 feet elevation, you branch right, climbing gently west through open yellow-pine forest. The pines here are predominantly Jeffrey pines, though for the first ¼ mile from the trailhead, similar looking ponderosa and Washoe pines add to the confusion. See the nature trail's post 6 information for some characteristics that help you identify each of these three species of yellow pine.

The grade quickly increases to moderate, and as we pass the 6400-foot elevation, we note that a few white firs appear among the Jeffrey pines. Chinquapin soon appears in the understory, followed by pinemat man-

zanita and occasional squaw currant. By 7300 feet Jeffrey pines and white firs have almost entirely disappeared, replaced with many red firs and a fair number of western white pines. The white firs disappear for good as we climb onward, but Jeffrey pines make a few more sporadic appearances before yielding to a prime red-fir belt.

Just above 8000 feet our trail switchbacks northeast up the south flank of Prospect Peak's summit cinder cone, which was active perhaps a few thousand years ago. Views begin to appear as red firs yield to Jeffrey pines and shrubs, both able to tolerate the drier, rocky soils found near the summit. Watch for sagebrush, goldenbush and rabbitbrush (all sunflowers), bitterbrush and cream bush (both roses), and alpine prickly currant (a saxifrage). The trail ends by circling clockwise along the rim of the cinder cone. The cone has a depression that harbors snow and a shallow lakelet, both lasting into mid-July, and the vegetation reflects this improved groundwater condition. Western white pines growing along the cone's rim give way to lodgepole pines growing in the cone's depression. Conditions are most severe on the rim's cold, shady, windswept north-facing slope. Here, at trail's end by an abandoned fire-lookout station, mountain hemlocks flourish among long-lasting snowfields.

The views from Prospect Peak's summit are best before 9 a.m., when the air is still and clear. From the lookout site, on an exceptionally clear day, you can see as far north as pyramidal Mt. McLoughlin and to the right of it, the Crater Lake rim, both in southern Oregon and both to the right of snow-capped Mt. Shasta. Mt. McLoughlin is 138 miles away, Crater Lake rim is 163; Mt. Shasta is a mere 72. West Prospect Peak is much closer, just 2 miles to the northwest, and a small cinder cone, perhaps less than 1000 years old, stands on its lower east slopes at the head of an equally young lava flow. On the northwest skyline, Magee, Crater and Fredonyer peaks are the high summits just left of West Prospect, and Burney Mountain is the high summit between it and Mt. Shasta. Sugarloaf Peak stands above and just left of Shasta. Magee Peak and adjacent peaks make up the rim of an extinct volcano.

As you walk clockwise along Prospect Peak's cinder-cone rim, you should easily ecognize L-shaped Butte Lake, Cinder Cone nd its bleak, dark Fantastic Lava Beds, and ;nag Lake, immediately south of, and dam-ned by, the lava beds. Red Cinder Cone is the ⅃ighest point on the southeast horizon, ꞁtanding roughly above the east base of Cin-ꞁer Cone. Lower Mt. Hoffman rises from ;nag Lake's east shore, barely reaching the kyline, while Mt. Harkness rises in the dis-ance beyond and to the right of Snag Lake's ᴠest shore. Lassen Peak, to the southwest, is ⅃he most domineering peak of all, and is ⅃anked on the east by Reading Peak and on ꞁhe north by Chaos Crags. A rolling, forested ꞁandscape lies between us and Lassen Park's ꞁkyline peaks, and it contains more than two ꞁozen lakes that are hidden from our view. ⅃owever, Rainbow Lake, located due south ⲟf us and lying at the southeast base of Fair-ield Peak, is open to view. This landscape ᴠas covered by an ice cap as recently as ꞁbout 11,000 years ago, the ice ranging in ꞁhickness from about 800 feet over the Butte ⅃ake area to only about 100 feet in the Badger ꟻlat area. Earlier ice caps were probably ꞁhicker, but eruptions in the last 50,000 ᶓears, such as from Prospect Peak, have ꞁuried most of the older glacial evidence in ꞁhe north half of the park.

Cinder Cone and West Shore of Snag Lake

Trailhead See this chapter's Introduction.

Distances 1.4 miles (2.3 km) to north base of Cinder Cone

4.0 miles (6.5 km) to northwest shore of Snag Lake via shortest route

4.6 miles (7.5 km) to Rainbow Lake

5.0 miles (8.1 km) for entire Cinder Cone Nature Trail and to northwest shore of Snag Lake via Cinder Cone's summit

5.3 miles (8.5 km) to Soap Lake

5.5 miles (8.9 km) to southwest shore of Snag Lake and to Lower Twin Lake

13.5 miles (21.7 km) for Snag Lake-Butte Lake loop via shortest route

14.4 miles (23.2 km) for Snag Lake-Butte Lake loop via Cinder Cone's summit

Trail description The first part of this hike is along part of the self-guiding Cinder Cone Nature Trail, which is the last trail described in Chapter 10. This trail begins in front of the Butte Lake Ranger Station and quickly descends to the start of the Nobles Trail, a pioneer route, which you meet at the northwest tip of Butte Lake. Along this pioneer route the nature trail traverses 0.4 mile southwest to a junction with the Prospect Peak trail, then continues 0.9 mile more to a junction with the southward-climbing nature trail. Consult Chapter 10 if you want to climb to the top of Cinder Cone. This route is about one mile longer than the shortest route to Snag Lake, described below. However, if you haven't climbed Cinder Cone before, don't pass up the opportunity to do so.

The shortest route stays on the Nobles Trail, climbing and then descending along a 0.4-mile stretch to a second junction with the nature trail. Visitors hiking only the nature trail will climb up to this junction, then head back toward the ranger station. We stay on the Nobles Trail for 0.2 mile more, enjoying glances up at Cinder Cone and across to Painted Dunes, both features only several hundred years old. At the next junction we leave the Nobles Trail, which goes 3⅓ miles to Soap Lake and another 1⅔ miles beyond it to Badger Flat, both described in Chapter 11. The trail south takes us quickly to the base of Painted Dunes, where we meet a short trail east, giving those with second thoughts another chance to climb Cinder Cone.

If you avoid the temptation, continue southward along the base of Painted Dunes, crossing a grassy flat before reaching yet another junction. An early-season creeklet, coming from Twin Lakes, flows across the flat until about mid-spring, when there is still plenty of snow in this summer-dry, almost lifeless area. After that, the creeklet's water sinks below the surface of the pumice and it flows beneath the Fantastic Lava Beds, later to resurface in Butte Lake. The porous pumice, several feet thick here, transforms this once-forested area into an almost lifeless desert landscape that makes it hard to believe this area several times lay under an ice cap hundreds of feet thick.

At the junction just past the flat, you veer right if you want to climb 2¼ generally view-less miles up to Rainbow Lake or beyond it to Lower Twin Lake (both mentioned in a

Chapter 11 hike starting at Summit Lake). Though viewless, the trail does offer you an interesting sight: about ½ mile before Rainbow Lake you pass through 20 acres of desolation—a red-fir forest leveled in an October 1962 storm. You'll find several campsites at Rainbow Lake and more along the east shore of Lower Twin Lake.

Most hikers, however, take the shorter, easier, rollercoaster trail over to the northwest shore of Snag Lake. After about a ¼-mile walk south on this pumice route, you lose sight of Cinder Cone for a while, where it disappears behind the Fantastic Lava Beds. Not far after it does, you may see some nearby waist-high squaw currants, just before you enter a forest of mostly lodgepole pines. The currants typically blossom forth in tiny pink flowers in mid- or late June, attracting droves of mosquitoes when they do so. It seems ironic to be hiking through a dry, almost lifeless area and then come upon a few bushes and be mobbed by mosquitoes! However, much as we may despise them, mosquitoes are important pollinators, and a lot of wildflowers might suffer without them.

For about one mile our trail parallels the boundary between the bleak, dark Fantastic Lava Beds, to our left, and a shady forest, to our right. This route climbs and descends across low slopes which, being laden with pumice, are about as hard to traverse as beach dunes. But then, the trail has been like this from the start and remains so almost to Snag Lake.

Snag Lake appears rather suddenly, and near some black cottonwoods at the lake's northwest corner you'll find a well-used campsite. This lake corner is a popular lunch spot, which you may share with a spotted sandpiper, killdeer or California gull, or with a variety of forest-edge birds. Although Snag Lake is the park's second largest lake, it is uncommonly shallow for its size, being about 20-25 feet deep along the south margin of the Fantastic Lava Beds. Grassy Creek used to flow north through a wide, flat, glaciated valley down to Butte Lake until about 1720 A.D., when an outpouring of lava flowed south to its present position, dam-

ming the creek and drowning a forest. Early settlers saw many snags still standing from this traumatic event—hence the lake's name. None of the few snags you see today date back to the lake's creation. The lake today still drains north to Butte Lake, albeit beneath the Fantastic Lava Beds.

By mid-July the lake is warm enough for swimming, particularly in the south and east lobes, both averaging 5-10 feet in depth. By late summer the lake level drops a few feet and these two areas decrease noticeably in size. As you hike south along the lake's west-shore trail, you'll see several good campsites. The best ones, however, are on a west-shore peninsula that juts out ⅓ of the way across the lake. You'll come to it about 1.1 miles beyond the lake's northwest corner, as the trail approaches the shoreline after having briefly deviated from it to pass through a snag-strewn forest. The peninsula has enough potential campsites to hold a Boy Scouts convention. This peninsula and the protruding point on the east shore are both parts of a moraine left by a retreating glacier. The water between these two protrusions is quite shallow, the lake bottom almost breaking the surface midway across.

The west-shore trail leads inland around the peninsula, depriving you of a lake view. Just past the peninsula you reach a junction with a steep trail that climbs 2 miles west to Rainbow Lake. This is a trail you'll want to descend, not ascend, so if you plan to visit Rainbow Lake, take the previously mentioned trail southwest from the Painted Dunes area and then descend to Snag Lake.

If you plan to make a loop trip around Snag Lake and back to your starting point via Butte Lake, you'll continue south about ⅔ mile to a junction, from where a trail climbs 2.4 miles south to the Horseshoe Lake Ranger Station. From this junction, you wander eastward ¼ mile to a bridge over energetic Grassy Creek, then traverse northeast ½ mile to Snag Lake's southeast shore, passing a trail to Cameron Meadow midway along this stretch. The following hike describes the route from Butte Lake south to Snag Lake. See Chapter 13 for details of trails and terrain south of Snag Lake.

Right: Cinder Cone and its lava flow appear unearthly, viewed from Butte Lake. Prospect Peak's fire lookout, as it appeared in 1980. Butte Lake, viewed from an uplifted butte at the lake's north shore. Prospect Peak's summit views include West Prospect Peak (center), Thousand Lakes Wilderness summits (left of it) and snowy Mt. Shasta (right of it).

Butte Lake and East Shore of Snag Lake

Trailhead   See this chapter's Introduction.

Distances   0.8 mile (1.3 km) to Butte Lake's outlet
2.1 miles (3.4 km) to south shore of Butte Lake
5.0 miles (8.1 km) to northeast shore of Snag Lake
5.7 miles (9.1 km) to Cameron Meadow
6.5 miles (10.5 km) to southeast shore of Snag Lake
7.0 miles (11.3 km) to Grassy Creek bridge
9.7 miles (15.6 km) to Juniper Lake Ranger Station via Cameron Meadow

Trail description   This hike starts from the east end of a parking area above the northwest tip of Butte Lake. Our route is a footpath: if you are an equestrian, you'll have to take a horse trail to the left, which climbs to Bathtub Lake before descending to Butte Creek and climbing back up its east bank to Butte Lake's outlet. This route is 0.6 mile longer than the footpath. Our route starts along a short road to a nearby generator station, quickly leaving it for a trail that traverses through a mature forest of ponderosa, Jeffrey and Washoe pines (see Cinder Cone Nature Trail, post 6).

Your eastbound trail stays above the cottonwood-lined north shore of Butte Lake, then climbs shortly to a spectacular viewpoint at the south end of a narrow ridge. Here, among mountain mahoganies, you'll note the lake's asymmetrical configuration: an almost straight, forested east shore versus a highly lobed, unvegetated west shore. From the lake's south tip a fault runs north-northwest halfway up the east shore, where it apparently splits, with one fault branch veering north along the shore to the lake's outlet and beyond, and the other branch continuing straight ahead along the west side of the fault-bound ridge we're on. Three series of events caused Butte Lake to evolve to its current configuration. First, land gradually subsided along one or more faults, creating a primordial Butte Lake and its east-shore escarpment. Glaciers might have preceded this faulting, and they were likely active for long periods during the faulting. Without doubt they were active over most of the last 100,000 years, burying the Butte Lake area with as much as 800 feet of ice as they flowed north to the Butte Creek Campground vicinity. These glaciers certainly scraped and enlarged the faulted basin, leaving a larger, deeper lake when the last glacier retreated, perhaps about 11,000 years ago. Finally, Cinder Cone erupted, and with it occurred some lava flows, this volcanic activity occurring several times from about 1567-1851 A.D. The bulk of the flows making up the Fantastic Lava Beds came from eruptions in the 1700s, flowing south and east from Cinder Cone. These dammed up Grassy Creek, creating Snag Lake, and they pushed eastward into Butte Lake, substantially reducing its size. The last flow, in the winter of 1850-51, barely reached the lake's western shore. Assuming no more lava flows occur in the near future—a risky assumption—we can expect to see the Fantastic Lava Beds eventually covered with a pine forest—in about 2000 years.

Some of the landmarks you see from your trail's shrubby ridgecrest viewpoint include Sunrise Peak, an eroded cinder cone atop Butte Lake's east escarpment. Rising beyond the lake's southeast tip is Ash Butte, also an eroded cinder cone, as are Red Cinder Cone and Red Cinder, partly hidden behind the butte's west and east flanks, respectively. Mt. Hoffman stands beyond Butte Lake's west shore.

Steep slopes of loose rocks prevent the trail from descending immediately to Butte Lake's outlet, so the trail first climbs momentarily north before making a switchbacking plunge. The trail ends a few yards below the outlet, and you pick your way along driftwood logs over to the horse trail on the opposite side. This is usually no problem except at high water in early summer, when you may have to wade.

Once on the horse trail, you traverse south along Butte Lake's east shore, passing in ⅓ mile a miniature island with several conifers that beautifully frame Cinder Cone, 2 miles to the southwest. Southward, you get unobstructed views of the Fantastic Lava Beds and of Prospect Peak, north of them, whose gentle slopes yield to steeper slopes that delineate a cinder cone capping its summit. Along the trail you may see the spoor of bears, who make occasional forays into Butte Lake Campground. In the lake's shallow water you'll probably see the spoor of fishermen—beer cans lying on the lake bottom. Evidently some fishermen, particularly those in boats, have nothing better to do in this trout-stocked lake.

As we near the south end of Butte Lake, willows and aspens appear, by which you can camp. In late summer, after the lake level drops a couple of feet, this shallow end dries up, and one can then walk west on exposed land over to the nearby edge of the Fantastic Lava Beds. Old maps show a trail going southwest along the edge of the lava beds, but this route was abandoned years ago. Just past Butte Lake we reach a junction from which a trail branching right climbs 2¾ miles over to Snag Lake while the trail continues along Butte Lake's east-shore fault before veering up to Widow Lake, 1.4 miles from our junction. The following hike describes that route.

We branch right and make a 1¾-mile viewless though not unpleasant climb to a shallow divide, then drop one mile on a rather steep grade to Snag Lake's northeast lobe. If you are looking for secluded campsites, explore the forested peninsula ¼ mile west of the trail and the shoreline north to the south edge of the Fantastic Lava Beds.

A glade of giant aspens highlights our trail's start clockwise around Snag Lake's east lobe. You may see several campsites as you head southwest toward the lake's south shore, but most of them are illegally close to the water. One that isn't is just west of a creek that descends to the wide mouth of the east lobe. Another, about ⅓ mile farther, is on a small point that juts into the lake. This point is part of a recessional moraine that goes across the lake's prominent west-shore peninsula, which has the best sites. As we approach Snag Lake's very shallow end, which dries up in mid- and late summer, we veer away from the shore, climbing briefly and crossing two creeklets before reaching a junction. From it you can head 300 yards west over to the Grassy Creek bridge and beyond (see the previous hike). Or you can climb 1.1 miles south to Cameron Meadow, then continue 1.9 miles beyond it to Juniper Lake Ranger Station or 2.0 miles beyond the meadow to Jakey Lake's west shore. See Chapter 13 for trails to Horseshoe Lake, Grassy Creek, Cameron Meadow and Jakey Lake.

Widow Lake and Red Cinder Cone

Trailhead See this chapter's Introduction.

Distances 3.6 miles (5.8 km) to Widow Lake
6.9 miles (11.1 km) to Red Cinder-Red Cinder Cone saddle
9.5 miles (15.3 km) to east shore of Jakey Lake
11.7 miles (18.9 km) to Cameron Meadow via Jakey Lake
12.6 miles (20.3 km) to Juniper Lake Ranger Station via Jakey Lake
19.7 miles (31.6 km) for Widow Lake-Jakey Lake-east shore Snag Lake loop

Trail description You can make a Widow-Jakey-Snag lakes loop, but most hikers bound for Widow Lake—who aren't that many—go no farther. The previous hike describes the first 2¼ miles of trail to a junction just south of Butte Lake. From the junction we continue straight ahead along Widow Lake's ephemeral outlet creek, which more or less descends along Butte Lake's east-shore fault. This fault, probably inactive, may have once extended southward along the west base of unseen Ash Butte and then south along the west base of Red Cinder Cone. These two summits plus Butte Lake's Sunrise Peak and three other summits make up a row of cinder cones. However, this row of cones is not nearly as prominent as a row of more than a dozen cones that stretch 7 miles south-southeast from Highway 44's Poison Lake. Another 7-mile stretch of about a dozen cones is found mostly within Thousand Lakes Wilderness (Chapter 17), extending from Eiler Butte south-southeast to Bear Wallow Butte. The unseen cones along our Widow Lake route lie along a similar compass orientation, which is the typical bearing of faults in northeastern California.

About 0.4 mile from the junction we cross Widow Lake's usually dry outlet creek—the first of several fords—and soon shift hiking gears as our easy climb becomes a moderate one. Pines and firs, however, shade our way as well as provide ideal lighting conditions for snow plant, pinedrops and other "root parasites" (see Cinder Cone Nature Trail, post 18, and Boiling Springs Lake Nature Trail, post 16—both trails in Chapter 10). Our moderate climb reaches a glade abounding in corn lilies and bracken ferns; then the trail becomes quite steep as it climbs beside a bouldery talus slope up to a glacial moraine that dams Widow Lake. Widow Lake drains through the moraine, not over it, and first appears on the surface near the base of the talus slope. Widow Lake, at about 6800 feet elevation, has the usual share of willows and lodgepole pines to be expected at this elevation, but it also has a few black cottonwoods, which are rare this high up.

The lake appears small at first, but then you see first only the lake's "forebay." You'll find a campsite near the lake's south shore, but more-secluded ones are along its north and east shores. The only easy cross-country route from Lassen Park to adjoining Caribou Wilderness begins at the lake's east shore and heads east to a gully, which one then follows up to a broad divide between Black Butte and cinder cone 7467, both in the wilderness. An almost level traverse east takes one to the northwest shore of Triangle Lake. When hiked in reverse, this cross-country route is considerably harder to follow, and one can easily end up north of Widow Lake. From the author's viewpoint, a Widow Lake-Triangle Lake trail would be very desirable, as would a Jakey Lake-Long Lake trail, a few miles south.

To reach Jakey Lake, you climb south from Widow Lake, soon leaving all the white firs and most of the Jeffrey pines below you as the forest shifts toward red firs, western white pines and lodgepole pines—the park's commonest forest assemblage. Midway along your ascent you pass a sizable swimming hole on your right, which provides reasonable drinking water in early and mid-season. Purify if in doubt. You pass a tiny pond ½ mile later and soon see your first mountain hemlocks—indicators of long-lasting snowfields. Your trail to the pass can have snow problems until mid-July, though even in the dead of winter you could successfully funnel up to the pass without worrying about losing your way.

Red Cinder Cone stands ¼ mile due west of the sometimes windy 7660-foot pass, and one is tempted to scramble up boulders and brush to its 8008-foot summit. An easier approach is to descend briefly south and then climb up a gully to the north side of a knoll that is ¼ mile south of Red Cinder Cone. You then walk west to a rocky bench with views and decide whether you still want to climb 250 more vertical feet to the cone's summit. From the rocky bench, Snag Lake is hidden behind Mt. Hoffman; no lake is in sight. Your rather disappointing view, however, does include most of snowy Lassen Peak, to the west, and finlike Bonte Peak and spreading Mt. Harkness, both to the south. But if you climb to the north summit of twin-coned Red Cinder Cone, a new panorama opens before you, dominated by the Fantastic Lava Beds, Cinder Cone, Butte Lake and Prospect Peak.

Red Cinder, to the east of Red Cinder Cone, involves a hardy struggle up steep, often brushy slopes. Only the most ardent peak-baggers will want to make this 700-foot climb. However, at 8374 feet, it is the highest summit for miles around and it provides an unobstructed view of most of Lassen Park, of the entire Caribou Wilderness, and of numerous features beyond the wilderness. Lake Almanor, to the south, is perfectly obvious, but bring along a Forest Service map to identify the numerous summits to the northeast. Crater Mountain is the foremost peak, lying 14 miles distant. It is a large shield volcano, like Prospect Peak and Mt. Harkness; this fairly youthful volcano grew smack in the middle of a large valley, mostly obliterating it. The mountain's summit collapsed in its later days, forming a caldera, or deep pit, today occupied by Crater Lake and the Crater Lake Campground. Lying halfway to Crater Mountain is the row of cinder cones previously mentioned in this hike.

From the Red Cinder-Red Cinder Cone pass your trail descends 2½ miles to the east shore of Jakey Lake. Only the first ¾ mile is moderately steep, and then the route is a gently rolling one past ponds and lakelets to Jakey Lake. See Chapter 13's last hike, "Jakey Lake and Red Cinder Cone," for details.

15 Lassen Park's South and West Borderlands

Introduction The roads, trails and lakes of the lands bordering Lassen Park's south and west margins receive little use except by locals and "those in the know." In deer season, however, the area can be "crawling" with hunters. While definitely less scenic than Lassen Park's backcountry, this area does have subtle attractions; they just aren't advertised all that well.

This chapter's trails are described in a clockwise manner, starting south of Lassen Park with the Pacific Crest Trail, which heads south to Highway 36 (and thence to the Mexican border) and north into Lassen Park (and thence to the Canadian border). Next, a short trail provides the easiest path to Lassen's Little Willow Lake and Terminal Geyser. Farther west, a jeep road goes almost to Lassen's boundary and, with a brief cross-country jaunt, you can easily reach Lassen's Twin Meadows. Other nearby short cross-country routes take you to Duck, Blue and Ridge lakes. Equestrians may be attracted to Childs Meadows Trail, which provides a longer route to Twin Meadows. Next, trail descriptions give you three choices to Heart Lake, the prime attraction beyond Lassen Park's southwest corner. Farther north, the Blue Lake Trail, totally isolated and within the park, takes you up Lassen's seldom visited Blue Lake Canyon. The chapter ends with a visit to Deep Hole, a large volcanic crater similar to those found in the Hawaiian Islands.

Pacific Crest Trail, Domingo Spring south to Highway 36

Trailhead From Chester, drive 8.4 miles to Domingo Spring Campground. You start this drive just north of the town's bridge over the North Fork Feather River, leaving town on Feather River Drive. This road branches in ⅔ mile, and you go left, driving 5½ miles to a second major branch. The paved road right goes to Warner Valley and Drakesbad. You keep left, go 2.3 miles to Domingo Spring Campground, and then continue 0.4 mile to where the Pacific Crest Trail crosses your road. The trail is obscure, but it leads northwest onto a road spur angling right. Park on it. If you miss this spot, you'll reach a major road intersection 0.2 mile west of the trail. From that intersection the main road goes 7.8 miles west to Highway 36, ending as the Wilson Lake Road. This road leads east from Highway 36 at a point 6.3 miles southeast along the highway from the Lassen Park Road junction and 5.9 miles northwest along it from the Highway 32 junction. At the major road intersection, the road north is the one you'll want for Little Willow Lake.

Distances   0.9 mile (1.5 km) to North Fork
              Feather River
              3.6 miles (5.7 km) to North
              Stover Mountain summit
              6.7 miles (10.8 km) to Stover
              Camp
              9.9 miles (16.0 km) to Highway
              36

Trail description   Don't expect to find
spectacular scenery, for the terrain is subdued and much of the forest has been logged.
However, do expect to find one of the best-
planned, best-engineered trails to be found
anywhere. From the main road west of
Domingo Spring Campground the Pacific
Crest Trail (PCT) meanders southeast about
0.4 mile, crossing a one-lane road en route to
crossing a major one. Immediately beyond it
we head across a narrow, linear clearcut,
then continue our stroll across forested flat-
lands. Soon we angle west to descend into a
small gorge, our trail leading us to a large
horsebridge across the North Fork Feather
River. Here you'll find campsites just upstream, and some hikers may want to go no
farther.

A moderate, winding climb over the next
half mile gets us to a point from where we
have our first good view of Lassen Peak,
whose summit is one mile above us and 12
miles northwest. At this point we cross a
bend in a well-used logging road, and then
we climb 1⅔ miles to North Stover
Mountain's broad, viewless summit, which
lies about 0.1 mile south of the area covered
by this guide's Lassen Park map. Along our
ascent we have several opportunities to admire Lassen Peak. On this stretch, note the
sugar pines and Douglas-firs, two conifers
rarely seen in Lassen Park.

The hike south to North Stover Mountain
makes a plesant day hike, but south from it
the PCT wanders mostly through old logging
lands. These we encounter immediately as
we begin an easy descent south. In ⅔ mile we
cross a saddle, exchanging Plumas County
for Tehama County and USFS land for Collins Almanor Forest land. In 120 yards we
leave the private land and gently descend as
we parallel an abandoned logging road
south-southeast. In just under a mile we
cross it and then climb ½ mile east-southeast
to a major USFS road. About ¼ mile beyond
it we cross a low divide, re-enter Plumas
County, drop ¼ mile to an abandoned road,

and then drop another ½ mile to lovely,
spring-fed Stover Camp. This USFS primitive camp is most often used in September,
when deer hunters frequent it. Before then,
particularly during the week, you may have
the camp all to yourself.

The well marked 3¼-mile stretch of PCT
south to Highway 36 is, like the part to here,
mostly through old logging areas and across
roads of varying use and condition. About
1½ miles before the highway you diagonal
across Marian Creek, which for most of the
hiking season is little more than a line of dry
boulders. Where the trail crosses Highway
36, about ½ mile east of a signed county line,
no parking is available. So if you want to
hike the PCT north or south from the highway, park your car by a road intersection
about 0.2 mile east of the signed county line
and walk 0.4 mile east to the trail.

Pacific Crest Trail, Domingo Spring north to Drakesbad

Trailhead   Same as in previous hike.
Distances   4.8 miles (7.7 km) to Little
              Willow Lake
              5.3 miles (8.5 km) to Terminal
              Geyser
              7.1 miles (11.4 km) to Boiling
              Springs Lake
              8.2 miles (13.1 km) to Drakes-
              bad trailhead

Trail description   There are shorter and
easier routes to Little Willow Lake and Terminal Geyser, but the northbound Pacific
Crest Trail (PCT) provides the more solitary
route "less traveled by." The trail north begins along a short, abandoned road spur,
which makes a convenient place to park your
car. Staying quite level, the trail traverses
along the base of a volcanic-rubble slope,
then climbs briefly onto a closed road. Up it
you count off 80 yards before the trail resumes. It switchbacks once across this
steeply ascending road, then joins it where
the road's gradient reduces to moderate. We
now follow the road 0.4 mile, to where its
gradient sharply increases and our trail
branches off its west side. This 2.8-mile trail
segment is somewhat shaded by ponderosa
and sugar pines, incense-cedars and white

firs—all but the last species being rather uncommon inside Lassen Park. Our PCT climbs to a ridge—visited occasionally by deer and bear—crosses it three times, then arrives at the brink of an east-west trending secondary ridge, from which we can see Willow Lake northeast below us and Lassen Peak northwest above us.

When botanist William H. Brewer first visited this area in September 1863, he came up the Willow Lake valley and at the lake caught his first trout. His traveling companions caught about 200. Today, however, the lake is not as inviting, for a herd of cattle grazes along its shore. Furthermore, an abandoned trail to the lake and a road to it both cross private land.

From your viewpoint, note the bedrock exposures below you that extend intermittently from the lake up-canyon into nearby Lassen Park: these rocks are the park's oldest rocks. In 1980 the U.S. Geological Survey began radiometrically dating the Lassen area's volcanic rocks, but it had not yet dated these, which the author believes to be 1-2 million years old. Before leaving your spot, note the lakelet ¼ mile to the east. This was ponded up behind sediments left by a glacier descending through Willow Lake valley. Previous glaciers buried this valley under at least 600 feet of ice, and earlier ones overrode your viewpoint.

Beyond the point, the trail contours west, descends to a saddle on the main ridge, crosses it, and traverses northwest across the west slope. Up the canyon to the west, a private road climbs to a broad saddle, where your now-descending trail almost touches it, then finally joins it after a 0.1-mile paralleling descent northwest. Follow the road 50 yards to where it forks. The quickest way to Terminal Geyser is to branch right and follow the road 1.2 miles to its end at the geyser. It was along this road in 1978 that Phillips Petroleum Company brought in a large drilling rig and drilled an exploratory geothermal well. The company no longer plans to develop this site, an action that would have destroyed Terminal Geyser, but the capped well still remains.

If you're bound for Little Willow Lake, stay on the PCT, which resumes on the west side of the left fork. The trail parallels the road toward the lake's outlet creek, then climbs steeply up along this seasonal creek to a

junction near the "lake's" outlet. Only during snowmelt does a knee-deep lake fill the basin, and when it does, mosquitoes are superabundant. By late season the lake has retreated to the basin's southwest corner, and wet meadow pervades the rest. The mucky basin tends to fascinate only hardcore nature lovers. The trails from Little Willow Lake and Terminal Geyser north to Boiling Springs Lake and the Drakesbad area are well marked, and these are described, albeit in a southern direction, in Chapter 12.

Little Willow Lake and Terminal Geyser via Stump Ranch Road

Trailhead First see the trailhead directions in this chapter's first hike. At the "major road intersection" mentioned in them, you start north (right turn, if you're coming from Domingo Spring), and drive 0.8 mile to a junction with Stump Ranch Road, branching right. To reach the trailhead, follow the road 4⅔ miles to a tiny parking/turnaround area at road's end.

Distances 0.1 mile (0.2 km) to Little Willow Lake

1.6 miles (2.6 km) to Terminal Geyser

3.7 miles (5.9 km) to Drakesbad trailhead

Trail description The trail to Little Willow Lake is short and easy, just up and over the saddle you see from road's end. As implied in the previous hike, Little Willow Lake appeals more to mosquitoes than to people, so until early August, be prepared for hordes of them. By then the lake has already begun shrinking and is certainly not photogenic. The lake probably owes its origin to a small glacier descending Sifford Mountain's east slope perhaps 11,000-20,000 years ago. Basaltic Sifford Mountain, formerly called Red Mountain, is itself fairly new to the Lassen scene, for this shield volcano is about 60,000 years old—merely a drop in the geologic bucket of time.

To reach Terminal Geyser, head to Little Willow Lake's outlet, where you'll meet the Pacific Crest Trail. Take it north for a one-mile-long, totally unnecessary climb and drop over a ridge. Had the trail been properly surveyed in the early 1970s, the trail today would have contoured effortlessly over to the present trail junction. From that junction a trail upslope immediately divides into two branches, which rejoin by Boiling Springs Lake, about 1½ miles away. You, however, descend ¼ mile southeast to a road, meeting a spur trail midway along your descent. This short trail goes over to a Terminal Geyser viewpoint, but the geyser is better viewed from below. Therefore, follow the road north 180 yards to the roaring geyser, at road's end. Continually churning out steam, it is technically a fumarole, not a geyser. Observe it with caution.

Where your trail ends at the road, you might note that it continues downslope from the road's opposite side. This rarely used segment descends 0.7 mile to the north edge of Willow Lake meadow. The park border is not much farther, and private land lies immediately beyond it.

Twin Meadows via North Arm Rice Creek

Trailhead See this chapter's first hike for the location of Wilson Lake Road. Leaving Highway 36, drive 3.0 miles up this road to a county-line road intersection atop a crest saddle. Turn left and take the Wild Cattle Mountain road 5⅔ miles to a junction with a dead-end spur road, branching left. This junction is about 250 yards before a bridge across the South Arm of Rice Creek. Drive 1¼ miles up the spur road to where it obviously becomes a steep, narrow jeep road. Although the spur road is good all the way to its end, it has a short, steep section at about midpoint, and this stops some drivers.

Distance 1.6 miles (2.6 km) to Twin Meadows

Trail description Older maps show a trail leading to Twin Meadows. In fact, no such trail exists. However, you can still easily reach the meadows by taking the jeep road, which remains steep for the first ¼ mile. The grade abates to moderate along the second ¼ mile, then it levels as it approaches Spencer Meadow, a cow pasture on private land. Just south of the meadow a short spur road branches west, quickly reaching the Childs Meadows Trail. You keep to the main road, which veers northeast at the meadow's north

end, then quickly dies out. Now only yards away from the park border, the route is simple: strike northeast over the nearby crest saddle, from which you see meadow spreading out below. Off the beaten track, Twin Meadows may see more cows than humans, the illegal aliens entering the park from Spencer Meadow or from the North Arm of Rice Creek. If you're an equestrian, keep in mind that in the Lassen Park backcountry you're not allowed to keep horses overnight.

Older maps show a trail descending the North Arm, then climbing to Drake Lake. Though spurts of cattle paths exist, the hiking trail doesn't, and in places you sink to your ankles in mud as you hack your way through row after row of dense alders. It is unfortunate that Lassen Park doesn't have a loop trail encircling its perimeter and connecting Twin Meadows with Drake Lake. Should you try to make the Twin Meadows-Drake Lake connection, bear due east—a route that avoids the alder groves and a lot of elevation loss and gain.

Duck, Blue and Ridge Lakes

Trailhead See the previous hike for directions to a deadend spur road. For Duck and Blue lakes, drive about ½ mile up it, stopping in a nearly level area. The road immediately ahead is quite steep. For Ridge Lake, continue past the spur road, bridging the South Arm of Rice Creek in about 250 yards (5.8 miles from the county-line junction). Continue 1⅓ miles east beyond the creek to another junction with a deadend spur road, up which you drive 2.2 miles to road's end.

Distances 0.4 mile (0.6 km) to Ridge Lake
0.5 mile (0.8 km) to Duck Lake
0.6 mile (1.0 km) to Blue Lake

Trail description Trails to these lakes are nonexistent, though at the rate roads have been built in the upper Feather River basin, you may soon be able to drive to them. The cross-country route to Duck and Blue lakes is quite simple: strike east across the flat up to a low ridge. If you've kept true to your bearing, you'll see Duck Lake to the south, below you. A brief walk up the ridge will reveal Blue Lake. Like Ridge Lake, neither sees many

Little Willow Lake is definitely more meadow than lake. Blue elderberries (described on page 40) grow in rocky places. A Pacific Crest Trail bridge crosses the North Fork Feather River.

visitors except perhaps a few during September's deer season. Ridge Lake is a bit harder to find. From road's end maintain a west-northwest course up a currently well-forested, amorphous ridge.

Childs Meadows Trail

Trailhead By the stables at the east end of Childs Meadows Resort. This Highway 36 resort, probably the largest in the Lassen area, is about 4½ miles east of the Lassen Park Road junction and about 7½ miles northwest of the Highway 32 junction.

Distances   5.0 miles (8.0 km) to Spencer Meadow
6.1 miles (9.8 km) to Twin Meadows

Trail description Although open to the public, this trail is essentially for the benefit of the resort's equestrians. Few hikers would care to struggle up the lower part of this mostly viewless route. Climbing out of a 1000-foot-deep glacial canyon requires some effort and, offering few switchbacks, the trail forces you to confront the challenge without a break. For the first half mile the forested path's grade is moderate, but beyond a usually flowing creeklet it becomes steep, then very steep. About 1.4 miles from the trailhead you cross a spring, then quickly reach a bouldery creekbed that you cross and follow up for ¼ mile.

Just before a logged-out area you veer north for a much easier climb along and between crests of lateral moraines. The black oaks, incense-cedars and ponderosa pines seen near the trailhead are now replaced with Jeffrey pines, lodgepole pines and red firs; only the white firs remain. In this thinner forest, mat and green manzanitas thrive in the summer-dry soils.

After 3.1 miles of easy progress, most of it as gentle ascent, you come to a junction with the abandoned Hanna Trail, which once descended Canyon Creek. Then in several minutes you meet a short spur road curving north to nearby Spencer Meadow, an unfenced cow pasture on private land. If you're continuing on to Twin Meadows, follow the spur road briefly east to the "Main" road, a jeep road, and see the description of the "Twin Meadows via North Arm Rice Creek" route.

Heart Lake via Glassburner Meadow

Trailhead From the Highway 172 junction in Mineral, drive 2¼ miles east on Highway 36 to a road junction beside Nanny Creek. If you're coming from the east, this junction is 2¼ miles west from the Highway 36/Lassen Park Road (Highway 89) junction. Drive 2.2 miles up the road to a junction, from where Road 29N22 traverses 3.0 miles northeast to the Lassen Park Road and Road 30N16 traverses 6.5 miles west over to Road 17. You turn left and drive 2.0 miles on Road 30N16 to a trailhead in Plantation Gulch.

Distances   2.0 miles (3.2 km) to Glassburner Meadow
4.1 miles (6.6 km) to Lassen Park's south boundary
6.7 miles (10.8 km) to Digger Creek trail junction
7.0 miles (11.3 km) to Heart Lake, southeast shore

Trail description Since this trail is about three times longer than either of the other two trails to Heart Lake, few will want to take it, particularly since it climbs well above the lake and then drops, rather steeply, almost 1000 feet to it. The first 0.4 mile of route is actually a jeep road, but this yields to a definite trail—Trail 3E10—just before you cross the Plantation Gulch creeklet. This trail climbs up a brushy, youthful looking moraine left behind by a glacier as few as 10,000 years ago. The glacier was on the west side of the moraine and it flowed down to Martin Creek, reaching it about ¼ mile below your trailhead. In a previous glaciation, a much larger glacier inundated the area, including the high ridge east of Plantation Gulch, and this glacier extended down-canyon all the way to Mineral.

Your trail crosses the moraine near its upper end, then rollercoasters ½ mile north to a meadow, the first of three, along a spring-fed creek. Hikers have camped here and at the second one, Glassburner Meadow, which is ¼ mile farther. You reach the waterlogged third meadow in another ¼ mile, then soon cross a cascading creek that feeds it. Ahead lies ½ mile of moderate climbing, followed by ¼ mile of nearly level walking. Your trail climbs up a linear gully before swerving east and then starting a northward

½-mile climb to Lassen Park's south border. Through a forest of red firs, western white pines and some mountain hemlocks, you now climb ½ mile to a low crest on the park's west border. Having climbed to here for naught, you now drop several hundred feet over the next mile, but at least get several views of the Twin Meadows-Rocky Peak-Heart Lake area below you. Along the last ⅓ mile of this stretch you cross three spring-fed creeklets, the last two flowing through a sloping corn-lily meadow.

Immediately beyond the meadow we reach a small rocky crest, over which a trail once descended to the Cabin Spring road. Our trail turns left and winds down the crest ¼ mile before turning northwest to descend somewhat brushy slopes. After ½ mile, a meadow heralds another change in trail direction, and from it we drop steeply southwest 0.2 mile to a trail junction near Heart Lake. If you hike ⅓ mile east on a trail, you'll come to several good campsites on a shady flat by the lake's southeast shore. The trail west from the junction immediately forks, giving rise to the South Fork and Digger Creek trails, described next.

Heart Lake via South Fork Digger Creek

Trailhead USFS Road 17, running 21.7 miles across Lassen Park's western borderlands, connects Highway 36 with Highway 44. This major road leaves Highway 36 at the east end of the Battle Creek bridge, this junction being 0.1 mile east of Battle Creek Campground and 1.1 miles west of the Lassen Park headquarters. Drive 9.7 miles up Road 17 to this hike's trailhead at South Fork Digger Creek. If you're coming from the north, you'll find the Road 17/Highway 44 junction 1.1 miles west of 44's junction with the Lassen Park Road (Highway 89). From 44, Road 17 goes 2.4 miles southwest to the Deep Hole jeep road, 2.7 miles more to the Brokeoff Meadows road, an additional 0.2 mile to the Viola road, 5.5 miles to the Digger Creek trailhead, and finally 1.2 miles to the South Fork trailhead.

Distance 2.4 miles (3.9 km) to Heart Lake

Trail description This trail and the following one are, for all practical purposes, equally long and climb an equal amount.

The author prefers this trail, however, for the scenery along it is more diverse. The first 0.4 mile of trail is along the north bank of the well-shaded South Fork, and then the trail veers away, climbing in 0.8 mile to a wet meadow trapped between two glacial moraines. The height of these moraines above the South Fork indicates that the last glacier down this canyon was at least 400 feet thick.

With the meadow marking the trail's midpoint, we now gently climb ¼ mile east, then steeply up to a small saddle near Rocky Peak. Here our course turns northeast and, after a minute's walk, we cross a second small saddle and descend in a few minutes to a creek fed by Rocky Peak's two tarns. From it we traverse ¼ mile over a low, broad surface, then see Heart Lake. When you do, you can either go to campsites along the lake's west shore or strike east to sites along its southeast shore. Though mostly shallow, this trout-stocked lake does have a deep center that one old-timer insists is "bottomless."

Heart Lake via Digger Creek

Trailhead Just 1.2 miles north along Road 17 from previous hike's trailhead.

Distance 2.3 miles (3.7 km) to Heart Lake, northwest shore

Trail description This trail is very direct, for it follows Digger Creek up toward Heart Lake. The route starts a few yards north of the creek's bank and climbs through a white-fir/incense-cedar forest that has a few sugar pines and, in brushy spots, Jeffrey pines. By the time this viewless trail reaches a trail junction near the northwest shore of Heart Lake, the vegetation has shifted to lodgepole pines, red firs and western white pines. About ½ mile before this junction the trail crosses 100 yards of very wet ground that is even soggy in late summer.

From the trail junction, Trail 3E10 climbs northeast, the South Fork trail peels south to the lake's west shore, and your trail continues ⅓ mile east, curving around the lake's very shallow east arm and then dying out at good campsites by the southeast shore. The three trails leading to Heart Lake are not well maintained, though they are, by and large, easy to follow. A problem, however, can arise at the junction near Heart Lake if there is downed timber and hikers and horsemen make their own routes. Then, one could mistakenly go down the South Fork trail when he wanted to go down the Digger Creek trail. Therefore, if you see Heart Lake after a minute's walk "west" from the junction, you'll know you're on the South Fork trail.

Blue Lake Trail

Trailhead Drive to Brokeoff Meadows road, following the trailhead directions in the "Heart Lake via South Fork" hike. Go 2.3 miles up this road to a junction, curve left at it, and in 0.1 mile reach the Blue Lake Canyon road. This poor road goes 1.8 miles up the North Fork of Bailey Creek to the Lassen Park boundary, but few will want to drive it all the way. In particular, you'll hit a short, muddy stretch about ½ mile before the park boundary.

Distance 1.0 mile (1.6 km) to unnamed lake

Trail description From the road's end, Trail 3E08 climbs gently ½ mile up Bailey Creek, then steeply up above it for several hundred yards. After several hundred more yards of nearly level, creekside trail, the trail crosses Bailey Creek—a raging torrent in early season—and shortly dies out among meadow grasses. Although officially called the Blue Lake Trail, this trail doesn't visit that lake but rather goes to another one about ⅓ mile west of it. If you plow southeast about 200 yards through the meadow's lush growth, you'll reach this unnamed, rather plain lake. Its formation, the author believes, is quite unusual. Note the winter-avalanche tracks down the steep slopes immediately south of the lake. Perhaps a large rockslide came down the avalance tracks and stopped in the meadow. Later avalanches added rocks to these, eventually constructing a wall that now makes up the rocky north shore of the lake. If you're geologically inclined, hike up to the lake and see what you conclude.

If you've hiked to the unnamed lake, you might go cross-country to miniscule Blue Lake, atop a rocky bench. From the north end of the bench look at the slopes immediately east and north of you. A large landslide, perhaps several centuries old, dropped north to Bailey Creek, then west ¼ mile down it to the grassy meadow's northeast end.

Deep Hole

Trailhead See the "Heart Lake via South Fork" trailhead description to the Deep Hole jeep road.

Distance 0.7 mile (1.1 km) to Deep Hole, west rim

Trail description If you've got a *narrow* 4WD, a high-clearance compact pickup, or a motorcycle, you should be able to drive east up to the rim, then north and south along it. Otherwise, plan to hike up it, for though the road's steepest part is its first 200 yards, it later surprises unwary drivers with a projecting rock or two. Worse, dense brush is encroaching upon the road, and it can really scratch your vehicle's paint. Given time, the brush will narrow the road to a trail.

Brush also lines most of Deep Hole, and this can hamper your efforts to reach its flat, forested bottom. Should you want to descend into it, head south about 200 yards up the rim road, then struggle about 100 yards east through brush before dropping past trees. Deep Hole is an anomaly in Lassen country, being a pit crater formed by collapsing lava. This crater, which may be only several thousand years old, is a kind of feature more common in the Hawaiian Islands. There are no other pit craters in the Lassen area.

16   Caribou Wilderness

Introduction   Lacking caribou but possessing dozens of lakes, lakelets and ponds, this wilderness should have been named "Thousand Lakes Wilderness." Unfortunately, a lake-deficient wilderness (described in the next chapter) already has claim to that title. However, Caribou Wilderness does have one iron-clad claim: of all the wilderness areas in California, none can match it for easy hiking. For the most part, its trails are either level or gently ascending or descending. Of the area's 25½ miles of maintained trail, only ⅓ mile is steep—and another trail bypasses that short stretch. With lakes only an hour or two away from its trailheads, this lightly used, 30-square-mile wilderness is ideal for novice backpackers or adults with young children. Nevertheless, be forewarned: the same gentle terrain which makes hiking so easy also makes off-trail routefinding hard—due to lack of prominent landmarks. Although most of the trails are easy to follow, don't let your children wander off by themselves, since they can easily lose their bearings. Properly supervised, they can have an extremely enjoyable outdoor experience.

Good roads lead to the area's three trailheads, which are Hay Meadow, Caribou Lake and Cone Lake. The area's southern trails are described under Hay Meadow, its central trails under Caribou Lake, and its northern trails under Cone Lake. None of these three trailhead-and-trail groups is superior to the other two. Each trailhead has ample parking space and all become snow-free about the same time, generally in mid-June. All trails climb through modest terrain to nearby, usually shallow lakes. Therefore, what trailhead you start from and what trails you hike on must be purely subjective decisions.

Hay Meadow Trails

Trailhead   Along the east side of Hay Meadow, which is about ½ mile below the south boundary of Caribou Wilderness. Reach it from Chester (measure mileage from the Drakesbad/Juniper Lake turnoff) by driving 5.0 miles east on Highway 36 to USFS Road 10, opposite southbound County Road A13. If you're driving west from Susanville, you'll find the Road 10 junction 8.1 miles west of the County Road A21 junction. Northbound Road 10 quickly turns west, immediately crosses Bailey Creek, then continues north again. After 9.6 miles on Road 10, you recross Bailey Creek and in 0.4 mile reach a junction with Hay Meadow road (Road 30N72). Follow the road 1.6 miles to a large parking area at road's end.

If you plan to drive to Silver Lake, Caribou Lake Trailhead or Cone Lake Trailhead, continue north on Road 10. Just 0.6 mile past the Hay Meadow junction, Road 10 turns east while wide, newer Road 32N10 continues straight ahead past Echo Lake, which has a primitive camping area along its west shore. Currently this road deadends in 1.0 mile, but ultimately it may replace the Trail Lake trail. Trail Lake, incidentally, is mostly waist-deep or less—hardly a fisherman's lake.

You'll find better fishing at Shotoverin Lake, along Road 10. Road 10 winds above the south shore of unseen Echo Lake, then winds down to a junction with Road 30N11, 2.6 miles past the previous junction. Continue straight ahead and in 0.6 mile veer up and left as a wider road branches right for a 4.2-mile descent to County Road A21. After 2.5 miles, Road 10 makes a sharp left; if you were to continue ahead, you'd reach A21 in 2.6 miles, joining it at a point 0.2 mile south of Silver Lake Road. Road 10 climbs west 1.6 miles to Shotoverin Lake, then another 0.8 mile to the Trail Lake trailhead. In 0.7 mile you reach Rocky Knoll Campground. Silver Beach Picnic Area, along the northeast lobe of Silver Lake, is just west. Road 10 jogs briefly east (right) to a junction from which the Silver Lake Road (Road 110) descends 5.0 miles east to Road A21. On Road 10, curve west 0.5 mile to another junction, from which you could drive 0.2 mile southwest to Silver Bowl Picnic Area or just past it to Silver Bowl Campground. This campground is better than Rocky Knoll Campground, for it is more level and has fewer mosquitoes. After a 0.3-mile climb north on Road 10, you'll reach a spur road that climbs briefly west to a large parking area by the Caribou Lake Trailhead. See that trailhead description for driving directions from Caribou Lake to Cone Lake.

Distances   2.0 miles (3.2 km) to Beauty Lake
2.1 miles (3.4 km) to Hidden Lake No. 5 via Indian Meadows
2.4 miles (3.9 km) to Hidden Lake No. 5 via Beauty Lake trail
2.6 miles (4.2 km) to Evelyn Lake
2.7 miles (4.4 km) to Long Lake via shortest route
2.9 miles (4.7 km) to Long Lake via Indian Meadows
3.2 miles (5.1 km) to Posey Lake
3.8 miles (6.1 km) to Long Lake via Beauty Lake trail
7.4 miles (11.9 km) for Beauty-Long-Hidden lakes semiloop
8.7 miles (14.0 km) to Caribou Lake Trailhead by shortest route
10.4 miles (16.8 km) to Cone Lake Trailhead by shortest route

Trail description   Hiking in the Caribou Wilderness is so easy that almost anyone can make a 10-lake, 7.4-mile semiloop hike without much effort. Until early August, hordes of mosquitoes will probably speed you along your way around the northeast edge of Hay Meadow. Just ⅓ mile from the trailhead, the trail forks at the swampy south end of Indian Meadow, it too with pre-August mosquito hordes. The right trail is the shortest trail to the Hidden Lakes, but it has more mosquitoes and contains the only steep stretch of trail to be found in the wilderness. This trail parallels the meadow's east edge, crosses through its northeast corner, parallels a meandering creek northwest, then climbs steeply to a junction by Hidden Lake No. 1.

The main trail—the recommended route—goes past the meadow's southwest edge then climbs moderately to a second junction. The trail branching right, which is the recommended return route, climbs 0.4 mile to Lake No. 1 and a junction with steep trail just described. Most hikers would probably rank the Hidden Lakes inferior to the other named lakes found nearby, for they are generally smaller and shallower, and certainly have fewer campsites. Lakes Nos. 1 and 3 are warm, oversized wading pools; Lake No. 2 is a bit deeper and is great for swimming; Lakes Nos. 4 and 5 are best, with good camping on the land separating them. The author, when hiking to Long Lake, prefers to visit Beauty Lake and other lakes first, then return to Hay Meadow via the Hidden Lakes. This way one can have a nice warm swim in shallow Hidden Lakes Nos. 1 or 2, then have an easy downhill hike back to the trailhead.

Beyond the second trail branching right to the Hidden Lakes, the main trail climbs ¼ mile north-northwest to a third junction. The shortest route to Long Lake is along the trail branching right, which reaches the south shore of that lake in just over one mile. The most scenic, and longest, route to Long Lake is via Beauty Lake, which you reach after a ½-mile moderate climb northwest from the third junction. This lake's most popular campsites are along its west shore just north of where the trail leaves the lakeshore. Though good sized, Beauty Lake is shallow, providing warm, enjoyable swimming before the afternoon wind whips it up.

Top: North Caribou (just left of center) and South Caribou (far right) stand above large, shallow Long Lake. Bottom: Gem Lake is rimmed with sloping land, making camping impractical.

About ¼ mile beyond Beauty Lake you reach a small, linear lake, around whose south end an often wet trail segment bends west to the north shore of nearby Evelyn Lake. A good camp lies on high ground just north of the lake and its shoreline trail. Near the camp you can dive off a low west-shore cliff into the linear lake's refreshing water. Larger Evelyn Lake may appeal more to fishermen.

From Evelyn Lake the trail climbs north over a low ridge to Posey Lake which, except in early season, is composed of a southern large, neck-deep wading pond barely separated from a northern, larger, shallow lake. Camp either on Posey's southwest peninsula or above its north shore. Beyond the lake, the trail rolls over to Long Lake, reached just

after you pass a bilobed lakelet. From the trail junction at Long Lake's southwest shore, the hiker has several options: return the way you came; return via the short trail; return via Hidden Lakes; continue north through the wilderness. The short trail begins from the lake's south shore. You'll probably find two trails starting south, the eastern one crossing through an ephemeral shallow pond along the lake's seasonal outlet creek. The two trails reunite by the pond's south end. The Hidden Lakes trail is obvious, passing by four sometimes murky ponds before reaching the divide between Lakes Nos. 4 and 5.

The trail north past Long Lake's west shore offers several campsites (the large lake has many), some with a view of North and South

Caribou, two very glaciated peaks. North Caribou, the highest, is most easily climbed from Cypress Lake. North of Long Lake the trail ambles 1.9 miles across easy terrain up to South Divide Lake, passing a shallow lakelet, then a knee-deep pond along the way. See the next section for hikes in the central Caribou Wilderness.

Caribou Lake Trails

Trailhead Near Caribou Lake's dam, which is about ½ mile below the east boundary of Caribou Wilderness. Reach it from Chester by first driving 13 miles east on Highway 36 to a junction with County Road A21. Here is your last opportunity for gas and food. If you're driving west from Susanville, you'll reach this junction 15½ miles west of the Highway 44 junction. Drive 13¾ miles north on A21 to a junction with Silver Lake Road. This junction is 4½ miles south of A21's north end at Highway 44, which in turn is 28 miles east of the Highway 44E/89 junction near Old Station. No supplies are available east of that junction. On Silver Lake Road, drive 5.0 miles west up to a junction. Rocky Knoll Campground, Silver Beach Picnic Area and Silver Lake are just ahead. You, however, turn right and follow Road 10 0.5 mile to a junction with a road to Silver Lake's north shore. On that road you'll reach Silver Bowl Picnic Area in 0.2 mile and Silver Bowl Campground just beyond it. This campground is better than Rocky Knoll Campground, for it is more level and has fewer mosquitoes. After an 0.3-mile climb north on Road 10, you'll reach a spur road that climbs briefly west to a large parking area by the Caribou Lake Trailhead.

If you want to drive from the Silver Lake/Caribou Lake area south to the Hay Meadow Trailhead, follow in reverse the driving directions given in its "Trailhead" section. If you want to drive north from the Caribou Lake Trailhead to the Cone Lake Trailhead, then follow Road 10 3.6 miles to its junction with Road 31N36, coming in on the right. In ¼ mile Road 10 makes a sharp turn to the right and then goes 6.2 miles northeast down to Highway 44. From the sharp turn, continue straight ahead for 1.0 mile, then turn left and follow another road 1.8 miles to its end at Cone Lake.

Distances   0.8 mile (1.3 km) to Cowboy Lake
1.8 miles (2.8 km) to Emerald Lake
2.0 miles (3.2 km) to Jewel Lake
2.2 miles (3.5 km) to Eleanor Lake
2.3 miles (3.7 km) to Gem Lake
2.8 miles (4.5 km) to Rim Lake
3.1 miles (5.0 km) to North Divide Lake
3.4 miles (5.5 km) to South Divide Lake
3.5 miles (5.6 km) to Cypress Lake and to Black Lake via Jewel Lake
3.6 miles (5.8 km) to Turnaround Lake
3.8 miles (6.1 km) to Black Lake via North Divide Lake
4.5 miles (7.2 km) to northeastern Twin Lake
5.4 miles (8.7 km) to Triangle Lake, north shore
6.0 miles (9.6 km) to Long Lake southwest shore
7.2 miles (11.6 km) to Cone Lake Trailhead by shortest route
8.7 miles (14.0 km) to Hay Meadow Trailhead by shortest route

Trail description From the parking lot brief trail climbs up to an outhouse and main trail above the southeast shore of heavily fished Caribou Lake. After a 0.4-mile westward traverse, you'll meet a feeder trail. This trail, meeting ours just yards outside the wilderness, ascends 0.4 mile from Silver Lake, and it is largely used by Silver Lake's summer residents. There is no room for parking at its trailhead. Continuing briefly westward, the hiker rounds a pond, glimpses Caribou Lake's west end, then comes to a second junction. A left turn starts you on your way toward Emerald, Rim, Cypress and Gem lakes, the Divide Lakes, and lakes usually visited from the Hay Meadow Trailhead. Continuing ahead ultimately gets you to the Cone Lake Trailhead, and this route will be described first.

1. Cowboy Lake to Triangle Lake. Just beyond the second junction the trail ahead comes to and circles around shallow Cowboy Lake, which is mostly too shallow for

wimming. The trail then wanders through a
hady forest for ½ mile before switchbacking
p an escarpment and shooting up a gully to
ewel Lake. Above this lake's north shore
ou'll find good legal campsites as well as
nes near the southwest shore of Eleanor
ake, which is a short off-trail walk to the
orth. At least two unofficial footpaths go to
. Both of these shallow lakes have their
harms—Jewel, with its setting and greater
epth, Eleanor, with its relative isolation.
ast Jewel, the trail winds through an open
orest on a nearly level bench, then climbs
est along the base of a brushy escarpment.

highly vegetated pond marks the end of
ur short climb and heralds an approaching
ail junction. Descending to it in a few min-
tes, we face a choice: south, north, or back
e way we came. Black Lake lies 200 yards
outh and, though pleasant, it lacks notable
atures. All pleasant, level campsites are too
ose to the lake's edge to be legal. However,
ou could enjoy a swim or engage in angling,
en either backtrack to the trailhead or
osey ¾ mile south down to North Divide
ake. North of the junction, larger Turn-
ound Lake presents the same campsite
roblem, though some hikers have made
gal campsites above the lake's north and
outh shores. Turnaround Lake is one of the
ilderness area's largest lakes, and the butte
ove its west shore adds a pleasant accent.
win Lakes and Triangle Lake are described
the Cone Lake Trailhead section.

Gem Lake and Divide Lakes. From the
econd junction, the hiker quickly reaches,
en rounds, a wade-across, bilobed lake.
eyond it is an escarpment, which the trail
oon tackles, switchbacking up it to an easier
imb 0.2 mile west to a third junction.
merald Lake lies just 180 yards up a
outhwest-climbing trail and is certainly
orth the effort even if you don't plan to
ontinue beyond it. West from the third junc-
on the main trail gradually levels, and in
4 mile, just past a narrow, gravelly flat, it
aches a fourth. If you veer right, you'll
ake a moderate 0.2-mile climb to
emmed-in Gem Lake, with no suitable
ampsites. But as usual, it does provide good
ay-use fishing and swimming. Those look-
g for camping potential should veer left
d climb one easy mile to knee-to-waist-
eep North Divide Lake. Don't camp by this
ke's shore or in its surrounding meadow
t rather among the lodgepoles near the

trail junction or along the trail leading north
from it toward Black Lake. The best
campsites, however, are above the west
shore of deeper though still shallow South
Divide Lake, which is found after a few minutes' walk southwest from the trail junction.
Beyond the lake you have a 1.9-mile descent
to the northwest shore of Long Lake, with a
lakelet providing a midway thirst quencher.

3. Emerald Lake to Cypress Lake. Emerald
Lake, mentioned in the previous paragraph,
is one of the area's deeper lakes. A low, rocky
bench sits above its north shore and is ideal
for camping or sunbathing. The trail to Rim
and Cypress lakes is a circuitous one, winding far more than necessary. To avoid an
escarpment, the trail meanders southeast ½
mile and tackles it at its lowest point. This
eastward migration does have one advantage, for it provides you with a view of Silver
and Caribou lakes and the lands beyond
them. The trail then winds—and I do mean
winds—up to Rim Lake. This stretch is up
sparsely forested bedrock slabs, and at times
the trail is hard to follow. Look for "ducks"
(little rock piles) marking the route. With a
scarcity of trees, trail blazes are few, and if
you are going to get lost on any of the area's
trails, it will be along this stretch. However,
if you proceed west upslope for about ½
mile, you're almost certain to encounter Rim
Lake. If you don't, walk north over to the
brink of the nearby escarpment and take a
bearing on Emerald Lake, below you. Rim
Lake is a pleasant sight on a hot day, for as
shallow as it appears at its east end, it does
have some deep water midway along its
south shore—and diving rocks to make entry
more enjoyable. Camp, if you want to, just
south or west of these rocks.

Another ½-mile hiking stretch rewards
you with an unnamed lake, mostly waist-
deep or less, which is blessed with a beautiful backdrop, a prominent escarpment. The
trail swings around the lake's south arm—
itself at the brink of an escarpment—then
rolls over a low divide to Cypress Lake. From
this divide you can map a logical cross-
country route up to the summit of North
Caribou peak, about an hour's hike away.
Cypress Lake, rockbound and attractive like
the other lakes along this trail, was probably
named for a few junipers that grow nearby;
cypress trees are nonexistent herabouts.
Look for campsites among the small slabs
and gravelly flats tucked around the lake.

Cone Lake Trails

Trailhead   At Cone Lake, which is about ¾ mile below the north boundary of Caribou Wilderness. From Chester or Westwood, follow directions in the Caribou Lake section up to the start of the Silver Lake Road. You can then continue to follow those directions to the Cone Lake Trailhead—that route all along graded roads—or you can continue 4.5 miles north on A21 to its end at Highway 44. If you're coming from Susanville, you'll want to take 44 all the way to this junction. Now drive 4.6 miles northwest on the highway, mostly in flat, broad Pine Creek Valley, to a junction with Crater Mountain road, starting east, and Road 10, starting west. If you enter forest again and reach a roadside rest, you've driven 0.1 mile too far. Approaching this junction from the west, you'll follow Highway 44 about 23½ miles from its junction with Higway 89 near Old Station. Watch for the roadside rest, which you reach moments before Road 10 at the northwest edge of Pine Creek Valley. Now drive 6.2 miles up Road 10 to where it angles sharply left. If you were to continue south on it, you'd reach the Caribou Lake Trailhead spur road in 3.7 miles and Silver Lake 1.0 mile farther. Rather, continue ahead for 1.0 mile, turn left, and drive 1.8 miles up a broad, well-graded road to a moderately large parking area at road's end.

Distances   1.8 miles (2.9 km) to Triangle Lake, north shore
2.6 miles (4.2 km) to northeastern Twin Lake
3.2 miles (5.1 km) to Turnaround Lake
3.9 miles (6.3 km) to Black Lake
4.8 miles (7.8 km) to North Divide Lake

7.2 miles (11.6 km) to Caribou Lake Trailhead by shortes route
10.4 miles (16.8 km) to Hay Meadow Trailhead by shortes route

Trail description   Cone Lake, which is wais deep after winter's snowmelt and merely a meadow by hunting season, offers little at traction, much less drinking water. However, the usually dry hike to Triangle Lake starts out easy, climbing through an open forest with Jeffrey pines before entering a shadier one of lodgepoles and red firs. Just before coming to a junction by Triangle Lake's outlet, we meet an overflow pond usually dry. Branching right, a trail takes 1¼ miles to weave leisurely around the lake's west shore, finally ending at the main trai just north of a shallow pond. The main trail skirting along the lake's east shore, reaches this spot in ⅔ mile. The west-shore trail however, offers better camping. In fact, two of its campsites, both perched on a tree-shaded rocky bench and straddling the border of Sections 20 and 29, may be the best in the whole wilderness. The lake's two southern arms, however, are quite shallow and are not too esthetic in late season after the water level drops.

Just after the west-shore trail meets the main trail, you pass a pond and reach the north edge of the northeastern Twin Lake. Its other "twins"—there are two more—are shallow and undesirable. No legal campsites exist by the main lake's shore, though you could make one midway between it and the southernmost lobe of Triangle Lake. Turnaround Lake, ½ mile south of the main Twin Lake, offers more selection, though most of its campsites are illegally close to the water. Beyond it you reach a junction described in the Caribou Lake section. See that section for trails and lakes of the central part of the wilderness.

7 Thousand Lakes Wilderness

Introduction   Thousand Lakes Wilderness leaves something to be desired: lakes. About 990 lakes short of its claimed number, this 25½-square-mile wilderness is certainly misnamed. And of the 10 or so lakes present, only three are first-rate. Lake Eiler, easily the largest and most popular, is snow-free after mid-June. However, Magee and Everett lakes, the area's two other respectable trailside lakes, don't shed the last of their shoreline snow until early or mid-July. Barrett and Durbin lakes are largely waist-deep or less and semistagnant by late season. The same is true of oversized Box Lake, encircled by, but unseen from, the nearby trails. Upper Twin Lake barely gets your knees wet, though its twin, just an easy off-trail jaunt southeast, is a great swimming hole. Hufford Lake and the smaller lake ¾ mile above it would be worth a visit if a trail were built to them. The cross-country routes to them are brushy and/or steep. About two dozen ponds lie in the area's Thousand Lakes Valley, and these produce daily hordes of mosquitoes through most of July. Perhaps the magnitude of these hordes led early visitors to conclude there must be at least a thousand lakes actively producing them.

By August the mosquitoes have abated and the lakes have entered their prime. But with good lakes few in number, the wilderness can seem crowded even with only two dozen camping parties. Fortunately, however, the wilderness is not close to any major highway and, although it has been publicized in the past, it receives relatively few visitors except on summer weekends. Unlike its slightly larger relative, Caribou Wilderness, Thousand Lakes Wilderness is mountainous and its scenery is therefore more diverse and photogenic. In particular, the summit views from Magee Peak and other nearby peaks justify a visit to the wilderness. Most of this introduction may seem overcritical of the wilderness, but the criticism is aimed at its misleading name, not as its features. As long as you don't expect to see a lot of pristine, sparkling lakes, you won't be disappointed. Mile for mile, its scenery certainly equals that of the Lassen Park backcountry.

Entry into the wilderness is via four trailheads: Bunchgrass Trailhead by the south border, Magee Trailhead by the southwest border, Cypress Trailhead by the northwest border, and Tamarack Trailhead by the east border. Excellent roads lead to the two southern trailheads; steep and narrow but well maintained ones lead to the east and northwest ones. The Tamarack Trailhead is closest to the heart of the wilderness, but many visitors will rightfully balk at driving up the last 1.5 miles to it. The best trailhead for lakebound visitors, therefore, is the Bunchgrass Trailhead, which you can expect to be snow-free from mid-May through late October. Use the Magee Trailhead if you're only interested in scurrying up to Magee Peak and back. It should be snow-free by mid-June. Trails are described under the trailhead most appropriate for each.

Bunchgrass Trails

Trailhead If you're coming from Lassen Park or Redding, note your odometer reading where Highways 44 and 89 merge, just outside the park. After a 4.0-mile drive north, turn left on USFS Road 16, which has a parking lot and restrooms by its start. These facilities were built primarily for Ashpan Snowmobile Park. If you're driving south up Hat Creek Valley, you'll reach this road 9.4 miles past the junction where Highways 44 and 89 merge, just northeast of Old Station. On Road 16 drive 6.4 miles west to Road 32N45 and follow it 2.1 miles to its end at a moderately large parking area.

Distances   3.3 miles (5.3 km) to Hall Butte
4.7 miles (7.5 km) to Durbin Lake
5.2 miles (8.4 km) to Barrett Lake
6.3 miles (10.1 km) to Lake Eiler, west shore
6.8 miles (10.9 km) to Lake Eiler, southeast shore
7.6 miles (12.2 km) to Upper Twin Lake
7.8 miles (12.6 km) to Everett Lake
8.1 miles (13.0 km) to Magee Lake and to Tamarack Trailhead
8.3 miles (13.4 km) to Cypress Trailhead
9.9 miles (15.9 km) to Magee Peak
13.1 miles (21.0 km) to Magee Trailhead

Trail description For the first 2 miles, the moderately climbing trail stays within forest cover, following a gully that separates the ancient, extinct Thousand Lakes volcano, on the left, from far more recent lava flows, on the right. These flows, primarily basalt, originated from the Tumble Buttes, cinder cones which, from about 20,000 to 5,000 years ago, probably erupted several times. These well-vegetated flows hide sparsely vegetated Devils Rock Garden, an andesite flow that originated just south of the Tumble Buttes as recently as 1000 years ago. Shrubs dominate the next mile of trail as you climb toward Hall Butte. This cinder cone may have erupted as recently as 500 years ago, and apparently has been active at least three times in the last several thousand years. It cannot be considered a dead cone.

Forest shade returns for good as the trai veers away from the cone. You soon cross a ill-defined saddle and enter a lush forest c lodgepole pines, red firs and western whit pines; this combination will stay with yo through most of the wilderness. Beyond th saddle you drop slightly into a flat, hangin, valley whose east side has apparently falle victim—literally—to a fault. A half-mil pleasant traverse through the valley give way to a brief climb to a shallow saddl through which the hiker enters Thousan Lakes Valley. You now make a moderat half-mile descent to the south shore of shal low Durbin Lake. You'll find an adequat campsite or two above the lake's northwes shore, and you'll find another on a con spicuous trail that starts west from the lake dying out after several hundred yards.

If Durbin Lake is too shallow for your lik ing, you'll probably be disappointed witl Barrett Lake, ½ mile north of it, which also i mostly waist-deep or less. Mosquitoes wai in ambush along the lodgepole-pine flat be tween the two lakes, which is unfortunate since it is one of the better places fo wildflower study. Among mosquitoes an lodgepoles you'll find an adequate campsit near the trail junction above Barrett Lake' shore. From this junction you can head eas on a wandering one-mile trail segment, pass ing a knee-deep lakelet one third of the wa to a junction with Tamarack Swale Trail From the junction, a ½-mile traverse aroun the base of Eiler Butte takes you up to Lak Eiler. See the "Tamarack Trails" section fo more on the Lake Eiler environs.

Magee Peak by the back door is probabl the area's most scenic hike. From the Bunch grass Trailhead, this route is a good two-da hike, round trip. Plan to camp either at Twin Everett or Magee Lakes so that you'll be rest ed and ready for the final assault. From the Barrett Lake trail junction, strike northwes ⅔ mile, veer left at another junction and after several minutes, veer left at yet another. Ahead now is a 3.6-mile, moderate to moderately steep climb south to a crest junc tion with the Magee Trail. Quickly, a set of switchbacks appear to aid your ascent up a steep slope, then a steady haul for a mile sees you to a second set, these ultimately taking you up to knee-deep Upper Twin Lake. Should you camp here, choose a spot away from the lake's fragile shoreline, perhaps up on the low divide that separates Upper from

Lower Twin Lake. Lower Twin is an ideal swimming hole after it warms up in late July, but hemmed-in as it is, it offers little camping possibility.

Everett Lake, a brief struggle above Upper Twin Lake, rivals the Oregon Cascades lakes in its setting. It is particularly beautiful in early morning when the sunlit cliffs south of the lake are mirrored in its placid water. Another confined lake, Everett offers little space for legal camping; you really have to search to find an acceptable site that is more than 100 feet from water.

Magee Lake, a quick jump up to the south, has several west-shore sites, though these can be snowbound through mid-July. The lake's basin, situated near the head of a glaciated valley, was deeply scoured by past glaciers, and consequently the lake is deep and cold—too chilly to suit most visitors. Welcome to the subalpine realm. Mountain hemlocks are now present, and they'll stay with us, along with lodgepoles and western white pines, almost to the Magee Peak crest.

The climb southwest from Magee Lake is a stiff one, particularly if you're wearing a backpack. Nevertheless, it is not excruciatingly steep, and the average hiker will probably reach the crest in about an hour's time if he's traveling light. A set of short, gravelly switchbacks caps the climb to the crest. Before late July, however, these may be partly buried in snow, and then your best bet is to head south directly up a snowy bowl to the crest and its junction with the Magee Trail. The next section describes the remaining ¼ mile of your hike and the views you attain from the summit.

Magee Trail

Trailhead As in the Bunchgrass Trailhead directions, drive west on USFS Road 16, but follow it 10.0 miles, almost to a gap. Here a road branches left over toward nearby Latour State Forest, but Road 16, which has been descending over the last 1.6 miles, swings right across the gap and immediately reaches Road 32N48. Turn right and follow this road 1.3 miles up to the large parking area at its end.

Distances 3.7 miles (5.9 km) to Magee Peak
5.0 miles (8.1 km) to Magee Lake
9.4 miles (15.1 km) to Cypress Trailhead
10.7 miles (17.2 km) to Tamarack Trailhead
13.1 miles (21.0 km) to Bunchgrass Trailhead

Trail description The Magee Trail, a utility trail up to a now-gone fire lookout, was designed for mules not people. It is steep, bouldery, very direct and, usually, waterless. Snow patches, however, linger near the trail's upper section well into August and sometimes into mid-September. You won't want to take this trail if you're carrying a heavy pack; it is best suited for day-hiking to Magee Peak and environs.

From a forested ridge you start down an abandoned jeep road that ends shortly in a shady gully. This gully lies along a fault that goes at least from Dry Burney Creek, in the northwest, to Bunchgrass Valley, which you drove through, in the southeast. From the gully a trail takes you quickly into the wilderness and your climb, moderate-to-steep, remains so all the way to the summit.

By the 6800-foot level, sugar pines and white firs are replaced by western white pines and red firs, which, with a smattering of Jeffrey pines and lodgepoles, comprise the forest cover to the 7800-foot level. At that elevation, about 1/6 mile above the trail's bend northwest, you emerge from the forest cover and have your first respectable views. The views improve as you struggle upward through brush and past wind-cropped trees. By the time you reach the crest, up at 8420 feet, weatherbeaten whitebark pines have become the primary vegetative cover. Forming a dense, bushlike cover, they sometimes impede your progress over the remaining ¼-mile walk up the crest to the summit.

From the summit most of the Thousand Lakes Wilderness lies exposed below you. You can look northeast down the deep, broad canyon, down which glaciers inched to the Freaner Peak area and beyond. Late in the glacial epoch, Freaner Peak came into a fiery existence, and subsequent glaciers flowing down-canyon were diverted largely to the northwest, down to the vicinity of Cypress Trailhead. Standing atop Magee Peak, you may rightly note that it is not the area's highest peak; Crater Peak, at 8677 feet, tops it by 127 feet, and consequently it totally blots out Burney Mountain, a young volcano 8 miles north of you. However, you can get an unrestricted view of that mountain by ambling ¾ mile along the

Red Cliff and the gentle crest of Magee Peak reflect in Everett Lake. A Magee Peak summit vie includes Thousand Lakes Valley and the switchbacking trail out of it up to Magee Peak. Freaner Pe is to the left, peak 8446 is right of center. Lassen Peak, in bottom photo, dominates Magee Peal southward views.

windy crest to Crater Peak. Though Crater Peak's views are better, they are second to those from Peak 8446, to the east, which puts the best views. From it you have an unencumbered perusal of Thousand Lakes Valley, an excellent appraisal of the semicircular Magee Peak crest, and a sweeping command of the lands from Lassen Peak north past the Hat Creek Rim escarpment to Burney Mountain. You can also study the line of cinder cones extending south from Freaner Peak, starting with Eiler Butte and ending, past desolate Devils Rock Garden, with Bear Wallow Butte. For revealing views of Twin, Everett and Magee lakes, descend ½ mile northeast to point 8224, at the brink of Red Cliff.

Tamarack Trails

Trailhead If you have a 4WD, a high-clearance vehicle, or an ordinary car and a lot of nerve, you can drive all the way to the small trailhead. Hope that loose boulders haven't fallen on the narrow road to block your way, for there are precious few spots where you can turn around. And, backing down the road is nerve-racking at best. Until the last 1.5 mile of road is improved, most drivers will prefer to walk up this stretch and preserve their vehicles and/or sanity. Our route to this trailhead starts from the Hat Creek Ranger Station on Highway 89. This station is located 10.9 miles north of the Highway 44 junction near Subway Cave and 10.8 miles south of the Highway 299 intersection east of Burney. Pick up your wilderness permit at the ranger station, then drive south 1.8 miles to Honn Campground and another 1.2 miles to an easily missed junction with Road 33N25, which you'll find just before the highway curves left and up. Turn right and take Road 33N25 1.6 steep miles up to a near-saddle junction, from where your road curves right and climbs 0.9 mile to an intersection with Road 35N35. You can reach this intersection from another route, namely, going 0.4 mile north from the ranger station and turning left onto steep Road 34N75, on which you climb 3.7 miles to Road 35N35, then take this almost level road 2.9 miles south to the intersection.) Now diagonal across Road 35N35 and make a steep climb up to a small hanging valley. After 2.9 miles of driving since cross-

ing Road 35N35, most of it along a fault, you reach, in Tamarack Swale, a one-lane road branching right. You've been forewarned, so you decide if you want to drive the steep, rocky 1.5 miles up to the trailhead parking area, with room for 8-10 cars, at road's end. If you walk, add 1.5 miles and 350 feet elevation change—each way—to your hiking itinerary.

Distances
1.9 miles (3.1 km) to Eiler Butte
2.4 miles (3.9 km) to Lake Eiler, southeast shore
2.9 miles (4.6 km) to Barrett Lake
3.3 miles (5.3 km) to Lake Eiler, west shore
3.4 miles (5.5 km) to Durbin Lake
5.2 miles (8.4 km) to Upper Twin Lake
5.5 miles (8.8 km) to Everett Lake
5.7 miles (9.2 km) to Magee Lake and to Cypress Trailhead
7.5 miles (12.1 km) to Magee Peak
8.1 miles (13.0 km) to Bunchgrass Trailhead
10.7 miles (17.2 km) to Magee Trailhead

Trail description The trail begins a stone's throw from the wilderness boundary, starting west past white firs, Jeffrey pines and a few tamaracks (lodgepole pines). Through a shady forest we climb up a gully cut between a pre-Ice Age volcanic knoll on our left and a post-Ice Age lava flow, originating from Eiler Butte, on our right. We climb to a forested ridge and, rather than hike along it, drop unnecessarily to a nearby junction with an abandoned trail south to Cornez Spring. The trail then climbs northwest up a second gully, and we encounter Eiler Butte lava of a more recent eruption—probably several thousand years old. The gully bends west and deadends at the base of Eiler Butte; we climb over a low, broad ridge to a junction immediately south of the butte. Fork left if you're bound for any destination other than Lake Eiler or Cypress Trailhead. The trail left goes 1.0 mile to a junction by Barrett Lake; consult the "Bunchgrass Trails" route descriptions for features south and west of the lake. About two thirds of the way to that junction the trail skirts along the north shore of a knee-deep lakelet, where you could leave the trail and head briefly cross-country north over a low ridge to Box Lake, which is mostly a waist-deep oversized wading pond, but a thorough investigation of it does have its rewards.

Many, if not most, hikers ascending our Tamarack Swale Trail head over to Lake Eiler, which is reached after an easy clockwise ascent around the southwest base of conical Eiler Butte. At this large lake you'll find pleasing campsites along its east, southwest and north shores. Since it is so easily reached and is, overall, the best lake in the wilderness, you can expect company. By the lake's west end a trail begins a 0.4-mile climb southwest up to the first junction northwest of Barrett Lake. Immediately beyond the west tip of Lake Eiler a *de facto* shoreline trail strikes east, passing an ample number of campsites before curving south toward the lake's southeast tip. See the next section for trails west of Lake Eiler.

Cypress Trails

Trailhead See the previous section's trailhead directions to the Hat Creek Ranger Station, which issues wilderness permits. From it drive 0.4 mile north, turn left onto Road 34N75 and drive 3.7 miles—most of them steeply up—to a junction with Road 35N35 in one of the area's many fault-related hanging valleys. Turn right and drive 1.3 miles to an intersection with Road 34N19, on which you turn left. After winding southwest for 2.9 miles, your road deadends. Road 34N14 goes north but you turn left and follow Road 34N22 2.0 miles south up to the signed Cypress Trailhead, a small parking area just before a bouldery ford of a seasonal creek. Unless you've got a 4WD or pickup, don't attempt to drive farther.

Distances 2.4 miles (3.9 km) to Lake Eile west shore
3.1 miles (5.0 km) to Barrett Lal
3.6 miles (5.8 km) to Durb Lake
3.9 miles (6.2 km) to Upper Tw Lake
4.1 miles (6.6 km) to Evere Lake
4.3 miles (7.0 km) to Magee Lak
5.7 miles (9.2 km) to Tamara Trailhead
6.1 miles (9.9 km) to Magee Pea
8.3 miles (13.4 km) to Bunc grass Trailhead
9.4 miles (15.1 km) to Mag Trailhead

Trail description Immediately beyond th trailhead's seasonal creek, a pickup roa branches left. We keep right and in a mome branch left on a second pickup road, whic we tread 0.2 mile over to a bouldery crossi of double-channeled, seasonal Eiler Gul Creek. On its east bank we start up the Cy ress Camp Trail and pass a fe "cypresses"—actually, western junipers- before the trail increases its gradient moderate-plus. The grade stays that way f one mile and, since the route is brushy, yc won't want to climb it in the heat of th afternoon. The trail almost levels as it ente forest cover near a junction. Straight ahea the Cypress Camp Trail goes 0.8 mile east Lake Eiler's west shore (see "Tamarac Trails"). Branching left, another tra traverses ⅓ mile to a second junction; go le if you're bound for Barrett or Durbin Lake right if you're bound for Twin, Everett Magee Lakes. See "Bunchgrass Trails" f descriptions to these destinations an others.

18 Hat Creek Valley Trails

Introduction In the last three chapters, roads have been described in the "Trailhead" section of each hike, for those roads are used chiefly by visitors just to get to a trailhead. Few roads of those areas go to campgrounds or to fishing areas, and none go to picnic grounds, vista points or sites of geologic interest. Not so for the roads of Hat Creek Valley, particularly those in the Hat Creek Valley Recreation Area. Therefore, an entire section, Chapter 9, was devoted to the valley's main road, Highway 89, and to the roads branching from it. On these secondary roads you can visit attractions such as the West Prospect Peak Fire Lookout Station, the University of California's Hat Creek Radio Astronomy Observatory and the Crystal Lake State Fish Hatchery.

This chapter deals only with the trails in and around Hat Creek Valley. These fall into three groups: nature trails, valley hiking trails and the Pacific Crest Trail. The Spatter Cone Nature Trail is a convenient one for campers staying at the Hat Creek Campground, for the trail begins right across from it. But even if you're just passing through the area, take an hour or so to hike it. It's a big hit with children, who like to climb around the spatter cones, as is the second hike, Subway Cave, which requires a lantern (a flashlight will do in an emergency). Both hikes can be potentially dangerous, so children must be kept under supervision.

The Hat Creek Trail is the valley's most popular hiking trail. Staying close to the creek, it provides access points for fishermen, who are the trail's primary users. Near the trail's north and south ends, other trails strike east across the valley, climbing to the Pacific Crest Trail, which traverses the Hat Creek Rim. Using all these trails, one can put together a loop route, the "Hat Creek Valley Loop," which presents the hiker with a diversity of terrain: creekside vegetation, dry, shrubby lava beds, and an open forest with rim views of Lassen Peak, Mt. Shasta and other peaks.

The Pacific Crest Trail, noted for its generally high elevation and spectacular scenery, doesn't live up to expectations in the area north of Lassen Park. The trail's route, mostly along Hat Creek Rim, is typically dry and waterless. In fact, once you leave Lassen Park, you won't find any fresh, year-round trailside drinking water until you reach the Baum Lake area, more than 40 miles away. But from April through early June, wildflower displays can make a walk along part of this trail a delightful experience. At this time both Lassen and Shasta are mantled with snow, as are the high peaks of Thousand Lakes Wilderness and, to its north, Burney Mountain. All present photogenic views, particularly if you have a field of colorful wildflowers in the foreground. The trail is described in four hikes, starting near Lassen Park's north boundary and working north to Highway 299.

Spatter Cone Nature Trail

Trailhead At the south edge of Hat Creek Campground's sewage-disposal station— see Chapter 9, mile 11.9/23.2.

Distance 1.6 miles (2.6 km) for entire loop

Trail description Like the Lassen Park self-guiding nature trails, which are described in Chapter 10, this nature trail has numbered posts. The trail is mostly shadeless, so be prepared for hot temperatures if you hike it on a summer afternoon. It is also waterless, so take a good drink at the fountain by the trailhead. You can do the hike in an hour or less, but plan for two. Tennis shoes are fine if you stick to the trail, but boots are advisable if you plan to scramble around the spatter cones. Children in particular love to do this, but since the rock is loose, there are plenty of opportunities for minor (occasionally major) falls; parental supervision is a must. Please do not collect samples or break off rocks.

1 These conifers are ponderosa pines, which are the commonest trees in upper Hat Creek Valley. However, on the lava flow, particularly north of Subway Cave, they are replaced by western junipers and digger pines—both conifers—and by curlleaf mountain mahogany, a rose. Sagebrush and its associated vegetation also thrive on the flow's dry, thin soils. One such associate is bitterbrush, or antelope bush, which is a rose bush with small, three-lobed leaves, and it grows by this post.

2 You'll see a matted, spreading bush, the squaw carpet, about 50 yards before this post and, beyond it and a trail fork, you'll see sagebrush. About one-half dozen species of sagebrush grow in Hat Creek Valley or on Hat Creek Rim, and these aromatic, late blooming sunflowers are easily recognized by their light gray-green leaves. Greenleaf manzanita, with smooth, dark-red bark, grows near the post. A few Jeffrey pines also grow in this area. They closely resemble ponderosa pines, but Jeffrey's cones are usually more than 5 inches long while ponderosa's are usually less. Furthermore, if you stick your nose in a bark fissure of a mature tree, it will smell like butterscotch if it is a Jeffrey, like sap if it is a ponderosa.

Keep right at a trail fork. You'll be returning on the left.

3 This is spatter cone 1. Its crater is 33 feet across and there is a secondary vent 25 feet to the east. This spot provides fine views, particularly to the northwest. The prominent peak you see in this direction is Sugarloaf Peak, which is a youthful volcano that has likely made its appearance in the last 20,000 years, perhaps much sooner. Close to its base (and just opposite Hat Creek Campground) is a brush-covered, reddish cinder cone, the northernmost of a series of five along a 3-mile long north-south line. The last two are the Potato Buttes. This line of cones indicates the presence of a fault, and if one were to extend this line northward beneath Sugarloaf Peak, it would connect with a major fault extending beyond this volcano's northwest base. Molten material within the earth's crust probably has worked up along this fault, giving rise to the volcano and the cinder cones.

An even longer fault, starting around the east base of Badger Mountain and heading Northwest past the west base of Wilcox Peak, has yielded no such recent eruptions, but it has raised the land east of the fault with respect to the land west of it, which is the typical fault pattern in this area. Badger Mountain is the spreading mass about 8 miles south of the Potato Buttes and lying to the left of Lassen Peak. Two substantial faults cut up the mountain's slopes, creating two shallow clefts on its broad, almost flat summit. Wilcox Peak is the forested peak immediately left of the cinder cone at the base of Sugarloaf Peak.

4 Here are some small pockets and domes

5 This is a collapsed lava tube, one of perhaps many hundreds of tubes in this Hat Creek Valley lava flow. The largest known lava tube in the area is Subway Cave, which is at least 2300 feet long and is described in the following hike. The second largest is Christmas Tree Cave, and is at least 950 feet long. Most lava tubes, however, are much smaller.

6 Spatter cone 2.

7 Mountain mahogany is the dominant plant on the low hill to the south.

8 Deer browse on the nearby bitterbrush, sagebrush and manzanita, and they bed down in this area. Stay out of the tick-infested brush.

9 Here, just before the next spatter cone, you get a good view to the south, of the

Lassen Peak area. Desolate Chaos Crags stand above the peak's right side, while to its left are Badger Mountain and West Prospect Peak, the latter largely hiding Prospect Peak.

10 Spatter cone 3. You get an even better view from the rim of this cone.

11 There has been a red-ant mound here for a number of years.

12 Spatter cone 4.

13 Spatter cones 5 through 10. In the next 200 feet you will pass a group of six craters.

14 This small hole resulted when the top of a lava tube collapsed. To your left is one of the largest spatter cones, having a 20-foot-deep crater. You'll see it on your way back along the trail that branches left just beyond it. You keep right.

15 Spatter cones 11, 12 and 13.

16 Spatter cone 14 is 40 yards off to the north-northeast. From its rim you have a view north of Hat Creek Valley, including a view of Old Station. With a crater about 70 feet across and 20 feet deep, spatter cone 14 is the largest one you'll see.

17 This blowhole in spatter cone 15 is about 35 feet deep. Don't try to descend into it, for the rock is loose. If you want to explore a real cave, visit Subway Cave instead.

18 Spatter cones 16 and 17, two overlapping craters.

To return, go back to the trail junction just north of post 14 and head west through a nearby gap. You immediately pass just north of a large spatter cone. Climb to its north rim for a view of its large crater. The trail then descends quite steeply, switchbacking down to more-level ground before reaching the junction between posts 2 and 3.

Subway Cave

Trailhead At the end of a spur road that branches east from Highway 89 only 0.3 mile north of the Highway 44 junction, near Old Station, in Hat Creek Valley (Chapter 9's road-log mile 13.7/21.4).

Distance 0.6 mile (1.0 km) for entire trail loop

Trail description The most popular trail in Hat Creek Valley may be the cool walk through Subway Cave. The cave, usually at or near 46°F, extends for about 2300 feet, but

only 1300 feet is open to the public, the northern half blocked off for your safety. In the part open to the public, the ceiling ranges from about 6-16 feet in height, and it is lower near the sides, so you may hit your head if you don't watch where you're going. The thickness of the lava roof over the cave ranges from 8-24 feet. The roof was evidently thin at today's entrance and exit, for both are sites of collapsed roof. Bring a sweater or jacket for, as mentioned earlier, the cave is cool. Also bring a lantern, though a flashlight or two will do in an emergency. In early 1962 Shasta County's Civil Defense Office considered using Subway Cave and several smaller caves near it as emergency fallout shelters. During the Cuban missile crisis of October 22-28, 1962, with nuclear war seeming imminent, they almost got put to use.

The Subway Cave trail starts at the north end of the parking loop, and you'll find the cave's entrance just beyond a set of stairs. Descend another set to the floor of the cave and let your eyes get adjusted to the dimmer light. About half of your traverse through the cave will be in absolute darkness. The first part of the cave is called, appropriately enough, Stubtoe Hall, perhaps because visitors don't expect the rough floor, which may have solidified a few hundred to 2000 years ago, just after this huge basalt flow—the latest of a series—flooded Hat Creek Valley. In the Subway Cave area, the surface of this lava flow was the first to cool, but lava continued to flow in a channel beneath it, soon draining to leave a cave. There must be hundreds of caves in the extensive flow, but most of them are minor tunnels you'd have to crawl through.

When you emerge from Subway Cave, you can either take a trail that winds northwest back to the cave's entrance or take a longer, more evident trail clockwise back to the south end of the parking loop. Along it you have views of the Hat Creek Rim, to the east, and Sugarloaf Peak, to the west. The Hat Creek Valley floor usually averages about 3 miles in width, but here it is only one mile wide because the volcano has grown atop the western floor.

From a small flat where your trail turns from southwest to northwest, Trail 5E27 starts south for a 2.9-mile climb to the Pacific Crest Trail. This is part of the "Hat Creek Valley Loop."

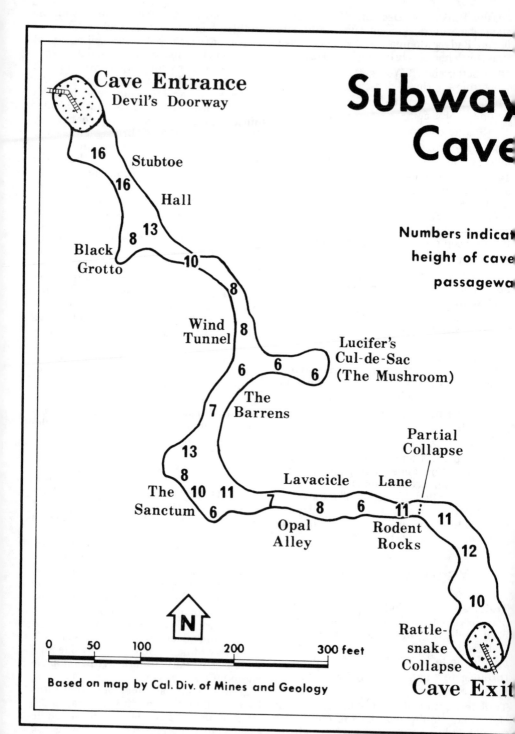

Cave Entrance
Devil's Doorway

Subway
Cave

16 Stubtoe

16 Hall

8 13

Black
Grotto 10

8

Wind 8
Tunnel

Lucifer's
Cul-de-Sac
(The Mushroom)

6 6
6

The
Barrens

7

Partial
Collapse

13

8 Lavacicle Lane

The 10 11
Sanctum 6 7 8 6 11 11

Opal Rodent 12
Alley Rocks

10

N

Rattle-
snake
Collapse

0   50   100   200   300 feet

Cave Exit

Based on map by Cal. Div. of Mines and Geology

Numbers indicate
height of cave
passageway

Partial
Collapse

The Subway Cave vegetation is largely that of a sagebrush plant community, though as soils develop in time, a ponderosa-pine forest may eventually spread across the entire floor of Hat Creek Valley—if there are no future lava flows. At Subway Cave you'll see the same vegetation seen along the Spatter Cone Nature Trail, near Hat Creek Campground. In addition to the shrubs mentioned at its first 2 posts, there are rabbitbrush, squaw currant and Wood's rose. If you are very fortunate, you may see a few lavender-flowered sagebrush mariposa tulips, blooming in May and early June, or yellow-flowered blazing stars, blooming in August and September. Neither is all that common, but you can't miss either if you come across them while they are in flower.

Hat Creek Trail

Trailheads   There are five possible starting points. See Chapter 9's road-log miles: 13.7/21.4 (Cave Campground), 14.2/20.9 (Sugarloaf Picnic Ground), 15.0/20.1 (road branching west), 16.7/18.4 (Rocky Campground) and 17.4/17.7 (Bridge Campground). The trail description starts at Cave Campground, since the trail near this spot receives greater usage. The following distances are measured from this spot.

Distances   0.6 mile (0.9 km) to Sugarloaf Picnic Ground
1.5 miles (2.4 km) to bridge across to spur road
3.3 miles (5.3 km) to Rocky Campground
3.8 miles (6.1 km) to Bridge Campground

Trail description   This trail was built primarily for fishermen, for Hat Creek provides some of the best fishing to be found in the area covered by this book. The trail usually stays within a stone's throw of the creek, but this doesn't mean you have access to it along every foot of the way. Dense brush and steep-walled minigorges deter many fishermen, hence most tend to congregate at the more accessible spots. Wildflower lovers will find that June is the best month for flowers, particularly the first half of the month. Swimmers can find up to a dozen or more minor swimming holes, but the water is far too cold for enjoyable swimming and the creek's current can be treacherous.

At its south end the Hat Creek Trail begins from the west side of Cave Campground. The trail immediately bridges Hat Creek at one of its deeper, narrower spots, then in 25 yards angles right. Your trail now stays on the creek's west bank all the way to its end. Ponderosa pines, white firs and incense-cedars provide shade at first, but greenleaf manzanitas take over by the time your trail enters Sugarloaf Picnic Ground. A bridge across the creek provides access to both its banks as well as to nearby Highway 89. The road starting east from Highway 89 is part of the old abandoned Highway 44 route. It goes about 0.9 mile to the base of Hat Creek Rim, where it is blocked off. From that point a minor, closed road curves southwest to Subway Cave and the closed highway climbs up to the Pacific Crest Trail. These two closed roads are part of the "Hat Creek Valley Loop," described in the following hike.

About 40 yards beyond the Sugarloaf Picnic Ground bridge, Hat Creek bounds tumultuously through a miniature lava gorge that is only 6 feet wide at one point. You would certainly not want to raft through it and over its low, turbulent waterfall. The route ahead is now a sunny one, mostly through stretch after stretch of manzanitas. After about 1¾ miles we reach a footbridge that goes across the creek to a 0.1-mile-long Highway 89 spur road, the road and bridge providing midpoint access to the Hat Creek Trail

A few Jeffrey pines, junipers and aspens add diversity here, but alders and willows continue to dominate along the creek's banks and manzanitas continue to dominate along our trail. Just beyond the bridge we pass by another minigorge then have a shadeless traverse until about midway to Rocky Campground. As we enter a grove of pines and firs, the vegetation changes dramatically to moist varieties such as miner's lettuce, false Solomon's seal, snow plant and thimbleberry. However, the shady traverse is momentary, and we again have manzanitas as our trailside companions.

Not far past the forest grove you'll hear the creek, and if you seek out the source of the muted roar, you'll see a small waterfall where the creek cuts through columnar basalt. The creek mostly runs along the western edge of the Hat Creek Valley basalt flow, which may be as young as a few hundred years or as old as two thousand. The flow originated from a series of spatter cones near Hat Creek Campground (see this chapter's first hike). To the north, the creek has cut a fairly deep gorge—40 feet or more—and soon after seeing this gorge we descend into its shady confines, reaching a bridge over to Rocky Campground in a few minutes. The creek, particularly along this stretch, is the prime habitat for the dipper, a small, chunky gray bird that typically hunts insect larvae along the bottom of swift streams.

Along the last half mile of trail to Bridge Campground, the gorge gets even deeper, and one can revel in the verdant display of forest species. Among the water-loving trees and shrubs you may see two large lilies, both usually blooming in June. The leopard lily has brilliant orange flowers with purple spots and the plant may grow to head height or higher. The Washington lily has white flowers, but these are enormous by wildflower standards, usually 3-4 inches long.

The trail ends on the brink of the Hat Creek gorge along the eastern edge of Bridge Campground. If you are taking the following hike, head over to the Highway 89 bridge and head 0.1 mile southeast on the highway to a road branching east.

Hat Creek Valley Loop

Trailheads   There are at least nine possible starting points. See Chapter 9's road-log miles: 13.4/21.7 (Pacific Crest Trail parking area), 13.7/21.4 (Subway Cave, Bridge Campground), 14.2/20.9 (Sugarloaf Picnic Ground), 15.0/20.1 (road branching west), 16.7/18.4 (Rocky Campground), 17.3/17.8 (road branching east), and 17.4/17.7 (Bridge Picnic Ground, Bridge Campground). The trail description begins at Subway Cave, and the following distances are measured counterclockwise from this spot.

Distances   3.0 miles (4.8 km) to Pacific Crest Trail parking area
6.2 miles (10.0 km) to leaving the Pacific Crest Trail
8.6 miles (13.8 km) to Highway 89 bridge over Hat Creek
8.8 miles (14.2 km) to start of Hat Creek Trail in Bridge Campground
9.3 miles (15.0 km) to Rocky Campground
12.0 miles (19.4 km) to Sugarloaf Picnic Ground

12.6 miles (20.3 km) to end of Hat Creek Trail in Cave Campground
12.9 miles (20.8 km) for complete loop

Trail description   In 1980 the Forest Service built two short trail segments that connected to existing roads and trails, thereby creating a 12.9-mile hiking loop known as Trail 5E27. On this loop you sample various environments: Hat Creek, which can be cool, moist and shady or hot and dry; Hat Creek Valley lava flow, which is often hot and mostly shadeless; and Hat Creek Rim, which supports a brushy, open forest. Not many hikers make the entire loop, especially since the only water available is along Hat Creek and at Subway Cave. That leaves 8.6 waterless miles. Furthermore, after late June the rim trail can be hard to follow in several places due to herbs obscuring the faint path. About the only respectable time to hike this route is in the spring, when you can admire the snowy peaks from your waterless rim route. Wildflowers are best on the valley's floor and rim during May, and are best along Hat Creek in early and mid-June.

The only part of this route that sees much use is along Hat Creek—the previous hike. The remainder, being little used, will only be briefly described. If you start about 7-8 a.m. from Subway Cave and follow the trail counterclockwise, you can climb up to the rim, traverse along it, and descend to Bridge Picnic Ground before noon. Then, after an extended picnic beside Hat Creek, you can leisurely spend the hot afternoon taking many stops as you progress up a creekside trail to your starting point.

Start at the end of the Subway Cave trail, this point being at the beginning of the cave's parking loop. First tank up on water then head southeast on the trail, going about 0.1 mile to another trail and following it 0.2 mile south to an old road that is blocked off at its west end. On this closed road you arc 1.1 miles counterclockwise northeast to the blocked-off east end of a linear road, old Highway 44. If you were to follow it west, you'd reach Sugarloaf Picnic Ground in about one mile. Instead, turn right on old 44 and follow its winding course 0.7 mile up to where the road is blocked off. Here you'll note a path, your route, which meanders 0.9 mile north to the Pacific Crest Trail's Highway 44 trailhead parking area.

Immediately north of the parking area you start a 3.2-mile stretch of Pacific Crest Trail. Ponderosa pines, Jeffrey pines and incense-cedars are the major shade trees, though an occasional western juniper may also provide some cover. Brush abounds, especially mountain mahogany, sagebrush, rabbitbrush, bitterbrush and greenleaf manzanita. About ¾ mile beyond the parking area you have your first good views, then in another ¾ mile you veer in and out of a major gully, getting another view as the trail reaches the rim. You see Lassen Peak to the south, Sugarloaf Peak to the southwest, the peaks of Thousand Lakes Wilderness to the west, Burney Mountain to the northwest, and Mt. Shasta in the distant north-northwest. In spring these peaks are snowy and present an inspiring sight.

Just beyond the major gully you duck into a second one and quickly meet a trail descending west. On it you plunge 0.3 mile down to a road, walk 115 yards north on it,

then branch left on a trail and drop 0.3 mile to a trail junction. The trail climbing east goes back up to the Pacific Crest Trail then dead ends at Grassy Lake, just east of that trail. From the junction you plunge west down the faulted Hat Creek Rim escarpment. The excessive steepness of these two "plunges" is ample reason for not hiking the loop in the opposite direction. Once your trail reaches the base of the escarpment you have an easy, mostly shadeless 1⅓-mile walk west to Highway 89, your trail widening to a road midway to the highway. The sparsely foliated pines you see along this stretch are digger pines, these usually found at lower elevations, but thriving well up here in this hot, dry environment.

On Highway 89 walk north 0.1 mile to Hat Creek and just past it to Bridge Picnic Ground and adjacent Bridge Campground. From that campground's far (east) side, the Hat Creek Trail climbs 3.8 miles up to a bridge over to Cave Campground, and that

Left: a churning Hat Creek fall. Right: a small reservoir north of Road 22—the ONLY trailside water along the entire Hat Creek Rim. Bald Mountain is in the background.

campground's entrance is opposite the entrance to Subway Cave.

Pacific Crest Trail, Road 32N12 south to the Nobles Trail

Trailhead   See chapter 9's road log, mile 8.1/27.0.

Distances   3.3 miles (5.3 km) to Lassen Park boundary
3.6 miles (5.8 km) to the Nobles Trail
3.7 miles (6.0 km) to horse camp
5.4 miles (8.7 km) to Badger Flat

Trail description   There is only one backcountry horse camp in all of Lassen Park, and the shortest route in to it is along the southbound Pacific Crest Trail. This trail crosses Road 32N12 just 40 yards northwest of the Plantation Loop Road, which no longer is a loop road. After a ½-mile climb south up your "PCT" along a forest's fringe, you hit a lateral road and walk 30 yards east on it to the loop road. Your waterless route is now shadeless as it climbs up the closed road, this road staying close to the base of denuded Badger Mountain. At least the lack of trees allows you to note the long linear ridge along the lower flank of the mountain. This is a lateral moraine left by a glacier that retreated up-canyon probably more than 50,000 years ago. That chilly thought is little consolation on a hot summer day.

After about 1.3 miles the loop road reaches the head of your sloping plain, and it curves northwest for a descent. Here you leave the road to make a moderate climb past dense brush up to a ridge atop a moraine left by a younger glacier. You enter forest cover and angle into a gully just before Lassen Park's signed boundary, at which you'll come to a trail junction. The spur trail right rolls 0.4 mile across glacial moraines to a fine Hat Creek campsite, the previously mentioned horse camp. The Pacific Crest Trail climbs 0.3 mile up the gully to a junction with the Nobles Trail, on which you can then head east to Badger Flat. See Chapter 11's "Nobles Trail to Badger Flat and beyond" for hiking possibilities. Remember, you'll need a wilderness permit if you spend the night camped in the park's backcountry.

Pacific Crest Trail, Road 32N12 north to Highway 44

Trailheads   See Chapter 9's road log, miles 8.1/27.0 and 13.4/21.7.

Distances   9.0 miles (14.5 km) to Baker Lake
12.8 miles (20.6 km) to Highway 44
13.5 miles (21.7 km) to Highway 44's trailhead parking area

Trail description   This waterless, largely logged stretch is perhaps the least inviting part of Pacific Crest Trail to be found in the Lassen area. Carry water! You do have two consolations: a very easy trail grade and some rewarding views.

From Road 32N12, just 40 yards northwest of the Plantation Loop Road, the Pacific Crest Trail climbs northeast through a selectively logged forest, crossing several old roads before finally reaching a more used one in 1.1 miles. Up this road you walk but 40 yards to the trail's resumption, almost on a saddle, and on the trail you climb 0.8 mile southeast up a faulted escarpment. Along this leg the avid photographer will stop several times to capture the beauty of Lassen's north face exquisitely framed by trailside ponderosa, Jeffrey and sugar pines, plus white firs and incense-cedars. Don't use up all your film here, for there are more views to come.

From a low point on the escarpment, your sometimes vague trail wanders 2.4 miles over to a major east-west logging road. From it you follow a road north to a curve northeast, enter a forest's edge and soon make contact with trail, about 0.6 mile past the logging road. Your trail route is now a long, winding traverse northeast past some steeply descending spur roads. Just after you cross the last logging road, about 1.6 miles from the start of your latest "PCT" tread, you begin a series of long, easy switchback legs up the faulted Hat Creek Rim escarpment. Once again you see Lassen Peak and its bleak associates, the Chaos Crags. Below to the west lie the Potato Buttes and their sparsely vegetated lava flows. Your trail reaches the Hat Creek Rim just before a gate across a well maintained logging road, then it winds ½ mile northwest to a junction with a spur trail. This goes east, first 160 yards to the logging

:oad, then 190 yards beyond it to a PCT :amp, which is fenced in to keep the cattle and horses out. The site, for desperate PCT trekkers, has piped-in water—the worst-tasting water the author has ever tasted. Hopefully, it will improve with time. Should the spigot be dry when you visit it (due to a possible broken pipe), you can always check its source, Baker Spring, which seeps at a cattle-plagued meadow's far side, about 125 yards east of the camp.

Beyond the spur trail the PCT stays along the escarpment paralleling it about 3 miles before turning east and then descending north ½ mile through a logged area to a crossing of Highway 44. A somewhat vague tread then arcs ¾ mile westward to the highway's trailhead parking area, the start of the next hike.

Pacific Crest Trail, Highway 44 north to Road 22

Trailheads See Chapter 9's road log, miles 13.4/21.7 and 24.5/10.6 (its last paragraph).

Distances 3.2 miles (5.1 km) to loop trail
4.8 miles (7.7 km) to Grassy Lake trail
7.1 miles (11.4 km) to Porcupine Reservoir access road
11.6 miles (18.7 km) to Hat Creek Rim Fire Lookout
14.4 miles (23.2 km) to Road 22

Trail description Like the preceding hike, this stretch of Pacific Crest Trail is waterless, but is easy to hike and has some rewarding views. However, in spots the tread can be vague. Hike it in May to see snowy peaks and blossoming wildflowers. The route can be excessively hot in summer.

From the Pacific Crest Trail parking area near Highway 44, Trail 5E27 descends 3.0 miles southwest to Subway Cave—part of the Hat Creek Valley Loop. We take a trail north that goes but a few yards to the Pacific Crest Trail, or "PCT." On it you snake down to the Hat Creek Rim, reaching it in about ¾ mile. Here you get your first good views of Lassen Peak to the south, Sugarloaf Peak to the southwest, the peaks of Thousand Lakes Wilderness to the west, Burney Mountain to the northwest, and Mt. Shasta in the distant

north-northwest. About 2¼ miles from the trailhead the PCT descends ¼ mile east into a major gully then takes ½ mile to climb back out to the escarpment. You have a fine momentary view, then curve back into another forested gully, in which you meet a westbound trail, also part of the Hat Creek Valley Loop.

Our PCT curves around the second gully, once again heading out to the rim, but this it quickly forsakes for a higher rim, which, like the first, is the result of uplift along a north-south fault. A ½-mile winding traverse on the rim ensues, soon bringing us to a shallow depression in which a stock trail from Hat Creek Valley strikes northeast ¼ mile to usually dry Grassy Lake, polluted when it isn't dry.

The trail again ventures to the rim and winds north along it to the brink of Lost Creek canyon, which has an audible spring-fed creek flowing down its lower section. Rather than descend to it, our trail stays high and follows this canyon's rim 1½ miles east to a usually dry crossing of the upper canyon, now just a gully with spring wildflowers. Just 250 yards beyond it we reach a gate and a narrow road. If you need water, take this road northeast ¼ mile to Road 33N21, pace 50 yards east on it, and then follow a road that heads up the creek ½ mile to Porcupine Reservoir, with polluted water, as at Grassy Lake.

Back at the roadside gate the PCT starts to follow yet another fault-formed rim, almost touching Road 33N21 where the trail crosses a spur road that heads west down to Little Lake, which is generally dry. With one more mile behind us, we continue our dry-rim traverse toward Mt. Shasta. Though we hike through a forest of mostly ponderosa pines, it is a sparse one that offers little protection from the soaring temperatures of summer afternoons. After several more miles of winding to and from rim views, we eventually spy and reach the Hat Creek Rim Fire Lookout. Water is usually not available. Views, however, are among the best. The top of the tower is almost precisely one mile in elevation.

The trail ahead now begins a long drop along an increasingly dry rim. By mid-June most of the wildflowers have blossomed, the flowers transforming into a myriad of nasty "stickseeds." You can get literally hundreds of them in your socks, so high boots and long pants are very desirable, or wear gaitors over your socks. Over 2¾ miles you descend more than 500 feet along the rim's escarpment, eventually reaching Road 22 about 100 yards west of a small pass along the Hat Creek Rim. Along this last stretch from the fire lookout, you have an almost continual line of views, for your trail never veers far from the rim. Every escarpment you see around you is due to faulting, which in this area goes hand in hand with vulcanism. Cinder Butte, a sparsely vegetated conical hill to the northwest, is, like Sugarloaf Peak to the south, a young volcano.

Pacific Crest Trail, Road 22 north to Highway 299

Trailheads See Chapter 9's road log, mile 24.5/10.6 (its last paragraph) for the Road 22 trailhead. The trail crosses Highway 299 about ¼ mile northeast of the highway's junction with the Cassel-Fall River Mills Road, this junction in turn being about 2¼ miles northeast of the junction of Highways 89 and 299.

Distances 8.8 miles (14.2 km) to Cassel-Fall River Mills Road
about 11.0 miles (17.7 km) to Baum Lake
about 14.6 miles (23.5 km) to Highway 299

Trail description Of the four Pacific Crest Trail segments mentioned in this chapter, this one is the lowest, hottest and driest. It also tends to have the most wildflowers, which is great in May and early June, but after that, the wildflower gardens become annoying weed patches. The growth of "weeds" can get so thick it not only obscures the tread, it also hides rattlesnakes. And this is tick and rattlesnake country. In short, this route, despite all its excellent rim views, will appeal to few.

From Road 22 about 100 yards west of a low pass, the trail climbs northwest to a knoll on the rim that evidently has been used as a takeoff spot for hang gliders. And why not, for here the escarpment rises a full 1100 feet above Murken Bench. This is the highest unbroken escarpment along the entire rim, an inducement to glider pilots. Furthermore, it is fairly accessible by road, has an un-

obstructed takeoff into the wind, and has a level, open landing space, Murken Bench —all on public land.

From the knoll the trail makes a drop of its own, nearly 600 feet down to a reservoir just 200 yards west of a Hat Creek Rim road, Road 36N18. About 1.9 miles from Road 22, you might plan to enjoy a swim, then climb back up the way you came. Don't drink the water. Ahead, the trail wanders for almost 1.2 miles before breaking through to the rim at a spectacular viewpoint. The wildflower gardens along the way to it can be fantastic in May, but by late June the flowers turn just plain sticky. After 1.9 scenic miles of rim traverse you come to a gate. Here's another fine place to turn around or to scramble 80 yards upslope to Road 36N18.

Ahead, the trail leaves the rim and gets hard to follow. Nothing good can be said about it. From the gate the trail takes a complex 2.4-mile course over to the Cassel-Fall River Mills Road, then parallels it 1.4 miles west through brush before finally crossing it.

Ahead, the PCT meanders westward across a youthful lava flow with caves, then in about ½ mile, as we leave Section 3, we leave Forest Service land—no camping ahead. The trail heads northwest through a dry, open woodland, and one has views of Mt. Shasta until you cross a road to Conrad Ranch. Shaded by ponderosa pines, you first climb ⅓ mile to a low gap, then drop ¼ mile west to a gully, then traverse southwest over to a road that is just above Rock Spring creek—the first *fresh, trailside* water along the PCT since Lassen Park's Lower Twin Lake, 51½ miles back. Your route soon crosses the creek, passes a PG&E powerhouse, and then bridges Rising River/Hat Creek, popular with fishermen.

Next we meet Crystal Lake State Fish Hatchery and swerve over to the lake's dam, which spills east into adjacent Baum Lake. This lake attracts fishermen, who frequent its south-shore picnic area. Beyond the Crystal Lake spillway, you walk 0.9 mile along the west shore of Baum Lake, leaving most of the fishermen behind. Ahead, the route is waterless. In 0.4 mile you climb and then traverse to a jeep road, then spend 1.8 miles traversing along the east and north rims of an oak-and-pine-vegetated lava plateau before dropping for 0.8 mile to Highway 299. Onward, the PCT winds 6.7 miles across viewless, waterless land—some of it private—before reaching Highway 89 in McArthur-Burney Falls Memorial State Park.

19 McArthur-Burney Falls Memorial State Park

Introduction This state park is really outside the Lassen area. However, it is included because many people visiting Lassen Park or its peripheral areas may also want to visit Burney Falls. The falls are, after all, higher, wider and more spectacular than any other waterfall in the Lassen area. Furthermore, a relatively short nature trail introduces you to many of the plants you'll see in lower Hat Creek Valley. This trail is the only one described in this chapter. You can also take a trail up Burney Creek to its spring-fed source, take trails north down to Lake Britton, or take a brief segment of the tri-state Pacific Crest Trail, which more or less makes an east-west traverse of the park. All these trails are shown on the back side of this guidebook's map.

Many visitors come just to camp, fish and relax. The park has a beach and a boat ramp along the south shore of Lake Britton, but fishing and swimming aren't all that good. Trout do poorly in the lake, and there are algae blooms, these making a swim unattractive though still safe. Fishing is better above the lake on the Pit River and along Hat Creek. Swimming is better in the warmer, cleaner waters of the lakes in Lassen Park, Caribou Wilderness and Thousand Lakes Wilderness. You can camp year round in the state park, though the campground's showers lack hot water except during the busy summer months. Visit the park in May for the best show of wildflowers.

Burney Falls Nature Trail

Trailhead At a parking lot immediately left of the park's entrance station.

Distance 1.0 (1.6 km) for entire loop

Trail description This trail introduces you to some of the natural history of McArthur-Burney Falls State Park. The numbers that

follow refer to numbered posts along the trail.

1 Self-Guiding Nature Trail. This trail takes about a half hour to walk, considerably more if you stop and study all the trailside features. The second post is 100 feet to the right, at the observation point.

2 Burney Falls and Burney Creek. As you can see, Burney Falls is two tiered. This is because there is a thick layer of basaltic lava that water can't penetrate. Water therefore has to flow either along its upper surface or beneath its lower surface, which is what happens. A thin layer of volcanic sediments lies immediately beneath the lava flow, and this layer is very porous and permeable. Hence, water flows easily through it, gushing out as a spring line midway up the falls. Below this layer of sediments is another impermeable layer that water can't penetrate, and this explains why you don't see water gushing out from rocks near the base of the falls.

Most of the water flowing over the rim of the falls is spring fed. Springs can be found as much as ¾ mile above the falls, but beyond the last one, Burney Creek is usually dry during summer and early fall. Looking at Burney Falls in summer, you'd find this hard to believe, since the voluminous water pours

Top row, left to right: Burney Falls (post 2), Oregon white oak (post 4), thimbleberry (post 7). Bottom row: Sierra currant (post 10), white alder (post 11), vine maple (post 12).

over the rim. From the falls, about 200 million gallons of water flow north down Burney Creek every day.

With so much water pouring over the rim and out from the spring line, erosion is inevitable. Although the face of the falls hasn't noticeably changed since the 1940s, a substantial collapse of the thick basalt flow could occur at any time. Perhaps when the "nose" at the base of the falls is washed away, a hunk of the basalt flow will break loose. This nose is made of volcanic rock known as tuff-breccia (*tuff* being fine particles, *breccia* being large angular pieces). This rock unit was uplifted and slowly eroded away in part before the basaltic lava, atop it today, flowed across it. Perhaps several million years elapsed from the time the tuff-breccia was deposited to the time the basalt flow covered it.

Top row, left to right: creek dogwood (post 11), squaw bush (post 16), poison oak (post 16). Bottom row: greenleaf manzanita (post 19), mountain misery (post 19), western redbud (post 20).

In the last two million years—perhaps substantially less—the rim of the falls has retreated about 1¼ miles from the Pit River (now Lake Britton, behind a Pacific Gas and Electric Company power dam). The rim will continue to retreat upcanyon. In the distant future, when it retreats past the uppermost spring, Burney Falls will take on a new look. It will then have a springtime-only creek flowing over a rim with a spring line (today's spring-fed creek) emerging immediately beneath it. Lower down, it will have the spring line we see today. In summer, the rim will be dry, but water will gush from the two spring lines; it should present quite an interesting sight.

3 Lava layers. As you descend the path you will be able to read the area's geologic history by studying its rocks. The younger rocks lie atop older ones, and as you descend you go back in time. Try to see where the thick Burney Falls basalt flow gives way to an older layer of rock.

The rocks of our part of the Cascade Range are quite young, mostly under 20 million years old. And most of the uplift of the range in the Burney Falls area is even younger, perhaps mostly in the last 10 million years, which is just a few ticks of the geologic clock. If all of the earth's geologic history could be compressed into a one-year period, then this uplift began on the year's very last day, about four in the morning. The Cascade Range is still very active today, and we can expect it to continue erupting and faulting for millions of years to come.

Between posts 3 and 5 you will see evidence of several separate flows of basalt. Basalt is low in silica and hence tends to flow more freely than volcanic rocks high in silica. It spreads out like hot fudge, covering broad areas rather than piling around a vent to form a "Shasta" or "Lassen." Note that the basalt here is porous and that it breaks into hexagonal columns, these caused by contraction from relatively rapid cooling. Water readily sinks into this band of basalt and, in winter, freezes in the cracks and pores, expanding as it does so. This cracks the rock, which, together with chemical weathering by ground water and decomposition by plants, transforms the rock into soil.

4 California black oak and Oregon white oak. On the left is an Oregon white oak, a tree common to this area but absent south in upper Hat Creek Valley, where California black oaks take over. Both can be found in this state park, which lies in a transition zone between Cascade and Sierra species. Both oaks are quite similar, but the lobes of black-oak leaves are usually angular and pointed while those of white-oak leaves are usually smooth and rounded. See the botany chapter for more information on some of the plants mentioned along this nature trail.

5 Rock strata. While you pause here, note the several separate flows of basalt lava above you. A few feet back along the path is a stratum of lake-bed sediments so recent that it has not yet been compressed into shale by the weight of the rock upon it. The lake beds, of course, were deposited horizontally, but in the Burney Falls area, the oldest strata are quite tilted, their surfaces dipping to the northeast. Younger strata, deposited after some uplift had already occurred, aren't tilted as much, and the youngest strata, deposited after uplift ceased, are essentially horizontal.

Lake sediments indicate that in the past a lake existed here. Perhaps many such lakes have formed in the Pit River-Hat Creek Valley area over the last few million years, for lava typically flows down canyons and valleys, blocking streams and thereby ponding up lakes.

6 Douglas-fir. The larger trees in the gorge are Douglas-firs. Although they have the thick, roughly fissured bark characteristic of firs, they are not true firs. True firs have cones perched erect on branches, but Douglas-firs have cones that hang and are spruce-like. Furthermore, the tree has soft needles, not rigid ones. The Douglas-fir is the commonest lumber tree in the Pacific Northwest, but here in the Lassen area it is a minor constituent. It thrives well in our state park only in this cool, moist Burney Falls gorge.

7 Thimbleberry. This rose, with leaves somewhat resembling those of maples, has white flowers that give way to pink or scarlet berries. You see it along shady stream banks up to about 6500 feet elevation.

As you continue down the trail, note the natural air conditioning made possible by Burney Falls and the resulting thick forest cover. During the summer the temperature in the gorge rarely exceeds 70°F, even when it may be over 90°F in the park's campground.

8 Ground water. Normally a lot of water flows underground. A stream is, so to speak, an "outcrop" of ground water. The spring line on Burney Falls is also an outcrop, and it is fed by a tremendous underground reservoir that rivals the largest ones made by man. Hence Burney Falls flows year-round even long after all this area's creeks have dried up.

9 Burney Falls pool. The pool at the base of the falls varies between 18-24 feet deep. The bottom is littered with large boulders that broke off from the lava flow above. Erosion causes the waterfall to slowly retreat upstream, and the pool retreats upstream along with it. Good-sized trout may be caught in this pool as well as downstream and also between the falls and the springs upstream. The pool, fed with chilly spring water, is too cold for swimming, for it ranges from about 42-48°F.

Swifts and swallows are two kinds of highly acrobatic birds that forage for insects in the air. The largest swift, though considerably smaller than a jay or robin, is the relatively rare black swift. It has a restricting habit of nesting only on sea cliffs or on cliffs by waterfalls, the nests constructed from nearby algae and moss. This highly maneuverable bird spends its time either airborne or in its inaccessible nest, nowhere else. Therefore, its predators are extremely few, as can be garnered by its low fecundity rate. It lays only one egg per year compared to 3-8 eggs laid by the other species of swifts and swallows. Where you find waterfalls, particularly in the Sierra Nevada, you can expect to see this very specialized bird.

10 Sierra currant. This common creekside shrub with maple-like leaves produces a very tasty berry. The shrub, however, has the undesirable habit of hosting a blister rust (a fungus) to which sugar pines are particularly susceptible. There are only a few of these pines in the park.

Snakes sometimes seen in the park include two harmless kinds, the gopher snake and the mountain king snake. The gopher snake, if frightened, sometimes shakes its rattleless tail like a rattlesnake. King snakes sometimes feed on rattlesnakes. In the park, rattlesnakes are quite rare, though they can

be quite common along parts of the Hat Creek Rim and in parts of Hat Creek Valley.

A flowing stream such as Burney Creek typically erodes backwards, as evidenced by the slowly retreating Burney Falls. But to some degree, a stream also cuts downward. The backward and downward cutting has produced a steep-walled gorge, and the black lava flow exposed along the rim has been made unstable, particularly since softer strata beneath it are eroding away. Therefore, a lot of blocks have broken from the lava flow, forming a talus slope.

11 White Alder and creek dogwood. The alder's leaves have saw-toothed margins while those of the dogwood are smooth. Also, alder leaves alternate along a branch while dogwood leaves are usually opposite each other on a branch. Along the creek you may see tall leopard lilies, with dangling bright-orange flowers.

12 American dipper. Along the stream you might see a gray, wren-like bird bobbing or dipping as it moves about rocks and branches. This is the dipper, America's only bird that forages along the bottom of swift creeks. Its oversized feet aid it as it prowls along the bottom in search of insect larvae. The bird then pops out of the water to resume its bobbing motion.

Vine maples grow in this vicinity. These are usually shrubs but can grow to be a small tree. In autumn its leaves turn a beautiful yellow with a tinge of red.

13 Cliff and talus slope. Here, as before, you see a talus slope composed of rocks broken off from the cliff above. The self-guiding nature tail crosses the bridge at this point.

14 White fir. This is the most important lumber tree in the Lassen area, growing to a height of 200 feet or more. At about 6000 feet elevation it yields to red fir, a similar species that is dominant in Lassen Park and its nearby mountain areas. In our state park the white fir is limited by generally dry soil conditions that prevail over most of the park.

15 Pacific dogwood. This tree is most beautiful in the spring, when it displays large white petal-like bracts, and in the fall, when Jack Frost's handiwork colors the leaves pale yellow or dusty rose.

16 Squaw bush. Although closely related to poison oak, this shrub is not poisonous.

Like that plant, squaw bush has three leaflets per leaf, but they are slighly hairy, not shiny. Also, the squaw bush produces yellow flowers and red fruits, not white flowers and fruits. The squaw bush, growing here at about 2800 feet elevation, is close to its upper elevation limit. In middle and upper Hat Creek Valley, the shrubs that look like poison oak *are* poison oak.

17 Height of Burney Falls. You are now about level with the brink of Burney Falls, which is about 129 feet above the pool. Note the dark, impervious basalt flow at this level. Below this lava is a thin bed of sediments, and springs gush out from it.

18 Volcanic soil. Bedrock weathers to soil largely due to action by ground water, bacteria, fungi, lichens, plant roots and tunneling insects. The soil has a high mineral content, which is the usual case for volcanic soils, and this certainly aids the vegetation. Although the soil can be quite dry during the summer, the millions of tiny root hairs of oaks and pines are still able to extract some water. In very dry soil, hardy shrubs, such as greenleaf manzanita, become locally predominant.

19 Greenleaf manzanita. This shrub is one of the commonest in the Lassen area, particularly below 6500 feet elevation. In Spanish, *manzanita* means "little apple." Its specific scientific name, *patula*, in Greek means "bearing grapes." Both names refer to the berry-like, usually pulpy fruit. Although prized by birds and mammals, the fruit is quite bitter to humans. Manzanita is very fire resistant, but it burns hot once ignited. After a fire, new growth quickly springs up from the roots. Its heartwood, veneered in smooth, dark-red bark, is extremely hard. Its round leaves are somewhat leathery to promote water conservation.

In early spring you may see Indian warriors, with purplish-red flowers, blooming at the base of a manzanita. Before summer they die back, going unnoticed. These herbs are root parasites, getting some of their nutrients by tapping into manzanita roots.

Mountain misery also grows here, and you can recognize it by its pungent odor and sticky, fernlike leaves. This species ranges from the Burney Falls area south to the lower mountain slopes of the southern Sierra.

20 Western redbud. This round-leaved shrub announces the coming of spring with a brilliant display of pink blossoms. These later give way to large pea pods as its leaves begin to appear. Unfortunately, most visitors see this plant long after it has gone to seed.

21 Springs. For most of the year, Burney Creek is dry about ½-¾ mile above this point. The stream's water, with the exception of the springtime runoff, emerges from hundreds of springs along the stream bed. Near the headwaters the springs may be easily observed. A trail to them begins just above this point.

A favorite food for deer is aptly named deer brush. In spring this robust shrub has large clusters of lilac-like flowers that fill the air with a sweet aroma.

22 Incense-cedar. This tree ranks third in the park's conifer population, behind ponderosa pine and Douglas-fir. Its wood is used for fence posts, roofing and pencils, but it rots too readily to be used as lumber. Indians were able to hew dugout canoes and make planks from the soft wood. Note that this "cedar" does not have needles, as true cedars do, but rather has tiny, scaly leaves. It belongs to the cypress family.

23 Ponderosa pine. This is the commonest lumber tree in the Burney Falls area. It differs from the sugar pine in having three rather than five needles to a bundle. Also, its cones are usually 3-5 inches long rather than 10-16 inches. Sugar pines, rare in the park, have long, rather thin branches high up their trunks and long cones hanging from the ends of these branches.

24 Ponderosa pine stump. This ponderosa pine attained an age of nearly 400 years before dying after a 1972 lightning strike. The rings indicate that growth was rapid for the first 50 years and then slower as the tree matured.

Books and Articles on the Lassen Area

Hiking, Touring and History

Amesbury, Robert. 1967. *Nobles' Emigrant Trail*. Self published: Sold through Loomis Museum Association (Mineral). 37 p.

Brewer, William H. 1930 (1966). *Up and Down California in 1860-1864*. Berkeley: University of California Press, 583 p.

Egenhoff, Elizabeth L. 1970. "Lassen—a page from history." California Division of Mines and Geology, *Mineral Information Service*, v. 23, p. 225-227.

Matteson, Stephen H. 1963. *Lassen Trails*. Mineral: Loomis Museum Association. 56 p.

Muir, John. 1894 (1961). *The Mountains of California*. New York: Doubleday. 300 p.

Schulz, Paul E. 1954. *Indians of Lassen Volcanic National Park and Vicinity*. Mineral: Loomis Museum Association. 176 p.

Schulz, Paul E. 1979. *Road Guide to Lassen Volcanic National Park*. Mineral: Loomis Museum Association. 40 p.

Strong, Douglas H. 1973. *"These Happy Grounds;" a History of the Lassen Region*. Mineral: Loomis Museum Association. 101 p.

Swartzlow, Ruby J. 1964. *Lassen, His Life and Legacy*. Mineral: Loomis Museum Association. 90 p.

Geology

Anderson, Charles A. 1940. "Hat Creek lava flow." *American Journal of Science*, v. 238, p. 477-492.

Aune, Quintin A. 1964. "A Trip to Burney Falls." California Division of Mines and Geology, *Mineral Information Service*, v. 17, p. 183-191.

Clynne, Michael A. 1984. *Stratigraphy and Major Element Geochemistry of the Lassen Volcanic Center, California*. Washington: U.S. Geological Survey Open-File Report 84-224. 168 p. plus 2 geologic maps.

Crandell, Dwight R. 1972. "Glaciation near Lassen Park, northern California." Washington: U.S. Geological Survey, Pro-fessional Paper 800-C, p. C179-C188.

Crandell, Dwight R., and Donal R. Mullineaux. 1970. *Potential geologic hazards in Lassen Volcanic National Park, California*. Washington: U.S. Geological Survey (unpublished administrative report for National Park Service). 54 p.

Crandell, Dwight R., and others. 1974. "Chaos Crags eruptions and rockfall-avalanches, Lassen Volcanic National Park, California." U.S. Geological Survey, *Journal of Research*, p. 49-59.

Evans, James R. "Geology of some lava tubes, Shasta County." California Division of Mines and Geology, *Mineral Information Service*, v. 16, no. 3, p. 1-7.

Finch, R.H. 1937. "A tree ring calendar for dating volcanic events at Cinder Cone, Lassen National Park, California." *American Journal of Science*, v. 33, no. 194, p. 140-146.

Heiken, Grant, and John C. Eichelberger. 1980. "Eruptions at Chaos Crags, Lassen Volcanic National Park, California." *Journal of Volcanology and Geothermal Research*, v. 7, p. 443-481.

Jones, David E. 1966. "Geology and rock magnetism of Cinder Cone lava flows, Lassen Volcanic National Park, California." *Geological Society of America Bulletin*, v. 77, p. 303–12.

Kane, Phillip S. 1975. *The Glacial Geomorphology of the Lassen Volcanic National Park Area*. Berkeley: University of California, Geography Department, Ph.D. Thesis. 224 p.

Kane, Phillip S. 1980. *Through Vulcan's Eye*. Mineral: Loomis Museum Association. 118 p.

Loomis, Benjamin F. 1926 (1971). *Pictorial History of the Lassen Volcano (Eruptions of Lassen Peak)*. Mineral: Loomis Museum Association. 96 p.

Macdonald, Gordon A. 1965. *Geologic Map of the Harvey Mountain Quadrangle, Lassen County, California*. Washington: U.S. Geological Survey, Map GQ-443.

Macdonald, Gordon A. 1966. "Geology of the Cascade Range and Modoc Plateau." In *Geology of Northern California* (Edgar H. Bailey, ed.). Sacramento: California Division of Mines and Geology, Bulletin 190, p. 65-96.

Macdonald, Gordon A. 1963. *Geology of the Manzanita Lake Quadrangle, California.* Washington: U.S. Geological Survey, Map GQ-248.

Macdonald, Gordon A. 1964. *Geology of the Prospect Peak Quadrangle, California.* Washington: U.S. Geological Survey, Map GQ-345.

Macdonald, Gordon A., and Takashi Katsura. 1965. "Eruption of Lassen Peak, Cascade Range, California, in 1915: example of mixed magmas." *Geological Society of America Bulletin*, v. 76, p. 475-482.

Williams, Howel. 1932. *Geology of the Lassen Volcanic National Park, California.* Berkeley: University of California, Department of Geological Sciences Bulletin, v. 21, p. 195-385.

Biology

Beedy, Edward C., and Stephen L. Granholm. 1985. *Discovering Sierra Birds.* Yosemite: Yosemite Natural History Association. 229 p.

California Department of Fish and Game. 1969. *Trout of California.* 56 p.

Gillett, George W., and others. 1961. *A Flora of Lassen Volcanic National Park, California.* The Wasmann Journal of Biology, v. 19, no. 1, p. 1-185.

Griffin, James R., and William B. Critchfield. 1972. *The Distribution of Forest Trees in California.* Washington: U.S.D.A., Pacific Southwest Forest and Range Experiment Station, Forest Service Research Paper PSW-82/1972. 114 p.

Grillos, Steve J. 1966. *Ferns and Fern Allies of California* (California Natural History Guide 16). Berkeley: University of California Press. 104 p.

Grinnell, Joseph. 1930. *Vertebrate Natural History of a Section of Northern California Through the Lassen Peak Region.* Berkeley: University of California, Publications in Zoology, v. 35. 594 p.

Horn, Elizabeth L. 1972. *Wildflowers 1: The Cascades.* Beaverton, OR: Touchstone Press. 160 p.

Horn, Elizabeth L. 1976. *Wildflowers 3: The Sierra Nevada.* Beaverton, OR: Touchstone Press. 128 p.

Ingles, Lloyd G. 1965. *Mammals of the Pacific States.* Stanford: Stanford University Press. 506 p.

Keator, Glenn. 1978. *Pacific Coast Berry Finder.* Berkeley: Nature Study Guild. 62 p.

Milne, Robert C. 1966. *Birds of Lassen Volcanic National Park.* Mineral: Loomis Museum Association. 48 p.

Munz, Philip A., and David D. Keck. 1968. *A California Flora and Supplement.* Berkeley: University of California Press. 1681 and 224 p.

Murie, Olaus J. 1975. *A Field Guide to Animal Tracks.* Boston: Houghton Mifflin. 375 p.

National Geographic Society. 1983. *Field Guide to Birds of North America.* Washington, D.C.: Nat. Geog. Soc. 464 p.

Nelson, Raymond L. 1962. *Trees and Shrubs of Lassen Volcanic National Park.* Mineral: Loomis Museum Association. 1971. 35 p.

Niehaus, Theodore F., and Charles L. Ripper. 1976. *A Field Guide to Pacific States Wildflowers.* Boston: Houghton Mifflin. 432 p.

Ornduff, Robert. 1974. *An Introduction to California Plant Life* (California Natural History Guide 35). Berkeley: University of California Press. 152 p.

Peterson, Roger Tory. 1961. *A Field Guide to Western Birds.* Boston: Houghton Mifflin. 366 p.

Showers, Mary Ann, and David W. Showers. 1981. *A Field Guide to the Flowers of Lassen Volcanic National Park.* Mineral: Loomis Museum Association. 112 p.

Stebbins, Robert C. 1972. *Amphibians and Reptiles of California* (California Natural History Guide 31). Berkeley: University of California Press. 152 p.

Sudworth, George B. 1908 (1967). *Forest Trees of the Pacific Slope.* New York: Dover Publications, Inc. 455 p.

Watts, Tom. 1973. *Pacific Coast Tree Finder.* Berkeley: Nature Study Guild. 62 p.

Weeden, Norman. 1986. *A Sierra Nevada Flora.* Berkeley: Wilderness Press. 406 p.

Whitney, Stephen. 1983. *A Field Guide to the Cascades & Olympics.* Seattle: The Mountaineers. 288 p.

Whitney, Stephen. 1979. *A Sierra Club Naturalist's Guide to the Sierra Nevada.* San Francisco: Sierra Club Books. 526 p.

Index